The Handbook of Information Systems Research

Michael E. Whitman
Kennesaw State University, USA

Amy B. Woszczynski
Kennesaw State University, USA

IDEA GROUP PUBLISHING

Hershey • London • Melbourne • Singapore

Acquisition Editor: Mehdi Khosrow-Pour
Senior Managing Editor: Jan Travers
Managing Editor: Amanda Appicello
Development Editor: Michele Rossi
Copy Editor: Elizabeth Arneson
Typesetter: Jennifer Wetzel
Cover Design: Michelle Waters
Printed at: Integrated Book Technology

Published in the United States of America by
        Idea Group Publishing (an imprint of Idea Group Inc.)
        701 E. Chocolate Avenue, Suite 200
        Hershey PA 17033
        Tel: 717-533-8845
        Fax: 717-533-8661
        E-mail: cust@idea-group.com
        Web site: http://www.idea-group.com

and in the United Kingdom by
        Idea Group Publishing (an imprint of Idea Group Inc.)
        3 Henrietta Street
        Covent Garden
        London WC2E 8LU
        Tel: 44 20 7240 0856
        Fax: 44 20 7379 3313
        Web site: http://www.eurospan.co.uk

Library of Congress Cataloging-in-Publication Data

Whitman, Michael E., 1964-
 The handbook of information systems research / Michael E. Whitman and
Amy B. Woszczynski.
     p. cm.
 ISBN 1-59140-144-5 (hardcover) -- ISBN 1-59140-145-3 (ebook)
 1. Management information systems--Handbooks, manuals, etc. I.
Woszczynski, Amy B., 1965- II. Title.
 T58.6.W49 2003
 658.4'038'011--dc21
                              2003008880

Paperback ISBN 1-59140-228-X

British Cataloguing in Publication Data
A Cataloguing in Publication record for this book is available from the British Library.

All work contributed to this book is new, previously-unpublished material. The views expressed in this book are those of the authors, but not necessarily of the publisher.

The Handbook of Information Systems Research

Table of Contents

Preface

Every major project has its story, and this project is no different. The text as you see is not in the form envisioned, nor is it the complete work needed. The editors originally set out to answer the same question all PhD researchers face: *What are the seminal and exemplary works in research in our field, so that I may refer to them and their successors in my research?*

As all researchers do, we also were required to familiarize ourselves with a general understanding of the best and most wide-reaching works both in information systems (IS) in general and in our specific area of research in particular. However, there is a wealth of information in other research areas that we may only find when we begin to examine studies in those areas. As we moved from graduate students to instructors of graduate students, we felt it important to capture in a single document or collection of chapters those works determined by the discipline to be the most exemplary. There are hundreds of excellent works on numerous topics within the field of IS, but as we prepared for the conduct of an IS research methods class, we wondered in the limited time we have these students which studies MUST we show the students to provide a solid foundation for their future research.

So we set out to determine this list of works. First we examined the available research published in the traditional IS venues, finding little. We then networked with our colleagues, classmates, and former instructors, securing a number of personal preference listings, finding a few commonalities, but still finding a general hodgepodge of articles. This is when we came to the determination that the only way to obtain this list was to develop it in the traditions of IS research—examine the literature, build a survey and administer it, and collect and analyze the results—and then we would have our listing.

CHAPTER REVIEWS

The first chapter in this text highlights this study. As indicated, there are hundreds of exemplary works in the many subdisciplines within IS research; however, in order to concentrate on those most beneficial to our self-serving needs, a research survey course, we felt it best to restrict the candidates to those on IS research rather than on a subdiscipline. This greatly reduced the field to some 250 to 300 potential candidates and made the task less Herculean in nature. The resulting list of more than 50 articles was examined in a number of ways, and the results of each, as well as a combined listing, are provided. First the survey was posted to the Web, and established author and promising graduate students alike were permitted to cast a ballot on the most important. This was then tempered with a co-citation analysis, which unfortunately favors older articles. The multiple listings permit the reader to draw their own conclusions as to the best method of interpreting the resulting ranking. The findings provide an initial method of comparing articles, although future studies are clearly needed not only to validate our study but also to update the field of IS research over time.

Every author with an article on this listing should be proud, as they were nominated by their peers for their work in the field. The resulting ranking should not be construed to disparage those listed lowly, as to be ranked among the recognized greats in our field should be considered an honor in and of itself.

Once the listing was complete, it was our intention to first simply collect these articles and use them in our class. We were so inundated with requests for the list that we considered a traditional avenue of making the required readings available to the academic community—a collection of previously published readings, that is, the best studies on IS research. Unfortunately journals have begun capitalizing on their intellectual property to the point of several hundred dollars per article in some cases, making the publication of such an anthology virtually infeasible at a price equivalent to the work's value. We then stumbled on the second best thing, creating a follow-on work of articles on the various aspects of IS research, coupled with an enhanced report of the listing, and making that available to others in the discipline. Idea Group Publishing approved our proposal and thus this work was born.

As we began assembling the collection of works, several themes emerged, and we used those themes to group chapters into meaningful sections. After the introductory chapter that describes our search for exemplary articles on IS research, we move to a theme that many IS researchers will find relevant to their work. Quantitative analysis using survey data remains a popular subject in the IS field. For this reason, the second section of the book deals with "Issues in Survey Research." First, Boudreau, Ariyachandra, Gefen, and Straub provide an excellent assessment of the current state of instrument validation in IS research—an update to previous works on the same topic. They provide promising results which indicate that the IS research community has improved instrument validation as compared to earlier time periods.

Second, Masterson and Rainer discuss multitrait-multimethod data analysis techniques—a technique that has been applied by IS researchers over the years. They illustrate the use of confirmatory factor analysis with multitrait-multimethod matrices to determine the convergent and discriminant validity, as well as the presence of method variance, in two commonly used instruments to measure end-user computing satisfaction and computer self-efficacy. Their results indicate satisfactory convergent and discriminant validity in the instruments studied, but a disturbing presence of method variance that accounts for a significant portion of variance is explained.

Third, Im and Grover provide a primer on the application of structural equation modeling in IS research. They describe how structural equation modeling has been used in IS research in the past and they evaluate empirical applications of structural equation modeling in leading IS journals. They also provide recommendations for appropriate applications of the technique.

This section concludes with Woszczynski and Whitman providing an analysis of common method bias in IS research. They research leading IS journals to determine if method bias is a potential problem in IS research. After determining that a substantial portion of IS research may contain method bias, they provide recommendations to IS researchers in overcoming this potential problem.

The third section of this text deals with a topic of interest to IS researchers and practitioners alike—"Rigor and Relevance." This topic is hotly debated in many forums, including journals, conferences, *ISWorld*, and the like. In the first chapter on this topic, Gasson describes qualitative, interpretive approaches to generating grounded theory, an analysis technique that is often criticized for its lack of rigor. After introducing the grounded theory research approach, she provides a comprehensive set of recommendations for appropriately applying grounded theory techniques in qualitative field studies.

Next, McDonagh discusses an approach to work towards achieving more relevance in IS research. He contends that much IS research has failed to adequately address how to effectively undertake strategic change involving IT, a common and enduring problem in the business environment. McDonagh then describes clinical inquiry and outlines how this technique provides a relevant approach for investigating IT-enabled business change.

Beachboard provides a unique practitioner-turned-academic perspective in the third chapter in the text's "Rigor and Relevance" section. He proposes a multi-paradigmatic research framework to meet the scientific rigor requirements while also achieving relevance in IS research. This chapter describes his motivation for pursuing practitioner-oriented research, along with observations on some of the advantages of the multi-paradigmatic approach.

The fourth section of the text deals with "Virtual Research Issues," an area that has recently become important to IS researchers. First, Rennecker describes ethnography as a valid approach for studying today's virtual project teams. Using results of an ethnographic study of a multi-site automotive firm, she describes some of the challenges and limitations of this approach. After discussing potential alternatives to ethnographic research, she then concludes with caution and optimism regarding the future of ethnographic and similar research techniques.

The second entry in this section comes from Robey and Jin, who describe empirical techniques for gathering data on virtual teams and related communities. They discuss some of the challenges of gathering data in a virtual work setting and provide guidance on appropriate methodological approaches for studying virtual teams.

With the increasingly global workforce, we felt that the fifth section of this book, "Global Issues," was certainly relevant. Karahanna, Evaristo, and Srite provide the first chapter in this section, discussing important methodological considerations when conducting cross-cultural research. They conclude by providing recommendations for overcoming potential methodological problems when conducting cross-cultural research.

Tan and Gallupe follow with a framework for developing research into global information management. Development of the framework helps identify areas that have been understudied in global information management. Further, the framework identifies areas that have been extensively studied, thus providing direction to future researchers in this area.

The last section of the text is entitled "Emerging Issues." Although all of the topics are not new (for example, simulation), their use in IS research has been somewhat limited or their potential for application in IS research has not yet been recognized. In Chapter 13, Poole and DeSanctis describe structuration theory in IS research. They indicate that structuration theory, which comes to IS through organization studies, has specific requirements and options applicable to IS researchers. Further, they discuss methodological controversies and directions to be considered when applying structuration techniques in IS research.

In Chapter 14, Vitolo and Coulston discuss simulation—a technique often used in other disciplines but underutilized in IS research. By using an example, they describe how simulation can be useful when conducting IS research.

Tan and Hunter discuss the repertory grid as a viable option for IS researchers in Chapter 15. They describe the various ways that the technique can be used in IS studies. Further, they illustrate how the repertory grid can be applied by analyzing published studies in IS and management fields.

In Chapter 16, Hunter provides an excellent discussion of qualitative research in information systems. After describing qualitative research use and applications, he then surveys current usage of qualitative research in IS. Further, he describes each of the methods and provides examples from the literature.

The next chapter in this section, Chapter 17, describes an interesting topic for IS researchers—that of studying failures in information systems. Dalcher suggests applying case study techniques to learn more about failures in IS. He contends that this approach provides a better understanding of stakeholder conflicts and issues in IS failures.

In the final chapter, Chapter 18, Carlsson provides the final chapter in the text, discussing an interesting alternative approach to standard IS research methodologies—that of critical realism. Carlsson describes the roots of critical realism and examines how this technique can be used in IS research.

As those familiar with IS research will note, the papers published in this work come from two sources. First are the "invited established authors"—individuals of note who have graciously donated their time and effort to contribute to this work. They are listed in the "Acknowledgments" following the "Preface." We would like to thank them for their contributions. The second group consists of the remainder of the articles—individuals who have had their works competitively evaluated for inclusion in this text. While all works are reviewed, these are the best of those submitted—having been accepted on their academic merit and interest. We would also like to congratuled and thank them. We hope you find this collection of value and interest. Should it be openly welcomed, we will consider subsequent editions, with additional works from both invited and competing authors. If you have any questions or comments about this text, please feel free to contact us at the addresses listed below. Enjoy.

Michael E. Whitman, PhD
Computer Science & Information Systems Department
Kennesaw State University
1000 Chastain Road, MS 1101
Kennesaw GA, 30144
P: (770) 423-6005
F: (770) 423-6731
mwhitman@kennesaw.edu

Amy B. Woszczynski, PhD
Computer Science & Information Systems Department
Kennesaw State University
1000 Chastain Road, MS 1101
Kennesaw GA, 30144
P: (770) 423-6005
F: (770) 423-6731
awoszczy@kennesaw.edu

Acknowledgments

The editors would like to thank the following individuals without whom this text would not be possible. Each author also served as a reviewer and provided valuable insights to improve their colleagues' works. Special thanks go to Patrice Hagans for her assistance in the administration and collection of these works, and to the Chair of our department, Merle King, for his assistance and tolerance of the process.

Invited Authors

Gerardine DeSanctis

Roberto Evaristo

R. Brent Gallupe

Varun Grover

Marshall Scott Poole

Daniel Robey

Detmar W. Straub

Felix B. Tan

Authors

Thilini Ariyachandra

John C. Beachboard

Marie-Claude Boudreau

Sven A. Carlsson

Chris Coulston

Darren Dalcher

Susan Gasson

David Gefen

M. Gordon Hunter

Kun Shin Im

Leigh Jin

Elena Karahanna

Michael J. Masterson

Joe McDonagh

R. Kelly Rainer, Jr.

Julie Rennecker

Mark Srite

Theresa M. Vitolo

And to Jacek Plodzien for his kind offer to review.

SECTION I

ISSUES IN SURVEY RESEARCH

Chapter I

Exemplary Works on Information Systems Research

Michael E. Whitman
Kennesaw State University, USA

Amy B. Woszczynski
Kennesaw State University, USA

ABSTRACT

With the quantity and quality of available works in information systems (IS) research, it would seem advantageous to possess a concise list of exemplary works on IS research in order to enable instructors of IS research courses to better prepare students to publish in IS venues. To that end, this study seeks to identify and rank a collection of works that is widely viewed as among the best in the field on the subject of research in IS. The study examined more than 460 such candidate works and was subsequently refined to a list of 58 exemplary studies. This list was formatted into an online survey and administered to the IS academic community. The resulting list of ranked articles provides an excellent supplement to a course on IS research, providing examples of quality in research methodology.

INTRODUCTION

The field of IS research is replete with outstanding works focused on specific areas of research. With calls for research and presentations of analyses in areas of group support systems (Benbasat & Lim, 1993), keyword classification schemes (Barki, Rivard, & Talbot, 1993), information technology planning (Boynton & Zmud, 1987), co-citations (Culnan, 1987), and other valued areas, the numbers of available sources of research information are staggering. It has become a monumental effort to identify and prioritize key works in order to include them in fields of study and specific courses. Given the specific content criteria and limited timeframe of the typical graduate course, it is virtually impossible to cover the breadth and depth of materials available. We have thus determined that there is a need for research to identify and rank exemplary works on IS research. The resulting list should provide individuals instructing graduate and undergraduate courses on research in IS with a specific collection of articles suitable for adoption whole or in part as a reading list or as a reference for research support.

PREVIOUS WORKS

We have found no study previously conducted and published that has attempted to do what this study has done. Many manuscripts have ranked IS journals using combinations of citation analysis, expert opinion, and quality of research published (i.e., Gillenson & Stutz, 1991; Hardgrave & Walstrom, 1997; Holsapple, Johnson, Manakyan, & Tanner, 1994; Mylonopoulos & Theoharakis, 2001; Walstrom, Hardgrave, & Wilson, 1995; Whitman, Hendrickson, & Townsend, 1999). In fact, the practice is so popular, there is an entire section of the IS World portal dedicated to the subject: Journal Rankings (see http://www.bus.ucf.edu/csaunders/newjournal.htm).

Recent citation analyses have also attempted to include underrepresented media, such as electronic publishing outlets, when analyzing research productivity in computer science (Goodrum, McCain, Lawrence, & Giles, 2001). Previous articles have also examined research productivity by author and institution in IS (Athey & Plotnicki, 2000) and in real estate (Dombrow & Turnbull, 2002). Other research has examined publishing patterns based on graduate school attended (McCormick & Rice, 2001), as well as evaluating the economic value of an IS paper publication to the author (Gill, 2001). However, no other study exists that seeks to specifically identify and rank the top quality articles available in the IS research arena.

Other studies have examined the development of fields within IS research, including Ives, Hamilton, and Davis (1980), Ives and Olson (1984), Jarvenpaa, Dickson, and DeSanctis (1988), Culnan (1987), and Culnan and Swanson (1986), to name a few. Several of these used co-citation analysis to quantify the value of journal articles (i.e., Culnan, 1987), then aggregated these values by research stream. However, the general thrust of this body of research was to examine where the new areas of study were in the discipline rather than identify best practice works.

Even outside of IS, only a very few works specifically address exemplary articles related to a particular topic or discipline. In accounting, Brown (1996) used citation analysis to determine influential accounting articles, individuals, graduate institutions, and faculties, while Leigh, Pullins, and Comer (2001) identified the top 10 sales articles of the 20th century using a combination of survey and citation analysis methodologies.

Perhaps the dearth of studies of this type reflects the sensitivity of individuals not desiring to raise or lower the worth of their peers as authors on the subject. Or, perhaps, it is because "all good researchers know what the best articles are." In any case, this study provides a short list of those studies which we recommend should be included in a survey of IS research topics. It also provides a list that can be distributed to our students for reference in their studies.

STUDY METHODOLOGY

To provide a quality evaluation of exemplary works on IS research, we decided to poll IS academicians and other IS experts. As indicated previously, no other article exists that seeks to identify and rank the top quality articles available in the IS research arena. Given the large numbers of available articles and broad categories of topics, the researchers initially identified the primary focus of such works as journal articles or book chapters in themed collections of readings, specifically focused on IS research in general. By IS research, we are specifically referring to articles that address fundamental concepts that investigators should consider when conducting IS research—that is, statistical testing, validity and reliability of measurement scales, and the like. While academicians may feel that any course on research methodology should include such seminal works as Churchill (1979), Cook and Campbell (1976), and Schwab (1980), we decided to concentrate on collections of works on IS research in order to provide as focused a collection as possible to stimulate student research resulting in publication in IS journals, conferences, and so forth.

The identification of this criterion enabled the researchers to cull the overwhelming collection of papers into a somewhat more manageable list. Initially the researchers found more than 462 articles focusing on IS research. The first list was then reduced to 137 by restricting the list to journal articles and works in books identified as collections of articles specifically on IS research. These 137 articles were then rated on a 3-point scale by three researchers knowledgeable in IS research and methodology. After calculating a weighted average for each article, the resulting list provided a natural break at 2.0 points—out of a maximum of 3.0 points—leaving the researchers with 58 articles that met the criterion identified and initially screened as exemplary works.

SURVEY DATA COLLECTION

Once the 58 articles were identified, an online instrument was created to provide members of the IS community an opportunity to rate the works on a 5-point scale, with a 1 indicating "a good article, optional reading for an IS research methodology class" and a 5 indicating "an exemplary article, mandatory reading for an IS research methodology class." Each of the citations posted included a hyperlink to an abstract of the article, providing respondents with additional information to help refresh their memory. Five spaces were also provided to allow respondents to add articles of interest they felt the researchers might have overlooked. Additional demographic questions were posed, collecting information on the respondent's professional experience, research record, and university, as well as a feedback block for comments.

Once the online instrument was complete and pilot tested, we posted an invitation to the ISWorld list server, an organization supporting information systems research around the world. At the time of this paper, there were more than 2,750 subscribers to the list. The invitation included details on accessing the survey and responding.

Findings

The survey resulted in 70 usable responses. The breakdown of respondents by academic position is presented in Table 1. As is evident, the bulk of respondents were full-time tenure track.

Table 1. Respondents by Position.

	Frequency	Percent
Full-Time Tenure Track	55	78.6
Full-Time Nontenure Track	3	4.3
PhD Student	6	8.6
Subtotal	64	91.4
Missing	6	8.6
Total	70	100.0

Next, respondents were asked to categorize their research productivity based on three categories: refereed articles, non-refereed articles, and conference presentations. The results are presented in Table 2. The results indicate a bipolar spread between high-productivity researchers (more than 25 publications in each category) and beginning or low-productivity researchers (less than 10 publications in each category).

Table 2. Respondent Research Productivity.

	Refereed Articles		Non-refereed Articles		Conference Presentations	
	Frequency	**Percent**	**Frequency**	**Percent**	**Frequency**	**Percent**
None	10	14.3	29	41.4	6	8.6
1-5	24	34.3	19	27.1	8	11.4
6-10	8	11.4	7	10.0	16	22.9
11-15	8	11.4	4	5.7	9	12.9
16-20	3	4.3	0	0.0	8	11.4
21-25	3	4.3	2	2.9	6	8.6
26+	14	20.0	9	12.9	17	24.3
Total	70	100.0	70	100.0	70	100.0

Respondents were then asked to indicate the amount of professional experience in academia and industry. The results are presented in Table 3. The respondents indicated an even spread of academic experience.

Table 3. Professional Experience.

Years	Academia		Industry	
	Frequency	Percent	Frequency	Percent
None	6	8.6	13	18.6
1-3	11	15.7	23	32.9
4-6	10	14.3	18	25.7
7-9	9	12.9	7	10.0
10-12	7	10.0	3	4.3
13-15	11	15.7	2	2.9
16+	16	22.9	4	5.7
Total	70	100.0	70	100.0

Of the respondents, 91.4% had taught an IS course, but only 44.3% of those had taught an IS research course. The final demographic question asked respondents to indicate the Carnegie classification for their current university. The Carnegie classification (see Carnegie, 2002) provides a means for categorizing institutions based on the number of degrees they offer at the highest level. The results are presented in Table 4. The dominant groups of respondents were from institutions considered traditional "research" institutions, possessing doctoral programs.

Table 4. Respondents' Institutions by Carnegie Classification.

	Frequency	Percent
Doc/Research Extensive	40	57.1
Doc/Research Intensive	11	15.7
Master's I	11	15.7
Master's II	5	7.1
Baccalaureate Liberal Arts	0	0.0
Baccalaureate General	1	1.4
Baccalaureate/Associate's	0	0.0
Associate's	0	0.0
Specialized	1	1.4
Missing	1	1.4
Total	70	100.0

The remainder of the survey was dedicated to a presentation of the 58 abbreviated citations for the candidate exemplary works. Each respondent was asked to rate the article on a 5-point scale of 1 = "good article/optional reading" to 5 = "exemplary article/ mandatory reading." For each article, a simple mean was conducted of the 5-point ratings. Table 5 presents a ranking of the simple means.

Table 5. Exemplary Articles Ranked by Means.

	N	Mean	Std Dev
Klein & Myers (1999)	53	4.02	1.26
Lee (1999)	56	3.93	1.14
Baroudi & Orlikowski (1989)	57	3.88	1.21
Orlikowski & Baroudi (1991)	56	3.88	1.15
Lee (1989)	56	3.84	1.26
Benbasat & Zmud (1999)	57	3.75	1.24
Straub (1989)	56	3.70	1.28
Jarvenpaa et al. (1985)	47	3.68	1.30
Robey (1996)	49	3.67	1.20
Benbasat et al. (1987)	55	3.64	1.22
Benbasat & Weber (1996)	51	3.55	1.27
Lee et al. (1997)	48	3.52	1.34
Kaplan & Duchon (1988)	49	3.51	1.19
Robey (1998)	47	3.51	1.23
Myers (1999)	50	3.40	1.25
Walsham (1995)	47	3.32	1.34
Lyytinen (1999)	45	3.31	1.31
Ives et al. (1980)	51	3.29	1.50
Gefen et al. (2000)	48	3.25	1.44
Galliers & Land (1987)	55	3.24	1.45
Darke et al. (1998)	48	3.23	1.28
Baskerville & Wood-Harper (1996)	50	3.22	1.33
Jarvenpaa (1988)	50	3.22	1.28
Mason & Mitroff (1973)	49	3.22	1.58
Sethi & King (1991)	43	3.16	1.23
Weill & Olson (1989)	43	3.16	1.23
Gable (1994)	44	3.14	1.25
Grover et al. (1993)	43	3.14	1.19
Westfall (1999)	43	3.12	1.24
Lacity & Janson (1994)	45	3.11	1.27
Hufnagel & Conca (1994)	41	3.07	1.40
Straub et al. (1994)	47	3.06	1.37
Chin & Todd (1995)	48	3.04	1.35
Pinsonneault & Kraemer (1993)	45	3.04	1.31
Dickson et al. (1977)	54	2.94	1.51
Hwang (1996)	44	2.93	1.35
Cavaye (1996)	43	2.91	1.46
Weber (1987)	41	2.83	1.20
Segars (1997)	41	2.80	1.33
Silverman (1998)	42	2.79	1.18
Zmud (1978)	41	2.76	1.43
Drury & Farhoomand (1997)	45	2.69	1.20
Nolan & Wetherbe (1980)	47	2.68	1.38
Benbasat et al. (1984)	49	2.67	1.26
Cheon et al. (1993)	42	2.64	1.21
Hamilton & Ives (1982a)	40	2.60	1.22
Alavi & Carlson (1992)	49	2.57	1.14

Table 5.   (continued) Exemplary Articles Ranked by Means.

	N	Mean	Std Dev
Klein et al. (1997)	42	2.57	1.25
Barki et al. (1993)	52	2.52	1.43
Remenyi & Williams (1996)	42	2.50	1.31
Swanson et al. (1993)	48	2.44	1.18
Hamilton & Ives (1982b)	44	2.41	1.24
Teng & Galletta (1990)	44	2.41	1.17
Culnan & Swanson (1986)	46	2.35	1.22
Culnan (1987)	49	2.29	1.15
Holsapple et al. (1994)	40	2.18	1.15
Nurminen (1999)	37	2.03	1.04
Cooper et al. (1993)	39	1.92	1.06

Next, in order to compensate for the number of individuals reviewing each article, a weighted ranking was calculated by multiplying the number of reviewers by the simple means of the ratings. This was deemed necessary to prevent a few respondents from giving high marks to one article and that overriding a well-received article with lower ratings. Table 6 provides a ranking of the result of this operation.

Table 6.   Exemplary Articles Ranked by Means and Number of Respondents (N).

	N	Mean	Std Dev	N * Mean
Baroudi & Orlikowski (1989)	57	3.88	1.21	221.16
Lee (1999)	56	3.93	1.14	220.08
Orlikowski & Baroudi (1991)	56	3.88	1.15	217.28
Lee (1989)	56	3.84	1.26	215.04
Benbasat & Zmud (1999)	57	3.75	1.24	213.75
Klein & Myers (1999)	53	4.02	1.26	213.06
Straub (1989)	56	3.7	1.28	207.2
Benbasat et al. (1987)	55	3.64	1.22	200.2
Benbasat & Weber (1996)	51	3.55	1.27	181.05
Robey (1996)	49	3.67	1.2	179.83
Galliers & Land (1987)	55	3.24	1.45	178.2
Jarvenpaa et al. (1985)	47	3.68	1.3	172.96
Kaplan & Duchon (1988)	49	3.51	1.19	171.99
Myers (1999)	50	3.4	1.25	170
Lee et al. (1997)	48	3.52	1.34	168.96
Ives et al. (1980)	51	3.29	1.5	167.79
Robey (1998)	47	3.51	1.23	164.97
Baskerville & Wood-Harper (1996)	50	3.22	1.33	161
Jarvenpaa (1988)	50	3.22	1.28	161
Dickson et al. (1977)	54	2.94	1.51	158.76
Mason & Mitroff (1973)	49	3.22	1.58	157.78
Walsham (1995)	47	3.32	1.34	156.04
Gefen et al. (2000)	48	3.25	1.44	156
Darke et al. (1998)	48	3.23	1.28	155.04
Lyytinen (1999)	45	3.31	1.31	148.95
Chin & Todd (1995)	48	3.04	1.35	145.92
Straub et al. (1994)	47	3.06	1.37	143.82
Lacity & Janson (1994)	45	3.11	1.27	139.95
Gable (1994)	44	3.14	1.25	138.16

Table 6. (continued) Exemplary Articles Ranked by Means and Number of Respondents (N).

	N	Mean	Std Dev	N * Mean
Pinsonneault & Kraemer (1993)	45	3.04	1.31	136.8
Sethi & King (1991)	43	3.16	1.23	135.88
Weill & Olson (1989)	43	3.16	1.23	135.88
Grover et al. (1993)	43	3.14	1.19	135.02
Westfall (1999)	43	3.12	1.24	134.16
Barki et al. (1993)	52	2.52	1.43	131.04
Benbasat et al. (1984)	49	2.67	1.26	130.83
Hwang (1996)	44	2.93	1.35	128.92
Nolan & Wetherbe (1980)	47	2.68	1.38	125.96
Alavi & Carlson (1992)	49	2.57	1.14	125.93
Hufnagel & Conca (1994)	41	3.07	1.4	125.87
Cavaye (1996)	43	2.91	1.46	125.13
Drury & Farhoomand (1997)	45	2.69	1.2	121.05
Silverman (1998)	42	2.79	1.18	117.18
Swanson et al. (1993)	48	2.44	1.18	117.12
Weber (1987)	41	2.83	1.2	116.03
Segars (1997)	41	2.8	1.33	114.8
Zmud (1978)	41	2.76	1.43	113.16
Culnan (1987)	49	2.29	1.15	112.21
Cheon et al. (1993)	42	2.64	1.21	110.88
Culnan & Swanson (1986)	46	2.35	1.22	108.1
Klein et al. (1997)	42	2.57	1.25	107.94
Hamilton & Ives (1982b)	44	2.41	1.24	106.04
Teng & Galletta (1990)	44	2.41	1.17	106.04
Remenyi & Williams (1996)	42	2.5	1.31	105
Hamilton & Ives (1982a)	40	2.6	1.22	104
Holsapple et al. (1994)	40	2.18	1.15	87.2
Nurminen (1999)	37	2.03	1.04	75.11
Cooper et al. (1993)	39	1.92	1.06	74.88

The final results of this study are presented in Table 7. This table presents the top 24 articles, breaking at the 150-point level. Full citations are presented in the Appendix.

CONCLUSION

So what does the list in Table 7 tell us? Are we left to assume that these articles are the only important readings for those interested in IS research? Certainly not. This list simply provides a starting point for learning about the history of IS research and current issues—that is, current issues relevant as of the time of this writing. This list will certainly have to be updated over time, but it does provide a useful starting point for beginning

Table 7. Exemplary Works on IS Research.

Citation		N	Mean	Std Dev	Weighted Rank N * Means
Baroudi & Orlikowski (1989)	I3	57	3.88	1.21	221
Lee (1999)	I35	56	3.93	1.14	220
Orlikowski & Baroudi (1991)	I42	56	3.88	1.15	217
Lee (1989)	I34	56	3.84	1.26	215
Benbasat & Zmud (1999)	I8	57	3.75	1.24	214
Klein & Myers (1999)	I32	53	4.02	1.26	213
Straub (1989)	I50	56	3.70	1.28	207
Benbasat et al. (1987)	I6	55	3.64	1.22	200
Benbasat & Weber (1996)	I7	51	3.55	1.27	181
Robey (1996)	I45	49	3.67	1.20	180
Galliers & Land (1987)	I19	55	3.24	1.45	178
Jarvenpaa et al. (1985)	I29	47	3.68	1.30	173
Kaplan & Duchon (1988)	I30	49	3.51	1.19	172
Myers (1999)	I39	50	3.40	1.25	170
Lee et al. (1997)	I36	48	3.52	1.34	169
Ives et al. (1980)	I27	51	3.29	1.50	168
Robey (1998)	I46	47	3.51	1.23	165
Baskerville & Wood-Harper (1996)	I4	50	3.22	1.33	161
Jarvenpaa (1988)	I28	50	3.22	1.28	161
Dickson et al. (1977)	I16	54	2.94	1.51	159
Mason & Mitroff (1973)	I38	49	3.22	1.58	158
Gefen et al. (2000)	I20	48	3.25	1.44	156
Walsham (1995)	I54	47	3.32	1.34	156
Darke et al. (1998)	I15	48	3.23	1.28	155

graduate students of IS, instructors of future IS researchers, and the IS research community as a whole. We do not begin to present this list as inclusive of all worthy studies on IS research. Indeed, more recent research may not have yet achieved its deserved place of prominence among the works listed. Moreover, older research may not be as recognized by current researchers, yet may be equally relevant. What began as a simple question of which articles on IS research are most important has only led us to a beginning, a point from which we can continue to ponder and reflect upon exemplary works on IS research.

REFERENCES

Athey, S., & Plotnicki, J. (2000). An evaluation of research productivity in academic IT. *Communications of the Association for Information Systems*, *3*(7).

Barki, H., Rivard, S., & Talbot, J. (1993). A keyword classification scheme for IS research literature. *MIS Quarterly*, *17*(2), 209-226.

Benbasat, I., & Lim, L. H. (1993). The effects of group, task, context and technology variables on the usefulness of group support systems: A meta-analysis of experimental studies. *Small Group Research*, 430-462.

Boynton, A. C., & Zmud, R. W. (1987). Information technology planning in the 1990's: Directions for practice and research. *MIS Quarterly, 11*(1), 59-71.

Brown, L. D. (1996). Influential accounting articles, individuals, Ph.D. granting institutions and faculties: A citational analysis. *Accounting, Organizations and Society, 21*(7,8), 723-754.

Carnegie Foundation for the Advancement of Teaching. (2002). *Carnegie classification of institutions of higher education.* Retrieved December 20, 2002 from: http://www.carnegiefoundation.org/Classification/CIHE2000/defNotes/Definitions.htm.

Churchill, G. A. (1979). A paradigm for developing better measures of marketing constructs. *Journal of Marketing Research, 16*, 64-73.

Cook, T. D., & Campbell, D. T. (1976). Four kinds of validity. In M. D. Dunnette (Ed.), *Handbook of Industrial and Organizational Psychology.* Chicago, IL: Rand McNally. (Reprinted from *The design and conduct of quasi-experiments and true experiments in field settings.*)

Culnan, M. J. (1987). Mapping the intellectual structure of MIS, 1980-1985: A co-citation analysis. *MIS Quarterly, 11*(3), 341-353.

Culnan, M. J., & Swanson, E. B. (1986). Research in management information systems, 1980-1984: Points of work and reference. *MIS Quarterly, 10*(3), 289-302.

Dombrow, J., & Turnbull, G. K. (2002). Individuals and institutions publishing research in real estate, 1989-1998. *Journal of Real Estate Literature, 10*(1), 45-92.

Gill, T. G. (2001). What's an MIS paper worth? (An exploratory analysis). *Data Base for Advances in Information Systems, 32*(2), 14-33.

Gillenson, M., & Stutz, J. (1991). Academic issues in MIS: Journals and books. *MIS Quarterly, 15*(4), 447-452.

Goodrum, A. A., McCain, K. W., Lawrence, S., & Giles, C. L. (2001). Scholarly publishing in the Internet age: A citation analysis of computer science literature. *Information Processing & Management, 37*(5), 661-675.

Hardgrave, B., & Walstrom, K. (1997). Forums for MIS scholars. *Communications of the ACM, 40*(11), 119-124.

Holsapple, C., Johnson, L., Manakyan, H., & Tanner, J. (1994). Business computing research journals: A normalized citation analysis. *Journal of Management Information Systems, 11*(1), 131-140.

Ives, B., & Olson, M. H. (1984). User Involvement in Information Systems: A critical review of the empirical literature. *Management Science, 30*(5), 586-603.

Ives, B., Hamilton, S., & Davis, G. (1980). A framework for research in computer-based management information systems. *Management Science, 26*(9), 910-934.

Jarvenpaa, S., Dickson, G., & DeSanctis, G. (1985). Methodological issues in experimental IS research: Experiences and recommendations. *MIS Quarterly, 9*(2), 141-156.

Kleijnen, J. P. C. (2000). Measuring the quality of publications: New methodology and case study. *Information Processing & Management, 36*(4), 551-570.

Leigh, T., Pullins, E. B., & Comer, L. B. (2001). The top 10 sales articles of the 20th century. *The Journal of Personal Selling & Sales Management, 21*(3), 217-227.

McCormick, J. M., & Rice, T. W. (2001). Graduate training and research productivity in the 1990s: A look at who publishes. *PS: Political Science & Politics, 34*(3), 675-680.

Mylonopoulos, N. A., & Theoharakis, V. (2001). Global perceptions of IS journals. *Communications of the ACM, 44*(9), 29-33.

Schwab, D. P. (1980). Construct validity in organizational behavior. *Research in Organizational Behavior, 2*, 3-43.

Walstrom, K., Hardgrave, B., & Wilson, R. (1995). Forums for management information systems scholars. *Communications of the ACM, 38*(3), 93-102.

Whitman, M. E., Hendrickson, A., & Townsend, A. (1999). Academic rewards for teaching, research and service: Data and discourse. *Information Systems Research, 10*(2), 99-109.

APPENDIX

The Exemplary Works on IS Research

Alavi, M., & Carlson, P. (1992). A review of MIS research and disciplinary development. *Journal of Management Information Systems, 8*(4), 45-62.

Barki, H., Rivard, S., & Talbot, J. (1993). A keyword classification scheme for IS research literature: An update. *MIS Quarterly, 17*(2), 209-226.

Baroudi, J., & Orlikowski, W. (1989). The problem of statistical power in MIS research. *MIS Quarterly, 13*(1), 87-106.

Baskerville, R., & Wood-Harper, A. (1996). A critical perspective on action research as a method for information systems research. *Journal of Information Technology, 11*, 235-246.

Benbasat, I., & Weber, R. (1996). Research commentary: Rethinking "diversity" in information systems research. *Information Systems Research, 7*(4), 389-399.

Benbasat, I., & Zmud, R. (1999). Empirical research in information systems: The practice of relevance. *MIS Quarterly, 32*(1), 3-16.

Benbasat, I., Dexter, A., Drury, D., & Goldstein, R. (1984). A critique of the stage hypothesis: Theory and empirical evidence. *Communications of the ACM, 7*(5), 476-485.

Benbasat, I., Goldstein, D., & Mead, M. (1987). The case research strategy in studies of information systems. *MIS Quarterly, 11*(3), 369-386.

Cavaye, A. (1996). Case study research: A multi-faceted research approach for IS. *Information Systems Journal, 6*(3), 227-242.

Cheon, M., Grover, V., & Sabherwal, R. (1993). The evolution of empirical research in IS: A study of IS maturity. *Information & Management, 24*(3), 107-119.

Chin, W., & Todd, P. (1995). On the use, usefulness, and ease of use of structural equation modeling in MIS research: A note of caution. *MIS Quarterly, 19*(2), 237-246.

Cooper, R., Blair, D., Pao, M., & Pao, L. (1993). Communicating MIS research: A citation study of journal influence. *Information Processing & Management, 24*(1), 73-102.

Culnan, M., & Swanson, E. (1986). Research in management information systems, 1980-1984: Points of work and reference. *MIS Quarterly, 10*(3), 288-302.

Culnan, M. J. (1987). Mapping the intellectual structure of MIS, 1980-1985: A co-citation analysis. *MIS Quarterly, 11*(3), 341-353.

Darke, P., Shanks, G., & Broadbent, M. (1998). Successfully completing case study research: Combining rigour, relevance and pragmatism. *Information Systems Journal, 8*(4), 273-289.

Dickson, G., Senn, J., & Chervany, N. (1977). Research in management information systems: The Minnesota experiments. *Management Science, 23*(9), 913-923.

Drury, D., & Farhoomand, A. (1997). Improving management information systems research: Question order effects in surveys. *Information Systems Journal, 7*(3), 241-251.

Gable, G. (1994). Integrating case study and survey research methods: An example in information systems. *European Journal of Information Systems, 3*(2), 112-126.

Galliers, R., & Land, F. (1987). Choosing appropriate information systems research methodologies. *Communications of the ACM, 30*(11), 900-902.

Gefen, D., Straub, D., & Boudreau, M. (2000). Structural equation modeling and regression: Guidelines for research practice. *Communications of the AIS, 4*(7), 1-70.

Grover, V., Lee, C., & Durand, D. (1993). Analyzing methodological rigor of MIS survey research from 1980-1989. *Information & Management, 25,* 305-317.

Hamilton, S., & Ives, B. (1982a). Knowledge utilization among MIS researchers. *MIS Quarterly, 14*(2), 3-14.

Hamilton, S., & Ives, B. (1982b). MIS research strategies. *Information & Management, 5*(6), 339-347.

Holsapple, C., Johnson, L., Manakyan, H., & Tanner, J. (1994). Business computing research journals: A normalized citation analysis. *Journal of Management Information Systems, 11*(1), 131-140.

Hufnagel, E., & Conca, C. (1994). User response data: The potential for errors and biases. *Information Systems Research, 5*(1), 48-73.

Hwang, M. (1996). The use of meta-analysis in MIS research: Promises and problems. *Data Base for Advances in Information Systems, 27*(3), 35-48.

Ives, B., Hamilton, S., & Davis, G. (1980). A framework for research in computer-based management information systems. *Management Science, 26*(9), 910-934.

Jarvenpaa, S. (1988). The importance of laboratory experimentation in information systems research. *Communications of the ACM, 31*(12), 1502-1504.

Jarvenpaa, S., Dickson, G., & DeSanctis, G. (1985). Methodological issues in experimental IS research: Experiences and recommendations. *MIS Quarterly, 9*(2), 141-156.

Kaplan, B., & Duchon, D. (1988). Combining qualitative and quantitative methods in information systems research: A case study. *MIS Quarterly, 12*(4), 571-587.

Klein, B., Goodhue, D., & Davis, G. (1997). Can humans detect errors in data? Impact of base rates, incentives, and goals. *MIS Quarterly, 21*(2), 169-195.

Klein, H., & Myers, M. (1999). A set of principles for conducting and evaluating interpretive field studies in information systems. *MIS Quarterly, 23*(1), 67-94.

Lacity, M., & Janson, M. (1994). Understanding qualitative data: A framework of text analysis methods. *Journal of Management Information Systems, 11*(2), 137-155.

Lee, A. (1989). A scientific methodology for MIS case studies. *MIS Quarterly, 13*(1), 33-50.

Lee, A. (1999). Rigor and relevance in MIS research: Beyond the approach of positivism alone. *MIS Quarterly, 21*(1), 29-33.

Lee, B., Barua, A., & Whinston, A. (1997). Discovery and representation of causal relationships in MIS research: A methodological framework. *MIS Quarterly, 21*(1), 109-136.

Lyytinen, K. (1999). Empirical research in information systems: On the relevance of practice in thinking of IS research. *MIS Quarterly, 23*(1), 25-27.

Mason, R., & Mitroff, I. (1973). A program for research on management information systems. *Management Science, 19*(5), 475-487.

Myers, M. (1999). Investigating information systems with ethnographic research. *Communications of the AIS, 2*(23), 1-20.

Nolan, R., & Wetherbe, J. (1980). Toward a comprehensive framework for MIS research. *MIS Quarterly, 4*(2), 1-19.

Nurminen, M. (1999). Research notes—Information systems research: The "infurgic" perspective. *International Journal of Information Management, 19*(1), 87-94.

Orlikowski, W., & Baroudi, J. (1991). Studying information technology in organizations: Research approaches and assumptions. *Information Systems Research, 2*(1), 1-28.

Pinsonneault, A., & Kraemer, K. (1993). Survey research methodology in management information systems: An assessment. *Journal of Management Information Systems, 10*(2), 75-105.

Remenyi, D., & Williams, B. (1996). The nature of research: Qualitative or quantitative, narrative or paradigmatic? *Information Systems Journal, 6,* 131-146.

Robey, D. (1996). Research commentary: Diversity in information systems research: Threat, promise, and responsibility. *Information Systems Research, 7*(4), 400-408.

Robey, D. (1998). Beyond rigor and relevance: Producing consumable research about information systems. *Information Resources Management Journal, 11*(1), 7-15.

Segars, A. (1997). Assessing the unidimensionality of measurement: A paradigm and illustration within the context of information systems research. *Omega, 25*(1), 107.

Sethi, V., & King, W. (1991). Construct measurement in information systems research: An illustration in strategic systems. *Decision Sciences, 22,* 455-472.

Silverman, D. (1998). Qualitative research: Meanings or practices? *Information Systems Journal, 8*(1), 3-20.

Straub, D. (1989). Validating instruments in MIS research. *MIS Quarterly, 13*(2), 147-169.

Straub, D., Soon, A., & Evaristo, R. (1994). Normative standards for IS research. *Data Base, 25*(1), 21-34.

Swanson, E., Burton, R., & Neil, C. (1993). Information systems research thematics: Submissions to a new journal, 1987-1992. *Information Systems Research, 4*(4), 299-330.

Teng, J., & Galletta, D. (1990). MIS research directions: A survey of researchers' views. *Data Base, 22*(1&2), 53-62.

Walsham, G. (1995). The emergence of intrepretism in IS research. *Information Systems Research, 6*(4), 376-394.

Weber, R. (1987). Toward a theory of artifacts: A paradigmatic base for information systems research. *Information Systems,* (Spring), 3-19.

Weill, P., & Olson, M. (1989). An assessment of the contingency theory of management information systems. *Journal of Management Information Systems, 6*(1), 59-85.

Westfall, R. (1999). An IS research relevance manifesto. *Communications of the AIS, 2*(September), Article 14.

Zmud, R. (1978). On the validity of the analytical-heuristic instrument utilized in "The Minnesota experiments". *Management Science, 24*(10), 1088-1090.

Chapter II

Validating IS Positivist Instrumentation: 1997-2001

Marie-Claude Boudreau
University of Georgia, USA

Thilini Ariyachandra
University of Georgia, USA

David Gefen
Drexel University, USA

Detmar W. Straub
Georgia State University, USA

ABSTRACT

Research quality depends on appropriate statistical validity, a major aspect of which is appropriate instrumentation. This survey examines the quality of IS instrumentation in five leading journals for a five-year period and concludes that much has been done to improve IS research quality through better instrument validation since the last two benchmark studies. Additional recommendations dealing with the current weak spots are discussed.

INTRODUCTION

The issue of rigor has been the subject of much discussion among information systems (IS) scholars. It has been argued that IS lacks the distinctiveness and rigor usually associated with scientific disciplines and remains institutionally weak (Avgerou,

2000). A specific area where rigor should be improved is the extent of instrument validation, as demonstrated in the work conducted by Straub and his colleagues (e.g., Boudreau, Gefen, & Straub, 2001; Straub, 1989). In Straub's article, it was reported that 19% of the articles in three IS journals over a three-year period had utilized either a pretest or a pilot test, 17% had reported reliability of their scales, 14% had validated their constructs, and only 4% had assessed content validity. These disappointing findings compelled Straub to issue a call for rigorous instrument validation, which was reassessed about a decade later. Boudreau et al.'s study, which expanded the number of sampled articles through the inclusion of additional journals, determined that "some real progress has been made in validating IS research." Indeed, their study showed that 47% of the sampled articles used a pretest or a pilot test, 63% reported reliability, 37% validated their constructs, and 23% assessed content validity. Although such improvements are considerable, Boudreau and her colleagues believed that these percentages were insufficient, and that "the field still has ground to make up to reach more comfortable levels of validation."

Enhancing instrument validation, we argue, will improve the overall process of conducting quantitative research because it is an elementary building block of statistical validity without which the results of any research are questionable (Cook & Campbell, 1979). In that spirit, this study seeks to provide an up-to-date assessment of the extent to which instrument validation is done rigorously. Our goal is to verify if IS researchers, considering their most recent publications, better validate their research instruments than they did before. We believe that in the past two years many researchers and journal editors have responded to the challenge of rigor in instrument validation as they now better understand its importance. This up-to-date assessment considers the same five journals as in Boudreau et al.'s (2001) work but extends the period of coverage to include five full years (i.e., from January 1997 to December 2001). The findings resulting from this inquiry lead us to highlight our strengths and weaknesses, which should be considered by IS researchers, reviewers, and journal editors. The basic premise of this evaluation is that the quality of research design directly manifests itself in the importance of the research findings and that without good design the conclusions may be unwarranted.

METHOD

The method used in the current research replicates the one used in Boudreau et al. (2001). Accordingly, articles were sampled from the same five journals: *MIS Quarterly, Information Systems Research, Journal of Management Information Systems, Management Science,* and *Information & Management.* Although the original journal selection was mainly based on Nord and Nord's (1995) study, it is consistent with more recent rankings (i.e., Mylonopoulos & Theoharakis, 2001; Whitman, Hendrickson, & Townsend, 1999), which consider these five publishing outlets as being important ones within the field of MIS.

Sampling and Coding Procedures

Articles from these five journals were reviewed, read, and coded for a period of inquiry starting in January 1997 and ending in December 2001. As in Straub (1989) and in Boudreau et al. (2001), the qualifying criteria for the sample were that the article employed either: (a) correlational or statistical manipulation of variables or (b) some form of quantitative data analysis, even if the data analysis was simply descriptive statistics. Studies utilizing archival data (e.g., citation analysis) or unobtrusive measures (e.g., computer system accounting measures) were omitted from the sample unless it was clear from the methodological description that key variable relationships being studied could have been submitted to validation procedures.

Eleven attributes were coded for each surveyed article. Each one of these attributes is briefly presented here (additional information on the rationale for collecting each one of these attributes can be found in Boudreau et al., 2001). The first attribute collected was the *type of research,* which enabled differentiating between confirmatory research (which tests prespecified relationships) and exploratory research (which defines possible relationships in only the most general form).

The second attribute examined was the *research method*. Research was classified into one of four research methods based on Stone (1978, 1979): (1) laboratory experiments, (2) field experiments, (3) field studies, and (4) case studies.

The third and fourth attributes examined dealt with whether the study employed a *pretest* and/or a *pilot* study. Alreck and Settle (1995) define a pretest as a preliminary trial of some or all aspects of the instrument to ensure that there are no unanticipated difficulties. This is to be distinguished from a pilot study, which these authors describe as a brief preliminary survey, often using a small, convenience sample.

The fifth and sixth attributes collected dealt with whether the study checked *content validity* and *construct validity*. Content validity is the extent to which the items in a test produces consistent or error-free results (Cronbach, 1971; Rogers, 1995). Construct validity is the extent to which the operationalization of a construct measures the concepts that it purports to measure (Straub, 1989; Zaltman, Duncan, & Holbek, 1973). Subtypes of construct validity include convergent validity, discriminant validity, nomological validity, criterion-related validity, predictive validity, and concurrent validity (Bagozzi, 1980; Cronbach, 1990; Rogers, 1995).[1]

The seventh attributed coded was whether an assessment of instrument *reliability* was reported. As previously defined, reliability assesses measurement accuracy, i.e., "the extent to which an instrument produces consistent or error-free results" (Rogers, 1995). In addition to the traditional measures of reliability, covariance-based structured equation modeling (SEM) techniques also allow the assessment of unidimensionality, which assesses whether there is only one underlying construct within each latent construct (Gerbing & Anderson, 1988; Segars, 1997). That too was included in this attribute.

Manipulation checks constituted the eighth coded attribute. Manipulation checks are necessary in laboratory and field experiments to assess whether a treatment group indeed received accurately the treatment it was supposed to receive. Simply put, manipulation checks measure the extent to which a treatment was administered correctly, such as whether the subjects perceived what they were exposed to accurately (Bagozzi, 1977). It is crucial in experimental settings that subjects be "manipulated" as intended.

The *nature of the instrument* was the ninth coded attribute. A research instrument was identified as either based or not based on a preexisting instrument. If little information was provided about the source of the instrument, it was assumed that it was developed "from scratch."

The tenth coded attribute dealt with whether an *instrument validation section* was included in the study. As recommended by Straub (1989), such a section, detailing what validation steps were taken, should be included in the reporting of empirical research.

The eleventh and final collected attribute was the use of second-generation statistical techniques, namely structured equation modeling (SEM) tools such as LISREL, PLS, EQS, and AMOS. Boudreau et al.'s (2001) study pointed to the fact that instrument validation is often more comprehensive when done with SEM, and, therefore, the inclusion of this attribute was worthy in the current study as well.

It should be noted that each instrument was treated as a whole. For example, in the cases where reliability was done on at least one construct within an instrument, then the instrument in its entirety was considered as if it had been assessed for reliability. This was true for all criteria. Provided this procedure, the findings of this study tend to overestimate the extent to which the field is rigorous in its validation efforts.

Another factor that also contributed to the overestimation of our assessment was the a priori choice of publication outlets. Given that our choice of journals is representative of high-quality research in the field of IS, the findings of this study, again, tend to overestimate the validation efforts pursued in our field. One should thus keep that mind while pondering the meaning of the results.

STUDY RESULTS

Sample

A total of 293 articles were used in the analysis. Among the articles reviewed, 41 originated in *MIS Quarterly,* 38 in *Information Systems Research,* 119 in *Information & Management,* 78 in *Journal of Management Information Systems*, and 17 in *Management Science.* Whereas most (68%) were field studies, coded works also included laboratory experiments (22%), case studies (5%), and field experiments (5%). In only 23% of the sampled articles, students (undergraduate or graduate) filled out the instrument. In the remainder of the articles, workers (sometimes in conjunction with students) were the ones to whom the instrument was administered. As far as the different techniques for data collection, it is worth mentioning that the majority (85%) of our sampled studies have collected data through the use of surveys (questionnaires). The conduct of an interview was the second most used technique, with 17% of the sampled articles using it. The use of more than one technique to capture data occurred in 31% of the studies.

Validation of Coding

Inter-rater was assessed to verify that our coding was reliable (Miles & Huberman, 1994). A second, independent coder thus coded a subset of the sampled articles. For the 11 coded attributes, the following percentages of agreement were obtained: *type of research—77%; research method—85%; pretest—82%; pilot test—95%; content validity—90%; construct validity—85%; reliability—85%; manipulation check—95%; nature of the instrument—82%; instrument validation section—92%;* and *use of second-generation statistical technique—95%.*

Cohen's (1960) kappa coefficient was also calculated. This coefficient is known to be a more stringent measure than simple percentages of agreement. For all criteria, the

Table 1. Survey of Instrument Validation Use in MIS Literature.

Inst. Categories / Year	Straub (1989)	Boudreau et al. (2001)	Current Study
Pretest	13%	26%	31%
Pilot	6%	31%	31%
Pretest or Pilot [i]	19%	47%	51%
Previous Instr. Utilized	17%	42%	43%
Content Validity	4%	23%	26%
Construct Validity	14%	37%	45%
Reliability	17%	63%	68%

i = Because some articles used both a pretest and a pilot, the category Pretest or Pilot does not add up to Pretest plus Pilot.

average kappa was 0.76, which is above the recommended 0.70 inter-rater minimum reliability (Bowers & Courtright, 1984; Landis & Koch, 1977; Miles & Huberman, 1994). As usual, disagreements between coders were reconciled before further analysis was performed.

Overview of Findings

Table 1 clearly shows that, over the past 13 years, instrument validation has improved in *all* the categories we have assessed. In addition, in two specific categories (pretest/pilot and reliability), the proportion of published studies validating their instruments is now *greater* than the proportion of published studies not validating their instruments. When comparing with Boudreau et al. (2001), the most important improvement is for construct validity, which was then assessed in 37% of the studies compared to 45% of the studies today. Improvement up to an additional 5% is noticeable in all other categories. Overall, although improvement in instrument validation is modest when comparing Boudreau et al.'s results to the current study's results, it is still comforting to observe a *consistent* increase in the use of all validation techniques.

Reliability is the validation criterion that was the most frequently assessed, when compared to all other validation criteria taken singly, in both previous studies as well as this one. As was the case in Boudreau et al. (2001), a majority of studies assessing reliability of their instruments have done so through the standard coefficient of internal consistency, i.e., Cronbach's α (84%). The second most popular technique to assess reliability was inter-coder tests, which was reported by 15% of the studies that appraised the reliability of their instrument. Moreover, the use of more than one reliability method is still rare, as it was done by only 10% of the studies assessing reliability.

A closer look at the studies that assessed construct validity reveals that diverse approaches were used for that purpose. More specifically, convergent, discriminant, and nomological validity were determined, respectively, in 50%, 58%, and 6% of these studies. As to predictive and concurrent validity, they were reported in 7% and 1.5% of these studies. Construct validity, in itself (and not in one of its five components), was recounted in 80% of the studies that assessed this kind of validity.

Table 2. Studies with Previously Utilized Instruments vs. those with New Instruments.

Inst. Categories	Previous Instrument (n=127)		New Instrument (n=166)	
	Boudreau et al. (2001)	Current Study	Boudreau et al. (2001)	Current Study
Pretest or Pilot	43%	46%	50%	55%
Content Validity	20%	24%	25%	28%
Construct Validity	44%	50%	32%	42%
Reliability	74%	74%	54%	63%

Table 1 shows that the utilization of previously existing instruments has more than doubled over the last 13 years. Also, as detailed in Table 2, it appears that studies using existing instruments were sometimes more inclined to validate their instrument than studies developing their own instrument from scratch. Indeed, construct validity and reliability were more frequently assessed in studies using a previously utilized instrument than those that did not (50% vs. 42%; 74% vs. 63%). However, with regard to the use of pretest or pilot studies and content validity, these validities were assessed more often within studies creating a new instrument than within studies using an existing instrument (55% vs. 46%; 28% vs. 24%). This table reveals another interesting fact: Over the past two years, research articles that created their own instrument improved their validation practices to a greater extent than research articles that used a previously utilized instrument.

It is interesting to observe how confirmatory studies (133 articles, or 45% of total) compare to exploratory studies (160 articles, or 55% of total). The present survey indicates that, for all criteria except for the use of pretest or pilot studies, exploratory studies showed less interest in validating their instruments than confirmatory studies (see Table 3). Indeed, the extent to which content validity, construct validity, and reliability were assessed was more frequent among confirmatory studies than among exploratory studies. This represents the same trend that was observed in Boudreau et al. (2001).

The extent to which a research method has bearing on instrument validation constitutes an interesting observation. In Straub's (1989) original study, it was argued that experimental and case researchers were less likely to validate their instruments than

Table 3. Type of Research (Confirmatory vs. Exploratory Studies).

Inst. Categories	Confirmatory Studies (45%)		Exploratory Studies (55%)	
	Boudreau et al. (2001)	Current Study	Boudreau et al. (2001)	Current Study
Pretest or Pilot	47%	49%	47%	53%
Content Validity	35%	35%	17%	19%
Construct Validity	53%	61%	29%	33%
Reliability	69%	75%	60%	62%

Table 4. Field Studies vs. Lab/Field Experiments vs. Case Studies.

Inst. Categories	Field Studies (n=200)	Lab/Fields Experiments (n=80)	Case Studies (n=13)
Pretest or Pilot	59%	36%	31%
Previous Inst. Utilized	47%	38%	23%
Content Validity	32%	15%	15%
Construct Validity	55%	24%	38%
Reliability	69%	65%	62%

field study researchers. Boudreau et al.'s (2001) study showed a similar trend when comparing field studies to experimental studies, but not to case studies. The additional data used in the present study demonstrates that Straub's initial inference still holds true today on *all* of the previously introduced validity criteria (see Table 4). Indeed, field study researchers from our sample were more inclined to validate their instrument than experimental and case researchers. The most notable difference was for the use of construct validity, where a gap of 31% existed between experimental and field study research.

The inclusion of an Instrument Validation section, as originally suggested in Straub (1989), was tallied as frequently in the current study as it was in Boudreau et al.'s (2001) study. Indeed, only 24% of the surveyed articles included such a section. For this minority of articles, there was a greater extent of reporting a pilot or pretest study (80% vs. 42%), content validity (52% vs. 18%), construct validity (82% vs. 34%), and reliability (88% vs. 61%). These percentages are hardly surprising since if one feels compelled to include a specific section on instrument validation, it is because efforts have been done in this area. However, it is disappointing not to observe an increase in the percentage of studies that included a special section reporting their endeavor in instrument validation.

Noticeable improvement has occurred in the use of manipulation check in the past few years. As indicated in Table 5, among the field and laboratory experiments in our sample, 30% performed one or several manipulation checks of the treatments, compared to 22% in Boudreau's et al.'s (2001) study. Moreover, percentages have particularly increased in two journals, that is, *MIS Quarterly* (increase of 21%) and *Information Systems Research* (increase of 12%). The absence of manipulation checks in the experimental studies of *Management Science* may be due to the tendency for articles of this journal to use directly observable measurements, such as time, rather then latent constructs.

A greater percentage of studies from our sample used second-generation statistical techniques (e.g., structural equation modeling) rather than first-generation statistical techniques (regression, ANOVA, LOGIT, etc.). From 15% in Boudreau et al. (2001), this percentage increased to 19% in the present study (see Table 6). However, the extent of instrument validation did not change much when comparing first- to second-generation

Table 5.   Use of Manipulation Validity.

Journal	Boudreau et al. (2001)	Current Study
Information & Management	24%	25%
Information Systems Research	38%	50%
MIS Quarterly	29%	50%
Journal of Management Information Systems	17%	19%
Management Science	0%	0%
All Five Journals	22%	30%

techniques in the two studies. As was the case in Boudreau et al., studies making use of SEM techniques scored higher in all categories, particularly for construct validity and reliability. Among the studies using second-generation statistical techniques, the most commonly used tools were PLS (42%), LISREL (21%), and EQS (18%).

A possible reason for this difference is that SEM analyzes both the *structural model* (the assumed causation) and the *measurement model* (the loadings of observed items). As a result, validity assessment is an integral part of SEM. The validity statistics appear explicitly in the output, and the degree of statistical validity directly affects the overall model fit indexes. In first-generation statistical techniques, on the other hand, validity and reliability are performed in separate analyses that are not related to the actual hypothesis testing and, thus, do not determine the overall fit indexes.

Summary of Key Points

It should be considered good news that, in the short period of two years since the last study assessing instrument validation practices, IS researchers have improved the validation of their instrument. Granted, such an improvement is certainly not as signifi-cant as what had been observed when using Straub's (1989) study as the baseline, but this is understandable given that the time period was then much longer. Although better, the current validation practices are far from perfect, and it is still necessary to state that

Table 6.   First-Generation vs. Second-Generation Statistical Techniques.

	Boudreau et al. (2001)		Current Study	
Inst. Categories	First Generation (85%)	Second Generation (15%)	First Generation (81%)	Second Generation (19%)
Pretest or Pilot	44%	64%	48%	63%
Previous Inst. Utilized	42%	46%	43%	46%
Content Validity	19%	43%	23%	39%
Construct Validity	29%	82%	36%	86%
Reliability	57%	96%	61%	93%

IS researchers need to achieve greater rigor in the validation of their instruments and their research. More particularly, the following nine key findings should engage further reflection and action:

1. Over the past two years, instrument validation practices have steadily improved.
2. In two specific categories (pretest/pilot and reliability), the proportion of published studies validating their instruments is now *greater* than the proportion of published studies not validating their instruments.
3. The assessment of construct validity has improved the most over the past two years.
4. Published studies are increasingly using preexisting instruments; while doing so, reliability and construct validity are being more frequently assessed.
5. Confirmatory studies are more likely to assess reliability, content validity, and construct validity than exploratory studies.
6. Laboratory experiments, field experiments, and case studies lag behind field studies with respect to all validation criteria.
7. Although the inclusion of an Instrument Validation subsection warrants greater reporting of validation practices, it appears infrequently in empirical studies.
8. There has been a noticeable improvement in the use of manipulation check in the past few years; however, in some publications outlets, manipulation check is only done by a minority of IS experimenters.
9. Published studies making use of second-generation statistical techniques (SEM) are much more likely to validate their instruments than published studies making use of first-generation statistical techniques.

DISCUSSION

Research quality is a never-ending process of striving for improvement and a process of reexamination of previous methods. It is a crucial process, for it is through this constant cycle of self-assessment and consequential improvement that scientific methods are improved and the results of science become more reliable, valid, and significant. We are glad to report that this self-improvement process seems to be working in IS research. The study shows there is reason to be optimistic, although much still needs to be done. In all the aspects we examined, the results of this study show that there has been remarkable improvement in instrument validation practices since Straub's initial plea in 1989. Furthermore, even in the short time period of two years that differentiates this study from Boudreau et al.'s (2001) study, it is clear that validation practices have improved some, at least modestly. This seems to be at least in part because of the growing awareness of the need to ensure quality research in the IS community and the growing popularity of SEM tools (see Gefen, Straub, & Boudreau, 2000, for a comparison of these). It appears that researchers, reviewers, and journal editors have made a conscious effort in the past years to include more rigor in their work. This should, if the trend continues, help reduce the skeptical questions about the quality of the work conducted by IS researchers (e.g., Avgerou, 2000).

Looking at the half-empty part of the glass, we could also observe that instrument validation practices are yet to be carried out a majority of the time, except for the assessment of reliability and the use of a pretest/pilot study. In addition, one should realize that these results are overestimates (as explained earlier), and that instrument validation is likely to be done to a much lesser extent in less prestigious IS journals and conferences. In other words, one can surmise that, in many cases, research is being conducted (and later published) with little validation of the data collection instruments. What does that say about the quality of our work? We caution the IS research community not to have a false sense of complacency when looking at the results of the current study. Improvement has been noticed, yes, but much more lies ahead and needs to be done.

Perhaps one of the most noticeable changes has been in the increased application of SEM and with it the heightened attention researchers are forced to give to verifying construct validity and reliability. Where in first-generation tools researchers could figuratively sweep unwarranted variance under the carpet, with SEM researchers are forced to a much larger degree to face this unwarranted variance with SEM tools and account for it by improving their scales and model. Clearly, statistical analysis when done with an appropriate SEM tool is much better and more reliable and shows greater construct validity (Gefen et al., 2000; Hair, Anderson, Tatham, & Black, 1995). It is, in fact, hard to get a good structural model in SEM where the measurement model statistics, namely, reliability and construct validity, are not up to the standard. Indeed, the reporting of these two statistics is considerably higher with research based on SEM as its analysis tool.

CONCLUSION

Good research is built first and foremost on good research design and correct data analysis. Science will not progress without statistical validity that is brought about by a meticulous attention to instrument validation through pretesting and pilot testing, to reliability, to content and construct validity, and to the correct application of appropriate tools. With this in mind, the results of this survey are encouraging.

REFERENCES

Alreck, P. A., & Settle, R. B. (1995). *The Survey Research Handbook* (2nd ed.). Chicago, IL: Irwin.

Avgerou, C. (2000). Information systems: What sort of science is it? *Omega 28*(5), 567-579.

Bagozzi, R. P. (1977). Structural equation models in experimental research. *Journal of Marketing Research, 14*, 209-236.

Bagozzi, R. P. (1980). *Causal Methods in Marketing*. New York: John Wiley & Sons.

Boudreau, M.-C., Gefen, D., & Straub, D. (2001). Validation in IS research: A state-of-the-art assessment. *MIS Quarterly, 25*(1), 1-16.

Bowers, J. W., & Courtright, J. A. (1984). *Communication Research Methods*. Glenview, IL: Scott, Foresman.

Campbell, D. T. (1960). Recommendations for APA test standards regarding construct, trait, discriminant validity. *American Psychologist, 15*, 546-553.

Cohen, J. (1960). A coefficient of agreement for nominal scales. *Educational and Psychological Measurement, 20*, 37-46.

Cook, T. D., & Campbell, D. T. (1979). *Quasi Experimentation: Design and Analytical Issues for Field Settings.* Chicago, IL: Rand McNally.

Cronbach, L. J. (1971). Test validation. In R. L. Thorndike (Ed.), *Educational Measurement* (pp. 443-507). Washington, D.C.: American Council on Education.

Cronbach, L. J. (1990). *Essentials of Psychological Testing.* New York: Harper & Row.

Gefen, D., Straub, D., & Boudreau, M.-C. (2000). Structural equation modeling and regression: Guidelines for research practice. *Communications of AIS, 4*(7).

Gerbing, D. W., & Anderson, J. C. (1988). An updated paradigm for scale development incorporating unidimensionality and its assessment. *Journal of Marketing Research, 25*, 186-192.

Hair, J. F., Jr., Anderson, R. E., Tatham, R. L., & Black, W. C. (1995). *Multivariate Data Analysis with Readings.* Englewood Cliffs, NJ: Prentice Hall.

Landis, J. R., & Koch, G. G. (1977). The measurement of observer agreement for categorical data. *Biometrics, 22*, 79-94.

Miles, M. B., & Huberman, A. M. (1994). *Qualitative Data Analysis: An Expanded Sourcebook.* Thousand Oaks, CA: SAGE.

Mumford, M. D., & Stokes, G. S. (1992). Developmental determinants of individual action: Theory and practice in the application of background data measures. In M. D. Dunnette & L. M. Hough (Eds.), *Handbook of Industrial and Organizational Psychology* (2nd ed., pp. 61-138). Palo Alto, CA: Consulting Psychologists Press.

Mylonopoulos, N., & Theoharakis, V. (2001). On-site: Global perceptions of IS journals. *Communications of the ACM, 44*(9), 29-33.

Nord, J. H., & Nord, G. D. (1995). MIS research: Journal status assessment and analysis. *Information & Management, 29*(1), 29-42.

Rogers, T. B. (1995). *The Psychological Testing Enterprise.* Pacific Grove, CA: Brooks/Cole.

Segars, A. H. (1997). Assessing the unidimensionality of measurement: A paradigm and illustration within the context of information systems research. *Omega, 25*(1), 107-121.

Stone, E. F. (1978). *Research Methods in Organizational Behavior.* Glenview, IL: Scott, Foresman.

Stone, E. F. (1979). Research methods and philosophy of science. In S. Kiev (Ed.), *Organizational Behavior* (pp. 15-40). Columbus, OH: Scott, Foresman and Company.

Straub, D. W. (1989). Validating instruments in MIS research. *MIS Quarterly, 13*(2), 147-169.

Whitman, M., Hendrickson, A., & Townsend, A. (1999). Research commentary: Academic rewards for teaching, research and service: Data and discourse. *Information Systems Research, 10*(2), 99-109.

Zaltman, G., Duncan, R., & Holbek, J. (1973). *Innovations and Organizations.* New York: John Wiley & Sons.

ENDNOTES

[1]   Whereas some researchers conceptualize predictive validity as different from construct validity (e.g., Bagozzi, 1980; Campbell, 1960; Cronbach, 1990), others believe that predictive validity is an aspect of construct validity (Mumford & Stokes, 1992).

[2]   Because some articles used both a pretest and a pilot, the category Pretest or Pilot does not add up to Pretest plus Pilot.

Chapter III

A Multitrait-Multimethod Analysis of the End User Computing Satisfaction and Computer Self-Efficacy Instruments

Michael J. Masterson
United States Air Force, USA

R. Kelly Rainer, Jr.
Auburn University, USA

ABSTRACT

Researchers are employing confirmatory factor analysis (CFA) with multitrait-multimethod (MTMM) matrices to estimate parameters representing trait, method, and error variance, as well as parameters representing the correlations among traits (or factors). This study utilizes CFA with MTMM matrices to assess the convergent validity, discriminant validity, and the presence and effects of method variance in the end-user computing satisfaction instrument (EUCSI) and the computer self-efficacy instrument (CSE).

The results of the study indicate that, in these samples, the two instruments demonstrate adequate convergent and discriminant validity, but that method variance is present and accounts for a large proportion of the variance in both models. Further, the proposed factor structure of the EUCSI appears to be unstable as a result of the effects of multiple methods, while the proposed factor structure of the CSE remains stable in the presence of the methods.

INTRODUCTION

The development of constructs and instruments to operationalize them provide a theoretical basis for research in a discipline (Venkatraman & Grant, 1986). Indeed, concerns with management information systems as a cohesive research discipline have long included inadequate construct development and a lack of valid, reliable measurement constructs (see, e.g., Dickson, Benbasat, & King, 1980; Keen, 1980).

In the ongoing process of instrument validation, researchers are employing confirmatory factor analysis (CFA) with multitrait-multimethod (MTMM) matrices to estimate parameters representing trait, method, and error variance, as well as parameters representing the correlations among traits (or factors; Bagozzi & Yi, 1990; Byrne, 1994; Schmitt & Stults, 1986; Widaman, 1985). Using CFA with Widaman's (p. 6) taxonomy of covariance structure models allows researchers to test for statistically significant differences between hierarchically ordered, or nested, models. These tests permit researchers to assess convergent validity, discriminant validity, and the presence and effects of method variance (Bagozzi & Yi; Widaman).

Two instruments (among others), widely used in MIS studies, have research streams devoted to assessing their validity and reliability: the end-user computing satisfaction instrument (Doll & Torkzadeh, 1988; see Table 1) and the computer self-efficacy instrument (Murphy, Coover, & Owen, 1989; see Table 2). The purpose of this study is to utilize CFA with multitrait-multimethod matrices to assess the convergent validity, discriminant validity, and the presence and effects of method variance in these two instruments.

BACKGROUND

Convergent validity occurs when a measure correlates highly with other variables that should measure the same construct (Cronbach & Meehl, 1955). Discriminant validity occurs when a measure fails to correlate highly with measures of different, distinct constructs (Cronbach & Meehl).

Cronbach (1946) described the concept of method variance by noting that test responses may be influenced by variables other than the one ostensibly tested. Method variance is that variance attributable to measurement method rather than to the constructs of interest (Bagozzi & Yi, 1990; Campbell & Fiske, 1959). Researchers have concluded that method variance is common and accounts for substantial variance in research data collected from studies using only self-report questionnaires (Bagozzi & Yi; Spector, 1987; Williams, Cote, & Buckley, 1989).

Ideally, method variance would not be present or, if present, would not be statistically significant. Method variance is undesirable for two reasons. First, method variance reduces the validity of item responses. Second, when significant method variance is present, researchers cannot be confident that the instrument actually

Table 1. The End User Computing Satisfaction Instrument.

Content
- C1: Does the system provide the precise information you need?
- C2: Does the information content meet your needs?
- C3: Does the system provide reports that seem to be nearly exact to what you need?
- C4: Does the system provide sufficient information?

Accuracy
- A1: Is the system accurate?
- A2: Are you satisfied with the accuracy of your system?

Format
- F1: Do you think the output is presented in a useful format?
- F2: Is the information clear?

Ease of Use
- E1: Is the system user friendly?
- E2: Is the system easy to use?

Timeliness
- T1: Do you get the information you need in time?
- T2: Does the system provide up-to-date information?

measures the constructs that it is designed to measure. That is, the items may covary as a result of the influence of a latent variable and/or as a result of the influence of the method (Cronbach, 1946).

Research Stream on the End User Computing Satisfaction Instrument

Doll and Torkzadeh (1988) proposed, operationalized, and tested the EUCSI (see Table 1), which measured user satisfaction with specific computer applications. In their 1988 study, the authors gathered usable responses from 618 end users in 44 organizations. Using exploratory factor analysis (EFA), they extracted five factors, which they identified as content, format, accuracy, timeliness, and ease of use. Using the method proposed by Campbell and Fiske (1959), they assessed the convergent and discriminant validity of the EUCSI. They noted that method variance was present (Doll & Torkzadeh, p. 267), suggesting that the Campbell and Fiske method was not definitive in determining convergent and discriminant validity.

In follow-on research to the 1988 study, Doll, Xia, and Torkzadeh (1994) utilized the EUCSI to collect usable responses from 409 end users in 18 organizations. Using CFA, they confirmed the second-order factor model alluded to in 1988.

Table 2.   The Computer Self-Efficacy Instrument (Murphy, Coover, & Owen, 1989; Torkzadeh, Koufteros, & Pflughoeft, 1996).

Beginning Skills

B1: Entering and saving data (numbers or words) into a file	(Beg)
B2: Calling up a data file to view on the monitor screen ***	(Beg)
B3: Storing software correctly	(Beg)
B4: Handling a floppy disk correctly ***	(Beg)
B5: Escaping/exiting from a program or software ***	(Beg)
B6: Making selections from an on-screen menu ***	(Beg)
B7: Using the computer to write a letter or essay ***	(Beg)
B8: Moving the cursor around the monitor screen ***	(Beg)
B9: Working on a personal computer (microcomputer) ***	(Beg)
B10: Using a printer to make a "hardcopy" of my work ***	(Beg)

File and Software Skills

F1: Copying an individual file ***	(Beg)
F2: Getting rid of files when they are no longer needed ***	(Beg)
F3: Copying a disk	(Beg)
F4: Adding and deleting information from a data file ***	(Beg)
F5: Getting software up and running ***	(Beg)
F6: Organizing and managing files ***	(Beg)
F7: Explaining why a program (software) will or will not run on a given computer	(Adv)

Advanced Skills

A1: Understanding terms/words relating to computer software ***	(Adv)
A2: Understanding terms/words relating to computer hardware	(Adv)
A3: Describing the function of computer hardware (keyboard, disk drives, computer processing unit)	(Adv)
A4: Trouble shooting computer problems	(Adv)
A5: Understanding the three stages of data processing: input, processing, output ***	(Adv)
A6: Learning to use a variety of programs (software) ***	(Adv)
A7: Using the computer to organize information ***	(Adv)
A8: Writing simple programs for the computer	(Adv)
A9: Using the user's guide when help is needed	(Adv)
A10: Getting help for problems in the computer system	(Adv)
A11: Using the computer to analyze number data ++	(Adv)
A12: Learning advanced skills within a specific program (software) ++	(Adv)

Mainframe Skills

M1: Logging onto a mainframe computer system ***	(Mf)
M2: Logging off the mainframe computer system ***	(Mf)
M3: Working on a mainframe computer ***	(Mf)

*Note: Twenty-item version marked with ***
            Two items from original CSE marked with ++
            Beg, Adv, and Mf at the right margin are the original three-factor solution*

Research Stream on the Computer Self-Efficacy Instrument

Murphy et al. (1989) developed the 32-item CSE (see Table 2) and administered the instrument to a sample of 414 graduate students, adult vocational students, and nurses. Using EFA, they produced a three-factor model of the CSE, labeling the factors as beginning computer skills, advanced computer skills, and mainframe skills. The authors reported alpha reliabilities of 0.97, 0.96, and 0.92, respectively.

Harrison and Rainer (1992) administered the 32-item CSE to a sample of 693 salaried university personnel. Using EFA, they replicated the three-factor model of Murphy et al. (1989), reporting alpha reliabilities of 0.97, 0.95, and 0.98, respectively.

Torkzadeh and Koufteros (1994) administered a 30-item CSE to a sample of 224 undergraduate students, omitting two items from the Murphy et al. (1989) instrument as "less relevant to the study" (p. 815). Using EFA, Torkzadeh and Koufteros produced a four-factor solution, labeling the factors beginning skills, advanced skills, file and software skills, and mainframe skills. They reported alpha reliabilities of 0.94, 0.90, 0.91, and 0.96, respectively.

Torkzadeh, Koufteros, and Pflughoeft (1996) administered the 30-item CSE to a sample of 199 undergraduate students. Using CFA, they found that the sample data supported an acceptable fit with the hypothesized, four-factor model of the CSE. The authors, by examining the unidimensionality of the four constructs (see Anderson & Gerbing, 1982; Gerbing & Anderson, 1988), determined that the sample data also supported an acceptable fit with a 20-item, four-factor model of the CSE (see Table 2).

Widaman's Taxonomy

Widaman (1985) presented a taxonomy of covariance structure models for representing MTMM data. The taxonomy allows researchers to formulate hierarchically ordered, or nested, models for MTMM data. Significance tests of differences between competing, nested models permit researchers to assess the convergent validity and discriminant validity of model constructs and to assess the extent of method variance. The following hierarchical, nested models may be derived from Widaman's taxonomy:

Model 1: null model (Widaman's model 1A);
Model 2: one general factor (or trait; Widaman's model 2A);
Model 3: uncorrelated methods (Widaman's model 1B');
Model 4: correlated factors (or traits; Widaman's model 3A);
Model 5: correlated factors (or traits) and uncorrelated methods (Widaman's model 3B').

THE STUDY

A questionnaire containing the EUCSI and the 20-item CSE was administered to 407 junior, senior, and graduate students at a large university. The sample included 179 females and 228 males, who averaged 21.7 years of age and 5.5 years of computer experience.

To obtain multiple methods, each student was instructed to bring a "peer" to the administration. The peer was to be another student who was familiar with the original student's use of computers, knowledge about computers, and feelings about computers. Student pairs were separated while completing the questionnaires to ensure independent responses. Students received extra credit for their participation in the study.

Participants first completed the questionnaire about themselves (the "self" method) and then completed the questionnaire about their peers (the "peer" method). They responded to the EUCSI and the CSE on 7-point Likert scales ranging from 1 (strongly disagree) to 7 (strongly agree).

The questionnaire also included the following five items, which respondents answered on 7-point Likert scales:

- I am familiar with my peer's computer knowledge and expertise.
- I am confident that I can answer the following questions about my peer's computer usage.
- I know a great deal about my peer's computer skills.
- I know a great deal about my peer's computer usage.
- I know how my peer feels about using his/her computer.

The mean responses were 5.57 (s = 1.23), 5.66 (s = 1.20), 5.65 (s = 1.21), 5.80 (s = 1.18), and 5.74 (s = 1.20), respectively. These results suggest that the respondents felt that they were reasonably knowledgeable about their peers' computer knowledge, expertise, feelings, and usage.

DATA ANALYSIS

For each instrument, five CFA models were fitted (null, one general trait only, uncorrelated methods only, correlated traits only, and traits-and-methods). Convergent validity, discriminant validity, and the presence and effects of method variance were evaluated following the procedures outlined by Widaman (1985) and Bagozzi and Yi (1990). All confirmatory factor analyses were performed using the EQS/Windows statistical software package (Bentler, 1995). For a full explanation of the goodness-of-fit indices used in this study, see Bollen (1989) and Bentler (pp. 92-94). Data analyses were performed using the Satorra and Bentler procedure to correct for non-normal data (Bentler, p. 47).

The data analyses refer to various models derived from Widaman's taxonomy. These models are depicted in Figures 1 to 5. Due to space limitations, we show only the CSE in the figures (see Appendix).

- Figure 1: Null model, CSE (Model 1);
- Figure 2: One general trait, CSE (Model 2);
- Figure 3: Methods only, CSE (Model 3);
- Figure 4: Traits only, CSE (Model 4);
- Figure 5: Multitrait-multimethod, CSE (Model 5).

Convergent Validity

Convergent validity was assessed in two ways. *First*, model 1 (null) was compared with model 4 (correlated traits) to see if the addition of traits significantly improved the fit of the model (Bagozzi & Yi, 1990, p. 554). The χ^2 difference tests between model 1 and model 4 for both instruments are statistically significant (see Table 3): χ^2 difference $_{EUCSI}$ = 6802.7, 33 df, p < .001 and χ^2 difference $_{CSE}$ = 6512.9, 46 df, p < .001).

Second, because convergent validity results when a trait loading on a measure is statistically significant, the trait-item loadings of model 4 were examined (Bagozzi & Yi, 1990). For each item, a statistically significant trait-item loading indicates that the trait explains a statistically significant amount of variance in the item (Bagozzi & Yi; Widaman, 1985).

For the EUCSI, 15 of the trait-item loadings in model 4 are statistically significant at p < .001; C1 (self) and E1 (self) are statistically significant at p < .05; C2 (self), C3 (self), C4 (self), A2 (self), and T2 (self) are statistically significant at p < .01; and E2 (self) and T1 (self) are not statistically significant (p > .05). For the CSE, all trait-item loadings in model 4 are statistically significant (p < .001), with the exception of B8 (self), which is statistically significant (p < .05). Space limitations do not permit the trait-item loadings to be shown.

Table 3. Goodness of Fit Indices for the CFA Models.

End User Computing Satisfaction Instrument

	χ^2	(df)	χ^2/df	NFI	NNFI	CFI	GFI	AGFI	RMSR
Null Model	10160.2	276	36.8						
Model 2	4192.9	253	16.6	.305	.249	.243	.218	.073	.249
Model 3	1904.6	253	07.5	.721	.715	.683	.467	.368	.099
Model 4	3357.5	243	13.8	.484	.425	.402	.275	.105	.234
Model 5	510.9	219	02.3	.929	.936	.944	.868	.819	.062

Computer Self-Efficacy Instrument

	χ^2	(df)	χ^2/df	NFI	NNFI	CFI	GFI	AGFI	RMSR
Null Model	14233.8	780	18.3						
Model 2	8554.9	740	11.6	.399	.388	.419	.250	.169	.170
Model 3	3591.1	736	04.9	.748	.775	.788	.650	.610	.058
Model 4	7720.9	734	10.5	.458	.448	.481	.259	.173	.170
Model 5	2066.4	694	02.9	.855	.885	.898	.780	.741	.037

Note: Model 2—*One general trait only*
         Model 3—*Uncorrelated methods only*
         Model 4—*Correlated traits only*
         Model 5—*Traits and methods*

Discriminant Validity

Discriminant validity was assessed for both instruments in two ways. *First*, model 2 (one general trait) was compared with model 4 (correlated traits) to determine if the addition of distinct traits significantly improved the fit of the model (Schmitt & Stults, 1986; Widaman, 1985). Model 2 constrains all intertrait correlations to 1.00 while model 4 allows the intertrait correlations to be estimated. A perfect correlation between two latent variables means that it is impossible to empirically discriminate or distinguish between the variables. A significantly better fit of model 4 over model 2 suggests that the intertrait correlations are not equal to 1.00. The χ^2 difference tests between model 2 and model 4 for both instruments are statistically significant (see Table 3): χ^2 difference $_{EUCSI} = 835.4$, 10 df, p < .001 and χ^2 difference $_{CSE} = 834$, 6 df, p < .001.

Second, the correlations among traits and their standard errors were examined. Discriminant validity among traits is attained when an intertrait correlation is less than 1.00 by an amount greater than twice the standard error (Bagozzi & Yi, 1990). Six of the 10 intertrait correlations in the EUCSI demonstrate discriminant validity. The exceptions are content-format, content-timeliness, accuracy-format, and format-timeliness (see Table 4). Five of the six intertrait correlations in the CSE exhibit discriminant validity, with the exception of file-advanced (see Table 4).

Table 4. Correlations Among Traits and Standard Errors.

End User Computing Satisfaction Instrument (Model 3--Correlated traits)

	Accuracy	Content	Format	Ease of Use
Accuracy				
Content	.920 (.019)			
Format	.991 (.015)	.993 (.017)		
Ease of Use	.826 (.034)	.770 (.032)	.840 (.029)	
Timeliness	.938 (.022)	.996 (.015)	.995 (.023)	.780 (.035)

Computer Self-Efficacy Instrument (Model 3--Correlated traits)

	Basic Skill	File Skill	Advanced Skill
Basic Skill			
File Skill	.904 (.015)		
Advanced Skill	.863 (.018)	.990 (.009)	
Mainframe Skill	.541 (.039)	.701 (.030)	.685 (.031)

Method Variance

The presence and effects of method variance were examined in five ways. *First*, the overall fit of model 5 (traits and methods) was examined. For the EUCSI, the goodness-of-fit indices (see Table 3) show that model 5 demonstrates an excellent fit to the data, with the exceptions that the χ^2 value is statistically significant and the GFI is below 0.9. Thirteen of the 24 trait-item loadings are statistically significant at p < .001. C1, C2, C3, C4, F2, T1, and T2 (peer) and A1, A2, E1, and E2 (self) are non-significant, p > .05. All method-item loadings are statistically significant (p < .001).

For the CSE, the goodness-of-fit indices (see Table 3) show that model 5 demonstrates an adequate fit to the data, with the exceptions that the χ^2 value is statistically significant, the GFI is less than 0.9, and the AGFI is less than 0.8. All trait-item and method-item loadings are statistically significant (p < .001).

Further, the square of the trait-item and method-item loadings is the proportion of the item variance (R^2) accounted for by the trait and by the method. The R^2 value can be used to estimate the reliability of each item, with R^2 values above 0.50 suggesting acceptable reliability (Bollen, 1989). However, Bagozzi and Yi (1990) used a more relaxed criterion for reliability, stating that if a loading is greater than twice the value of its standard error, then it is statistically significant, and the variance explained by the trait for that item is statistically significant.

For the EUCSI, the statistically significant trait-item and method-item loadings demonstrate reliability using Bagozzi and Yi's (1990) criterion. No trait-item loadings, but all method-item loadings, demonstrate reliability using Bollen's (1989) criterion.

For the CSE, all trait-item and method-item loadings demonstrate reliability using Bagozzi and Yi's (1990) criterion. Using Bollen's (1989) criterion, two trait-item loadings and 18 method-item loadings demonstrate reliability.

Second, model 3 (uncorrelated methods) was compared with model 1 (null) to determine if the addition of the two method factors significantly improved the fit of the model. The χ^2 difference tests between model 3 and model 1 for both instruments are statistically significant (see Table 3): χ^2 difference $_{EUCSI}$ = 8255.6, 23 df, p < .001 and χ^2 difference $_{CSE}$ = 10642.7, 44 df, p < .001.

Third, model 4 (correlated traits) was compared to model 5 (traits and methods) to determine if the addition of the method factors significantly improved the fit of the model (Widaman, 1985). The χ^2 difference tests between model 4 and model 5 for both instruments are statistically significant (see Table 3): χ^2 difference $_{EUCSI}$ = 2846.6, 24 df, p < .001 and χ^2 difference $_{CSE}$ = 5654.5, 40 df, p < .001.

Fourth, the specific effects of the method factor were assessed by examining the statistical significance of the individual method-item loadings in model 3 (Bagozzi & Yi, 1990). All individual method-item loadings in model 3 for both instruments are statistically significant at p < .001.

Fifth, CFA enables the variance of the model to be partitioned between the variance attributable to trait, to method, and to error. A comparison of the relative amounts of variance explained suggests the relative importance of method variance in the EUCSI and CSE data sets. The five traits of the EUCSI account for 6.8% of the variance and the two methods explain 68.3% of the variance, with the remaining 24.9% of the variance attributable to error. The four traits of the CSE account for 22.7% of the variance and the two methods explain 41.1% of the variance, with the remaining 36.2% of the variance attributable to error.

DISCUSSION AND CONCLUSIONS

The findings clearly suggest that both instruments demonstrate convergent validity. First, the addition of traits to the null model significantly improved the fit of the model to the data, and second, 22 of 24 EUCSI trait-item loadings and 39 of 40 CSE trait-item loadings were statistically significant.

The findings indicate that the CSE demonstrates discriminant validity. The correlated-traits model provides a significantly better fit than the one general trait model, and five of six intertrait correlations discriminate according to Bagozzi and Yi (1990). The findings for the discriminant validity of the EUCSI are somewhat less clear. The correlated-traits model does provide a significantly better fit than the one general trait model, but only six of 10 intertrait correlations discriminate.

The findings strongly show that method variance is present and accounts for a large proportion of the variance in both the EUCSI and CSE data sets. First, the traits-and-methods model provides the best fit to the data of the five models. Second, the addition of the two methods to the null model resulted in significantly improved fits to the data. Third, the addition of the two methods to the correlated-traits model also resulted in significantly improved fits to the data. Fourth, all individual method-item loadings in the uncorrelated-methods model and the traits-and-methods model are significant. Finally, the methods explain 68.3% of the variance in the EUCSI and 41.1% of the variance in the CSE.

Interestingly, 22 of 24 of the EUCSI trait-item loadings are statistically significant when methods are not considered. However, when methods are considered, only 13 of 24 trait-item loadings are statistically significant. All trait-item loadings for the CSE remain statistically significant whether methods are considered or not.

This study provides both favorable and unfavorable results. Favorably, the findings provide evidence that, in these samples, the traits of the 20-item CSE and those of the EUCSI demonstrate two important aspects of construct validity; i.e., convergent validity and discriminant validity. Unfavorably, method variance is present in both samples and accounts for a large amount of variance. In addition, the factor structure of the EUCSI appears to be less stable in the presence of the methods and deserves more study. In fact, these results suggest a study examining the unidimensionality of the EUCSI.

Most research in MIS involves self-report measures, meaning that it is likely that method variance is present and that the constructs used might be affected. Therefore, method variance should be examined in studies using self-report measures. Multiple methods may be obtained by the use of peers, as in this study, or through the use of alternate scaling methods, such as semantic differential, Likert, and/or paired-comparison formats.

REFERENCES

Anderson, J. C., & Gerbing, D. W. (1982). Some methods for respecifying measurement models to obtain unidimensional construct measurement. *Journal of Marketing Research, 19*, 453-460.

Bagozzi, R. P., & Yi, Y. (1990). Assessing method variance in multitrait-multimethod matrices: The case of self-reported affect and perceptions at work. *Journal of Applied Psychology, 75*(5), 547-560.

Bentler, P. M. (1995). *EQS Structural Equations Program Manual.* Encino, CA: Multivariate Software.

Bollen, K. A. (1989). *Structural Equations with Latent Variables.* New York: John Wiley & Sons.

Byrne, B. M. (1994). *Structural Equation Modeling with EQS and EQS/Windows.* Thousand Oaks, CA: SAGE.

Campbell, D. T., & Fiske, D. W. (1959). Convergent and discriminant validation by the multitrait-multimethod matrix. *Psychological Bulletin, 56*(1), 81-105.

Cronbach, L. J. (1946). Response sets and test validity. *Educational and Psychological Measurement, 6*, 475-494.

Cronbach, L. J., & Meehl, P. E. (1955). Construct validity in psychological tests. *Psychological Bulletin, 52*, 281-302.

Dickson, G. W., Benbasat, I., & King, W. R. (1980). The management information systems area: Problems, challenges, and opportunities. In E. R. McLean (Ed.), *Proceedings of the First International Conference on Information Systems* (pp. 1-7). Philadelphia, PA.

Doll, W. J., & Torkzadeh, G. (1988). The measurement of end-user computing satisfaction. *MIS Quarterly, 12*(2), 259-273.

Doll, W. J., Xia, W., & Torkzadeh, G. (1994). A confirmatory factor analysis of the end-user computing satisfaction instrument. *MIS Quarterly, 18*, 453-461.

Gerbing, D. W., & Anderson, J. C. (1988). An updated paradigm for scale development incorporating unidimensionality and its assessment. *Journal of Marketing Research, 25*, 186-192.

Harrison, A. W., & Rainer, R. K., Jr. (1992). An examination of the factor structures and concurrent validities for the computer attitude scale, the computer anxiety rating scale, and the computer self-efficacy scale. *Educational and Psychological Measurement, 52*, 735-745.

Keen, P. G. W. (1980). MIS research: Reference disciplines and a cumulative tradition. In E. R. McLean (Ed.), *Proceedings of the First International Conference on Information Systems* (pp. 9-18). Philadelphia, PA.

Murphy, C. A., Coover, D., & Owen, S. V. (1989). Development and validation of the computer self-efficacy scale. *Educational and Psychological Measurement, 49*, 893-899.

Schmitt, N., & Stults, D. (1986). Methodology review: Analysis of multitrait-multimethod matrices. *Applied Psychological Measurement, 10*, 1-22.

Spector, P. E. (1987). Method variance as an artifact in self-reported affect and perceptions at work: Myth or significant problem? *Journal of Applied Psychology, 72*(3), 438-443.

Torkzadeh, G., & Koufteros, X. (1994). Factorial validity of a computer self-efficacy scale and the impact of computer training. *Educational and Psychological Measurement, 54*, 813-821.

Torkzadeh, G., Koufteros, X., & Pflughoeft, K. (1996). Structural equation modeling for confirming the self-efficacy instrument. *Proceedings of the Decision Sciences Institute*, 601-603.

Venkatraman, N., & Grant, J. H. (1986). Construct measurement in organizational strategy research: A critique and proposal. *Academy of Management Review, 11*(1), 71-87.

Widaman, K. F. (1985). Hierarchically nested covariance structure models for multitrait-multimethod data. *Applied Psychological Measurement, 9*(1), 1-26.

Williams, L. J., Cote, J. A., & Buckley, M. R. (1989). Lack of method variance in self-reported affect and perceptions at work: Reality or artifact? *Journal of Applied Psychology, 74*(3), 462-468.

APPENDIX

Figure 1. Null Model (CSE).

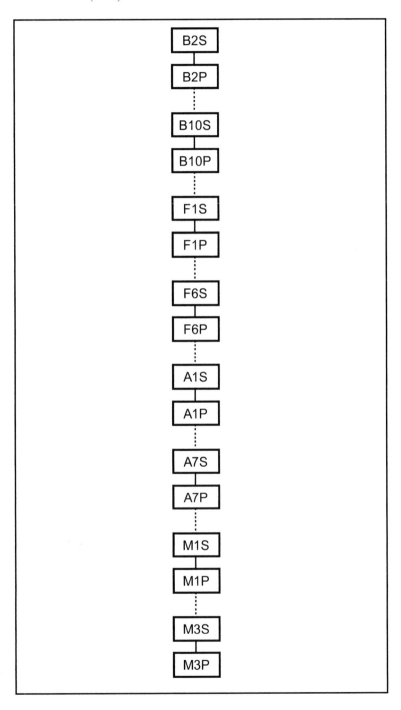

Figure 2. One General Trait (CSE).

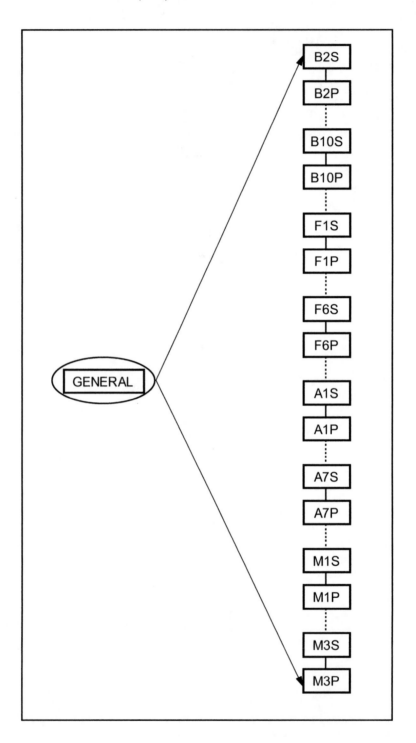

Figure 3. Trait Only (CSE).

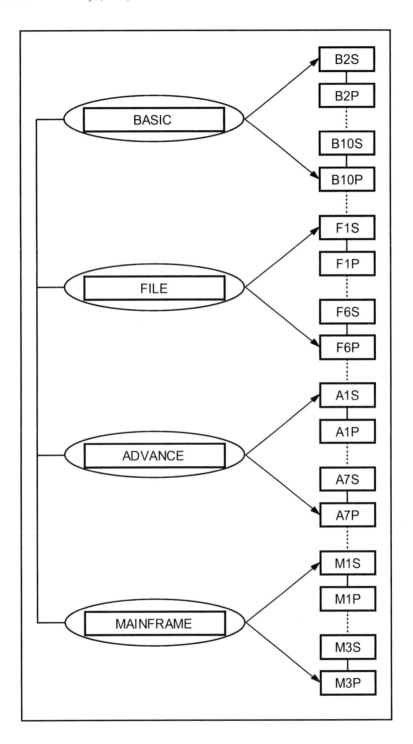

Figure 4. Method Only (CSE).

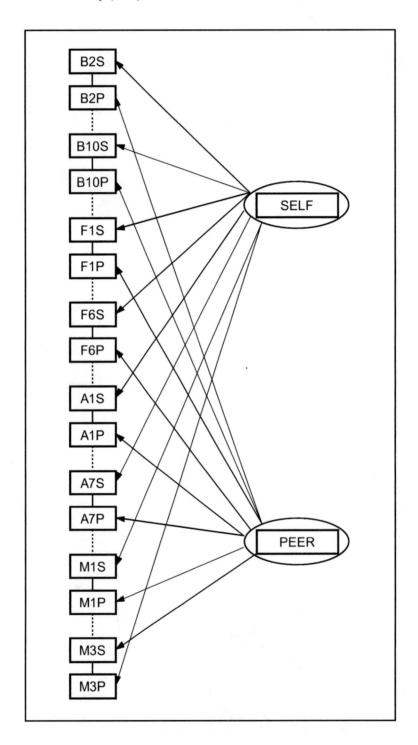

Figure 5.   Multitrait-Multimethod (CSE).

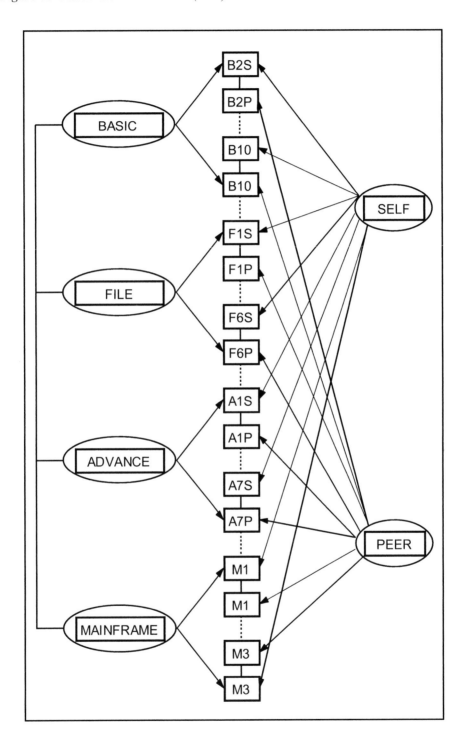

Chapter IV

The Use of Structural Equation Modeling in IS Research: Review and Recommendations

Kun Shin Im
Yonsei University, Korea

Varun Grover
Clemson University, USA

ABSTRACT

The structural equation modeling (SEM) technique has significant potential as a research tool for assessing and modifying theoretical models. There have been 139 applications of SEM in IS research published in major journals, most of which have been after 1994. However, despite its increasing use in the field, it remains a complex tool that is often difficult to apply effectively. The purpose of this study is to evaluate the previous IS applications of SEM and to suggest guidelines to realize the potential of SEM in IS research. The 72 empirical applications of SEM gathered from leading IS journals are reviewed and evaluated according to prescribed criteria. Avenues for improvement are suggested which can facilitate application of this important technique in IS theory development and testing.

INTRODUCTION

Structural equation modeling (SEM) has become an important and widely used research tool for theory testing and development in the social and behavioral sciences. One reason for the substantive use of SEM is that the confirmatory methods provide researchers with a comprehensive means for assessing and modifying theoretical models. In addition, the potential of SEM for comprehensive investigations of construct measurement is also generally acknowledged. Because of these merits of SEM, many researchers in the field of information systems (IS) have been using it for measuring constructs or developing and testing IS theories.

Anderson and Gerbing (1988) argue, however, that because of the relative sophistication of SEM, initial applications might be prone to misuse, which can inhibit theory development. This could be an acute problem in a younger field like IS, where erroneous theory development and testing could greatly inhibit the building of a cumulative tradition of research. Also, if the trend in more mature disciplines (e.g., marketing) is any indication, the use of SEM in IS research is only going to increase. Therefore, we believe it is important to take an introspective view of this important methodology.

The purpose of this study is to provide an in-depth analysis of a critical mass of SEM applications in seven leading IS journals and to suggest specific avenues for improvement. To our knowledge, no comprehensive survey of SEM applications in the IS field has been reported in the literature.

APPLICATIONS OF SEM IN THE IS FIELD

Seven widely regarded IS outlets were chosen for selection of SEM applications. These are *MIS Quarterly (MISQ), Information Systems Research (ISR), Journal of Management Information Systems (JMIS), Information & Management (I&M), Communication of the ACM (CACM), Decision Sciences (DS),* and *Management Science (MS)*. All issues of these seven journals between 1987 and 2001 were searched for empirical SEM applications. Theoretical papers dealing with issues related to SEM and papers using exploratory factor analysis, path analysis, structural modeling by regression analysis, and partial least square (PLS) models were excluded from the sample. The final sample of this study includes confirmatory measurement models, structural models with single indicator, and integrated measurement/structural models.

A total of 72 papers had applications that satisfied the selection criteria (see Table 1). The Appendix contains the listing of these papers. It seems apparent that the use of SEM in the leading IS journals has recently increased. More than 90% of the total number of papers were published after 1994. Most of these SEM application papers involve development of measures of system effectiveness and investigation of the relationship between system effectiveness and its antecedent variables. The SEM applications were fairly evenly published in six of the seven major IS journals (with the exception of *CACM*).

The vast majority of published studies have been conducted with cross-sectional data (96%). Only three studies were performed on longitudinal data (4%). It is generally believed that because of time-specific factors, using the cross-sectional data makes it difficult to establish causality (Malhotra & Grover, 1998). Therefore, the exclusive use of cross-sectional data to investigate structural relationships among constructs indi-

Table 1. SEM Application Articles in IS Outlets between 1987 and 2001.

	CACM	DS	IM	ISR	JMIS	MISQ	MS	Total (%)
1987	0	0	0	0	0	0	0	0 (0.0%)
1988	0	0	0	0	0	0	0	0 (0.0%)
1989	0	0	0	0	0	0	0	0 (0.0%)
1990	0	0	0	1	0	0	0	1 (1.4%)
1991	0	0	0	0	0	0	0	0 (0.0%)
1992	0	0	0	0	0	2	0	2 (2.8%)
1993	0	0	0	0	0	1	1	2 (2.8%)
1994	0	2	1	3	0	2	3	11 (15.3%)
1995	0	1	1	4	0	2	0	8 (11.1%)
1996	0	0	0	0	2	0	1	3 (4.2%)
1997	0	2	1	1	0	1	0	5 (6.9%)
1998	0	5	2	3	0	2	0	12 (16.7%)
1999	0	4	3	1	3	0	0	11 (15.3%)
2000	0	1	1	0	2	2	0	6 (8.3%)
2001	0	2	4	0	3	2	0	11 (15.3%)
Total	0	17	13	13	10	14	5	72
(%)	(0.0%)	(23.6%)	(18.1%)	(18.1%)	(13.9%)	(19.4%)	(6.9%)	(100.0%)

cates that special care should be taken in interpreting results derived from SEM using cross-sectional data. Most of the SEM applications were performed by using LISREL (57.6%), reflecting the popularity of this package. EQS was also used to perform SEM (20.1%). Recently, PROC CALIS procedure in SAS (8.6%) and AMOS in SPSS (7.9%) have been used for SEM in the IS field.

TERMINOLOGY OF STRUCTURAL MODELING AND UNIT OF ANALYSIS

Before discussing the methodological issues of SEM, it is useful to establish the commonly accepted terminology of SEM formulation.[1] A structural model can be represented by the following equations:

$$\eta = B\eta + \Gamma\xi + \zeta, \tag{1}$$
$$x = \Lambda^x\xi + \delta, \tag{2}$$
$$y = \Lambda^y\eta + \varepsilon. \tag{3}$$

Equation (1) is called the structural model. This equation represents the structural relationships among the endogenous and exogenous constructs. η indicates the endogenous constructs that are causally affected by other endogenous or exogenous constructs in the model. ξ represents exogenous constructs that are not influenced by other constructs in the model. While the structural coefficients among endogenous constructs are represented by B matrix, those between endogenous and exogenous constructs are represented by Γ matrix. The amount of unexplained relationship in each structural equation is referred to as error in equation and is denoted by ζ. Equations (2) and (3) are called measurement model. These equations represent how the constructs are related to their indicators (i.e., measured items). While y represents indicators of the endogenous

Figure 1. Sample Illustrations of Type I, Type II and Type III Applications.

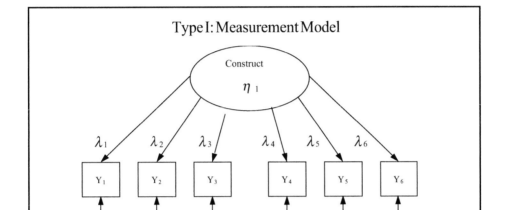

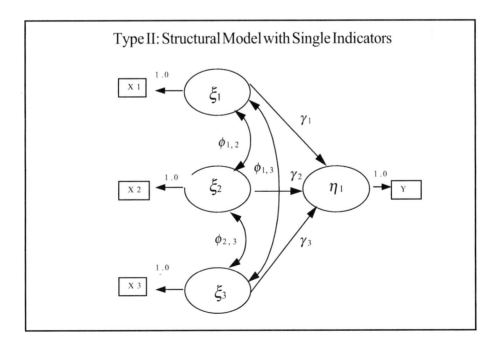

Figure 1. (continued) Sample Illustrations of Type I, Type II and Type III Applications.

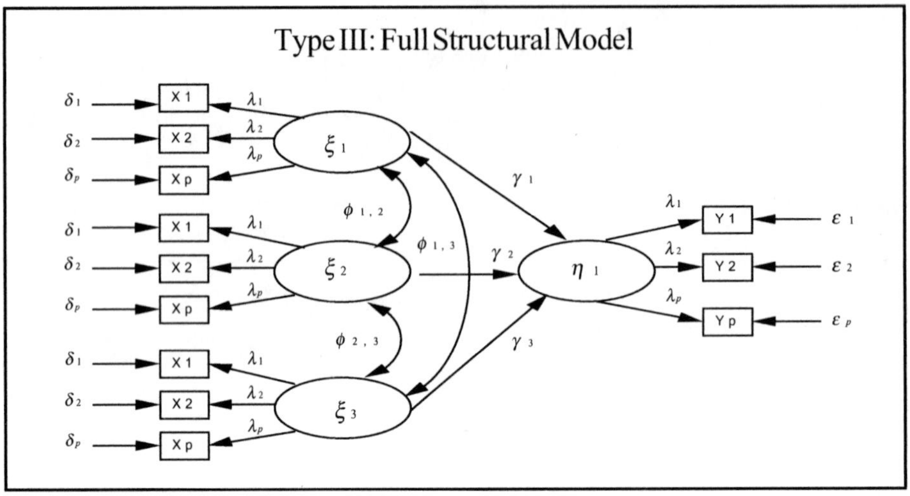

constructs (η), x represents indicators of the exogenous constructs (ξ). Λ^x and Λ^y show how y relates to η and x relates to ξ, respectively. δ and ε represent measurement errors.

To discuss methodological issues in the SEM applications, it is necessary that the unit of analysis be not a paper but a model. In some papers multiple models are estimated and analyzed: (1) a model is estimated on multiple samples for cross-validating; (2) different models are estimated on the same sample; or (3) different models are estimated on different samples. For example, separate measurement models are specified for different constructs, or a two-step approach by Anderson and Gerbing (1988) is conducted, separately estimating measurement model and structural model. In the first case, the data were averaged across replications in the analysis. In the other two cases, each distinct model was used separately in this study. As a result, a total of 139 models were analyzed.

A total of 78 models were confirmatory measurement models that solely investigate the measurement structure between indicators and endogenous or exogenous constructs, i.e., Equations (2) or (3) above. In five cases, SEM was used to examine only the structural relationships among constructs that are all measured by single indicators. These models were represented by only Equation (1). A total of 34 models were full structural equation models that include both measurement models and structural models, i.e., Equations (1), (2), and (3). In this paper, these confirmatory measurement models, single-indicator structural models, and full structural models will be referred to as Type I, Type II, and Type III, respectively. Figure 1 provides sample illustrations of these three types of models.

METHODOLOGICAL ISSUES

Four sets of methodological issues are considered in this paper. As shown in Figure 2, the issues closely parallel the recommended sequence of activities that need to be

Figure 2. A Four-Steps Approach of SEM and Methodological Issues.

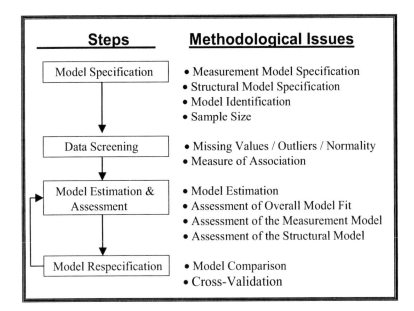

performed to conduct effective SEM: (1) model specification issues; (2) data screening issues; (3) model estimation and assessment issues; and (4) model respecification issues.

Model Specification Issues and Recommendations

With respect to the issues related to model specification, it is useful to classify them into the following four sub-issues related to: (1) measurement model specification; (2) structural model specification; (3) model identification; and (4) sample size (Bagozzi & Baumgartner, 1994).

Measurement Model Specification

A fundamental decision has to be made about how many indicators can be explicitly related to a construct. Technically, a latent factor may be assessed with just two indicators under certain conditions. However, models with only low indicator variables per factor often exhibit problems with identification and convergence (Hatcher, 1994). Therefore, it is recommended that each construct be measured with at least three indicators (Anderson & Gerbing, 1988; Bentler & Chou, 1987). In practice, researchers are advised to have at least four or five indicators for each latent factor, as it is often necessary to drop some of the indicators in order to arrive at a well-fitting measurement model (Hatcher).

Evaluation and Recommendation. Table 2 shows the descriptive statistics regarding the issues of model specification, both overall and by type of model. Overall, the median number of indicators across all applications of SEM was 11 and the median number of constructs was 4, resulting in a median ratio of indicators to constructs of

Table 2. Statistics-Model Specification Issues (Overall and by Type of Model)*. (Table entries are medians and those in parentheses are the 25th and 75th percentile, unless a percentage value is indicated.)

	Overall (N=139)	Type I (N=78)	Type II (N=5)	Type III (N=34)
Measurement Model Specification Issues:				
Number of indicators	11	10	9.5	13
	(7, 165)	(6,16)	(5, 15.5)	(10, 18)
Number of constructs	4	2.5	9.5	5
	(2, 6)	(1, 5)	(5, 15.5)	(4, 7)
Ratio of indicator to constructs	2.75	4.0	1.0	2.7
	(2.4, 5.0)	(3.0, 6.0)	(1.0, 1.0)	(2.0, 3.6)
Percentage of models containing at least one single-indicator construct	20.1	3.9	100.0	36.7
Percentage of models lacking unidimensional measurement	1.4	1.3	na	2.0
Percentage of measurement models lacking simple structure	1.4	1.3	na	2.0
Percentage of models with correlated measurement errors	32.4	46.2	na	16.3
Percentage of applications justifying correlated measurement errors	1.4	1.3	Na	2.0
Structural Model Specification Issues:				
Percentage of nonrecursive model	3.6	na	8.3	8.2
Percentage of models with elements above and below the diagonal of the β matrix	3.6	na	8.3	8.2
Percentage of models with correlated errors in equations	4.3	na	8.3	10.2
Percentage of applications justifying correlated errors in equations	0.7	na	0	2.0
Model Identification Issues:				
Percentage of applications in which evidence of model identification is presented	14.4	20.5	0	8.2
Degrees of Freedom Issues:				
Number of degrees of freedom	35	27	15	54
	(14, 84)	(9, 80)	(5, 104)	(24, 84)
Percentage of applications in which degrees of freedom are reported incorrectly	13.0	16.7	8.3	8.2
Contribution of measurement model to overall number of degrees of freedom (in %)	100.0	100.0	0	89.3
Contribution of structural model to overall number of degrees of freedom (in %)	0.0	0.0	100.0	10.7
Sample Size Issues:				
Sample size	193	216	103	174
	(119, 253)	(159, 253)	(60, 190)	(119, 335)
Number of parameters estimated	26.5	22	22	31
	(14, 40)	(11, 42)	(12, 40)	(22, 38)
Ratio of sample size to number of parameters estimated	7.0	9.0	4.8	5.9
	(3.9, 14.8)	(4.1, 18.1)	(3.5, 6.2)	(3.7, 8.7)
Percentage of models with a ratio of sample size to number of free parameters smaller than 5	30.4	28.6	33.3	32.6
Percentage of models with a ratio of sample size to number of free parameters smaller than 10	54.8	45.5	58.3	69.6

about 2.75. For Type II models, because all constructs are indicated by a single measure by definition, the ratio is one. The median ratios of indicators to constructs were 4 and 2.7 for Type I and Type III models, respectively. However, it should be noted that 20.1% of all SEM applications and 36.7% of Type III applications used one single-indicator construct.

A significant proportion of IS applications used single indicator constructs when three to four indicators per construct is desirable. Even though some of these cases used one composite-indicator construct, the use of single-indicator constructs is not recommended because single-indicator constructs ignore unreliability of measurement, which is one of the problems that SEM was specifically designed to circumvent (Baumgartner & Homburg, 1996). If there are too many items per construct, it is prudent to establish unidimensionality before aggregating indicators (Anderson & Gerbing, 1988). The unidimensional construct measurement is represented by models with simple structure and no correlated measurement errors (δ and ε). The simple structure indicates that each observed variable is related to a single latent variable. While not observed in this sample, items that load on two or more constructs should be avoided.

Structural Model Specification and Model Identification

At the structural model level the use of a nonrecursive model is one of the main issues. While a recursive model is one in which causation flows in only one direction, in a nonrecursive model causation may flow in more than one direction (Hatcher, 1994). A nonrecursive model is specified as one with correlated errors in equations or entries both above and below the diagonal in the B matrix. It is generally recommended that if nonrecursive models are specified, relevant issues such as model identification and the stability of reciprocal effects be addressed explicitly (Hatcher). In this study, only five models were nonrecursive models.

Once a theoretical model has been specified, it is necessary to consider its identification. A model is said to be underidentified if it is possible for two distinct sets of parameter values to yield the same population variance-covariance matrix (Hatcher, 1994). In an underidentification model, in other words, two different solutions for the same structure with widely differing theoretical implications can account for the data equally well. Therefore, it would be advisable to deal with identification explicitly.

Evaluation and Recommendation. Table 2 shows that very few researchers mention whether they checked identification. This result might reflect the fact that because most computer programs give a warning message when a model is underidentified, it is unnecessary to mention underidentification explicitly. A simple rule to avoid underidentification is that the number of parameters freely estimated should not exceed the number of distinct elements in the variance-covariance matrix of the observed variables (Sharma, 1996). Table 2 shows that the median number of degrees of freedom is 35 for all models. The figures for Type I, Type II, and Type III models were 27, 15, and 54, respectively. In 13% of all cases, degrees of freedom are reported incorrectly. One reason for this error might be that a correlation matrix is used as input to estimation and the scale of a latent variable is fixed by setting *both* (rather than only one) the loading of one reference indicator and the factor variance equal to unity yielding inflated degrees of freedom (Baumgartner & Homburg, 1996). Another issue regarding degrees of freedom is how much the measurement model contributes to the total number of degrees of freedom in Type III models. The fact that the contribution of the measurement model to the total number of degrees of freedom is relatively high indicates the dangers of interpreting a good overall fit of a model as support for the validity of one's theory (Fornell, 1983). The median contribution of the measurement model to the overall degrees of freedom is about 89% in Type III models, indicating that there is more testing of measurement taking place than the theory-based structure. Researchers should be careful about the domination of measurement as opposed to theoretical relationships between constructs.

Sample Size

Researchers should check whether the sample size is likely to be sufficient prior to actually conducting the study. Small sample sizes can result in nonconvergence and improper solutions (Anderson & Gerbing, 1988; Fornell, 1983). Simulation studies (Bearden, Sharma, & Teel, 1982; Boomsma, 1982) confirm the fact that small samples are not compatible with maximum likelihood estimation of covariance structure models. Anderson and Gerbing (1984) suggest that a sample size of 150 or more typically will be needed to obtain parameter estimates that have standard errors small enough to be of practical use. On the other hand, Bentler and Chou (1987) also provide the rule of thumb that under normal distribution theory the ratio of sample size to number of free parameters should be at least 5:1 to get trustworthy parameter estimates and higher (at least 10:1) to obtain appropriate significance tests.

Evaluation and Recommendation. Table 2 shows that for overall applications of Type I and Type III models, the median numbers of observations were larger than 150. However, the figure for Type II models was not larger than the minimally required number of sample size. With respect to the sample size per parameter to be estimated, the requirement of 5:1 was met in overall applications of Type I and Type III cases. The sample size per parameter for Type II did not meet the minimally required number. It should be noted that about 30% of all models for all cases had ratios smaller than 5:1.

Data Screening Issues and Recommendations

The raw data should be screened carefully before a variance-covariance matrix is computed. It is important to make sure that there are no coding errors and that missing values have been dealt with appropriately. Simple descriptive statistics can be used to check whether the minimum and maximum values for each variable fall within the admissible range (Bagozzi & Baumgartner, 1994). Since in the case of pairwise deletion the sample variance-covariance matrix may not be positive definite, listwise deletion is usually suggested as a proper method to deal with missing values. In this study it was found that most authors of SEM applications did not show particular concern for coding error and missing values.[2]

Outlier detection and the assessment of normality should be also considered prior to model estimation and testing (Baumgartner & Homburg, 1996). It is helpful to investigate possible distorting influences introduced by the presence of a few outliers. Since SEM requires the assumption of multivariate normality, it is also crucial to examine the normality of the raw data. It is generally recommended to check the outliers and the normality of the raw data by inspecting the data through histograms, stem-and-leaf displays or other graphical means and by computing univariate and multivariate measures of skewness and kurtosis (Bagozzi & Baumgartner, 1994). Only in 0.7% of all cases, whether outliers had been detected was reported. Also in 8.6% of all applications authors mentioned that they had checked the normality of data.

A final issue regarding data screening is which measure of association was used in the model estimation and testing. Researchers often use a correlation rather than a covariance matrix as input to model estimation and testing. However, since theoretically the maximum likelihood procedure for confirmatory factor analysis is derived for covariance matrices, it is recommended that a covariance matrix should be used as input to estimation (Sharma, 1996). Given the assumption that a correlation matrix is used by default, only 18.7% of applications have estimated using a covariance matrix. Therefore, it should be recommended that, in future research, all analyses of SEM be conducted on covariance matrices.

Model Estimation and Assessment Issues and Recommendations

Model Estimation

Maximum likelihood has been the predominant estimation method since the inception of SEM in the middle 1960s. Under the assumption of a multivariate normal distribution of the observed variables, ML estimators have the desirable asymptotic properties of being unbiased, consistent, and efficient so that significance testing of the individual parameters and overall model fit is possible (Anderson & Gerbing, 1988). Besides the ML estimation method, generalized least squares (GLS), unweighted least squares (ULS), and asymptotically distribution-free (ADF) methods have been used to obtain parameter estimates and test statistics. These methods have focused on relaxing the assumption of multivariate normality. However, these methods based on arbitrary theory have some limitations, such as constraints on model size and the need for larger sample size.

Evaluation and Recommendation. Researchers should consider the trade-offs between the reasonableness of an underlying normal theory assumption and the limitations of arbitrary theory methods. Table 3 shows that 61.2% of all models were estimated using ML. The percentages of models estimated by ML for the three types of models were 57.7, 50.0, and 69.4, respectively. The reason for the slightly low use of ML estimation in SEM applications seems to be that since ML is the default method in most computer packages, many authors of SEM applications did not explicitly report they used ML in their papers.

Assessment of Overall Model Fit

After estimating the model, a researcher would assess how well the specified model accounted for the data with one or more overall goodness-of-fit indices, such as χ^2 statistic, goodness-fit index (GFI), adjusted goodness-fit index (AGFI), root mean residual (RMR), comparative fit index (CFI), etc. Because the χ^2 statistic is sensitive to sample size, other size-insensitive indices such as normed fit index (NFI) and non-normed fit index (NNFI) should be also used to assess overall model fit.

Evaluation and Recommendation. Table 3 shows that the most commonly used fit index was the χ^2 statistic (about 92.1% of all models). Other common indices were GFI and

Table 3. Statistics-Model Estimation, Assessment and Respecification Issues (Overall and by Type of Model)*. (Table entries are medians and those in parentheses are the 25th and 75th percentile, unless a percentage value is indicated.)

	Overall (N=139)	Type I (N=78)	Type II (N=12)	Type III (N=49)
Model Estimation Issues:				
Percentage of models estimated by ML	61.2	57.7	50.0	69.4
Percentage of models in which convergence problems occurred	0.0	0.0	0.0	0.0
Percentage of models with improper solutions	0.7	0.0	0.0	2.0
Overall Fit Assessment Issues:				
Frequency of use of χ^2 test	92.1	91.0	100.0	91.8
Frequency of use of GFI	65.5	71.8	58.3	57.1
Frequency of use of AGFI	52.5	47.4	58.3	59.2
Frequency of use of RMR	48.2	56.4	66.7	38.8
Frequency of use of CFI	41.7	37.2	50.0	46.9
Frequency of use of NFI	32.4	18.7	25.0	32.7
Frequency of use of NNFI	32.4	26.9	25.0	42.9
Magnitude of χ^2 to degrees of freedom ratio	1.99 (1.53, 2.93)	1.99 (1.53, 2.91)	1.53 (1.14, 2.05)	2.30 (1.55, 3.52)
Magnitude of GFI	.94 (.90, .97)	.95 (.90, .97)	.97 (.93, .99)	.93 (.90, .95)
Magnitude of AGFI	.88 (.84, .92)	.88 (.84, .93)	.89 (.87, .94)	.87 (.84, .89)
Magnitude of RMR	.05 (.03, .07)	.04 (.03, .05)	.07 (.04, .09)	.06 (.04, .10)
Magnitude of CFI	.96 (.94, .97)	.96 (.95, .98)	.96 (.91, .99)	.95 (.94, .97)
Magnitude of NFI	.92 (.89, .96)	.92 (.89, .96)	.96 (.90, .99)	.92 (.88, .95)
Magnitude of NNFI	.95 (.92, .96)	.95 (.93, .96)	.97 (.92, 1.12)	.95 (.91, .96)
Measurement Model Assessment Issues:				
Percentage of models for which indicator and construct reliability were provided	27.3	39.7	25.0	30.6
Percentage of models for which convergent and discriminant validity were reported	59.0	78.2	25.0	40.8
Structural Model Assessment Issues:				
Percentage of models for which structural coefficients were provided	40.3	na	100.0	89.8
Percentage of models for which R² for structural equations were reported	20.1	na	25.0	51.0
Model Respecification Issues:				
Percentage of models for which specification searches were discussed	22.3	20.5	25.0	24.5
Percentage of models for which model comparisons were reported	20.9	19.2	25.0	22.5
Percentage of models that were cross-validated	7.2	5.1	16.7	8.2

AGFI. The size-insensitive indices (NFI and NNFI) were also used in about 32% of all models. These indices are automatically reported in most computer packages, which seem to explain their popularity. As a result, it is clear that most IS researchers using SEM applications employed multiple fit indices representing different types of measures along with χ^2 statistic. Table 3 also presents summary statistics on the distribution of the goodness-fit indices. The median ratio of χ^2 to degrees of freedom for all four cases was 1.99. The figures met the informed criterion that the χ^2 value should be less than twice the size of the degrees of freedom. Because this ratio is also sensitive to sample size, however, this criterion should be supplemented with other criteria that are not affected by sample size (Hatcher, 1994). The suggested cutoff values for the indices are summarized in Table 4. The acceptable cutoff value for RMR has not been discussed in the literature. Because a value of RMR ranges between 0 and 1, however, the value close to 0 is preferred and 0.1 is regarded as a suggested cutoff value for RMR. In this study, the medians of GFI, AGFI, CFI, RMR, NFI, and NNFI for all four cases were greater than their suggested critical value. In general, the applications reviewed did attempt to demonstrate model fit by using indices that were both sensitive and independent of sample size.

Assessment of the Measurement Mode

After the hypothesized model is accepted as a reasonable approximation to the data by assessing the overall model fit, it is important to check the quality of construct measurement. The quality of construct measurement may be ascertained by assessing the reliability and validity of the construct. Reliability refers to consistency of measurement. Reliability can be computed at the individual indicator level or at a given construct level. Indicator reliability indicates the percent of variation in the indicator that is explained by the factor that it is supposed to measure (Long, 1983). When a multiple-item scale is used, composite (or construct) reliability is usually more important, assessing the reliability of the indicators of a given construct (Sharma, 1996).

On the other hand, validity refers to the extent to which an instrument measures what it is intended to measure. Construct validity can be assessed by convergent and discriminant validity that collectively refer to whether the indicators within a construct are similar and yet sufficiently different from indicators within other constructs (Bagozzi, Yi, & Phillips, 1991; Campbell & Fiske, 1959; Churchill, 1979). While convergent validity can be assessed by testing the significance of estimated factor loadings, discriminant

Table 4. Acceptable Cutoff Values of Goodness-of-Fit Index.

Goodness-of-fit Index	Acceptable Cutoff Values
χ^2 to Degrees of Freedom Ratio	≤ 2.0
Goodness-of-fit Index (GFI)	$\geq .90$
Adjusted Goodness-of-fit Index (AGFI)	$\geq .80$
Comparative Fit Index (CFI)	$\geq .90$
Root Mean Residual (RMR)	$\leq .10$
Normed Fit Index (NFI)	$\geq .90$
Non-normed Fit Index (NNFI)	$\geq .90$

validity may be obtained through the use of a chi-square difference test (Anderson & Gerbing, 1988).

Evaluation and Recommendation. Overall, 27.3% of all applications reported both indicator and construct reliability. The figures for Type I and III models were 39.7% and 30.6%, respectively. For Type II models that represent single-indicator structural models, 25.0% of them mentioned indicator reliability. Based on these low figures, it is recommended that IS researchers assess and report both indicator and construct reliability in future studies. A total of 59.0% of all applications mentioned both convergent and discriminant validity. The figures for Type I, Type II, and Type III models were 78.2%, 25.0%, and 40.8%, respectively. These figures were greater than or equal to those in the case of reliability, which seems to be desirable because reliability is a necessary but not a sufficient condition for validity of construct measurement. However, it is still recommended that, in the future, IS researchers report *both* reliability and validity information.

Assessment of the Structural Model

The assessment of the structural model can be conducted by looking at the sign, size, and statistical significance of the structural coefficients. In addition to the significance test of structural coefficients, Bagozzi and Baumgartner (1994) argue that because the squared multiple correlations (R^2) for the endogenous constructs (variance fit) are different from χ^2 tests of overidentifying restrictions (covariance fit), it is useful to look at the variance fit of the structural models.

Evaluation and Recommendation. Table 3 shows that all Type II model applications reported the size and statistical significance of structural coefficients. About 90% of Type III model applications provided structural coefficients. Overall, 20.1% of all cases reported the squared multiple correlations (R^2). The figure for Type II models was 25.0%. Because a model might fit well (covariance fit) but have little explanatory power at the structural level (variance fit) or conversely fit poorly but exhibit high explanatory power (Baumgartner & Homburg, 1996), it is important that variance fit (R^2) be reported for all SEM applications.

Model Respecification Issues and Recommendations

Most often the theoretical model that is initially specified is modified until the model adequately represents the empirical data. It should be noted, however, that modifications of the model should not be based on statistical considerations alone but rather in conjunction with theory and content considerations (Anderson & Gerbing, 1988).

Model respecification may be necessitated by nonconvergence, an improper solution, or unacceptable overall fit. These problems could be solved by respecifying indicators that do not load on the target factor, load on another factor, or load on multiple factors simultaneously. There are four basic ways to respecify these indicators: (1) relate the indicator to a different factor; (2) delete the indicator from the model; (3) relate the indicator to multiple factors; or (4) use correlated measurement errors (Anderson & Gerbing, 1988). Two useful tools for identifying which indicators should be respecified are modification indices and residual analysis. Based on modification indices and standardized residuals that are reported routinely in the output of most computer packages, researchers can conduct specification searches and possibly improve the overall fit of a model. It should be noted again that model respecification suggested by inspecting the modification indices and the standardized residuals *should be guided by theory* since there is always the danger of capitalizing on chance (MacCallum, 1986).

Model comparison and cross-validation have been suggested in order to choose the most parsimonious model. Based on sequential chi-square difference tests, model comparisons are conducted among different plausible models that are nested in each other and can be justified theoretically (Anderson & Gerbing, 1988). In contrast, under the cross-validation approach, the complete sample is split randomly into a calibration sample and a validation sample, and model selection is based on the criterion of minimum discrepancy in fit between the validation-sample observed covariance matrix and the calibration-sample estimated covariance matrix (Cudeck & Browne, 1983).

Evaluation and Recommendation. Table 3 shows that in 22.3% of all applications researchers conducted some form of specification searches. These included specifications on the basis of preliminary explorations of the data, addition of structural paths or correlated errors in structural equations, and modifications by the four basic ways for respecifying the indicators that did not work as planned. Model comparisons were performed in 20.9% of all cases and cross-validation with a new set of data was conducted in only 7.5% of the cases. The low usage of model comparison and cross-validation in SEM applications of the IS field could be explained by the difficulty in conducting the model comparison and in collecting a large sample. However, besides the danger of delving into specification searches not guided by theory, such validation reduces the mistaken notion that a good fit indicates the most plausible representation of the data (Baumgartner & Homburg, 1996).

RECOMMENDATIONS

The use of SEM in IS research has increased in recent years. Fornell (1983) argues that whenever a new methodology appears in substantive applications, it seems inevitable that it will not always be appropriately used. Therefore it is necessary to evaluate IS applications of SEM and to suggest ways to better utilize the powerful technique. Based on the review of previous empirical applications of SEM in the leading IS journals between 1987 and 2001, some general guidelines to take full advantage of the SEM technique have been suggested.

1. *Specification:* Model specification issues should be considered before empirical data are collected: those related to the number of indicators per construct, unidimensionality, nonrecursive model, sample size, and identification. More importantly, model specification should be based on relatively well-developed theory whenever possible because the primary purpose of SEM is to test hypothesized models that are truly specified a priori.

2. *Screening:* As in the case of most empirical research, careful screening of raw data is necessary (and not often done) before estimating and testing. Since missing values, outliers, and non-normal data could cause several problems in estimating SEM, such as nonconvergence and improper solutions, data screening should be more carefully considered. Furthermore, because the SEM technique was initially developed to explain the covariance structure of the model containing observable and unobservable variables, researchers should use a covariance matrix rather than a correlation matrix as input to SEM analysis.

3.   *Fit/Modification:* In order to assess the overall fit of the estimated model, researchers should not depend solely upon χ^2 statistics but consider various fit indices simultaneously. In addition, the reliability and validity of construct measurement, and squared multiple correlations for each structural equation and for all equations should be also considered to assess the model. Through specification searches based on theoretical grounds, modifications of the model should be conducted. Comparisons among the nested models and cross-validation are also recommended to ascertain how well the hypothesized model represents the empirical data.

It should be noted, however, that while the objective of this study is to provide guidelines to improve on the quality of SEM studies in the future, blind adherence to the individual guidelines is not recommended. It is possible that "other" evidence presented in individual studies (e.g., strong theoretical support) can more than offset any single quality criteria. Further, these criteria could be argued to vary depending on the purpose of the study. However, consistent violation of a number of criteria will generally result in a poor application of the technique and subsequently erroneous conclusions.

CONCLUSION

SEM is being prominently used in IS research. Its ability to improve measurement reliability in multi-item constructs and its ability to investigate theoretical frameworks with complex relationships make it a powerful technique. This, along with sophisticated yet easy-to-use software, makes it probable that the use of SEM will continue. However, as the results of this study suggest, judicious use of this technique is warranted in order to take full advantage of its ability.

On the other hand, there is a question of whether the increased use of SEM has had a positive influence on the practice of research in the IS field. Several authors have voiced critical comments in this regard (e.g., Martin, 1987). It could be argued that the introduction of a new methodology might place emphasis only on methodological aspects and divert attention from theory development. Particularly in the earlier applications of SEM, we found that researchers (ourselves included) often felt compelled to explain the basics of the new technique in great detail, and given the space constraints in journals, the result probably was a decreased concern with theory development. However, in the IS field where there are increasing demands on researchers' excellence in both theory and method, this new modeling technique is beginning to foster the development of IS theories. It is hoped that as familiarity with the SEM methodology increases, IS researchers will be able to present technical matters more succinctly and allow greater attention to substantive issues.

Finally, it should be noted that failure to apply SEM consistently and appropriately will result in islands of research that spend more time justifying and adding to the inconsistencies in prior work. We've all been there. We hope that our review of previous applications of SEM will further improve the quality of empirical research in the IS field and ultimately contribute to the better development of IS theory.

REFERENCES

Adams, D. A., Nelson, R. R., & Todd, P. A. (1992). Perceived usefulness, ease of use, and usage of information technology: A replication. *MIS Quarterly*, *16*(2), 227-247.

Agarwal, R., & Prasad, J. (1998). A conceptual and operational definition of personal innovativeness in the domain of information technology. *Information Systems Research*, *9*(2), 204-215.

Agarwal, R., & Prasad, J. (1999). Are individual differences germane to the acceptance of new information technologies? *Decision Sciences*, *30*(2), 361-391.

Anderson, J. C., & Gerbing, D. W. (1984). The effect of sampling error on convergence, improper solutions, and goodness-of-fit indices for maximum likelihood confirmatory factor analysis. *Psychometrika*, *49*(2), 155-173.

Anderson, J. C., & Gerbing, D. W. (1988). Structural equation modeling in practice: A review and recommended two-step approach. *Psychological Bulletin*, *103*(3), 411-423.

Bagozzi, R. P. (1984). A prospectus for theory construction in marketing. *Journal of Marketing*, *48*, 11-29.

Bagozzi, R. P., & Baumgartner, H. (1994). The evaluation of structural equation models and hypothesis testing. In R. P. Bagozzi (Ed.), *Principles of Marketing Research* (pp. 386-422). Cambridge, MA: Blackwell.

Bagozzi, R. P., Yi, Y., & Phillips, L. W. (1991). Assessing construct validity in organization research. *Administrative Science Quarterly*, *36*, 421-458.

Barki, H., & Hartwick, J. (1994). User participation, conflict, and conflict resolution: The mediating roles of influence. *Information Systems Research*, *5*(4), 422-438.

Barki, H., & Hartwick, J. (2001). Interpersonal conflict and its management in information system development. *MIS Quarterly*, *25*(2), 195-228.

Baumgartner, H., & Homburg, C. (1996). Applications of structural equation modeling in marketing and consumer research: A review. *International Journal of Research in Marketing*, *13*, 139-161.

Bearden, W. O., Sharma, S., & Teel, J. E. (1982). Sample size effects upon chi-square and other statistics used in evaluating causal models. *Journal of Marketing Research*, *19*, 425-430.

Becerra-Fernandez, I., & Sabherwal, R. (2001). Organizational knowledge management: A contingency perspective. *Journal of Management Information Systems*, *18*(1), 23-55.

Bentler, P. M., & Chou, C. (1987). Practical issues in structural modeling. *Sociological Methods & Research*, *16*, 78-117.

Bhattacherjee, A. (2001). Understanding information systems continuance: An expectation-confirmation model. *MIS Quarterly*, *25*(3), 351-370.

Boomsma, A. (1982). The robustness of LISREL against small sample sizes in factor analysis models. In K. G. Jöreskog & H. Wold (Eds.), *Systems Under Indirect Observation: Causality, Structure, Prediction* (pp. 149-173). Amsterdam: North Holland.

Boynton, A. C., Zmud, R. W., & Jacobs, G. C. (1994). The influence of IT management practice on IT use in large organizations. *MIS Quarterly*, *17*(3), 299-318.

Byrd, T., & Turner, D. (2000). Measuring the flexibility of information technology infrastructure: Exploratory analysis of a construct. *Journal of Management Information Systems*, *17*(1), 167-208.

Byrd, T., & Turner, D. (2001). An exploratory analysis of the value of the skills of IT personnel: Their relationship to IS infrastructure and competitive advantage. *Decision Sciences*, *32*(1), 21-54.

Campbell, D. T., & Fiske, D. W. (1959). Convergent and discriminant validation by the multitrait-multimethod matrix. *Psychological Bulletin*, *56*, 81-105.

Chang, M. K., & Cheung, W. (2001). Determinants of the intention to use Internet/WWW at work: A confirmatory study. *Information & Management*, *39*, 1-14.

Chau, P. (1996). An empirical assessment of a modified technology acceptance model. *Journal of Management Information Systems*, *13*(2), 185-204.

Chau, P. (1997). Reexamining a model for evaluating information center success using a structural equation modeling approach. *Decision Sciences*, *28*(2), 309-334.

Chau, P., & Hu, P. (2001). Information technology acceptance by individual professionals: A model comparison approach. *Decision Sciences*, *32*(4), 699-719.

Chin, W. W., & Newsted, P. R. (1995). The importance of specification in causal modeling: The case of end-user computing satisfaction. *Information Systems Research*, *6*(1), 73-81.

Chin, W. W., & Todd, P. A. (1995). On the use, usefulness, and ease of use of structural equation modeling in MIS research: A note of caution. *MIS Quarterly*, *18*(2), 237-246.

Chin, W. W., Gopal, A. & et al. (1997). Advancing the theory of adaptive structuration: The development of a scale to measure faithfulness of appropriation. *Information Systems Research*, *8*(4), 342-367.

Churchill, G. A. (1979). A paradigm for developing better measures of marketing constructs. *Journal of Marketing Research*, *16*, 64-73.

Cudeck, R., & Browne, M. W. (1983). Cross-validation of covariance structures. *Multivariate Behavioral Research*, *18*, 147-167.

Dishaw, M., & Strong, D. (1999). Extending the technology acceptance model with task-technology fit constructs. *Information & Management*, *36*, 9-21.

Doll, W. J., & Torkzadeh, G. (1991). The measurement of end-user computing satisfaction: Theoretical and methodological issues. *MIS Quarterly*, *15*(1), 5-10.

Doll, W. J., & Torkzadeh, G. (1998). Developing a multidimensional measure of system-use in an organizational context. *Information & Management*, *33*, 171-185.

Doll, W. J., Hendrickson, A., & Deng, X. (1998). Using Davis's perceived usefulness and ease-of-use instruments for decision making: A confirmatory and multigroup invariance analysis. *Decision Sciences*, *29*(4), 839-869.

Doll, W. J., Raghunathan, T. S., Lim, J.-S., & Gupta, Y. P. (1995). A confirmatory factor analysis of the user information satisfaction instrument. *Information Systems Research*, *6*(2), 177-188.

Doll, W. J., Xia, W., & Torkzadeh, G. (1994). A confirmatory factor analysis of the end-user computing satisfaction instrument. *MIS Quarterly*, *17*(4), 453-461.

Fornell, C. (1983). Issues in the application of covariance structure analysis. *Journal of Consumer Research*, *9*, 443-448.

Gatian, A. W. (1994). Is user satisfaction a valid measure of system effectiveness? *Information & Management*, *26*, 119-131.

Gelderman, M. (1998). The relation between user satisfaction, usage of information systems and performance. *Information & Management, 34*, 11-18.

Gold, A., Malhotra, A., & Segars, A. (2001). Knowledge management: An organizational capabilities perspective. *Journal of Management Information Systems, 18*(1), 185-214.

Goodhue, D. L. (1998). Development and measurement validity of a task-technology fit instrument for user evaluations of information systems. *Decision Sciences, 29*(1), 105-138.

Gopal, R., & Sanders, L. (1998). International software piracy: Analysis of key issues and impacts. *Information Systems Research, 9*(4), 380-397.

Hann, J., & Weber, R. (1996). Information systems planning: A model and empirical tests. *Management Science, 42*(7), 1043-1064.

Hartwick, J., & Barki, H. (1994a). Explaining the role of user participation in information system use. *Management Science, 40*(4), 440-465.

Hartwick, J., & Barki, H. (1994b). Hypothesis testing and hypothesis generating research: An example from the user participation literature. *Information Systems Research, 5*(4), 446-449.

Hatcher, L. (1994). *A Step-by-Step Approach to Using the SAS System for Factor Analysis and Structural Equation Modeling.* Carry, NC: SAS Institute.

Hong, W., Thong, J., Wong, W., & Tam, K. (2001). Determinants of user acceptance of digital libraries: An empirical examination of individual differences and system characteristics. *Journal of Management Information Systems, 18*(3), 97-124.

Hu, P., Chau, P., Liu Sheng, O., & Tam, K. Y. (1999). Examining the technology acceptance model using physician acceptance of telemedicine technology. *Journal of Management Information Systems, 16*(2), 91-112.

Hunton, J. E., & Beeler, J. (1997). Effects of user participation in systems development: A longitudinal field experiment. *MIS Quarterly, 20*(4), 359-388.

Jackson, C. M., Chow, S., & Leitch, R. A. (1997). Toward an understanding of the behavioral intention to use an information system. *Decision Sciences, 28*(2), 357-389.

Jiang, J., & Klein, G. (1999). Supervisor support and career anchor impact on the career satisfaction of the entry-level information systems professional. *Journal of Management Information Systems, 16*(3), 219-240.

Jiang, J., Klein, G., & Crampton, S. (2000). A note on SERVQUAL reliability and validity in information system service quality measurement. *Decision Sciences, 31*(3), 725-744.

Karahanna, E., & Straub, D. (1999). The psychological origins of perceived usefulness and ease-of-use. *Information & Management, 35*, 237-250.

Karimi, J., Bhattacherjee, A., Gupta, Y., & Somers, T. (2000). The effects of MIS steering committees on information technology management sophistication. *Journal of Management Information Systems, 17*(2), 207-230.

Kettinger, W., & Lee, C. C. (1994). Perceived service quality and user satisfaction with the information services function. *Decision Sciences, 25*(5/6), 737-766.

Kettinger, W., & Lee, C. C. (1995). Global measures of information service quality: A cross-national study. *Decision Sciences, 26*(5), 569-588.

Long, J. S. (1983). *Confirmatory factor analysis: A preface to LISREL* (Sage University

Paper Series No. 07-033). Beverly Hills, CA: SAGE.

MacCallum, R. (1986). Specification searches in covariance structure modeling. *Psychological Bulletin, 100*, 107-120.

Mak, B., & Sockel, H. (2001). A confirmatory factor analysis of IS employee motivation and retention. *Information & Management, 38*, 265-276.

Malhotra, M., & Grover, V. (1998). An assessment of survey research in POM: From constructs to theory. *Journal of Operations Management, 16*(4), 407-415.

Martin, J. A. (1987). Structural equation modeling: A guide for the perplexed. *Child Development, 58*, 33-37.

McHaney, R., & Cronan, T. P. (1998). Computer simulation success: On the use of the end-user computing satisfaction instrument: A comment. *Decision Sciences, 29*(2), 525-536.

McHaney, R., & Cronan, T. P. (2000). Toward an empirical understanding of computer simulation implementation success. *Information & Management, 37*, 135-151.

McHaney, R., Hightower, R., & White, D. (1999). EUCS test-retest reliability in representational model decision support systems. *Information & Management, 36*, 109-119.

Miriani, R., & Lederer, A. (1998). An instrument for assessing the organizational benefits of IS projects. *Decision Sciences, 29*(4), 803-838.

Moore, J. E. (2000). One road to turnover: An examination of work exhaustion in technology professionals. *MIS Quarterly, 24*(1), 141-168.

Nidumolu, S. (1995a). The effect of coordination and uncertainty on software project performance: Residual performance risk as an intervening variable. *Information Systems Research, 6*(3), 191-219.

Nidumolu, S. (1995b). Interorganizational information systems and the structure and climate of seller-buyer relationships. *Information & Management, 28*, 89-105.

Nidumolu, S., & Knotts, G. W. (1998). The effects of customizability and reusability on perceived process and competitive performance of software firms. *MIS Quarterly, 21*(2), 105-137.

Palvia, P., & Basu, S. C. (1999). Information systems management issues: Reporting and relevance. *Decision Sciences, 30*(1), 273-290.

Premkumar, G., & King, W. R. (1994). Organizational characteristics and information systems planning: An empirical study. *Information Systems Research, 5*(2), 75-109.

Raghunathan, B., & Raghunathan, T. S. (1994). Adaptation of a planning system success model to information systems planning. *Information Systems Research, 5*(3), 326-340.

Raghunathan, B., Raghunathan, T. S., & Tu, Q. (1999). Dimensionality of the strategic grid framework: The construct and its measurement. *Information Systems Research, 10*(4), 343-355.

Rai, A., & Patnayakuni, R. (1996). A structural model for CASE adoption behavior. *Journal of Management Information Systems, 13*(2), 205-234.

Rasch, R. H., & Tosi, H. L. (1992). Factors affecting software developers' performance: An integrated approach. *MIS Quarterly, 15*(3), 395-413.

Ravichandran, T., & Rai, A. (1999). Total quality management in information systems development: Key constructs and relationships. *Journal of Management Information Systems, 16*(3), 119-155.

Sabherwal, R. (1999). The relationship between information system planning sophistication and information system success: An empirical assessment. *Decision Sciences*, *30*(1), 137-167.

Segars, A. H., & Grover, V. (1993). Re-examining perceived ease of use and usefulness: A confirmatory factor analysis. *MIS Quarterly*, *17*(4), 517-525.

Segars, A. H., & Grover, V. (1998). Strategic information systems planning success: An investigation of the construct and its measurement. *MIS Quarterly*, *21*(2), 139-163.

Segars, A. H., Grover, V., & Teng, J. T. C. (1998). Strategic information systems planning: Planning system dimensions, internal coalignment, and implications for planning effectiveness. *Decision Sciences*, *29*(2), 303-345.

Sethi, V., & King, W. R. (1994). Development of measures to assess the extent to which an information technology application provides competitive advantage. *Management Science*, *40*(12), 1601-1627.

Sharma, S. (1996). *Applied Multivariate Techniques*. New York: John Wiley & Sons.

Sriram, V., Stump, R. L., & Banerjee, S. (1997). Information technology investments in purchasing: An empirical study of dimensions and antecedents. *Information & Management*, *33*, 59-72.

Stone, R., & Good, D. (2001). The assimilation of computer-aided marketing activities. *Information & Management*, *38*, 437-447.

Straub, D., Limayem, M., & Karahanna-Evaristo, E. (1995). Measuring system usage: Implications for IS theory testing. *Management Science*, *41*(8), 1328-1342.

Straub, D. W. (1990). Effective IS security: An empirical study. *Information Systems Research*, *1*(3), 255-276.

Subramanian, G. H. (1994). A replication of perceived usefulness and perceived ease of use measurement. *Decision Sciences*, *25*(5/6), 863-874.

Swanson, E. B., & Dans, E. (2000). System life expectancy and the maintenance effort: Exploring their equilibration. *MIS Quarterly*, *24*(2), 277-297.

Taylor, S., & Todd, P. A. (1995a). Assessing IT usage: The role of prior experience. *MIS Quarterly*, *18*(4), 561-570.

Taylor, S., & Todd, P. A. (1995b). Understanding information technology usage: A test of competing models. *Information Systems Research*, *6*(2), 144-175.

Teo, T., & Choo, W. Y. (2001). Assessing the impact of using the Internet for competitive intelligence. *Information & Management*, *39*, 67-83.

Van Dyke, T., Prybutok, V., & Kappelman, L. (1999). Cautions on the use of the SERVQUAL measure to assess the quality of information systems services. *Decision Sciences*, *30*(3), 877-891.

Wright, G., Chaturvedi, A., Mookerjee, R., & Garrod, S. (1998). Integrated modeling environments in organizations: An empirical study. *Information Systems Research*, *9*(1), 64-84.

Zaheer, A., & Venkatraman, N. (1994). Determinants of electronic integration in the insurance industry: An empirical test. *Management Science*, *40*(5), 549-566.

ENDNOTES

[1]   It should be noted that the goal of this study is not to provide a tutorial on SEM. Interested readers are referred to excellent treatment of the methodology in Bagozzi (1984), Anderson and Gerbing (1984), Bagozzi & Baumgartner (1994), and Sharma (1996).

[2]   The authors of SEM applications might not report various forms of data screening they performed to save space in the reported article for more important things.

APPENDIX

Sample Articles by Journal

Communication of the ACM (0 papers)	

Decision Science (17 papers)	
• Agarwal and Prasad (1999)	• Miriani and Lederer (1998)
• Byrd and Turner (2001)	• Kettinger and Lee (1994)
• Chau (1997)	• Kettinger and Lee (1995)
• Chau and Hu (2001)	• Palvia and Basu (1999)
• Doll, Hendrickson, and Deng (1998)	• Sabherwal (1999)
• Goodhu (1998)	• Segars, Grover, and Teng (1998)
• Jackson, Chow, and Leitch (1997)	• Subramanian (1994)
• Jiang, Klein, and Crampton (2000)	• Van Dyke, Prybutok, and Kappelman (1999)
• McHaney and Cronan (1998)	

Information & Management (13 papers)	
• Chang and Cheung (2001)	• McHaney and Cronan (2000)
• Dishaw and Strong (1999)	• McHaney, Hightower, and White (1999)
• Doll and Torkzadeh (1998)	• Nidumolu (1995)
• Gatian (1994)	• Siriam, Stump, and Banerjee (1997)
• Gelderman (1998)	• Stone and Good (2001)
• Karahanna and Straub (1999)	• Teo and Choo (2001)
• Mak and Sockel (2001)	

Information Systems Research (13 papers)	
• Agarwal and Prasad (1998)	• Premkumar and King (1994),
• Barki and Hartwick (1994)	• Raghunathan and Raghunathan (1994)
• Chin and Newsted (1995)	• Raghunathan, Raghunathan, and Tu (1999)
• Chin, Gopal, and Salisbury (1997)	• Straub (1990)
• Doll, Raghunathan, Lim, and Gupta (1995)	• Taylor and Todd (1995)
• Gopal and Sanders (1998)	• Wright, Chaturvedi, Mookerjee, and Garrod (1998)
• Nidumolu (1995)	

Journal of Management Information Systems (10 papers)	
• Becerra-Fernandez and Sabherwal (2001)	• Hu, Chau, Liu Sheng, and Tam (1999)
• Byrd and Turner (2000)	• Jiang and Klein (1999)
• Chau (1996)	• Karimi, Bhattacherjee, Gupta, and Somers (2000)
• Gold, Malhotra, and Segars (2001)	• Rai and Patnayakuni (1996)
• Hong, Thong, Wong, and Tam (2001)	• Ravichandran and Rai (1999)

MIS Quarterly (14 papers)	
• Adams, Nelson, and Todd (1992)	• Moore (2000)
• Barki and Hartwick (2001)	• Nidumolu and Knotts (1998)
• Bhattacherjee (2001)	• Rasch and Tosi (1992)
• Boynton, Zmud, and Jacobs (1994)	• Segars and Grover (1993)
• Chin and Todd (1995)	• Segars and Grover (1998)
• Doll, Xia, and Torkzadeh (1994)	• Swanson and Dans (2000)
• Hunton and Beeler (1997)	• Taylor and Todd (1995)

Management Science (5 papers)	
• Hann and Weber (1996)	• Straub, Limayem, and Karahanna-Evaristo (1995)
• Hartwick and Barki (1994)	
• Sethi and King (1994)	• Zaheer and Venkatraman (1994)

Chapter V

The Problem of Common Method Variance in IS Research

Amy B. Woszczynski
Kennesaw State University, USA

Michael E. Whitman
Kennesaw State University, USA

ABSTRACT

Many IS researchers obtain data through the use of self-reports. However, self-reports have inherent problems and limitations, most notably the problem of common method variance. Common method variance can cause researchers to find a significant effect, when in fact, the true effect is due to the method employed. In this chapter, we examined published research in leading information systems (IS) journals to determine if common method variance is a potential problem in IS research and how IS researchers have attempted to overcome problems with method bias. We analyzed 116 research articles that used a survey approach as the predominant method in MIS Quarterly, Information Systems Research, *and* Journal of Management Information Systems. *The results indicate that only a minority of IS researchers have reported on common method variance. We recommend that IS researchers undertake techniques to minimize the effects of common method variance, including using multiple types of respondents, longitudinal designs, and confirmatory factor analysis that explicitly models method effects.*

INTRODUCTION

Although non-positivist approaches have recently emerged as valid alternatives to traditional statistical techniques, many information systems (IS) researchers continue to rely heavily on self-reports to gather data. However, IS researchers must recognize the inherent problems associated with self-reports to assure that the results reported are due to the predicted effect and not due to common method variance. Common method variance comprises one part of the measured variance. Spector (1994) divided measured variance into three distinct components: trait variance, method variance, and error variance. Trait variance includes all of the variance associated with the variable being studied, while (common) method variance includes the variance associated with all systematic influences on the construct of interest, particularly as it relates to a common method used to gather data. Error variance is simply random measurement error, something that researchers must attempt to control in order to move closer to measuring true latent variance.

When self-reports are used, common method variance can be a serious problem and can, in fact, cause the researcher to find a significant effect when the only real effect is due to the method employed. Organ and Ryan (1995) note that a significant problem with self-reports may be unstable correlations, particularly with data measured at one point in time. Spector (1994) agrees, noting that self-reports are particularly unreliable when measuring variables that are correlated with one another. Moreover, moderators that are specific to the situation or temporary in nature may affect the accuracy of the results. These problems are particularly relevant to IS studies, which often use self-reports to gather data on system usage. Studies have shown that new models are needed to more accurately assess how people respond to frequency questions (Blair & Burton, 1987) and that IS researchers themselves do not generally agree how system usage should be measured (Straub, Limayem, & Karahanna-Evaristo, 1995). How should IS researchers test for common method variance? How can IS researchers attempt to minimize the potential bias associated with the method employed? The following section describes how the IS research community has examined the problem of common method variance and how other research communities have addressed the same issue. Further, the section provides an elementary overview of procedures that can minimize the common variance associated with the method employed. Then we move to the study methodology and results, followed by concluding remarks.

THEORETICAL BACKGROUND

Although a substantial number of IS research studies use self-reports to measure latent variance, few test for common method variance. Researchers from various disciplines have suggested multiple techniques to overcome bias associated with employing a common method—e.g., self-reports. First and foremost, IS researchers should use instruments that exhibit both reliability and validity, as per Boudreau, Gefen, and Straub (2001), Hufnagel and Conca (1994), and Straub et al. (1995). Certainly, researchers should also maximize response rates to include as many different respondents as possible and should minimize missing data within the sample (Roth & Campion, 1996). Obviously, a scale that is fraught with unreliable items, poor validity, and the like will probably yield invalid results, with or without considering common method bias. However, simply having instruments that exhibit both reliability and validity is not enough (Boone & de Brabander, 1997; Podsakoff & Organ, 1986). Researchers from all disciplines must do more to assure that results are not contaminated by extraneous factors.

What can IS researchers do to overcome the potential problem of common method variance? We present a series of actions that IS researchers can take to minimize the effects of common method variance. We start with what the IS researcher can do prior to and while collecting data and conclude with steps that the researcher can take after data collection.

First, when gathering data, researchers can secure multiple types of respondents for the same question (Boone & de Brabander, 1997; Spector, 1994). For example, peers, customers, supervisors, and direct reports can all respond to questions. This overcomes the problem of having a single respondent answering each question. By comparing answers from multiple categories of respondents, researchers can aggregate and/or average responses in hopes of improving latent variance measured.

Second, researchers can use multiple methods of gathering data in conjunction with self-reports to decrease the chances of common method bias (Conger & Kanungo, 1988; Spector, 1994). For example, qualitative analyses can support data gathered using self-reports. Moreover, quantitative analysis of objective data, such as sales figures, can provide support in addition to self-reports. Finally, conducting case studies, laboratory experiments, and the like in concert with gathering data through self-reports can provide additional support for results.

Third, when gathering information using self-reports, IS researchers should attempt to minimize social desirability bias, a common form of method variance (Jo, 2000; Kline, Sulsky, & Rever-Moriyama, 2000; Nunnally & Bernstein, 1994). That is, people tend to want to make themselves look good—high performer, team player, etc.—when answering survey questions. Allowing respondents anonymous responses may overcome some of the social desirability bias inherent in surveys. Further, researchers can model the social desirability construct into the survey if necessary, asking questions that measure the levels of social desirability exhibited by respondents. Then the researchers can partial out the social desirability factor (Podsakoff & Organ, 1986), thus yielding a more accurate estimate of the true effect.

Fourth, longitudinal designs can overcome some problems with self-reports (DeGroot, Kiker, & Cross, 2000; Spector, 1994). One major disadvantage of self-reports is that respondents answer questions at one point in time. If, instead, researchers ask questions over time to gauge change in beliefs, attitudes, intentions, etc., the results tend to be more accurate. Of course, longitudinal designs are more costly and time-consuming to manage, but the rewards may be worthwhile for the IS researcher.

Fifth, the IS researcher should consider and report any relevant mood connotations (Spector, 1992). Using care when administering surveys can help alleviate the common method variance associated with a survey. For example, asking employees their opinions of benefits offered by the company immediately after layoffs may yield very different results than surveys administered at other times. At the very least, the IS researcher should report and consider the mood of the survey respondents.

In addition to taking steps during data collection to minimize common method variance, researchers can also complete Harman's one-factor test (Harman, 1976;

Podsakoff & Organ, 1986) after data collection to test for the possible presence of method bias. The one-factor test provides a quick and easy way to check for potential common method variance. By conducting a factor analysis on all items at once, researchers can quickly note whether one factor emerges upon which most items load. If that is the case, then the common factor is probably the method employed. If, instead, multiple factors emerge, with items loading as predicted, then common method variance may not be a problem in the study being conducted. However, as Johns, Xie, and Fang (1992) note, simply having a one-factor solution does not necessarily mean that common method bias is a problem, just that the researchers should potentially investigate further.

Confirmatory factor analysis also holds great promise for addressing common method bias. However, researchers should explicitly model and test for common method bias in the models tested. Simply partialing out error variance and trait variance is not enough. Instead, researchers should compare models both with and without method bias to determine if common method variance presents a possible influence on the trait variance estimated (Cote & Buckley, 1987; MacKenzie, Podsakoff, & Rich, 2001; Williams, Cote, & Buckley, 1989).

Finally, after multiple studies have collected data on a topic of interest, IS researchers may employ meta-analysis techniques, which offer great possibilities for overcoming potential method variance (DeGroot et al., 2000; Organ & Ryan, 1995). Meta-analyses aggregate large amounts of data into a meaningful interpretation while separating method variance and error variance from true variance. Thus, researchers are able to provide stronger support using meta-analyses as compared to single studies.

Obviously, IS researchers can call upon various techniques to attempt to identify and overcome potential problems with common method variance. Many of the techniques are quick and simple. Logically, we would assume that IS researchers have used many of these techniques and have considered the potential problems of common method variance in research conducted. However, many IS researchers have ignored— or failed to report upon—the potential problem of common method bias.

Although many IS researchers have ignored the potential problems associated with common method variance, researchers from other disciplines have not. For example, Organ and Ryan (1995) completed a meta-analysis of 55 studies of the relationship between job satisfaction and organizational citizenship. Using the one-factor test, they found that the most significant moderator of the correlations was the use of self-reports. Similarly, using the one-factor method, Johns et al. (1992) found a potential problem with common method variance when testing a sample of job characteristics and attitudes. Further, Williams et al. (1989) used confirmatory factor analysis to test for the presence of trait, method, and error variance. They found that, in some studies, common method variance accounts for approximately 25% of explained variance. Cote and Buckley (1987) found even more alarming results. In their examination of 70 empirical studies, they found that measures contained 41.7% trait variance, 26.3% method variance, and 32.0% random error variance. Clearly, when trait variance may account for less than half of measured and reported variance, researchers should seek techniques to improve the estimate of latent variance.

There are, however, some studies that indicate that common method variance may not be a serious problem (Schmit & Allscheid, 1995) and that the degree of common method bias varies depending on the domain studied (Crampton & Wagner, 1994).

Therefore, we are left to ask if IS researchers should even be concerned about common method variance. Is common method variance even a problem in IS research? What specific steps—if any—have IS researchers undertaken to try to overcome common method variance? We examined published research in leading IS journals to determine if common method variance is a potential problem and if researchers have tested for common method variance. Specifically, we surveyed three top IS journals from 1996-2000 and analyzed empirical articles that use self-reports as the predominant method. After compiling a list of all articles that perform statistical analyses based mainly on self-reports, we then systematically analyzed the articles to determine if IS researchers have tested for common method variance and, if so, the techniques used to test for and overcome common method bias. Finally, we summarize findings and make recommendations to reduce the effects of common method variance.

STUDY METHODOLOGY
Journal Selection

Many studies have ranked IS journals in terms of citations or other measures (Hardgrave & Walstrom, 1997; Mylonopoulos & Theoharakis, 2001; Whitman, Hendrickson, & Townsend, 1999). By using these studies as a guideline and limiting the current study to strictly research journals (e.g., *Communications of the ACM* would not qualify) and by further limiting the study to specifically IS journals (i.e., *Decision Sciences* and *Management Science* would not qualify), we selected three journals to use in our sample: *MIS Quarterly, Information Systems Research*, and *Journal of Management Information Systems*. These three final selections were the top-ranked IS research journals in each of the above-mentioned studies. Other researchers (e.g., Boudreau et al., 2001) have used similar guidelines when selecting journals from which to sample. We also selected a relatively large time period to determine if researcher habits had changed over time. Therefore, we examined all articles in the three selected journals for the years 1996-2000.

Classification of Articles

Each article was grouped according to article type, as shown in Table 1. To initially classify an article, one of the authors would read the article and classify accordingly. Then the other author would also read the article and classify accordingly. Any articles for which there existed a disagreement among researchers, later discussions were able to resolve it so that the researchers agreed on the classification of all articles. In studies using more than one methodology, the predominant methodology was used to classify each article—that is, a case study that used a survey as a small part of the analysis would be classified as a case study, not a survey.

Of 428 total research articles published in the five-year period, 116 (27.1%) were classified as using a survey approach with self-reported data as the predominant method. Another 127 (29.7%) were classified as theory/system development, including research note/analysis/response, as well as secondary data analysis. No other category accounted for more than 13.8% (case study) of the articles. Clearly, with over one-fourth of the published research in the top journals categorized as using a survey methodology,

Table 1. Article Classification.

Type of Study	Journal (1996-2000)			
	Information Systems Research	*MIS Quarterly*	*Journal of Management Information Systems*	**TOTALS**
Survey/Questionnaire	31[1] 23.5%[2]	31 25.0%	54 31.40%	116 27.1%
Theory/System Development[3]	41 31.1%	29 23.4%	57 33.1%	127 29.7%
Case Study	11 8.3%	29 23.4%	19 11.1%	59 13.8%
Experiment	11 8.3%	5 4.0%	27 15.7%	43 10.1%
Mathematical Modeling[4]	16 12.1%	4 3.2%	9 5.2%	29 6.8%
Qualitative Analysis	3 2.3%	12 9.7%	2 1.2%	17 4.0%
Interviews	1 0.8%	5 4.0%	2 1.2%	8 1.9%
Event Study/Objective Data	4 3.0%	3 2.4%	0 0.00%	7 1.6%
Action Research	0 0.00%	1 0.8%	1 0.6%	2 0.5%
Delphi Method	0 0.00%	2 1.6%	0 0.00%	2 0.5%
Field Study	13 9.9%	2 1.6%	1 0.6%	16 3.7%
Electronic Brainstorming	1 0.8%	1 0.8%	0 0.00%	2 0.5%
TOTALS	132 100.0%	124 100.0%	172 100.0%	428 100.0%

Notes:[1] Number of articles by journal; [2] Percent of total articles by journal; [3] Includes research note/analysis/response; also includes secondary data analysis; [4] Includes simulation, algorithms, economic modeling, etc.

this approach appears important to the IS community. Therefore, common method variance, a potential confounding factor in survey research, should be of interest to the IS community at large. The next section describes how IS researchers have handled common method variance over the time period specified.

RESULTS

As we began our analysis, it became quite apparent that few IS researchers have tested for the presence of common method bias, as shown in Table 2. In fact, of the 116 articles that potentially had a problem with common method variance, only 12 of the articles explicitly mentioned common method variance, common method bias, method bias, single response bias, or method variation as it relates to the common method used

Table 2. Techniques Used to Check for and Overcome Common Method Variance[1].

Technique	Journal (1996-2000)			
	Information Systems Research	*MIS Quarterly*	*Journal of Management Information Systems*	**TOTALS**
Used multiple types of respondents	2[2] 6.5%[3]	4 12.9%	1 1.9%	7 6.0%
Used multiple methods of data gathering	17 54.8%	18 58.1%	14 25.9%	49 42.2%
Minimized social desirability bias	0 0.0%	1 3.2%	0 0.0%	1 0.9%
Used longitudinal designs	3 9.7%	6 19.4%	2 3.7%	11 9.5%
Reported mood connotations	0 0.0%	1 3.2%	0 0.0%	1 0.9%
Used confirmatory factor analysis—specifically mentioned the modeling of method variance	0 0.0%	3 9.7%	0 0.0%	3 2.6%
Completed Harman's one-factor test	0 0.0%	3 9.7%	0 0.0%	3 2.6%
Specifically mentioned common method variance or related terms	2 6.5%	9 29.0%	1 1.9%	12 10.3%

[1] *Note that some authors did not use any of the above techniques to test for/compensate for common method bias, while other authors used multiple techniques;* [2] *Number of articles by journal;* [3] Percent of total articles by journal*

to gather data. *MISQ* seemed to have the best record of discussing common method variance, with nine of the 31 articles that used self-reports to gather data mentioning potential problems with the method employed. Over the same 1996-2000 time frame, with 85 articles using self-reports in *ISR* and *JMIS* together, only *three* articles explicitly mentioned common method variance. So, although researchers may indeed be trying to minimize bias and may even be checking for common method variance effects, readers are rarely made aware of the potential for method bias or the steps that researchers have taken to attempt to overcome inherent problems with self-reports.

Of the recommended techniques to compensate for inherent problems with self-reports, authors most commonly used multiple methods of gathering data in addition to the self-reports. Of the 116 articles in this study, 49 used some sort of secondary method to substantiate data collected using self-reports. Some authors used additional data from sources such as organizational records, databases, and the like (Ang, 1998; Dewan, Michael, & Min, 1998; Freeman, Jarvenpaa, & Wheeler, 2000; Grover, Fiedler, & Teng, 1997; Hitt & Brynjolfsson, 1997; Hunton & Beeler, 1997; Montazemi, Cameron, & Gupta, 1996; Palmer & Markus, 2000; Swanson, 2000; Truman, 2000), while others used interviews, case studies, or other qualitative methods to support self-reported data (Burke, 1999; Karahanna & Straub, 1999; Vandenbosch & Higgins, 1996).

The second most common technique to compensate for potential problems with self-reported data was the use of longitudinal designs, which 11 of the articles used to some extent, including Burke (1999), Chidambaram (1996), Compeau and Higgins (1999), Devaraj and Kohli (2000), Hunton and Beeler (1997), Moore (2000), Simon, Grover, Teng, and Whitcomb (1996), Vandenbosch and Ginzberg (1997), Venkatesh (2000), and Venkatesh and Morris (2000). Authors using longitudinal designs tend to decrease the bias of having a single respondent answer questions at one point in time. Over time, the bias from using the common method tends to fade. Obviously, however, longitudinal designs are sometimes impractical because of cost constraints, loss of participants over time, and other confounding factors.

The third most common technique—and the remaining technique that at least 5% of the articles used—was using multiple categories of respondents. That is, peers, customers, managers, etc., were used in addition to self-reports to supplement the response from a single person. Authors using this technique include Armstrong and Sambamurthy (1999), Choe (1996), Guinan, Cooprider, and Faraj (1998), Janz, Wetherbe, Davis, and Noe (1997), Nelson and Cooprider (1996), Nidumolu and Knotts (1998), and Webster (1998).

Another interesting point learned from our analysis is the limited use of Harman's one-factor test to analyze the potential for common method bias. Although researchers in other fields commonly use this test to check for method variance problems, IS researchers have tended to avoid this simple test. In fact, of the 116 articles surveyed in this study, only three used Harman's to check for method bias. If we omit *MISQ* from the analysis, not one of the other journals had any articles that discussed Harman's test. IS researchers should certainly consider expanded use of this relatively simple test as a tool for testing for and overcoming common method bias.

Although single techniques to reduce the effects of common method bias are admirable, the best researchers use multiple techniques to attempt to overcome effects due to the common method employed. There are relatively few examples of IS researchers who have effectively handled common method variance by clearly articulating the potential problems and working to overcome bias. However, a small number of IS researchers have done an exceptional job of testing for and adequately discussing common method variance. Other IS researchers are encouraged to emulate the standards set by these researchers. Three examples of excellent analysis and discussion of common method variance by IS researchers follow.

First, Igbaria, Zinatelli, Cragg, and Cavaye (1997) tested for common method variance using the one-factor test, as recommended by Podsakoff and Organ (1986). Since the results showed a 7-factor model accounting for a substantial portion of explained variance, they determined that common method variance was not a problem in the study.

Second, Nambisan and Agarwal (1999) used several techniques to try to minimize the effect of common method variance. They asked respondents to think about utilization in the last two years in an attempt to reduce recall errors. They also completed Harman's one-factor test and found no significant common method bias. Moreover, they attempted to control for social desirability bias.

Finally, Moore (2000) used multiple techniques to try to minimize the effect of common method variance. She completed Harman's one-factor test, and the results supported the belief that common method variance was not a problem in the study. Further, she used a longitudinal design to reduce self-report method effects, as well as using multiple methods of data analysis (quantitative and qualitative data analysis).

Finally, she controlled for negative affectivity. By using multiple techniques and a longitudinal design to overcome common method bias as well as explicitly checking for the presence of bias by using Harman's one-factor test, Moore truly exemplifies the best of attempting to compensate for self-report methods of gathering data. The next section provides a brief discussion of the results and recommendations for IS researchers.

CONCLUSION

Clearly, IS researchers—with few exceptions—have not adequately addressed the potential confounding effects of common method variance. By using a few simple techniques, IS researchers could strengthen the impact of their studies. Further, these same researchers might find results stronger and more compelling after trait variance is separated from common method variance. We have recommended simple techniques that IS researchers can employ to attempt to prevent and overcome common method bias in empirical studies. IS researchers have tended to use multiple methods of data gathering more often than any other technique we discussed, and this should decrease the likelihood of common method variance. However, without testing for and explicitly considering common method variance, we are left to wonder if the results are due to the trait effect predicted or the method employed. We are not recommending that IS researchers abandon self-reports as a valid technique for data collection and analysis, just that these same researchers carefully consider potential confounding effects, including common method variance. By expanding their repertoire of tools to include the use of multiple categories of respondents, the factoring of social desirability, and other techniques in the design and administration of data collection strategies, along with increased use of meta-analysis and confirmatory factor analysis that correctly considers method bias, IS researchers can provide more support for the theories developed and reported in leading research journals.

REFERENCES

Ang, S. (1998). Production and transaction economies and IS outsourcing: A study of the U.S. banking industry. *MIS Quarterly*, *22*(4), 535-552.

Armstrong, C. P., & Sambamurthy, V. (1999). Information technology assimilation in firms: The influence of senior leadership and IT infrastructures. *Information Systems Research*, *10*(4), 304-327.

Blair, E., & Burton, S. (1987). Cognitive processes used by survey respondents to answer behavioral frequency questions. *Journal of Consumer Research*, *14*(2), 280-288.

Boone, C., & de Brabander, B. (1997). Self-reports and CEO locus of control research: A note. *Organization Studies*, 18(6), 949-971.

Boudreau, M.-C., Gefen, D., & Straub, D. W. (2001). Validation in information systems research. *MIS Quarterly*, *25*(1), 1-14.

Burke, K. (1999). How much bandwidth is enough? A longitudinal examination of media characteristics and group outcomes. *MIS Quarterly*, *23*(4), 557-579.

Chidambaram, L. (1996). Relational development in computer-supported groups. *MIS Quarterly*, *20*(2), 143-165.

Choe, J. (1996). The relationships among performance of accounting information systems, influence factors, and evolution level of information systems. *Journal of Management Information Systems, 12*(4), 215-240.

Compeau, D., & Higgins, C. A. (1999). Social cognitive theory and individual reactions to computing technology: A longitudinal study. *MIS Quarterly, 23*(2), 145-158.

Conger, J. A., & Kanungo, R. N. (1988). Training charismatic leadership: A risky and critical task. In J. A. Conger & R. N. Kanungo (Eds.), *Charismatic Leadership: The Elusive Factor in Organizational Effectiveness*. San Francisco, CA: Jossey-Bass.

Cote, J. A., & Buckley, M. R. (1987). Estimating trait, method, and error variance: Generalizing across 70 construct validation studies. *Journal of Marketing Research, 24*, 315-318.

Crampton, S. M., & Wagner, J. A. (1994). Percept-percept inflation in micro-organizational research: An investigation of and effect. *Journal of Applied Psychology, 13*, 46-78.

DeGroot, T., Kiker, D. S., & Cross, T. C. (2000). A meta-analysis to review organizational outcomes related to charismatic leadership. *Canadian Journal of Administrative Sciences, 17*(4), 356-371.

Devaraj, S., & Kohli, R. (2000). Information technology payoff in the health-care industry: A longitudinal study. *Journal of Management Information Systems, 16*(4), 41-68.

Dewan, S., Michael, S. C., & Min, C. (1998). Firm characteristics and investments in information technology: Scale and scope effects. *Information Systems Research, 9*(3), 219-232.

Freeman, L. A., Jarvenpaa, S. L., & Wheeler, B. C. (2000). The supply and demand of information systems doctorates: Past, present, and future. *MIS Quarterly, 24*(3), 355-380.

Grover, V., Fiedler, K., & Teng, J. (1997). Empirical evidence on Swanson's tri-core model of information systems innovation. *Information Systems Research, 8*(3), 273-287.

Guinan, P. J., Cooprider, J. G., & Faraj, S. (1998). Enabling software development team performance during requirements definition: A behavioral versus technical approach. *Information Systems Research, 9*(2), 101-125.

Hardgrave, B. C., & Walstrom, K. A. (1997). Forums for MIS scholars. *Communications of the ACM, 40*(11), 119-124.

Harman, H. H. (1976). *Modern Factor Analysis* (3rd ed.). Chicago, IL: University of Chicago Press.

Hitt, L. M., & Brynjolfsson, E. (1997). Information technology and internal firm organization: An exploratory analysis. *Journal of Management Information Systems, 14*(2), 81-102.

Hufnagel, E. M., & Conca, C. (1994). User response data: The potential for errors and biases. *Information Systems Research, 5*(1), 48-73.

Hunton, J. E., & Beeler, J. D. (1997). Effects of user participation in systems development: A longitudinal field experiment. *MIS Quarterly, 21*(4), 359-388.

Igbaria, M., Zinatelli, N., Cragg, P., & Cavaye, A. L. M. (1997). Personal computing acceptance factors in small firms: A structural equation model. *MIS Quarterly, 21*(3), 279-302.

Janz, B. D., Wetherbe, J. C., Davis, G. B., & Noe, R. A. (1997). Reengineering the systems development process: The link between autonomous teams and business process outcomes. *Journal of Management Information Systems, 14*(1), 41-68.

Jo, M. (2000). Controlling social-desirability bias via method factors of direct and indirect questioning in structural equation models. *Psychology & Marketing, 17*(2), 137-148.

Johns, G., Xie, J. L., & Fang, Y. (1992). Mediating and moderating effects in job design. *Journal of Management, 18*(4), 657-678.

Karahanna, E., & Straub, D. W. (1999). Information technology adoption across time: A cross-sectional comparison of pre-adoption and post-adoption beliefs. *MIS Quarterly, 23*(2), 183-213.

Kline, T. J. B., Sulsky, L. M., & Rever-Moriyama, S. D. (2000). Common method variance and specification errors: A practical approach to detection. *Journal of Psychology, 134*(4), 401-421.

MacKenzie, S. B., Podsakoff, P. M., & Rich, G. A. (2001). Transformational and transactional leadership and salesperson performance. *Journal of the Academy of Marketing Science, 29*(2), 115-134.

Montazemi, A. R., Cameron, D. A., & Gupta, K. M. (1996). An empirical study of factors affecting software package selection. *Journal of Management Information Systems, 13*(1), 89-106.

Moore, J. E. (2000). One road to turnover: An examination of work exhaustion in technology professionals. *MIS Quarterly, 24*(1), 141-168.

Mylonopoulos, N. A., & Theoharakis, V. (2001). Global perceptions of IS journals. *Communications of the ACM, 44*(9), 29-33.

Nambisan, S., & Agarwal, R. (1999). Organizational mechanisms for enhancing user innovation in information technology. *MIS Quarterly, 23*(3), 365-395.

Nelson, K. M., & Cooprider, J. G. (1996). The contribution of shared knowledge to IS group performance. *MIS Quarterly, 20*(4), 409-432.

Nidumolu, S. R., & Knotts, G. W. (1998). The effects of customizability and reusability on perceived process and competitive performance. *MIS Quarterly, 22*(2), 105-137.

Nunnally, J. C., & Bernstein, I. H. (1994). *Psychometric Theory* (3rd ed.). New York: McGraw-Hill.

Organ, D. W., & Ryan, K. (1995). A meta-analytic review of attitudinal and dispositional predictors of organizational citizenship behavior. *Personnel Psychology, 48*, 775-802.

Palmer, J. W., & Markus, M. L. (2000). The performance impacts of quick response and strategic alignment in specialty retailing. *Information Systems Research, 11*(3), 241-259.

Podsakoff, P. M., & Organ, D. W. (1986). Self-reports in organizational research: Problems and prospects. *Journal of Management, 12*(4), 531-544.

Roth, P. E., & Campion, J. E. (1996). The impact of four missing data techniques on validity estimates in human resource management. *Journal of Business & Psychology, 11*(1), 101-112.

Schmit, M. J., & Allscheid, S. P. (1995). Employee attitudes and customer satisfaction: Making theoretical and empirical connections. *Personnel Psychology, 48*, 521-536.

Simon, S. J., Grover, V., Teng, J. T. C., & Whitcomb, K. (1996). The relationship of information system training methods and cognitive ability to end-user satisfaction, comprehension, and skill transfer: A longitudinal field study. *Information Systems Research, 7*(4), 466-490.

Spector, P. E. (1992). A consideration of the validity and meaning of self-report measures of job conditions. In C. L. Cooper & I. T. Robertson (Eds.), *International Review of Industrial and Organizational Psychology*. West Sussex, UK: John Wiley & Sons.

Spector, P. E. (1994). Using self-report questionnaires in OB research: A comment on the use of a controversial method. *Journal of Organizational Behavior, 15*, 385-392.

Straub, D., Limayem, M., & Karahanna-Evaristo, E. (1995). Measuring system usage: Implications for IS theory testing. *Management Science, 41*(8), 1328-1342.

Swanson, E. B. (2000). System life expectancy and the maintenance effort: Exploring their equilibrium. *MIS Quarterly, 24*(2), 277-297.

Truman, G. E. (2000). Integration in electronic exchange environments. *Journal of Management Information Systems, 17*(1), 209-244.

Vandenbosch, B., & Ginzberg, M. J. (1997). Lotus Notes and collaboration: Plus can change … . *Journal of Management Information Systems, 13*(3), 65-81.

Vandenbosch, B., & Higgins, C. (1996). Information acquisition and mental models: An investigation into the relationship between behavior and learning. *Information Systems Research, 7*(2), 198-214.

Venkatesh, V. (2000). Determinants of perceived ease of use: Integrating control, intrinsic motivation, and emotion into the technology acceptance model. *Information Systems Research, 11*(4), 342-365.

Venkatesh, V., & Morris, M. G. (2000). Why don't men ever stop to ask for directions? Gender, social influence, and their role in technology acceptance and usage behavior. *MIS Quarterly, 24*(1), 115-139.

Webster, J. (1998). Desktop videoconferencing: Experiences of complete users, wary users, and non-users. *MIS Quarterly, 22*(3), 257-286.

Whitman, M. E., Hendrickson, A. R., & Townsend, A. M. (1999). Research commentary: Academic rewards for teaching, research, and service: Data and discourse. *Information Systems Research, 10*(2), 99-109.

Williams, L. J., Cote, J. A., & Buckley, M. R. (1989). Lack of method variance in self-reported affect and perceptions at work: Reality or artifact? *Journal of Applied Psychology, 74*(3), 462-468.

SECTION II

RIGOR AND RELEVANCE

Chapter VI

Rigor in Grounded Theory Research: An Interpretive Perspective on Generating Theory from Qualitative Field Studies

Susan Gasson
Drexel University, USA

ABSTRACT

This chapter presents a set of principles for the use of Grounded Theory techniques in qualitative field studies. Some issues and controversies relating to rigor in Grounded Theory generation are discussed. These include: inductive theory generation and emergence, how theoretical saturation may be judged, the extent to which coding schemes should be formalized, the objectivist-subjectivist debate, and the assessment of quality and rigor in interpretive research. It is argued that Grounded Theory is often criticized for a lack of rigor because we apply positivist evaluations of rigor to research that derives from an interpretive worldview. Alternative assessments of rigor are suggested, that emphasize reflexivity in the inductive-deductive cycle of substantive theory generation.

INTRODUCTION

Grounded Theory research involves the generation of innovative theory derived from data collected in an investigation of "real-life" situations relevant to the research problem. Although Grounded Theory approaches may use quantitative or qualitative methods (Dey, 1999), the emphasis in this chapter is on qualitative, interpretive approaches to generating Grounded Theory, as it is this area that is most criticized for its lack of rigor. I will discuss some reasons for this and suggest some solutions. The chapter starts with an introduction to the Grounded Theory research approach. Some issues and controversies relating to rigor in Grounded Theory generation are then discussed, including inductive theory generation and emergence, how theoretical saturation may be judged, the extent to which coding schemes should be formalized, the objectivist-subjectivist debate, and the assessment of quality and rigor in qualitative Grounded Theory research.

The chapter concludes with a set of principles for the appropriate use of Grounded Theory techniques in qualitative field studies.

A BRIEF INTRODUCTION TO GROUNDED THEORY RESEARCH METHODS

Grounded Theory approaches to research are so called because contributions to knowledge are not generated from existing theory, but are *grounded* in the data collected from one or more empirical studies. In this chapter, I have described Grounded Theory as an approach rather than a method, as there are many alternative methods that may be employed. In Figure 1, a guiding process for Grounded Theory is presented, adapted from Lowe (1995), Pidgeon and Henwood (1996), and Dey (1999). The process model of Grounded Theory given in Figure 1 is presented as a *reflexive* approach because this process is centered around surfacing and making explicit the influences and inductive processes of the researcher.

The Grounded Theory approach (Glaser, 1978, 1992; Glaser & Strauss, 1967; Strauss, 1987; Strauss & Corbin, 1998) is designed "to develop and integrate a set of ideas and hypotheses in an integrated theory that accounts for behavior in any substantive area" (Lowe, 1996, p.1). In other words, a Grounded Theory approach involves the generation of *emergent* theory from empirical data. A variety of data collection methods may be employed, such as interviews, participant observation, experimentation, and indirect data collection (for example, from service log reports or help desk e-mails).

The uniqueness of the Grounded Theory approach lies in two elements (Glaser, 1978, 1992; Strauss & Corbin, 1998):

1.   Theory is based upon patterns found in empirical data, not from inferences, prejudices, or the association of ideas.
2.   There is constant comparison between emergent theory (codes and constructs) and new data. Constant comparison confirms that theoretical constructs are found across and between data samples, driving the collection of additional data until the researcher feels that "theoretical saturation" (the point of diminishing returns from any new analysis) has been reached.

Figure 1. A Reflexive, Grounded Theory Approach.

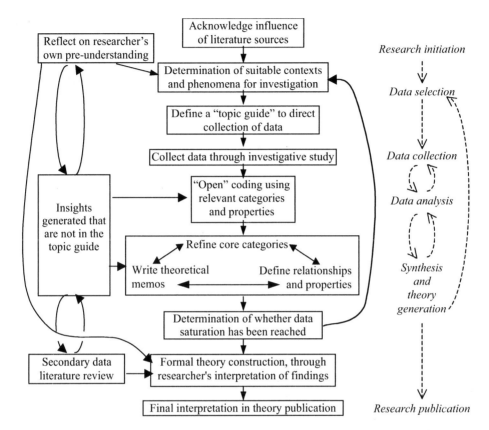

In the context of this chapter, there is not space for a thorough introduction to all of the many techniques for Grounded Theory analysis. The Grounded Theory approach is complex and is ultimately learned through practice rather than prescription. However, there are some general principles that categorize this approach and these are summarized here. For further insights on how to perform a Grounded Theory analysis, some very insightful descriptions of the process are provided by Lowe (1995, 1996, 1998) and Urquhart (1999, 2000). Most descriptions of Grounded Theory analysis employ Strauss's (1987; Strauss & Corbin, 1998) three stages of coding: open, axial, and selective coding. These stages gradually refine the relationships between emerging elements in collected data that might constitute a theory.

Data Collection

Initial data collection in interpretive, qualitative field studies is normally conducted through interviewing or observation. The interview or recorded (audio or video) inter-actions and/or incidents are transcribed: written in text format or captured in a form amenable to identification of sub-elements (for example, video may be analyzed second-by-second). Elements of the transcribed data are then *coded* into categories of what is being observed.

Open Coding

Data is "coded" by classifying elements of the data into themes or categories and looking for patterns between categories (commonality, association, implied causality, etc.). Coding starts with a vague understanding of the sorts of categories that might be relevant ("open" codes). Initial coding will have been informed by some literature reading, although Glaser and Strauss (1967) and Glaser (1978) argue that a researcher should avoid the literature most closely related to the subject of the research because reading this will sensitize the researcher to look for concepts related to existing theory and thus limit innovation in coding their data. Rather, the researcher should generate what Lowe (1995) calls a "topic guide" to direct initial coding of themes and categories based upon elements of their initial research questions. Glaser (1978) provides three questions to be used in generating open codes:
1.   What is this data a study of?
2.   What category does this incident indicate?
3.   What is actually happening in the data? (p. 57)

For example, in studying IS design processes, I was interested in how members of the design group jointly constructed a design problem and defined a systems solution. So my initial coding scheme used five levels of problem decomposition to code transcripts of group meetings: (1) high-level problem or change-goal definition, (2) problem subcomponent, (3) system solution definition, (4) solution subcomponent, and (5) solution implementation mechanism. I then derived a set of codes to describe how these problem-level constructs were used by group members in their discussions. From this coding, more refined codes emerged to describe the design process.

The unit of analysis (element of transcribed data) to which a code is assigned may be a sentence, a line from a transcript, a speech interaction, a physical action, a one-second sequence in a video, or a combination of elements such as these. It is important to clarify exactly what we intend to examine in the analysis and to choose the level of granularity accordingly. For example, if we are trying to derive a theory of collective decision-making, then analyzing *parts* of sentences that indicate an understanding, misunderstanding, agreement, disagreement, etc. may provide a relevant level of granularity, whereas analyzing a transcript by whole sentences may not. A useful way to start is to perform a line-by-line analysis of the transcribed data and to follow Lowe (1996), who advises that the gerund form of verbs (ending in -ing) should be used to label each identified theme, to "sensitize the researcher to the processes and patterns which may be revealed at each stage" (Lowe, 1996, p. 8). Strauss (1987) suggests that the researcher should differentiate between *in vivo codes*, which are derived from the language and terminology used by subjects in the study, and *scientific constructs*, which derive from the researcher's scholarly knowledge and understanding of the (disciplinary, literature-based) field being studied. This is a helpful way of distinguishing constructs that emerge from the data from constructs that are imposed on the data by our preconceptions of what we are looking for.

Axial Coding

Axial coding is the search for relationships between coded elements of the data. Substantive theories emerge through an examination of similarities and differences in these relationships, between different categories (or subcategories), and between categories and their related properties. Strauss (1987) suggests that axial coding should examine elements such as antecedent conditions, interaction among subjects, strategies, tactics, and consequences. Strauss and Corbin (1998) liken this process to fitting the parts of a jigsaw puzzle together. They argue that, by asking the questions who, when, where, why, how, and with what consequences, the researcher can relate structure to process. Glaser (1978) suggests applying the "six *C*s": causes, contexts, contingencies, consequences, covariances, and conditions. Whichever approach is taken (we are not limited to just one), we should carefully note the emergence of insights and explicitly reflect on how these insights are bounding the research problem through selecting some categories and not others. This can be achieved through the generation of theoretical memos.

Theoretical Memos

Theoretical memos "are the theorizing write-up of ideas about codes and their relationships as they strike the analyst while coding" (Glaser, 1978, p. 83). They reflect emerging ideas concerning relationships between data categories, new categories, and properties of these categories, cross-category insights into the process, mention of relevant examples from the literature, and many other reflections. They provide a way to capture those insights that we want to explore further and should be treated as a resource, triggering further constant comparison. Glaser (1978) recommends that a researcher should *always* interrupt coding to memo an idea that has just occurred to them. But constructs and relationships noted in theoretical memos must be related to other data in other samples for verification. At the end of the day, theoretical insights must be supported by further data analysis, or there is no theory—just speculation.

Selective Coding

"Selective coding is the process of integrating and refining categories" (Strauss & Corbin, 1998, p. 143) so that "categories are related to the core category, ultimately becoming the basis for the Grounded Theory" (Babchuk, 1996). Glaser (1992) emphasizes the importance of "core" categories: categories which lie at the core of the theory being developed and "explain most of the variation in a pattern of behavior" (p. 75). The Grounded Theory analysis process often involves moving up and down levels of analysis, to understand one core category at a time (Lowe, 1996). It is important to *explicitly state the research analysis objectives before and **during** coding*. Detailed objectives of the analysis—as distinct from the overall research problem—may well change as emerging insights become significant. A search for different types of theoretical models will lead to different category structures. For example, a *process* model involves stages of action, so the core categories would reflect these stages, with sub-categories and properties reflecting elements such as process stage-triggers, or states by which it is judged that the process is ended. A *factor* model, on the other hand, would focus on cause and effect: core categories that reflect antecedent conditions, influences on, and consequences of the construct being explored.

Research Iteration and Constant Comparison

Unlike more pre-designed research, data collection and analysis are interrelated: the analyst "jointly collects, codes and analyzes his data and decides what data to collect next and where to find them, in order to develop his theory as it emerges" (Glaser & Strauss, 1967, p. 45). This process is referred to as "theoretical sampling" (Glaser & Strauss). Grounded Theory generation is highly iterative, constantly cycling between coding, synthesis, and data collection. The generation of theory is achieved through *constant comparison* of theoretical constructs with data collected from new studies. Constant comparison lies at the heart of the Grounded Theory approach and differentiates a rigorous Grounded Theory analysis from inductive guesswork. The researcher must continually ask whether the analysis of new data provides similar themes and categories to previous data or whether other patterns emerge. Constant comparison requires continual research into the meaning of the developing categories by further data collection and analysis. The researcher may interview new respondents, study the situation in a different group of people, or observe the same group over a different period of time. As the analysis proceeds, new themes and relationships emerge and the researcher will find themselves recoding earlier data and reconceptualizing relationships between data elements. Urquhart (1999) provides an especially useful description of how codes and categories evolve and change to reflect reconceptualizations of core theoretical elements. It may be found that some of the ideas or relationships that constitute a part of the theory may originate from other sources, such as insights from readings, or a eureka flash of inspiration. Strauss and Corbin (1998) also suggest that literature (such as reports of other studies) may be used as a source of data for analysis. Whatever the source of the inspiration, Glaser and Strauss (1967) note that:

> *"The generation of theory from such insights must then be brought into relation with the data, or there is great danger that theory and empirical world will mismatch"* (p. 6).

Grounded Theory closure is guided by the concept of saturation. Theoretical saturation is reached when diminishing returns from each new analysis mean that no new themes, categories, or relationships are emerging and new data confirm findings from previous data. At this point, it should be possible to abstract a formal theory from the findings.

Progress from Substantive to Formal Theory

Glaser and Strauss (1967) differentiate *substantive* theory from *formal* theory by associating substantive theory generation with empirical research, whereas formal theory is associated with theoretical or conceptual work. Substantive theories are seen as emergent—by saturating oneself in the analysis of appropriate data, where the direction and quantity of data collection are driven by emerging patterns in the data, rather than by predetermined research "design," one can generate original theories concerning human behavior (Glaser & Strauss, 1967). The ultimate end of Grounded Theory research, however, is to generate formal theories: theories that may be generalizable at an abstract level. **A formal theory can only emerge from sufficient data analysis in sufficient cases for the researcher to be sure that they are not merely describing the**

case in a single situation. A single Grounded Theory research study would not be expected to generate formal theory. Formal theory emerges over time (Glaser, 1978) and with reflection (Strauss & Corbin, 1998). It derives from the conceptual abstraction of a substantive theory across multiple research studies.

So the process of grounded theory analysis moves:

- from an open coding of data to axial coding through the identification of core categories of the data,
- through the use of theoretical memos to capture insights on how categories are related,
- to the analysis of "networks" of interactions between categories (and their properties),
- to the construction of substantive theory, through a rigorous analysis of how core categories (and network models) fit with new data.

Over a period of time (often years), enough studies may be conducted to justify the proposal of a formal theory.

ISSUES, CONTROVERSIES AND PROBLEMS OF GROUNDED THEORY

Inductive Theory Generation and Emergence

One of the major criticisms of Grounded Theory is that it is not "scientific" (deductive) in its analysis of the data but based on inductive conclusions from a superficial analysis of collected data. But research in psychology tells us that all human reasoning is a balance of deductive and inductive reasoning (Simon, 1957). It is through inductive inference, based on our experience of the world, that we survive. If we put our hand on the stove and it is burned, we learn that hot stoves will burn us. But then it is through deduction from empirical evidence that we can identify and avoid hot stoves (this is the expected shape for a stove and it is turned on). Learning depends upon inductive-deductive cycles of analytical thinking.

So inductive research techniques are not indefensible per se. In fact they form the basis for most of the qualitative coding methods used, for example, in qualitative case study analysis. Inductive analysis is treated as suspect because it introduces subjectivity into research and so the findings can be challenged, from a positivist perspective, as not *measured from*, but *subjectively associated with* the situation observed. Strauss and Corbin (1998) recognize the role of inductive reasoning in Grounded Theory generation and deal with it as follows:

> *We are deducing what is going on based on data but also based on our reading of that data along with our assumptions about the nature of life, the literature that we carry in our heads, and the discussion that we have with colleagues. (This is how science is born.) In fact, there is an interplay between induction and deduction (as in all science). ... **This is why we feel that it is important that the analyst validate his or her interpretations through constantly comparing one piece of data to another.** (pp. 136-137)*

The use of constant comparison between emerging theoretical constructs and new data can be used to switch from inductive to deductive thinking to "validate" our constructs. But, as Glaser (1992) observes, there are two parts to constant comparison. The first is to constantly compare incident to incident and incident to theoretical concept. The second is to ask the "neutral" coding question: "What category or property of a category does this incident suggest?" (Glaser, 1992, p. 39). From the use of the word "neutral," Glaser obviously views this as a deductive process. But Pidgeon (1996) questions the assumption that qualitative researchers can directly access their subjects' internal experiences and so derive an objective coding scheme from the subjects' own terms and interpretations. He observes that some inductive use of *existing* theory is required, particularly at the beginning of analysis, to guide the researcher's understanding of the situation and so to guide them in what data to collect. The "emergence" of theory thus results from the constant interplay between data and the researcher's developing conceptualizations—a "flip-flop" (Pidgeon, 1996) between new ideas and the researcher's experience (deductive $\leftrightarrow$ inductive reasoning). This process is better described as theory *generation* than theory *discovery*. Although the issue of familiarity with the literature in one's field is contentious, Dick (2000) makes an interesting point. In an emergent study, the researcher may not know which literature is relevant, so it is not always feasible to read *relevant* literature until the study is in progress. In acknowledging the emergence of findings, it is important to understand that most non-grounded-theory approaches are not as planned and linear as they would appear when their findings are published. Many researchers are highly critical of any approach that is not "guided" by a planned schema (a research instrument). But an incredibly useful insight on research in general is best summarized by a quote from Walsham (1993):

> The actual research process did not match the linear presentation of this book whereby theory is described first, empirical research happens next, results are then analyzed and conclusions are drawn. Instead, the process involves such aspects as the use of theoretical insights at different stages, the modification of theory based on experience, the generation of intermediate results that lead to the reading of a different theoretical literature and the continuing revision or new enactment of past research results. (p. 245)

Judging Theoretical Saturation

One of the consequences of employing a highly iterative (and sometimes recursive) approach to data analysis and synthesis is the inability to judge when to stop. In the generation of Grounded Theory, data analysis is not an end of itself (as in other research approaches) but drives the need for further investigation, instigating new research questions and directions. It is very easy to fall into a state of hopeless confusion or, paradoxically, to terminate data collection and analysis before any rigorous support for theoretical insights has been obtained (in which case, the approach provides inductive insights rather than Grounded Theory). The point at which *theoretical saturation* (Glaser & Strauss, 1967) is achieved is best described as the point at which diminishing returns are obtained from new data analysis or refinement of coding categories. The point of diminishing returns comes when (and only when) theoretical constructs fit with existing data *and* the comparison of theoretical constructs with new data yields no significant new insights. Grounded Theory is continuing to gain acceptance in the IS field. But criticisms and suspicions of Grounded Theory are often well-deserved. Many analyses appear to have been terminated because of publication deadlines, boredom, or exhaustion. Such studies only serve to undermine efforts to formalize rigor differently for qualitative research.

Formalization of Data Coding and Analysis

At the core of the debate between Glaser (1992) and Strauss (1987; Strauss & Corbin, 1998) is the notion of whether theory emerges from flexible, inductively guided data analysis or whether theory is derived as the result of applying structured, analytical methods. Glaser (1992) argues that the generation of Grounded Theory emerges from categories and patterns suggested by informants and by socially constructed realities. Glaser views Strauss's method of applying a specific coding method (the categorization of causal conditions, context, action/interactional strategies, and consequences) as "forcing" theoretical constructs and challenges the resulting theories as being more descriptive than processual or structural. Strauss emphasizes "canons of good science" (Babchuk, 1996) to data analysis and coding, while Glaser argues that the codes should emerge from the data. To be fair to Strauss's position, Strauss (1987) does argue that his procedures should be considered as rules of thumb to be used heuristically. He advises researchers to modify the scheme as required. But Glaser (1992) makes the point that, in an endeavor to make Grounded Theory "rigorous," the researcher may well filter out elements within the data that might lead to a theory that would change the way we view the world.

Both authors appear to agree that the emergence of theory from data is central to employing a Grounded Theory approach. So the two authors are not diametrically opposed; the issue appears to be one of how to ensure rigor in the process of data analysis and selection. Glaser emphasizes the emergent, inductive nature of Grounded Theory generation and recommends constant comparison with the data and self-reflection (reflexivity on our role and influences in the research process) as a way of ensuring quality. Strauss emphasizes the need to apply rigorous, repeatable methods to data selection and analysis and recommends the structuring of method around formal coding schemes as a way of ensuring consistency and quality. The debate appears to boil down to whether the researcher believes that their work should be *defended* from a positivist or interpretive perspective. This is discussed in the next section.

The Objectivist-Subjectivist Debate

To employ Grounded Theory rigorously, it is important to understand that, like the case study method, this approach may be used successfully to support both positivist and interpretive research. The main area of debate between the positivist and interpretive positions lies in their respective definitions of "reality"—the objectivist-subjectivist debate (Burrell & Morgan, 1979; Walsham, 1993). The positivist position argues that reality is "out there," waiting to be discovered, and that this reality is reflected in universal laws that may be discovered by the application of objective, replicable, and "scientific" research methods. The interpretive position argues that the world is subjective and reality is socially constructed (Lincoln & Guba, 2000). The phenomena that we observe are only meaningful in terms of individual experience and interpretation: one person's shooting star may be another person's alien spacecraft. "Truth" is constructed within a community of research and practice interests, across which "knowledge" is defined and valued (Latour, 1987). This "consensus theory" thus reflects a shared reality (Lincoln & Guba, 2000). The distinction between the two worldviews of positivism and interpretive research is particularly critical when deriving *Grounded* Theory, as it is based in empirical data collection and analysis. In Glaser and Strauss (1967), the authors talk of the "discovery" of Grounded Theory. The authors clearly view these laws as "out there," waiting to be discovered (a positivist perspective). But it is apparent from both authors' later work that they have questioned and modified this view to some extent. Strauss and Corbin (1998, pp. 157-158) give an example where one of the authors found that "something seemed awry with the logic" of her theory concerning the management of high-risk pregnancies by mothers-to-be. The researcher realized that she was defining risk from her perspective as a health professional and understood that she needed to define risk intersubjectively, from the point of view of her subjects, in order to understand their behavior. Her research subjects perceived their level of risk differently than her own assessment and often assessed the same risk differently at different times during their pregnancy. This understanding reflects an *interpretive* research position: that a phenomenon (or research "variable," to use positivist language) cannot be defined objectively, according to a set of absolute criteria, but must be defined from a *specified* point of view. Phenomena need to be understood both externally *and* internally to a situation for a theory to be internally consistent. This distinction is critical for the Grounded Theory researcher performing interpretive, qualitative field studies and forms the basis of the reflective, inductive-deductive research cycle that is required for learning (Schön, 1983).

The existence of *multiple* perspectives is an important issue for interpretive research (Klein & Myers, 1999). We must be sensitive to different accounts of "reality" given by different participants in the research rather than trying to discover universal laws of behavior by fitting all the accounts to a single perspective. Often, the interesting element of social theories derives from accounting for differences between accounts of a process rather than from similarities. Strauss and Corbin (1998) stress the importance of internal consistency. A theory should "hang together" and make sense not to an "objective" external observer but to an observer who shares, intersubjectively, in the meanings of phenomena as perceived by the research subjects. To achieve this, we must report our findings in context, consistently, and with sufficient detail to allow our readers to share the subjects' experiences of the phenomena that we report.

Grounded Theory involves the generation of theory from an analysis of empirical data. We need to be absolutely clear, as researchers, about our beliefs about the nature of those theories, to guide appropriate data collection and analysis. If we use the positivist criteria of external validity to guide a qualitative study, we must apply "objective" definitions of the phenomena under study; this will exclude subjects' own perceptions of the phenomena. But if we abandon positivist criteria, we must substitute alternative notions of rigor that are equally demanding and that reflect the same notions of quality as those used in positivist research.

The distinction between positivist and interpretive worldviews represents two extremes of a spectrum that may be considered *incommensurable*: people experiencing one of these "life-worlds" can never understand the perspectives of the other. Different researchers strive in different ways to overcome the incommensurability of the two philosophical positions. But it must be said that there are some very muddled or unexamined views concerning the nature of Grounded Theory research to be found in the IS literature. By abandoning a positivist research method, many researchers appear to believe that they can abandon the rigorous application of method completely. Many "Grounded Theory" studies appear to report loosely associated, inductive insights that cannot be justified by any notion of rigor or evidence. The interpretive Grounded Theory researcher must consider the defensibility of their work more deeply than the positivist researcher, as interpretivism does not yet have a body of knowledge and tradition embedded into formalized procedures for how to perform rigorous, interpretive research.

Quality and Rigor in Qualitative Grounded Theory Research

Lincoln and Guba (2000) argue that qualitative research cannot be judged on the positivist notion of validity but should rather be judged on an alternative criterion of trustworthiness. This assertion is justified on the basis that the positivist worldview is incommensurable with the interpretive worldview. Thus different criteria of rigor and quality need to be developed to reflect the very different assumptions that interpretive researchers hold about the nature of reality and appropriate methods of inquiry. Interpretive alternatives to the four traditional quality measures used in positivist research are developed and summarized in Table 1, developed from those suggested by Miles and Huberman (1994) and Lincoln and Guba (2000). The criteria for rigor discussed here do not constitute an exhaustive set but are selected on the basis of agreement across some reputable, knowledgeable, and reflective references on qualitative research.

The substitution of alternative criteria for rigor in interpretive studies is not intended to imply that rigor is to be abandoned in favor of "interpretation." On the contrary, the interpretive criteria of confirmability, auditability, authenticity, and trans-ferability become paramount to making any claim to rigor. At every stage of the process, the researcher should subject their findings to both personal and external views on the basis of these criteria. Each of these issues is taken, in turn, to discuss criticisms of the Grounded Theory approach when it is used in qualitative field studies and to understand how quality and rigor may be maintained in interpretive, qualitative Grounded Theory generation.

Objectivity vs. Confirmability

We have discovered that the generation of Grounded Theory is not and cannot be totally objective. An important question to ask, therefore, is whether this makes theory generated in this way more or less **confirmable** (and therefore useful) than that generated by deductive, hypothesis-based research methods. One response is that, while the weakness of qualitative, inductive approaches to research lies in the data-analysis stage of the research life cycle, quantitative, hypothesis-based approaches are weakest in the research initiation and data selection stages. Even if the quantitative researcher is rigorously objective in their application of a consistent coding scheme and in the statistical analysis of data, inductive reasoning is involved in the selection of the research instrument and the selection or design of an appropriate coding or measurement scheme to operationalize the research instrument.

Table 1. Quality and Rigor Related to the Stages of a Theory-Building Research Life Cycle.

Issue of Concern	Positivist Worldview	Interpretive Worldview
Representativeness of findings	Objectivity: findings are free from researcher bias.	Confirmability: conclusions depend on subjects and conditions of the study rather than the researcher.
Reproducibility of findings	Reliability: the study findings can be replicated independently of context, time or researcher.	Dependability/Auditability: the study process is consistent and reasonably stable over time and between researchers.
Rigor of method	Internal validity: a statistically-significant relationship is established, to demonstrate that certain conditions are associated with other conditions, often by "triangulation" of findings.	Internal consistency: the research findings are credible and consistent to the people we study and to our readers. For authenticity, our findings should be related to significant elements in the research context/situation.
Generalizability of findings	External validity: the researcher establishes a domain in which findings are generalizable.	Transferability: how far can the findings/conclusions be transferred to other contexts and how do they help to derive useful theories?

As Silverman (1993) observes:

No hypotheses are ever "theory free." We come to look at things in certain ways because we have adopted, either tacitly or explicitly, certain ways of seeing. This means that, in observational research, data-collection, hypothesis-construction and theory-building are not three separate things but are interwoven with each other. (p. 46)

The claims to truth and knowledge provided by prior literature are socially constructed and so remain unquestioned (Latour, 1987). Overall, qualitative inductive approaches are no more subjective than quantitative deductive approaches. Subjectivity is merely introduced at a later, more visible stage of the research life cycle than with hypothesis-testing research approaches. The formalized ways by which we manage subjectivity are only problematic as they are based on positivist assessments of rigor. We need to substitute reflexive self-awareness for objectivity.

Reliability vs. Dependability/Auditability

Let me pose a question:

If two researchers are presented with the same data, will they derive the same results if they use the same methods, applied rigorously?

To answer this question, it is important to question our assumptions about reality. If we understand reality as being "out there"—that what we see and measure when we collect "data" is what exists independently of our interpretation of the situation (or of the influence that our presence imposes)—then we would naturally answer "of course they would." If we understand reality as being socially constructed—that what we see is our interpretation of the world and that what others report to us is their interpretation—then we would answer "of course they would not." In that "of course" lies the internal conflict that we all tussle with as researchers. *Because the problem is that all of us understand the world in both ways at once.*

So far, I have treated positivist and interpretive worldviews as though they are opposing and incompatible. Intellectually, they *are* incommensurable. The problem is that humans are subjective, inconsistent beings, who are quite capable of taking different positions at different times on different issues without realizing the inherent contradictions. So, to ensure **dependable and authentic findings**, we need to establish *clear and repeatable procedures* for research and to *reflect on the position that we take* as we perform them. In that way, we can at least minimize the impact of subjectivity on the process. This does not mean that we have to have highly structured procedures based on inflexible, preexisting theoretical frameworks. But we do need to understand (and to be able to define) what our data selection, analysis, and synthesis procedures actually *are*. We need to constantly reflect on and record the means by which we reach our theoretical constructs and the detailed ends that these means achieve.

Internal Validity vs. Internal Consistency

It is probably in a rejection of the notion of internal "validity" that interpretive research garners its most virulent critics. Validity in deductive hypothesis-based research is ensured by statistically testing correlations between data variables and by ensuring a statistically significant sample population. Such notions of mathematical proof have no equivalent in qualitative interpretive research because (a) collected data represent social constructs rather than measurable physical phenomena, and (b) data analysis is recognized as subjective and inductive-deductive rather than as deductively objective. However, the idea of *internal consistency* may be used instead (Strauss & Corbin, 1998) to ask, *Do all the parts of the theory fit with each other and do they appear to explain the data?* As a way of answering this question, the criteria of credibility and authenticity may be substituted for internal validity (Miles & Huberman, 1994).

While rigor is viewed as a quality to be desired in positivist research, the interpretive position on positivist views of rigor can be summarized by the Webster dictionary definition of the term: "the quality of being unyielding or inflexible." It is important to avoid just falling into a hierarchical coding scheme by default, as this type of scheme is too often used to fit the data to an individual's preconceived notions of how it should relate (see Alexander, 1966, for a fascinating discussion of this tendency in architectural planning). Additionally, Urquhart (2000) reinforces (with feeling) the Glaser and Strauss (1967) observation that lower level categories tend to emerge relatively quickly, with higher level categories emerging much later through the integration of concepts. A hierarchical coding scheme discourages the reordering of concepts and tends to act as a disincentive to think radically about reconceptualization of the core categories previously identified.

To achieve **credible** research, we need to constantly question where the theoretical constructs that we have adopted have come from. Whichever approach we take to the coding and analysis of data, we need to implement it reflectively and to reexamine it critically. We need to employ representational techniques that permit an explicit examination of the relationships between data elements on a periodic basis and to constantly question the assumptions that led us to search for those relationships.

External Validity vs. Transferability

Eisenhardt (1989) comments that the objective of hypothesis-testing (positivist) research is to randomly test samples from a large population, while the aim of Grounded Theory research is to deliberately select specific samples (cases) that will confirm or extend an emerging theory. So it should be understood that Grounded Theory claims to generalizability do not even reside in the same universe, never mind reflect the same worldview, as those of deductive hypothesis-based research. Taking an interpretive Grounded Theory approach leaves us with a significant question of how widely our theory can be applied, given that the process is interpretive and, as we saw above, subjective. How can we can make a claim to be generating generalizable theory from an external reality that we do not believe exists independently of ourselves? One of the best resolutions of this issue lies in understanding the detailed objectives of our analysis, for which Lowe (1998) provides a wonderfully comforting description:

> *The social organization of the world is integrated. This means that everything is already organised in very specific ways. The grounded theorist's job is to discover these processes of socialisation. There is no need for preconceived theorising because all the theoretical explanations are already present in the data. (p. 106)*

As interpretive researchers, we reject the "universal laws" (positivist) notion of reality in favor of discerning socially constructed norms and relationships that are located in a particular culture or context. Claims for **transferability and fit** between contexts must therefore arise through identifying similarities in factors that are part of the theoretical model and are consistent between different contexts for which the theory fits. Ultimately, we need to recognize that interpretive researchers cannot make the same claims to generalizability as positivist researchers and that to do so opens our research to attack because then we defend our research from a different worldview than that which governed the way in which it was performed. In using the language of positivism (e.g., claims to "triangulation" of findings or making claims for validity or universal generalizability), we lay ourselves open to criticisms of not following positivist methods to ensure these criteria are met. Positivism and interpretivism have no common language of quality or rigor. The findings from multiple data samples may be compared across contexts (for example, using multiple case studies for which contextual factors are similar). However, once any part of the method is admitted to be inductive, it becomes difficult to make claims for generalizable findings without investigating *very* large numbers of samples (case studies) across which findings can be compared statistically. But this may take years with such labor-intensive studies. Statistical correlations between intersubjectively-defined constructs are also meaningless, from both a positivist and an interpretive perspective. This issue is often fudged in publication; the generally acceptable minimum number of case studies for comparison appears to be four, which is indefensible from either worldview on any grounds except pragmatism (or a *huge* number of quantitative samples for each study, which is rarely the case). As a replacement for external validity, in qualitative research we could substitute the notion of external consistency. We need to adopt the discourse of *transferable* findings rather than that of generalizable results.

SOLUTIONS AND RECOMMENDATIONS
Objectivity vs. Confirmability

Core Issue: Findings should represent, as far as is (humanly) possible, the situation being researched rather than the beliefs, pet theories, or biases of the researcher.

Rather than focusing on repeatable surveys or experiments, interpretive Grounded Theory research approaches focus on reflexive self-awareness to acknowledge (and guard against) implicit influences, biases, and prejudices:

> *Positivist scientists favour objectivity—the putting aside of the researcher's own views and values in order to establish objective truths. ... Interpretive social scientists ... acknowledge that a researcher's findings will be influenced by their own values and outlook, and instead promote the idea that the researcher should explore and acknowledge them. The self-knowledge will still be imperfect because the researcher is too close to the subject, but at least contemplation is encouraged with the notion of reflexivity. (Mallalieu, Harvey, & Hardy, 1999, p. 42)*

The mechanistic application of constant comparison will not remove inductive bias (subjectivity) from our findings. The selection of data as significant to our theory (or the exclusion/filtering out of data) is an inductive process, driven by a researcher's understanding of what is relevant to the theoretical constructs that we expect to find. This understanding is often influenced by experiences outside of the research study (see Figure 1). The only way to deal with subjectivity is through constant, *explicit* processes of reflexivity. Reflexivity is a more active form of self-reflection, a conversation with oneself. The reflexive focus can be on the researcher, the participant, or both (Smith, 1996). There are two elements to reflexivity that are relevant here:
1.   Self-awareness as part of a social context affecting the phenomena under observation.
2.   Self-awareness as someone who applies biases, prejudices, cognitive filtering, and bounded rationality to the collection, analysis, and interpretation of data.

We can minimize the effect that these "distortions" have on our interpretation of data by making our assumptions and frameworks explicit. As new models and conceptualizations emerge, they should be written down and *justified*, so that we can examine their implications. For example, we may perceive a need for exploration of a new area of literature, a need to collect data from a different situation for comparison with our emerging constructs, or a need to change an inappropriate coding scheme. We should ask questions such as:

- Where did this concept come from—the literature, my experience, or the analyzed data?
- Does this concept or category apply to other data?
- What sort of theory do these relationships and categories represent?

Subjectivity sometimes yields wonderful insights. But we must acknowledge where our insights come from rather than pretending that they all came from "the data." We must be able to understand *how* we arrived at our findings at all stages of the research process and what sensitized us to examine certain patterns so that we can defend ourselves from the accusation that we just found what we set out to look for. This understanding should be recorded at the time that the research is performed. Lowe (1995) suggests the preparation of a "topic guide" for data selection and initial analysis (open coding). This topic guide *explicitly* recognizes our influences, detailed objectives, and pre-understandings (see Figure 1). Other ways of ensuring reflexivity during Grounded Theory analysis are (a) writing memos to yourself about the rationale underlying your constructs, (b) explaining what you are doing and why to someone outside of your field, or (c) presenting your intermediate research findings to a group of very critical colleagues.

Finally, we must *demonstrate* self-awareness to the reader. Any approach involving subjective assessment is indefensible in positivist terms and so we need to develop our own vocabulary and understanding of how we communicate rigor. We must justify our research method in terms of what we were trying to discover, and we must explain the analysis in such a way that the reader may confirm to themselves *how* the theory emerged from a sequence of analysis and insights and understand that this theory is consistent with the data because the data is presented to them. By following this discipline, we avoid any accusation that we have fabricated a theory which is not grounded in the data.

Reliability vs. Dependability/Auditability

Core Issue: The way in which a study is conducted should be consistent across time, researchers, and analysis techniques.

To ensure dependable and authentic findings, we need to establish *clear and repeatable procedures* for the way that we perform our research. The decision whether to use a formal (predefined) coding scheme or to let the coding be guided by categories that emerge from the data should be made on the basis of whether we perceive a need to defend our research on the grounds of reliability or on those of dependability/ auditability. If we take the interpretive view that rigorous procedures cannot ensure reliability (because we recognize that we apply and interpret social constructions of reality rather than an objective reality that can be reproduced in further studies), then a useful way of ensuring the dependability of our findings is by *making explicit the process through which they were derived.* To achieve dependability and auditability, we need to (a) define the procedures that we employ to collect and to analyze data, (b) understand the ends that these achieve in detail, and (c) ensure that these procedures are recorded so that others can understand them. We must ensure that we leave behind an "audit trail" of detailed analysis. When you reflect that you probably cannot remember what you had for dinner a week ago, what hope do you have of remembering how and why you merged two categories during data analysis? As qualitative researchers, we cannot defend our findings on the basis of objective data collection and analysis. We must be able to defend our findings by making explicit what we did and how we arrived at our conclusions. Whether we use a formal initial coding scheme or let this emerge, we must constantly reflect on and *record* where our ideas and influences came from. We should make explicit what we did at all stages of our analysis and provide enough information to permit others to see how our findings followed from our analysis of the data. Keeping a research journal is essential. We should save records of *all* analyses (including early and intermediate analyses). Describing how our findings emerged (if only to ourselves) is a critical part of rigorous research. Using network diagrams is an excellent way of articulating emergent theoretical concepts and so making them accessible for fitting (or discovering an absence of fit) with new data. An example of part of a network diagram is given in Figure 2. Network diagrams permit *explicit* comparison of emerging constructs with new data analysis and expose constructs that do not fit with new data very quickly.

Network diagrams are models that make explicit the relationship between various categories, subcategories, and category properties. Multiple network diagrams can be used to understand different parts of a theory. Relationships may indicate causality, association, process sequences, or any pattern that the researcher finds useful. One of the dangers of inductive research is that emerging models remain poorly articulated and therefore implicit and untested against new data. Network diagrams allow the development of fluid, hierarchical, and nonhierarchical models that explain the data and make these models explicit to our readers and to ourselves.

Internal Validity vs. Internal Consistency

Core Issue: How we ensure rigor in the research process and how we communicate to others that we have done so.

To achieve internal consistency, we need to explain how and from what data we derived our theoretical constructs and whose perspective these constructs reflect. Just as the data flows into and out of different "levels" of a data flow diagram must agree for the data flow model to be internally consistent, so must different views of our data agree. We must describe the source data in sufficient detail to demonstrate a fit between the theory and the data. We must also describe the process by which we performed a constant comparison between theoretical constructs and new data. Constant comparison is critical to research credibility (as well as confirmability) because it is only by constant comparison of theoretical constructs with the data across multiple sites and situations that we can detect systematic biases and distortions in our analysis. For example, some participants may describe their work processes in terms of formal work procedures rather than what they actually do. This can be very difficult to detect without using constant

Figure 2. An Example of a Partial Category Network Diagram.

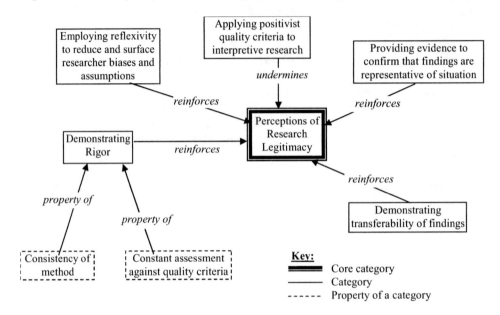

* *The key is my own way of representing different categories—there is no standard notation.*

comparison because the results appear to be consistent between informants. It is only when the findings are compared with findings from another company that we start to realize that a minority perspective of work processes could fit better with the new data than the majority perspective. This realization could drive new data collection: revisiting the previous company and asking participants about informal work processes or performing an observation study.

We must be explicit in explaining *how* data collection was driven by emerging constructs. In making claims for the authenticity of theories produced by grounded research, we should consider how to explain our assessment of data "saturation" (sufficient data collection and analysis for the theory to be considered substantively usable). Constant comparison can be performed using data from new informants (or subjects), new sites, new periods of time (as in a longitudinal study), or new situations that are comparable to previous situations in terms of the *core analytical categories* that we have identified as significant. The selection and collection of new data should be justifiable on analytical terms—i.e., driven by the emerging categories, properties, and relationships that result from the analysis. For example, collecting data samples over time (as for a longitudinal study) is justifiable if the core categories provide an explanation for *why* behavior changes with time. Figure 3 shows an example from my own research.

First, a behavioral factor model was developed from the data (this is a very simplified version of the model for illustration). Then the model was compared to meeting transcripts and informant interviews to identify elements of the model that were constant or

Figure 3. How a Process Theory may Develop through Constant Comparison over Time.

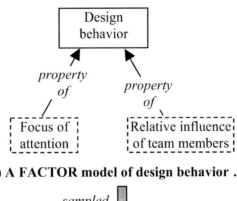

(a) A FACTOR model of design behavior ...

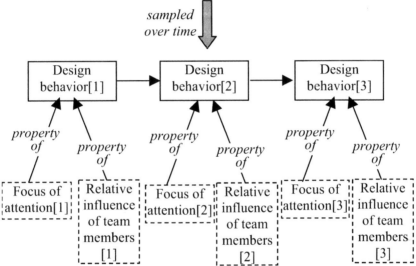

(b) ... develops into a PROCESS model of design behavior,
by constant comparison of multiple samples over time

changed over time. Through a process of constant comparison with additional data (I tape-recorded and observed design meetings over a period of 18 months, and I performed regular interviews with the core team members), I was able to interpret changes over time and to modify my original factor model. The factor model was then compared with earlier meeting data, to confirm that it fitted with these. But if open coding had started with categories that defined the "stages" of behavior shown in diagram (4b), using data samples from different time periods would not have provided an authentic way of analyzing the data. I would probably just have been sensitized to the data that fitted with these stage categories because these stages would have been what I was looking for in the data. I may well have missed evidence that defined these stages differently.

To guide data selection for constant comparison, we need to understand the detailed *ends* of our research. Some elements of reflexivity again come into play:

- Reflecting on the influence of our own background in forming perceptions of what may be important in the research problem.
- Acknowledging the influence of various literatures pertaining to the research problem.
- Clarifying and recording the *detailed* objectives of the research study (not just the overall aim) and how theoretical concepts achieving these objectives emerged from the data (recognizing that detailed research objectives are also emergent).
- Authenticating the research by explaining the process by which diminishing returns (theoretical saturation) were perceived and how this affected our data collection and analysis strategy.

External Validity vs. Transferability

Core Issue: How far a researcher may make claims for a general application of their theory.

Claims for **transferability and fit** depend on identifying similarities or differences in the context in which the theory is to be applied. This involves employing the constant comparison method to determine whether a substantive theory fits new data and how the context in which the new data was collected is similar to (or different from) the contexts in which previous data were collected. In this way, we can extend the theory to include contextual factors. For example, if we develop a substantive theory of how developers investigate new IS requirements and then discover that the theory fits with new data from one company but not another, we could ask what is different about the two companies. Are they both of comparable size? Are developers in both companies similarly trained and educated? Do they use similar methods? By using constant comparison in this way, we not only extend the substantive theory to include new factors such as size of firm or developer education, but we also provide a basis to generalize between firms that are comparable in these factors. We must also, however, recognize the limits of generalizability that our sample size imposes and be quite honest about the extent to which our theories may be generalizable or just constitute an interesting direction for future research.

Ultimately, claims for generalizability cannot be made using the same constructs as those used for positivist research, as dissimilar techniques to ensure application between contexts and different criteria for assessment are applied. Rather, claims for *transferability* may be made on the basis that constant comparison between data sets has yielded similar findings or that differences have enabled the researcher to extend their theory.

FUTURE TRENDS: ADVANCES IN GROUNDED THEORY CONSTRUCTION

A significant trend in IS research is the employment of multiple methodologies to generate deep or multilayer theoretical models. Many specific research methods can be used in information systems research but an interpretive approach requires methods which deal carefully with context and process (Walsham, 1993). To obtain an holistic view of any research question, multiple approaches must be employed which reflect (and thus question) differences between assumptions concerning the nature of the research problem and the generalizability of the data obtained for analysis. In the words of Cavaye (1995):

> *It is widely accepted that the selection of a research strategy entails a trade-off: the strengths of the one approach overcome the weaknesses in another approach and vice versa. This in itself is a powerful argument for pluralism and for the use of multiple research approaches during any investigation. (p. 229)*

It is possible to use multiple methods for data collection and analysis in Grounded Theory generation, and this may lead to much deeper insights than the mechanistic application of inductive coding. Eisenhardt (1989) comments on the richness of insights that the use of multiple methods can bring to data analysis in Grounded Theory generation. Gasson (1998) employed multiple methods such as hermeneutic analysis, discourse analysis, soft systems modeling, process modeling, and inductive categorization.

An increasingly common trend is the use of a software package for qualitative data analysis. This may be particularly helpful for Grounded Theory research because the constant comparison of data requires the researcher to constantly revise and evaluate emerging theoretical constructs on many different data sets. Category codes, property codes, theoretical memos, and network diagrams can be associated with transcripts and multimedia files using a software package for qualitative data analysis. Be sure to select a package that does not force you to use hierarchical coding structures (many older packages do), as you will certainly wish to change your initial coding structures—emergent (and therefore changing) theoretical constructs are fundamental to the Grounded Theory approach. Some of the newer packages even automate code generation, using natural language recognition and association to suggest category codes from the transcript. Many researchers argue that software packages constrain the free flows of thought and insight that are required for deep, analytical coding of qualitative data. I would argue that, at the end of the day, your theory should be just that—*your* theory. If you have used a computer package to generate it, you have played a very small role in its generation. Computers are excellent to automate the repetitive and labor-intensive tasks of data analysis and theory recording. But they are not capable of the inductive-deductive cycle that is integral to Grounded Theory generation.

CONCLUSION

Each of the issues discussed above resulted in a specific recommendation for the way in which Grounded Theory is performed, but notions of quality and rigor in interpretive Grounded Theory research are probably best explained using the metaphor of total quality management. Each of the quality mechanisms suggested will not guarantee quality or rigor. They must be considered as part of a holistic research approach and must be employed reflectively rather than mechanistically. In this spirit, I present the following guidelines for conducting qualitative Grounded Theory research:

1.   Make the process of research data collection and analysis explicit, both to yourself and to others, through your writing. Provide enough information to permit others to see how your findings followed from your analysis of the data.
2.   Provide an "audit trail" through the maintenance of research journals and by saving all analysis documents (including early and intermediate analyses).
3.   Explicitly acknowledge and integrate influences provided by literature sources, your own prior understanding, and theoretical insights generated through serendipity.
4.   Write formal memos, question theoretical constructs, employ category network diagrams, and employ explicit (written) theory justification as ways of making the implicit explicit.
5.   Continually define and redefine detailed objectives for the theory that you seek. As a staring point, this can be phrased in terms of "I am trying to generate a theory that explains how/what/why a, b, and c because I believe that d, e, and f are important in this situation."
6.   Understand the requirements for constant comparison and theoretical saturation to ensure sufficient and rigorous iteration between data collection, data analysis, and data selection and to avoid superficial inductive conclusions.
7.   Regularly justify emerging constructions to friends *and* to critical colleagues.
8.   Constantly use a research journal and explicit self-questioning to encourage and make explicit the role of self-reflexivity.
9.   Understand the limits of validity and generalizability that you can claim when using a qualitative Grounded Theory approach to research.
10.   Recognize that no research process is ever as planned as the literature would lead one to believe. Freed from the need to defend your research according to its ability to proceed as planned, you can apply the tenets of Grounded Theory freely and reflectively.

Klein, Hirschheim, and Nissen (1991) suggest that knowledge is achieved in the struggle between positivism and antipositivism, through the competing claims of those who advocate their chosen approach. A synthesis of the two approaches arises from this struggle, which creates a new dominant approach, to which emerges a new opposition, … and so on. This chapter has attempted to represent the current state of this struggle and to present qualitative Grounded Theory as a way of differentiating and making explicit the different aims of antipositivist research. But a Grounded Theory approach is not recommended unless you are *really* enthusiastic about your topic. It demands a great deal more energy, time, and commitment than any other method I know. One must be constantly critical and realistic about the theoretical application of one's research; sometimes it is better to settle for Walsham's (1995, p.79) "contribution of rich insight" than to make ill-founded claims that are pitifully easy for a knowledgeable reader to deconstruct.

An interpretive Grounded Theory approach is only relevant to research questions that are not well-explained by existing theoretical constructs. Grounded Theory is a way of deriving theory from data; it does not provide the deductive validation required to "prove" or to rigorously extend existing theory in positivist terms. It is best suited to the investigation of what theory might apply in a specific type of situation.

I have found it useful to observe the limitation that "any claim to truth is always at risk and subject to revision as one learns from the arguments of one's opponents" (Klein et al., 1991, p. 7). Through my research and reflection for this chapter, I have gained a deep insight into the fundamental differences between interpretive and positivist approaches to research. I have understood that it is not possible to justify either approach using the discourse of the other. Finally, I have appreciated that self-reflexivity is an essential part of understanding whether one has accomplished what one set out to do because one's own prejudices and biases creep in unawares! I have tried to remove those biases where I could and to declare them where I felt that they were an essential part of the explanation. This reflects the hermeneutic circle of inquiry, analysis, reporting, and reflection that is central to rigorous research.

REFERENCES

Alexander, C. (1966). A city is not a tree. *Design, 206*, 46-55.

Babchuk, W. (1996, October 17-19). *Glaser or Strauss?: Grounded Theory and adult education*. Paper presented at the Midwest Research-to-Practice Conference in Adult, Continuing, and Community Education, October 15-17, 1997. Retrieved from: http://www.anrecs.msu.edu/research/gradpr96.htm.

Burrell, G., & Morgan, G. (1979). *Sociological Paradigms and Organisational Analysis*. London: Heinemann.

Cavaye, A. L. M. (1995). User participation in system development revisited. *Information & Management, 28*, 311-323.

Dey, I. (1999). *Grounding Grounded Theory*. San Diego, CA: Academic Press.

Dick, B. (2000). *Grounded Theory: A Thumbnail Sketch*. Last revised December 29, 2002 and retrieved from: http://www.scu.edu.au/schools/gcm/ar/arp/grounded.html.

Eisenhardt, K. M. (1989). Building theories from case study research. *Academy of Management Review, 14*(4), 532-550.

Gasson, S. (1998). Framing design: A social process view of information system development. In *Proceedings of the Nineteenth International Conference on Information Systems* (pp. 224-236), Atlanta, GA: Association for Information Systems (AIS).

Glaser, B. G. (1978). *Advances in the Methodology of Grounded Theory*. Mill Valley, CA: Sociology Press.

Glaser, B. G. (1992). *Basics of Grounded Theory Analysis, Emergence vs. Forcing*. Mill Valley, CA: Sociology Press.

Glaser, B. G., & Strauss, A. L. (1967). *The Discovery of Grounded Theory*. New York: Aldine.

Klein, H. K., & Myers, M. (1999). A set of principles for conducting and evaluating interpretive field studies in information systems. *MIS Quarterly, 23*(1), 67-94.

Klein, H. K., Hirschheim, R., & Nissen, H.-E. (1991). A pluralist perspective of the information systems research arena. In H.-E. Nissen, H. K. Klein, & R. Hirshheim (Eds.), *Information Systems Research: Contemporary Approaches and Emergent Traditions* (pp. 1-26). Amsterdam: North-Holland.

Latour, B. (1987). *Science in Action*. Cambridge, MA: Harvard University Press.

Lincoln, Y. S., & Guba, E. G. (2000). Paradigmatic controversies, contradictions, and emerging confluences. In N. K. Denzin, & Y. S. Lincoln (Eds.), *The Handbook of Qualitative Research*, pp. 163-188 Beverly Hills, CA: SAGE.

Lowe, A. (1995). The basic social processes of entrepreneurial innovation. *International Journal of Entrepreneurial Behaviour and Research*, *1*(2), 54-76.

Lowe, A. (1996). *An explanation of Grounded Theory* (Working Paper). Glasgow, Scotland, UK: University of Strathclyde, Department of Marketing.

Lowe, A. (1998). Managing the post-merger aftermath by default remodelling. *Management Decision*, *36*(2), 102-110.

Mallalieu, G., Harvey, C., & Hardy, C. (1999). The wicked relationship between organisations and information technology. *Journal of End User Computing*, *11*(4), 40-50.

Miles, M. B., & Huberman, A. M. (1994). *Qualitative Data Analysis: An Expanded Sourcebook* (2nd ed.). Thousand Oaks, CA: SAGE.

Pidgeon, N. (1996). Grounded Theory: Theoretical background. In J. T. E. Richardson (Ed.), *Handbook of Qualitative Research Methods for Psychology and the Social Sciences*. Leicester, UK: British Psychological Society.

Pidgeon, N., & Henwood, K. (1996). Grounded Theory: Practical implementation. In J. T. E. Richardson (Ed.), *Handbook of Qualitative Research Methods for Psychology and the Social Sciences*, pp. 86-101. Leicester, UK: British Psychological Society.

Schön, D. A. (1983). *The Reflective Practitioner: How Professionals Think in Action*. New York: Basic Books.

Silverman, D. (1993). *Interpreting Qualitative Data*. London: SAGE.

Simon, H. A. (1957). *Models of Man: Social and Rational*. New York: John Wiley & Sons.

Smith, J. A. (1996). Evolving issues for qualitative psychology. In T. E. Richardson (Ed.), *Handbook of Qualitative Research Methods for Psychology and the Social Sciences*, pp. 189-202. Leicester, UK: British Psychological Society.

Strauss, A. L. (1987). *Qualitative Research for Social Scientists*. Cambridge, UK: Cambridge University Press.

Strauss, A. L., & Corbin, J. (1998). *Basics of Qualitative Research: Grounded Theory Procedures and Techniques* (2nd ed.). Newbury Park, CA: SAGE.

Urquhart, C. (1999). Themes in early requirements gathering: The case of the analyst, the client and the student assistance scheme. *Information Technology and People*, *12*(1), 44-70.

Urquhart, C. (2000). Strategies for conversation and systems analysis in requirements gathering: A qualitative view of analyst-client communication. *The Qualitative Report, 4*(1/2), January. Retrieved from: http://www.nova.edu/ssss/QR/QR4-1/urquhart.html.

Walsham, G. (1993). *Interpreting Information Systems in Organizations*. Chichester, UK: John Wiley & Sons.

Walsham, G. (1995). Interpretive case studies in IS research: Nature and method. *European Journal of Information Systems*, *4*(2), 74-81.

Chapter VII

Investigating the Dynamics of IT-Enabled Change: The Appeal of Clinical Inquiry

Joe McDonagh
University of Dublin, Ireland

ABSTRACT

Since the 1950s the process of introducing information technology (IT) into work organizations has posed formidable challenges all too frequently resulting in reports of significant underperformance and failure. On closer inquiry it emerges that such poor outcomes are due, in no small way, to a distinct inability to effect an integrated approach to change, an approach that concurrently attends to economic, technical, human, and organizational facets of change. Considering that extant research fails to adequately address this enduring dilemma, this chapter acknowledges weaknesses in dominant positivist approaches to inquiry and establishes the case for a more collaborative approach to inquiry, an approach that is firmly embedded in the post positivist tradition. In particular, the case for one such collaborative approach, clinical inquiry, as a legitimate and profoundly important research approach to investigating the dynamics of IT-enabled change is presented.

INTRODUCTION

Since the 1950s the process of introducing IT into work organisations has been marred by reports of significant underperformance and failure. While it emerges that such underperformance and failure is due, in no small way, to an inability to effect integrated strategic change, it is unfortunate that much IT-related inquiry has failed to adequately address this dilemma. Acknowledging the weaknesses of dominant positivist research approaches, this chapter outlines the case for clinical inquiry as a legitimate and profoundly important research approach relevant to investigating the dynamics of IT-enabled business change.

THE PLIGHT WITH INFORMATION TECHNOLOGY

Empirical studies over the last 25 years provide substantial evidence to support the assertion that underperformance and failure all too frequently mar the introduction of IT into work organisations (Standish Group, 1998). Unfortunately, the number of IT-related change initiatives that actually deliver espoused business benefits is in the order of 10% while the number of initiatives that fail or are abandoned completely is in the order of 50% (McDonagh, 1999). The impermeable and enduring nature of this dilemma is of concern to both investigators and practitioners alike.

Such underperformance and failure are rarely explained by way of attending purely to economic and technical criteria, yet such criteria appear to dominate the introduction of IT in work organisations (More, 1990). Executive management tends to view the introduction of IT as an economic imperative while IT specialists tend to view it as a technical imperative (McDonagh, 1999). Alas, this narrow techno-economic bias, sustained over time by the coalescent behavioural patterns of both the executive and IT communities, results in the human and organisational aspects of IT-related change being marginalized and ignored (McDonagh, 1999).

Such an outcome is rarely inconsequential since failing to attend to the human and organisational aspects of IT-related change is said to be responsible for the high incidence of underperformance and failure. Indeed, investigators are increasingly of the opinion that economic and technical aspects of IT account for less than 10% of underperformance and failure while human and organisational factors account for more than 90% (Isaacc-Henry, 1997). The nature of this dilemma is both obstinate and enduring.

This predicament is further compounded by an inability to effect integrated change due to the requisite knowledge and expertise being widely dispersed in organisational settings (McDonagh & Coghlan, 2000). Those organisational actors who understand the technology have little appreciation of the human and organisational aspects of IT. Similarly, those organisational actors who understand the human and organisational aspects of IT have little appreciation for the technology. Addressing this plight inevitably places a high premium on integrating different forms of knowledge and expertise (McDonagh, 1999).

DIVORCED FROM PRACTICE

Reflecting on the need to nurture a more integrated approach to IT-enabled change it seems prudent to consider the current state of research in the IT domain. Considering the perplexed nature of the domain it is hardly surprising that the fruits of inquiry have been seriously challenged in recent times (Benbasat & Weber, 1996; Galliers, 1997; Senn, 1998). Keen (1980, p. 15) contends that while "the world of practice is central not peripheral" the reality remains that "research is too divorced from practice" and "research issues arising from practice remain unstated." Galliers (1997, p. 154) notes that "It does appear that we IS researchers are pursuing somewhat different agendas than those of our colleagues in practice." More recently, the dilemma has been articulated with precision, noting that "a great deal of the academic research conducted in information systems is not valued by IT practitioners" and that such research "is not relevant, readable, or reachable" (Senn, 1998, pp. 23-24).

This relevancy crisis is not unique to the IT domain. In the context of research in the field of organisation science, Susman and Evered (1978, p. 582) note that "the findings in our scholarly management journals are only remotely related to the real world of practising managers." Indeed, it appears that this dilemma is rooted in positivist research approaches that dominate the field. Such approaches "are deficient in their capacity to generate knowledge for use by members of organisations" (Susman & Evered, p. 585). Supporting this contention Schein (1991, p. 2) posits that "we have largely adopted a traditional research paradigm that has not worked very well, a paradigm that has produced very reliable results about very unimportant things." In a similar vein, it has been argued that most research in the strategy domain is "irrelevant" since it is "increasingly and prematurely stuck in a normal science straightjacket" (Bettis, 1991, p. 315).

Empirical evidence of an overarching bias towards positivist research can be found in North American trends in empirical IT research methods during the 1970s and 1980s. Positivist methods such as cross-sectional studies were the dominant research approach during the 1980s, followed by laboratory experiments, case studies, and field tests (Cheon, Grover, & Sabherwal, 1993; Orlikowski & Baroudi, 1991). Static, one-shot, cross-sectional studies are clearly the predominant form of research in information systems (Orlikowski & Baroudi, 1991). Even the case study in IT research is more generally classified as a positivist, rather than a post-positivist, research approach (Knights, 1995).

On closer scrutiny, the dominance of positivism and the perceived lack of relevance in IT-related inquiry suggest the need for a rethink of both the process and intended contribution of such inquiry. Three distinct challenges emerge, including the need to concurrently (1) embrace the agendas of both practitioners and researchers, (2) establish spheres of mutual interest, and (3) contribute to effective social action and the development of robust social theory. The social nature of these challenges suggests the need for a more action-oriented approach to inquiry.

A CALL TO ACTION

Reflecting, once again, upon the need to nurture a more integrated approach to IT-enabled change, some writers contend that the study of organisational processes of change cannot be conducted well without affecting their very nature and therefore advocate the legitimacy of action-oriented philosophies to guide the research process (Argyris, Putnam, & Smith, 1985; Gummesson, 1991; Schein, 1991). In this regard, action research has received significant attention (Chakravarthy & Doz, 1992; Checkland, 1981; Huber & Van de Ven, 1995; Van de Ven, 1992) while clinical inquiry, a contemporary development of action research, has received relatively limited attention (Coghlan & McDonagh, 2001; McDonagh & Coghlan, 2000).

Advocating the legitimacy of action research Chakravarthy and Doz (1992) contend that organisational processes cannot be researched well without possibly affecting their very nature. "Rather than ignore the issue or only harp upon the occasional consulting dimension to process research, we believe action research should gain more legitimacy" (p. 10). Such advocacy is congruent with the core characteristics of action research, a theme that will be addressed later (Argyris et al., 1985; Eden & Huxham, 1996; Susman & Evered, 1978).

In a similar vein, Van de Ven (1992) contends that embracing an action research approach implies:

> *"significant investigator commitment and organisational access, which few investigators have achieved to date. One reason why gaining organisational access has been problematic is because investigators seldom place themselves into the manager's frame of reference to conduct their studies. Without observing a change process from a manager's perspective, it becomes difficult, if not impossible, for an investigator to understand the dynamics confronting managers who are involved in a strategic change effort, and thereby generate new knowledge that advances theory and practice" (p. 181).*

The appropriateness of action research in the study of organisational processes of change has been forcefully argued over the years (Argyris et al., 1985; Gummesson, 1991).

THE ASCENT OF ACTION RESEARCH

Undoubtedly, action research as a research strategy has increased in prominence in the last decade not only in the field of management and organisation studies (Eden & Huxham, 1996) but also in the field of IT studies (Avison, Lau, Myers, & Nielsen, 1999; Baskerville & Wood-Harper, 1996, 1998; Lau, 1997). Notwithstanding such increased prominence, identifying its distinctiveness has become somewhat of a challenge (Eden & Huxham, 1996).

This is a by-product of an emerging range of nuanced theories and practices. Action science, action learning, clinical inquiry, action inquiry, participatory action research, and normative action research share many of the core principles deeply embedded in action research (McDonagh, 1999). For instance, they are based on a collaborative problem-solving relationship between investigator and client system (Coghlan & McDonagh, 1997). The remainder of this section limits its attention to action research and clinical inquiry, a contemporary development of action research.

Kurt Lewin, the founding father of action research stressed:

"the limitations of studying complex, real social events in a laboratory"
and "the artificiality of splitting out single behavioural events from an
integrated social system" (Foster, 1972, p. 530).

Lewin stressed:

"the advantages of understanding the dynamic nature of change, by
studying it as it takes place" (Foster, p. 530)

and asserted that

"one cannot understand a human system without trying to change it. It is
in the attempt to change the system that some of the most important
characteristics of the system reveal themselves, phenomena that even the
most talented ethnographer would not discover unless he happened to be
present when someone else was trying to produce some change" (Schein,
1991, p. 4).

Action research, then, is founded and legitimised on the premise that
deliberate intervention in human activity systems is both the key to their
understanding and a preferred approach to research in social settings.
What is of the critical importance is not whether to intervene or not but
rather the nature of the desired intervention. "The illusion among some
investigators or ethnographers that they can go into organisations without
influencing them has been the source of a great deal of misunderstanding.
Instead of attempting to maintain this fiction or to argue for minimal
influence, why not acknowledge that any appearance of an outsider on the
organisation's doorstep is an intervention. The issue then is to decide what
kinds of intervention are desirable" (Schein, 1991, p. 10).

Action research is best conceptualised not as a single research approach but as a
family of approaches that share common characteristics. Identifying such characteristics, of necessity, involves, in the first instance, defining the concept of action research.
One of the most widely cited interpretations of action research is that of Rapport (1970)
who states: "Action research aims to contribute both to the practical concerns of people
in an immediate problematic situation and to the goals of social science by joint
collaboration within a mutually acceptable ethical framework" (p. 499). Eden and Huxham
(1996, p. 526) state that action research refers to "research which, broadly, results from
an involvement by the investigator with members of an organisation over a matter which
is of genuine concern to them and in which there is an intent by the organisation's
members to take action based on the intervention."

Various writers have sought to crystallise the distinctive nature of action research—e.g., Susman and Evered (1978), Argyris et al. (1985), Eden and Huxham (1996),
and Coghlan and McDonagh (1997). According to Argyris et al. (1985, pp. 8-9), Lewin's

concept of action research is characterised as follows: (1) Action research involves change experiments on real problems in social systems. It focuses on a particular problem and seeks to provide assistance to the client system. (2) Action research, like social management more generally, involves iterative cycles of identifying a problem, planning, acting, and evaluating. (3) The intended change typically involves *reeducation*, a term that refers to changing patterns of thinking and acting that are presently well-established in individuals and groups. The intended change is typically at the level of norms and values expressed in action. Effective reeducation depends on participation by clients in diagnosis and fact-finding and on free choice to engage in new kinds of action. (4) Action research changes the status quo from a perspective of democratic values. This value orientation is congruent with the requirements of effective reeducation (participation and free choice). (5) Action research is intended to contribute simultaneously to basic knowledge in social science and to social action in everyday life. High standards for developing theory and empirically testing propositions organised by theory are not to be sacrificed, nor is the relation to practice to be lost.

Susman and Evered (1978), among others, have all sought to crystallise the nature of action research. A synthesis of such writings reveals that action research is: diagnostic, problem focused, action oriented, collaborative, situational, cyclical, ethically based, experimental, scientific, naturalistic, normative, reeducative, emancipatory, eclectic and case-oriented, emergent, stresses group dynamic, balances research and social action, incorporates local knowledge, multidisciplinary, and contributes to human systems development.

Action research, "the most demanding and far-reaching method of doing case study research" (Gummesson, 1991, p. 102), is context-bound inquiry that is particularly suited to investigating organisational processes of change (Gummesson, 1991; Susman & Evered, 1978). It does not strive to formulate universally true laws, but rather situation specific insights (Susman & Evered). The real business of action-oriented case study research is particularisation, not generalisation.

A CONTEMPORARY DEVELOPMENT

Clinical inquiry, a contemporary development of action research as espoused by Lewin and his followers, has hitherto received relatively limited attention. Proposed by Schein (1987, 1991, 1995, 1999) as an appropriate philosophy to guide action-oriented inquiry into social systems, clinical inquiry embodies the general characteristics of action research but differs from it in an important respect. Clinical inquiry is first and foremost client centred since it is the client who requests some form of help and the investigator comes into the situation in response to the needs of the client, not her own needs to gather data (Schein, 1991). The investigator is not being facilitated by the client system, rather the client system is being "helped" by the investigator. This implies that the investigator has both research skills and helping skills. Indeed, it is the investigator's helping skills that are the prime attraction for the client system (Schein, 1991, 1995). The client-centred nature of clinical inquiry is its distinctive nuance since there is nothing in action research that focuses on client needs as a necessary condition for data to surface. Indeed, in the action research model, the client is involved in the investigator's agenda rather than vice versa (Schein, 1995).

In the clinical inquiry model, opportunities for learning about the client system are enhanced immensely. As Schein (1991, p. 5) has noted, "once the helping relationship exists, the possibilities for learning what really goes on in organisations are enormous if we learn to take advantage of them and if we learn to be good and reliable observers of what is going on." The enhanced learning opportunities for the investigator are directly related to the nature of the psychological contract between the investigator and the client in the clinical model. In the traditional situation, the client is facilitating the investigator since it is the investigator's agenda that is of the utmost importance. In this situation, the level of incentive for the client to reveal herself is extremely low, and "there is certainly nothing in the situation that would motivate her to reveal some of her deeper observations or attitudes" (Schein, 1991, p. 5).

In the clinical inquiry model, the nature of the exchange between the investigator and the client is significantly altered. "In the traditional situation the investigator wanted something from reluctant organisation members and has relatively little to offer in return" (Schein, 1991, p. 7). In the clinical situation, clients want something from the helper and are willing to "lay themselves open to being questioned by the clinician on matters that may be regarded under other circumstances as private or secret, or *dirty linen*" (Schein, 1991, p. 7). Indeed, the nature of the relationship is such that the client obligates to give answers and provide all pertinent information.

Schein's model of clinical inquiry is best characterised as follows: (1) The client wants help and is therefore more likely to reveal important data. (2) The investigator is expected to intervene, which allows new data about the client system to be surfaced. (3) The richness of the data allows the investigator to develop deep insights into the client system, particularly with respect to (i) the psychological defences operating in the organisation, (ii) the cultural assumptions that are driving the organisation, (iii) the interpersonal and group dynamics that are operating, and (iv) how power and authority operate in the organisation (Schein, 1991, p. 13).

Clinical inquiry is particularly challenging considering its intent of nurturing effective social action while concurrently focusing on the development of robust social theory (Coghlan & McDonagh, 2001; McDonagh, 1999; McDonagh & Coghlan, 2000). Attending to these twin challenges inevitably involves reconciling the dual roles of process consultant and investigator with their respective time frames and associated behavioural patterns (Gummesson, 1991).

With a view to nurturing effective social action, the investigator is primarily concerned with the needs of the client system wherein effective short-term social action is key. The investigator embraces the role of process consultant wherein he engages in a cyclical process of dialogue, action, and reflection with the client system with the explicit intention of releasing the client's own resources through self-diagnosis and self-intervention (Gummesson, 1991). This approach is based on the assumption that the resources to take action and implement change exist within the client's organisation.

Embracing the role of process consultant is not synonymous with "expert consultancy approaches in management" (Gummesson, 1991, p. 36). Unlike expert consultancy, which prescribes a solution for the client system, process consulting focuses on enabling the client system to determine the most appropriate course of action suited to its circumstances. More specifically, process consulting assumes: (1) clients know there is a problem but do not know what the problem is; (2) clients often do not know what help is available and which consultant might be best; (3) clients have constructive intent and are motivated by goals and values that the consultant can accept; (4) clients are capable of solving their own problems and want help in figuring things out for themselves; (5) clients learn from this process to work more effectively when such problems arise again; (6) clients benefit from participation in the diagnostic process; (7) the client owns the problem and is therefore the only one who ultimately knows what form of remedy will work; and (8) the client and consultant are equally committed to collaborative approaches to change.

With a view to developing robust social theory, the investigator embraces a longer term perspective on social inquiry wherein he engages in deep reflection and "maintains a distance from a change project, analyses it within a more general, long-term framework and develops concepts, categories, models, hypotheses, and theories" (Gummesson, 1991, pp. 106-107). Such deep reflection is reminiscent of higher level or double-loop learning, which involves a restructuring of mental models and involves significant changes in understanding.

Clinical researchers do not attempt to establish an absolute truth about their interpretations. The observations and interpretations are themes for learning and for further intervention into the ongoing situation. In clinical inquiry, diagnosis and intervention are simultaneous activities. As clinical researchers engage in inquiry, which enables clients to explore and diagnose their organisational situations, the responses themselves generate data for further questioning and exploration (Schein, 1999). The diagnostic process remains with the client throughout the consultation.

Action research and clinical inquiry are not synonymous. Clinical inquiry is a contemporary development of action research, with distinctive nuances. Unlike action research, clinical inquiry is primarily concerned with pursuing the client's rather than the investigator's agenda (Schein, 1991, 1995, 1999). This approach to research results in significantly enhanced organisational access (Gummesson, 1991) where "involvement with practitioners over things which actually matter to them provides a richness of insight which could not be gained in other ways" (Eden & Huxham, 1996, p. 526). The benefit of such rich insights is further amplified in the clinical inquiry model of action research where clients are generally willing to "lay themselves open to being questioned by the clinician on matters that may be regarded under other circumstances as private or secret, or *dirty linen*" (Schein, 1991, p. 7).

In clinical inquiry theory emerges from the ground up as action proceeds with constant cycling between data and theory development. Knowledge generation is dynamic and fluid with constant iteration between dialogue, action, and reflection (Eden & Huxham, 1996; Gummesson, 1991). In essence, theory development is grounded in organisational action, similar to Strauss and Corbin's concept of grounded theory.

THE MERITS OF CLINICAL INQUIRY

Reflecting on both alleged weaknesses in extant research approaches (Benbasat & Weber, 1996; Keen, 1980; Senn, 1998) and the need to nurture a more integrated approach to IT-enabled change, action-oriented inquiry emerges as a legitimate and profoundly important post-positivist family of research approaches relevant to exploring the dynamics of such change. Indeed, there appears to be an increased emphasis on the appropriateness of such approaches to inquiry for the study of IT more generally (Avison et al., 1999; Lau, 1997; Mansell, 1991).

Within action-oriented research paradigms, Schein's (1987, 1991, 1995) model of clinical inquiry is ideally placed to address research within the IT domain (Coghlan & McDonagh, 2001; McDonagh, 1999; McDonagh & Coghlan, 2000). More specifically, its focus on organisations as technical, political, and cultural systems enables a multidimensional approach to researching IT-enabled organisational change. Indeed, the clinical approach to exploring the dynamics of IT-enabled change offers unrivalled opportunities for gaining deep insights into the complex nature of such change. Having embraced the clinical approach when exploring the role of executive management in shaping large-scale IT-enabled business change, it is worth emphasising that clinical inquiry offers unrivalled opportunities for shaping effective social action and the development of robust social theory (McDonagh, 1999). A number of pivotal insights are of particular importance in this regard.

First, "clinical inquiry provides a legitimate basis for embracing the concerns of both practitioners and investigators alike" (McDonagh, 1999, p. 235). Both the practitioner and investigator are concerned with the immediacy of a particular problematic or challenging situation and are equally focused and committed to effective social action with a view to effecting change. By wholeheartedly embracing the world of the practitioner, the investigator develops deep insights that provide a sound basis for the development of robust social theory. Clinical inquiry therefore redresses the perceived lack of relevance in much extant research (Galliers, 1997; Keen, 1991; Senn, 1998). When investigating the role of executive management in IT-enabled business change, clinical inquiry facilitated the integration of the organisation's need to foster an integrated approach to change and the investigator's need to establish how executive management shapes IT-enabled change (McDonagh, 1999).

Second, "clinical inquiry is capable of embracing the dynamic and developmental nature of IT-enabled change" (McDonagh, 1999, p. 235). This is of particular importance since much extant research is excessively static, with Orlikowski and Baroudi (1991) noting that static, one-shot, cross-sectional studies are clearly the predominant form of research in information systems. Cross-sectional studies fail to capture the dynamic and developmental nature of change and equally fail to account for the actions, reactions, and interactions of key social actors that shape processes of change. The clinical approach to collaborative inquiry redresses this plight by attending to both the developmental nature of change and its sociopolitical context (McDonagh, 1999; McDonagh & Coghlan, 2000). When investigating the role of executive management in IT-enabled business change, clinical inquiry fostered a longitudinal perspective on change wherein understanding dynamic and developmental processes of change was an imperative (McDonagh, 1999).

Third, "with its processual focus, clinical inquiry is capable of facilitating the integration of diverse forms of knowledge and expertise that executive management uses to shape the introduction of IT" (McDonagh, 1999, p. 235). Clinical researchers proactively embrace the distinctive perspectives on IT-enabled change as embraced by executive management (McDonagh, 1999). Clinical researchers' knowledge of strategy, organisational behaviour, and IT enables them to embrace the multifaceted nature of executive behaviour in the context of IT-enabled change (McDonagh, 1999; McDonagh

& Coghlan, 2000). When investigating the role of executive management in IT-enabled business change, clinical inquiry facilitated the integration of diverse forms of knowledge and expertise which underpinned the four diverse roles of executive management, namely, architect, engineer, humanist, and broker (McDonagh, 1999).

Fourth, "clinical inquiry is capable of facilitating the integration of diverse requirements and demands that executive management places on the process of introducing IT" (McDonagh, 1999, p. 236). In particular, clinical researchers are capable of crafting a more integrated approach to the introduction of IT that accommodates the diverse demands of executive management which result in the need to concurrently embrace strategic, technical, social, and political perspectives on IT-related change. The clinical inquiry process enables the development of a shared dialogue between executive management (Schein, 1999). When investigating the role of executive management in IT-enabled business change, clinical inquiry facilitated the integration of diverse requirements and demands embedded in the four diverse roles of executive management, namely, architect, engineer, humanist, and broker (McDonagh, 1999).

Fifth, "clinical inquiry is capable of reconciling the diverse bases of power and influence that executive management uses to shape the introduction of IT" (McDonagh, 1999, p. 236). Clinical researchers embrace the role of negotiator when addressing this distinctive challenge. Inevitably, this may involve significant compromise since addressing the collective requirements and demands of executive management may not be feasible when all known constraints on change are accounted for. Clinical researchers rightfully recognise the diverse bases of power and influence and seek to negotiate a way forward that is acceptable to all executives. Clinical researchers do not take sides between conflicting groups; rather they build a trusting relationship with all parties so that they can act as brokers of inquiry, cooperation, and compromise. When investigating the role of executive management in IT-enabled business change, clinical inquiry reconciled reward and coercive power, technical expert power, affiliative power, and referent power (McDonagh, 1999).

Sixth, clinical inquiry is capable of uncovering, challenging, and changing the polarised patterns of cognition and action with respect to IT embodied in the executive and IT communities (McDonagh, 1999). The importance of explicating implicit theories, which guide informed human action with respect to IT, is of the utmost importance when one considers the unintended consequence of the economic and technical mind-sets of the executive and IT communities, respectively. As has been previously argued, the coalescent nature of these mind-sets is such that human and organisational aspects of IT are frequently marginalized and ignored. Considering the embedded nature of the executive and IT mind-sets with respect to IT, the effective introduction of IT necessitates real-time reeducation for both communities. Clinical inquiry wholeheartedly embraces this reeducative agenda as part of the investigative process, as demonstrated in the study of executive management and IT-enabled business change (McDonagh, 1999).

Seventh, "clinical inquiry is capable of nurturing a collaborative approach to change based on principles of partnership and participation" (McDonagh, 1999, p. 236). Recognising the rightful place of diverse forms of knowledge and expertise along with diverse requirements and demands, clinical researchers proactively cultivate a collaborative approach to change that accommodates the political realities of organisational life. Indeed, this is accomplished in a manner that attends to the introduction of IT in an integrated manner, concurrently attending to strategic, technical, social, and political considerations (McDonagh, 1999; McDonagh & Coghlan, 2000). McDonagh (1999), when investigating the role of executive management in shaping IT-enabled business change, demonstrated how clinical inquiry nurtured a collaborative approach to change, particularly within the executive suite.

In summary, the clinical approach to collaborative inquiry offers deep insights into the complex nature of IT-enabled change. More particularly, such insights arise from (1) the collaborative nature of the relationship between practitioners and investigators, (2) the emphasis on dynamic and developmental processes of change, (3) attempts to integrate different forms of knowledge and expertise, (4) attempts to integrate diverse requirements and demands, (5) attempts to reconcile diverse bases of power and influence, (6) uncovering, challenging, and changing the polarised patterns of cognition and action with respect to IT embodied in the executive and IT communities, and (7) attempts to craft a collaborative approach to change. Recognising the role of clinical researchers as helpers and facilitators of change, clinical inquiry offers unrivalled opportunities for shaping effective social action and the development of robust social knowledge.

A PAUCITY OF ACTION

Reflecting on both the increasing advocacy for the use of action-oriented approaches to inquiry and their inordinate value for research and practice, how prevalent are such approaches in the IT literature? Rare, to say the least. Once again, reflecting on North American trends in empirical research methods during the 1970s and 1980s as outlined in Figure 1, only one empirical study employed an action research approach during this period. In a separate review, not confined to North America, on the use of action research in IT studies over the last 25 years, Lau (1997) identifies 10 discussion papers and 20 field studies embracing action research, action science, participatory action research, and action learning. Unfortunately, none of these were published in mainstream IT journals such as *MIS Quarterly*, *Information Systems Research*, *Communications of the ACM*, or the *European Journal of Information Systems* (Lau, 1997). This finding is not inconsistent with the statistics outlined in Figure 1 since the latter confines itself to what are considered mainstream North American journals.

Outside North America, action-oriented research approaches have made more contributions to the literature of the IT research community (Baskerville & Wood-Harper, 1996, 1998). In particular, Checkland's work on soft systems methodology (Checkland & Scholes, 1990) has influenced IT research by linking action research and the systems development process. Similarly, soft systems methodology and action research have been applied to IS strategy development (Galliers, 1992).

While increased advocacy for the legitimacy of action-oriented approaches to inquiry for the study of IT is discernible, unfortunately "despite its overwhelming acceptance in organisation development, it is virtually nonexistent among North American IS research" (Baskerville & Wood-Harper, 1996, p. 235). In a European and Australian context it has been equally noted that "action research is not a predominant IS research method even in those geographic areas" (Baskerville & Wood-Harper, 1996, p. 235). How can a family of research approaches, which holds such promise, be embraced by so few?

"Action research can address complex real-life problems and the immediate concerns of practitioners. Yet, paradoxically, the academic community has almost totally ignored action research" (Avison et al., 1999, p. 95).

CONCLUSION

This chapter has usefully illustrated enduring dilemmas in both IT-enabled business change and IT-related inquiry. In the former, the practitioner's dilemma is rooted in a distinct inability to foster a highly integrated approach to change that concurrently attends to economic, technical, human, and organisational considerations. Addressing this challenge invariably necessitates embracing a systemic approach to change in organisational contexts. In the latter, the investigator's dilemma in rooted in an alleged inability to pursue inquiry that generates robust theory while concurrently informing and transforming practice.

Focusing on these twin dilemmas, the case for a more collaborative approach to inquiry was explicated, paying particular attention to the ascent of action-oriented research philosophies. Furthermore, as a contemporary development of action research, clinical inquiry was presented as a rather distinctive approach to inquiry ideally suited to addressing the twin dilemmas outlined in the chapter.

Seven pivotal benefits associated with the effective use of clinical inquiry were explicated in the context of investigating the dynamics of IT-enabled business change. Indeed, the author is convinced that the complex challenge of managing large-scale IT-enabled business change can be better understood and the associated issues addressed through the effective use of a collaborative approach to inquiry, particularly clinical inquiry (Coghlan & McDonagh, 2001; McDonagh, 1999; McDonagh & Coghlan, 2000).

REFERENCES

Argyris, C., Putnam, R., & Smith, D. (1985). *Action Science*. San Francisco, CA: Jossey-Bass.

Avison, D., Lau, F., Myers, M., & Nielsen, P. (1999). Action research. *Communications of the ACM, 42*(1), 94-97.

Baskerville, R. L., & Wood-Harper, A. T. (1996). A critical perspective on action research as a method for information systems research. *Journal of Information Technology, 11*, 235-246.

Baskerville, R. L., & Wood-Harper, A. T. (1998). Diversity in information systems action research methods. *European Journal of Information Systems, 7*(2), 90-107.

Benbasat, I., & Weber, R. (1996). Research commentary: Rethinking 'diversity' in information systems research. *Information Systems Research, 7*(4), 389-399.

Bettis, R. A. (1991). Strategic management and the straightjacket: An editorial essay. *Organisation Science, 2*(3), 315-319.

Chakravarthy, B. S., & Doz, Y. (1992). Strategy process research: Focusing on corporate self renewal. *Strategic Management Journal, 13*, 5-14.

Checkland, P. (1981). *Systems Thinking, Systems Practice*. Chichester, UK: John Wiley & Sons.

Checkland, P., & Scholes, J. (1990). *Soft Systems Methodology in Action*. Chichester, UK: John Wiley & Sons.

Cheon, M. J., Grover, V., & Sabherwal, R. (1993). The evolution of empirical research in IS—A study in IS maturity. *Information & Management*, 107-119.

Coghlan, D., & McDonagh, J. (1997). Doing section science in your own organization. In T. Brannick & W. K. Roche (Eds.), *Business Research Methods: Strategies, Techniques and Sources* (pp. 139-161). Dublin, Ireland: Oak Tree Press.

Coghlan, D., & McDonagh, J. (2001). Research and practice in IT-related change: The case for clinical inquiry. In R. Woodman & W. A. Pasmore (Eds.), *Research in Organization Change and Development* (pp. 195-211). Thousand Oaks, CA: SAGE.

Eden, C., & Huxham, C. (1996). Action research for the study of organizations. In S. Clegg, C. Hardy, & W. Nord (Eds.), *Handbook of Organization Studies* (pp. 526-542). Thousand Oaks, CA: SAGE.

Foster, M. (1972). An introduction to the theory and practice of action research in work organisations. *Human Relations, 25*(6), 529-556.

Galliers, R. D. (1992). Soft systems scenarios and the planning and development of information systems. *Systemist, 14*(3), 146-159.

Galliers, R. D. (1997). Reflections on information systems research: Twelve points of debate. In F. Stowell (Ed.), *Information Systems: An Emerging Discipline?* (pp. 141-157). Maidenhead, UK: McGraw-Hill.

Gummesson, E. (1991). *Qualitative Methods in Management Research* (Rev. ed.). London: SAGE.

Huber, G. P., & Van de Ven, A. H. (1995). *Longitudinal Field Research Methods—Studying Processes of Organisational Change*. London: SAGE.

Isaacc-Henry, K. (1997). Management of information technology in the public sector. In C. Barnes (Ed.), *Management in the Public Sector—Challenge and Change* (pp. 131-159). London: International Thomson Business Press.

Keen, P. G. W. (1980, December). *MIS research: Reference disciplines and a cumulative tradition.* Paper presented at the First International Conference on Information Systems, Philadelphia, Pennsylvania, USA.

Keen, P. G. W. (1991). Relevance and rigor in information systems research: Improving quality, confidence, cohesion, and impact. In H.-E. Nissen, H. K. Klein, & R. Hirschheim (Eds.), *Information Systems Research: Contemporary Approaches and Emergent Traditions* (2nd ed.), pp. 27-49. Amsterdam: North-Holland.

Knights, D. (1995). Refocusing the case study: Researching the politics of IT and the politics of IT research. *Technology Studies,* No. 3.

Lau, F. (1997). A review on the use of action research in information systems studies. In J. DeGross (Ed.), *Information Systems and Qualitative Research* (pp. 31-68). London: Chapman & Hall.

Mansell, G. (1991). Action research in information systems development. *Journal of Information Systems, 1*, 29-40.

McDonagh, J. (1999). *Exploring the role of executive management in shaping strategic change: The case of information technology*. Unpublished PhD dissertation, University of Warwick, Coventry, UK.

McDonagh, J., & Coghlan, D. (2000). The art of clinical inquiry in IT-related research. In P. Reason & H. Bradbury (Eds.), *Handbook of Action Research: Participative Inquiry and Practice* (pp. 372-378). London: SAGE.

More, E. (1990). Information systems: People issues. *Journal of Information Science, 16*, 311-320.

Orlikowski, W. J., & Baroudi, J. J. (1991). Studying information technology in organisations: Research approaches and assumptions. *Information Systems Research, 2*(1), 1-28.

Rapport, R. (1970). Three dilemmas of action research. *Human Relations, 23*, 499-513.

Schein, E. H. (1987). *The Clinical Perspective in Fieldwork*. Newbury Park, CA: SAGE.

Schein, E. H. (1991). *Legitimating Clinical Research in the Study of Organizational Culture* (WP# 3288-91-BPS). Cambridge, MA: Massachusetts Institute of Technology, Sloan School of Management.

Schein, E. H. (1995). Process consultation action research and clinical inquiry: Are they the same? *Journal of Managerial Psychology, 10*(6), 14-19.

Schein, E. H. (1999). *Process Consultation Revisited—Building the Helping Relationship*. Reading, MA: Addison-Wesley.

Senn, J. (1998). The challenge of relating IS research to practice. *Information Resource Management Journal, 11*, 23-28.

Standish Group. (1998). *Chaos*. Retrieved from: www.standishgroup.com/chaos.html.

Susman, G. I., & Evered, R. D. (1978). An assessment of the scientific merits of action research. *Administrative Science Quarterly, 23*.

Van de Ven, A. H. (1992). Suggestions for studying strategy process: A research note. *Strategic Management Journal, 13*, 169-188.

Chapter VIII

Rigor, Relevance and Research Paradigms: A Practitioner's Perspective

John C. Beachboard
Idaho State University, USA

ABSTRACT

A practitioner leaves behind the world of failed multimillion-dollar information systems projects to seek solutions in academe. In making the transition from IS practitioner to IS researcher, the author encounters two fundamental tensions regarding the conduct of social science. The first tension concerns the challenge of conducting research meeting the criteria of scientific rigor while addressing issues relevant to practitioners. The second tension centers on the debate concerning the suitability of positivist and non-positivist approaches to research in the social sciences. A review of the literature discussing these tensions led the author to the observation that the two tensions appear to be related. This insight led to the investigation of multi-paradigmatic research frameworks as a means of reconciling these related tensions. The essay provides a personalized account regarding the author's motivation for conducting practitioner-oriented research, the intellectual journey made through the literature to acquire tools of the social science field, and his observations concerning the advantages of multi-paradigmatic research in the IS field.

INTRODUCTION

I was not surprised to learn that the effort to transition from the world of practice to the world of research would be challenging. I was, however, unprepared for the discovery of the diversity of strongly held views regarding the nature of reality and what constitutes valid knowledge. Nor was I prepared to find multiple, seemingly contradictory, goals and approaches to the conduct of social science.

This chapter is essentially a story concerning my effort to understand these philosophical issues and wrestle with their implications regarding the conduct of research in the field of information systems (IS) generally and IS management specifically. My hope is that this analysis of philosophical and methodological issues, by a serious practitioner who wants to become a competent IS researcher, will prove useful to those seeking practical relevance in their research.

I have chosen to present my findings in a confessional narrative form (Schultze, 2000; Van Maanen, 1988). As Schultze (2000) explains, the *confessional* or *vulnerable* genre "exposes the ethnographer, rendering his/her actions, failings, motivations, and assumptions open to public scrutiny and critique" (p. 8). The confessional genre reveals personal motivations and assumptions underlying the author's thinking, thus helping readers to evaluate the text's relevance to their purposes.

WHY THE INTEREST IN I.S. RESEARCH?

It can almost be considered axiomatic that IS failures reflect management problems rather than problems with underlying technology. Accordingly, academicians and practitioners have invested considerable energy in developing policies and prescriptions to strengthen IS management practice (Feeny & Willcocks, 1998; Lewis, 1999; Rockart, Earl, & Ross, 1996; Sambamurthy & Zmud, 1994; Strassmann, 1995; Van Schaik, 1985). Yet, despite years of study and mountains of literature on the subject of IS management, large, medium and small IS management problems continue to occur.

My personal dissatisfaction with IS management practice stemmed from my work with the U.S. Department of Defense (DOD), where I participated in the development of multiple IS programs, each resulting in the waste of hundreds of millions of dollars. While the average taxpayer may find the financial aspects outrageous, what particularly struck me was that these programs failed despite significant investments made by the federal government and the DOD codifying how to manage large, complex programs. In every case, significant effort and expense had gone into complying with federal and DOD information technology (IT) management policies, policies largely consistent with the types of IS management prescriptions found in private-sector and academic literature. While the work was intellectually challenging, I was discouraged to see my colleagues' and my efforts come to naught with the demise of each successive program.[1]

Ironically, working on failed projects can prove financially rewarding to employees if not to employers. These two realities—failed projects and financial success—motivated and enabled me to return to graduate school. My goal was to better understand why, in the face of numerous and long-standing management prescriptions, IS management was so difficult. It did not seem that practitioners had the answers so, after 15 years in practice, I returned to academe to attain a better understanding of practice. I entered a master's degree program in information resources management.

Early in my studies, I observed two fundamental tensions in the conduct of information systems research. The first tension concerned the challenge facing IS researchers attempting to achieve acceptable levels of scientific rigor while conducting research relevant to practice. The second tension concerned the debate among proponents of traditional (positivist) social science research perspectives and social scientists espousing a wide variety of non-positivist[2] approaches to research. Early on, the thought occurred to me that these tensions might be related. Consequently, I labored to understand this debate so that I could select an appropriate perspective for pursuing my research agenda.

RESEARCH: RIGOR VS. RELEVANCE

As Benbaset and Zmud (1999) might have predicted, the academic literature was mostly irrelevant to my needs. I found myself literally nodding in agreement while reading Strassmann's (1995) assertion regarding the study of information management policy: "academics tend to shun this topic because it is too difficult to collect research data about policy-making that meet the publishing criteria of academic journals" (p. 5).

However, there has been research in the information management area. Research in IT management can be conceptualized as consisting of two distinct but interrelated streams. The first research stream concerns IT governance strategies and addresses questions concerning factors influencing decisions to adopt centralized, decentralized and, more recently, federal IT governance structures. Theoretical frameworks for predicting selection of IT governance style have become increasingly sophisticated (Boynton, Jacobs, & Zmud, 1992; Brown, 1997; Brown & Magill, 1994; Ein-Dor & Segev, 1982; King, 1983; Sambamurthy & Zmud, 1999; Tavakolian, 1989; Zmud, 1984). For example, Sambamurthy and Zmud (1999) have suggested a multiple-contingency model identifying factors jointly influencing the selection of governance arrangements employed to direct, control and coordinate three fundamental spheres of IT activities: IT infrastructure management, IT use management, and IT project management. The research produced in this IT governance stream is theoretically sound and has been conducted in a rigorous manner consistent with positivist-oriented methods and philosophical assumptions. I do not deny that this research stream has yielded useful insights. It has explicitly identified and categorized IT management activities as well as internal and external factors that can influence the selection of an organization's strategy for governing the conduct of those activities. However, this research addressed tangentially at best the issue and problems that I had encountered as an IS practitioner.

The second research stream identifies IT management processes and competencies associated with successful IT implementation and use. Much of this research is empirically based, practitioner oriented, and prescriptive in nature (Broadbent & Weill, 1997; Feeny & Willcocks, 1998; Rockart et al., 1996; Ross, Beath, & Goodhue, 1996). This research stream, based on the extensive interaction with senior industry IS management, exhibits a high degree of relevancy as witnessed by its being predominantly published in practitioner-oriented journals. I fully believe that such publications are highly commendable. But these venues do pose difficulties. Because they tend to lack adequate description of theory and method, it is difficult for the researcher to assess methodological rigor and the validity of the findings.

At the risk of revealing further personal biases, let me point out that I worked primarily as a mid-level IS manager and learned to treat the pronouncements of many senior IS managers with a degree of skepticism. Later exposure to academic literature discussing cognitive biases (Hogarth, 1981; Tversky & Kahneman, 1974; Wright, 1980) and the impact such biases can have on reported actions and behaviors (Golden, 1992; Huber & Power, 1985) have only reinforced that skepticism.

Furthermore, while the prescriptions resulting from this research were relevant to my interests, they were not necessarily helpful. Many of the prescriptions derived from these studies have tremendous face validity and can almost be considered truisms. Yet, these prescriptions were not sufficiently rich to reveal the subtleties that one would encounter in their implementation. In short, there is an abundant IT management literature. Yet much of the research that I found to be rigorous was not particularly relevant to my needs, while much of the research that was relevant failed to substantiate methodological rigor, thus undermining my confidence in its practical applicability.[3]

My introduction to the philosophical issues concerning the conduct of research came when I enrolled in a class on research methods required in my master's degree program. The professor assigned Orlikowski and Baroudi's (1991) paper "Studying Information Technology in Organizations: Research Approaches and Assumptions." This work introduced me to such concepts as ontology, epistemology, positivism, critical theory, and interpretivist philosophy. The article was disconcerting, largely because some of the arguments severely challenged my fundamental assumptions regarding reality and knowledge. Frankly, the article expressed some ideas that I was not prepared to accept. The ideas that "'objective' or 'factual' accounts of events and situations" are not possible and that scientists cannot achieve value neutrality were a bit too philosophical for this product of a Midwestern public school education to accept (Orlikowski & Baroudi, p. 5). However, it did not seem quite fair to discount something I did not comprehend, so I decided to do more reading and studying on the subject. It turned out to be a lot more: I entered a PhD program.

A PRACTITIONER STUDIES RESEARCH

The journey from practitioner to neophyte researcher began in earnest upon my acceptance into a doctoral program. In attempting to satisfy the curiosity stimulated by the Orlikowski and Baroudi paper, I discovered abundant literature discussing competing philosophies of science, the notion of research paradigms, and what has been referred to as the "paradigm war" (Gage, 1989). While it is not practical in this paper to comprehensively reference the literature I reviewed, two sources were particularly helpful. Denzin and Lincoln's (1994) *Handbook of Qualitative Research* provided a comprehensive treatment of the variety of philosophical foundations informing qualitative research performed under multiple paradigms. I also found Hammersley's (1995) summarization of research paradigms in his exploration of political dimensions of the "paradigm debate"[4] to be very helpful.

The literature surrounding the paradigm debate is extensive, not only in terms of sheer volume but also in that the debate has been conducted in many disciplinary domains. As I suspect many other budding researchers before me have done, I made a nonsystematic excursion through this vast literature, chasing citations whose titles caught my eye and taking the unmanly step of occasionally stopping to ask directions from professors and peers.

Following are some highlights observed along the way:

- I was not alone in my doubts regarding the relevancy of academic research. It turns out that academicians had been expressing similar concerns regarding research relevancy for some time (Churchman, 1971; Miner, 1984; Mitroff & Pondy, 1978). While some researchers are comfortable viewing research primarily as a means of increasing disciplinary knowledge, others clearly feel an obligation to produce practical or instrumental knowledge.

- The paradigm debate had political as well as philosophical dimensions. Hammersley (1995) claims that positivism is rejected "not just in intellectual but in moral and political terms" (p. 1). Not surprisingly, the response to non-positivist paradigms from those engaged in traditional research can be harsh: "The unbalanced and unquestioned equation of ethnographic or qualitative methods with phenomeno-logical or hermeneutical non-science contributes to an unfortunate reinvention of social science precepts" (Sandstrom & Sandstrom, 1995, p. 163).

- There appeared to be similarities in the criticisms of published research proffered by those concerned with the issue of relevancy and those who found positivist methods inappropriate to the study of social phenomena. Essentially, both groups are concerned that in the pursuit of methodological rigor, many of the contingent and situated factors relevant to social behavior are stripped away (Miner, 1984; Walsham, 1995).

- I found it ironic that non-positivists were arguing that traditional positivist-oriented research was too focused on prediction and control, overly emphasizing managerialist values. Conversely, critics concerned with relevancy worried that researchers were too focused on increasing disciplinary knowledge (knowledge for the sake of knowledge) without properly attending to practitioner needs (Guba & Lincoln, 1994; Hammersley, 1995; Miner, 1984; Zmud, 1996).

As the time to start my dissertation research approached, I was still unable to select an appropriate paradigmatic approach to addressing my substantive research topic. The reader will recall that my objective was to obtain a better understanding of the effectiveness (or, more accurately, the ineffectiveness) of accepted policies and prescriptions for addressing IS management problems. Furthermore, postmodernist writing had introduced doubt as to whether attempting this research was even worthwhile. I had become a methodological agnostic and lacked the experience required to firmly declare a position on these philosophical and methodological issues.

Happily, I encountered a stream of literature suggesting that it might be possible to straddle the methodological fence and perhaps sidestep the apparently insurmount-able philosophical differences. A number of researchers have suggested that it is not only possible but beneficial to integrate positivist and non-positivist perspectives (DeSanctis & Poole, 1994; Kaplan & Duchon, 1988; Lee, 1991; Orlikowski, 1992; Orlikowski & Robey, 1991). For example, several of these researchers have referenced Giddens's theory of structuration, which finds untenable the premise that subjectivism and objectivism are mutually exclusive (Giddens, 1984; Orlikowski & Robey, 1991). Structuration theory, in suggesting that objective (or institutional) properties of social systems recursively influence and are influenced by the "day-to-day routines of people in interaction" (Turner, 1986, p. 460), appeared to provide a reasonable theoretical basis for employing a multi-paradigmatic research approach. Thus, in postulating this "duality of structure," Giddens synthesized elements of structural theory without discounting human agency and motivation in enacting and reenacting social structures. By acknowledging this dual nature of social phenomena, Giddens implicitly recognized the usefulness of research methods associated with neo-positivism as well as various non-positivist philosophies.

The adoption of a multi-paradigmatic approach should provide the researcher with the opportunity to more completely study the phenomenon of interest and to design a study that capitalizes on the advantages and minimizes the disadvantages of positivist and non-positivist research paradigms. Fortunately, the research environment in my doctoral program was more supportive than that described by Applegate and King (1999) in their vignette concerning Professor Marilyn Moore's research experiences.[5]

Despite the difficulties associated with the approach (Creswell, 1994), I decided that my topic warranted pursuing a multi-paradigmatic research design. Such an approach promised to provide a richer understanding of what constitutes IS management practice, given the relative lack of theory relevant to the subject. Beyond my substantive research agenda, the selection of a multi-paradigmatic research design afforded me the opportunity to personally evaluate the strengths and weaknesses of positivist and non-positivist approaches as well as my own ontological and epistemological beliefs.

Consequently, I adopted a multi-paradigmatic research framework proposed by Lee. In his framework, Lee (1991) identifies three levels of understanding (p. 351)[6]:

- *Understanding at the first level* (subjective understanding) belongs to the observed human subjects. This understanding consists of the everyday sense and everyday meanings with which the human subjects see themselves and which give rise to the behavior that they manifest in socially constructed settings.
- *Understanding at the second level* (interpretive understanding) belongs to the observing, organizational researcher. This understanding is the researcher's reading or interpretation of the first-level, common sense understanding.
- *Understanding at the third level* (positivist understanding) also belongs to the organizational researcher. This understanding is the one the researcher creates and tests in order to explain the empirical reality that he or she is investigating.

Lee suggests that methodologies (phenomenological sociology, hermeneutics, ethnography, etc.) associated with interpretive research could be used to develop the researcher's second level of understanding. The second level, interpretive understanding, can then inform the development of testable propositions addressing institutional/structural aspects of the social phenomenon being studied. These patterns or themes, as represented by testable propositions, constitute a third level of understanding that can then be subjected to more conventional methods of scientific testing.

Having already confessed a degree of paradigmatic agnosticism, I must also admit that the adoption of a multi-paradigmatic research design hedged my methodological bet. While not necessitated by Lee's multi-paradigmatic approach, my study included structured surveys in the data collection effort. Consistent with Lee's model, I accepted in advance that I would be conducting subsequent phases of research using more positivistic-oriented research methods. Including structured survey data permitted me to evaluate data-quality issues associated with surveying key informants in large, complex organizations. I could additionally cite as an objective for this additional collection effort the desire to achieve data triangulation (Jick, 1979). However, more to the point, I was worried about my ability to conduct rigorous interpretivist-oriented research. I wanted to ensure that I would have data to analyze should my efforts at conducting unstructured interviews and analyzing the resulting data prove less than satisfactory.

A MULTI-PARADIGMATIC RESEARCH EXPERIENCE

My research site was a federal agency. My data-collection methods were multiple: I reviewed hundreds of documents, conducted three formal surveys (of IS managers, non-IS managers, and general agency staff), held 19 unstructured interviews with IS and non-IS managers (varying from 40 to 90 minutes in length), conducted several focus groups with IS managers, and had numerous short conversations and e-mail exchanges with agency staff. The surveys ensured that participants had an opportunity to provide their perceptions on a number of constructs identified in my literature review.

As noted above, the structured collection of data in the surveys gave me the confidence to conduct face-to-face interviews in an unstructured, conversational style. While I did provide the general topic of IS management challenges as a starting point, participants were encouraged to take the conversation in whatever direction they thought appropriate. My initial fears concerning data and analysis issues resulting from this unstructured approach proved groundless. The narrative data resulting from these naturalistic interviews (actually conversations) provided the primary basis for my constructing an understanding of IS management within the studied agency. With respect to Lee's (1991) model, this understanding represented my second-level interpretation of participant understandings. The analysis of these data, primarily taped transcripts and electronic mail, conformed to the canons of rigorous research as recommended by qualitative researchers (Miles & Huberman, 1994; Silverman, 1993).

Researchers espousing positivistic assumptions would likely be uncomfortable with such a naturalistic interviewing technique. How could I claim to control for personal biases and my influence on study participants? After all, I was entering the study with preconceived notions. I had 15 years of federal IT management experience. I had spent almost five years immersed in analyzing federal IT management policies and had read widely in the academic and practitioner literature concerning management and IT management. I had an emotional commitment to understanding the research question.

Consistent with a non-positivist approach to research, I recognized but did not seek to overtly control for researcher bias. Strauss (1987) warns against squashing experiential data in an attempt to minimize bias. "Mine your experience," he admonishes researchers. "There is potential gold there!" (p. 11). This idea is central to understanding non-positivist paradigms. I was not attempting to capture an unsullied representation of some external social reality. Rather I was constructing an understanding "with" the study participants.

The employment of multiple data collection and analysis methods provided the anticipated benefits of triangulation in the positivist sense of capturing "a more complete, *holistic*, and contextual portrayal of the unit(s) under study" (Jick, 1979, p. 603).[7] However, that benefit was minor in comparison to the benefits derived from not imposing my predetermined constructs on the participants. My results were similar to those reported by Trauth and Jessup (2000): The adoption of a non-positivist research perspective, as related to the application of qualitative methods, provided me access to phenomena and relationships I had not been seeking. In this case, the analysis interview data revealed the pivotal role that organizational culture played in determining the extent and quality of agency policy-compliance actions.

I had not insisted that study participants respond to theoretically imposed and sterilely operationalized constructs. Due to the non-positivist approach, the participants were able to identify their concerns in their own vocabulary. Because the findings were grounded in participant experience, the research product was relevant to the study participants[8] and much more likely to be relevant to practitioners who have had similar experiences. This was not simply the application of qualitative techniques applied within a positivist framework. The research process involved the study participants and researcher in a mutual creation of meaning that was quite different from uncovering a set of lawful relationships implied by exploratory research conducted under a positivistic paradigm.

CONCLUSIONS AND IMPLICATIONS

One could declare success with an application of non-positivist-oriented research as just described. Yet, I am not prepared to disavow research methods typically associated with neo-positivist epistemology and ontology. As a practitioner, I believe that non-positivists err to the extent that they adopt a radically constructivist stance, discounting completely the notion of objectivity and value neutrality and holding all knowledge to be paradigm-dependent. Human experience suggests the accuracy of the statement, "There is a world of empirical reality out there. The way we perceive and understand that world is largely up to us, but the world does not tolerate all understandings of it equally" (Kirk & Miller, 1986, p. 11). There do appear to be objective consequences to actions taken on the basis of our human understandings and misunderstandings of our social environment. This common sense view is echoed by Giddens's (1984, p. 343) assertion that:

> *Social life is in many respects not an intentional product of its constituent actors, in spite of the fact that day-to-day conduct is chronically carried on in a purposive fashion. It is in the study of unintended consequences of action that ... some of the most distinctive acts of social science are to be found.*

The advantage of Lee's (1991) multi-paradigm framework is that it recognizes that understandings gained through interpretivist analysis might provide a basis for developing testable propositions. Such propositions do not necessitate a belief in universal laws of social behavior. However, to the extent that evidence can be found supporting the validity of such propositions in other organizational settings, researchers may be able to provide useful insights or suggest changes in behavior beneficial to an organization and its stakeholders. The methods associated with positivism lend credibility to an assertion that insights obtained in one context might be usefully generalized or transferred, thus increasing the relevancy of those research findings to the practitioner community.

One can reject a correspondence theory of reality while accepting that individual and organizational behaviors often have predictable consequences. Positivist-oriented research techniques force researchers to consider sources of error that inevitably creep into human understanding, error that might well be defined in reference to instances when a person's behavior resulted in consequences inconsistent with his/her intent or interests. Considerable behavioral research has demonstrated a human predilection for certain types of judgmental errors (e.g., selective perception, illusion of control, prior hypothesis bias, adjustment and anchoring) that can lead to behavior in conflict with an individual's own goals or intentions, be that individual a practitioner or a researcher (Hogarth, 1981; Kleinmuntz, 1990; Tversky & Kahneman, 1974; Wright, 1980). Giddens (1984, p. 339) recognizes the issue in his distinction between "credibility criteria" and "validity criteria":

Credibility criteria refer to criteria, hermeneutic in character, used to indicate how the grasping of an actor's reasons illuminates exactly what they are doing in light of those reasons. Validity criteria concern criteria of factual evidence and theoretical understanding employed by the social sciences in the assessment of reasons as good reasons.

Thus, apprehending the actor's authentic reasons or beliefs as a motivation for action is distinct from assessing the accuracy of those reasons with respect to the consequences of that action. Both types of criteria are relevant to social theorizing. While hermeneutic methods pertain to ascertaining an actor's reasons, neo-positivist methods can still contribute to establishing the validity of those beliefs.

Furthermore, Giddens is not alone among social scientists in his recognition of objective and subjective dimensions of social life. Mingers (2001), crediting Habermas, suggests the existence of a multidimensional world—material, social and personal—each dimension having distinct epistemological possibilities. For Mingers, the implication of this perspective is that multi-method, multi-paradigm research designs are required "to deal effectively with the full richness of the real world" (p. 243).

To the extent that one is willing to adopt the perspective that these multiple dimensions impinge upon one another, multiple methods, informed by corresponding ontological and epistemological perspectives, are not simply desirable but necessary for achieving research rigor and relevance within the IS community. The selection of non-positivist approaches to research can improve relevancy by helping to focus the researcher's attention on problems and issues foremost in the minds of study participants as reflected by their speech and behavior. Researchers are not constrained to looking only at what they think they will be able to quantify and measure. While accepting that research necessitates subjective interpretation, the evolving standards for evaluating non-positivist research promise methodological rigor (Kirk & Miller, 1986; Klein & Myers, 1999; Miles & Huberman, 1994; Schultze, 2000), allowing the consumers of such research a means for evaluating the quality and relevance of those subjective interpretations to their own purposes.

Should the understandings gained from non-positivist research lend themselves to formulation as testable propositions, then let us test them. Researchers should not reject methods associated with positivism solely on the basis of epistemological or ontological disagreement. Those methods simply represent another source of data that require rigorous interpretation. Evidence gained through positivist-oriented methods may prove crucial for those researchers wishing to argue for the transferability of their research findings, thus increasing relevancy of the research to the practitioner community.

Falconer and Mackay (2000) have labeled multi-paradigmatic research as a cross-paradigm accommodation and found it to be problematic. They contend that papers which have been cited as exemplars of multi-paradigmatic research "did not address adequately ontological issues and they [the authors of these papers] subordinated non-positivist methods" (p. 1470). It is difficult to discount their fundamental argument regarding the incommensurability of diverse philosophical positions, particularly with respect to realist versus nonrealist ontologies. This remains the dilemma that initiated my philosophical inquiry: Can a social science legitimately endeavor to produce knowledge without holding a philosophically consistent ontology and epistemology?

Happily, more experienced minds than mine have pondered the issue. Again, I find solace in Giddens's perspective (1984, pp. xvii-xviii):

> *The main concern of social theory is the same as that of the social sciences in general: the illumination of concrete processes of social life. To hold that philosophical debates can contribute to this concern is not to suppose that such debates need to be resolved conclusively before worthwhile social research can be initiated. On the contrary, the prosecution of social research can in principle cast light on philosophical controversies just as much as the reverse. In particular, I think it is wrong to slant social theory too unequivocally toward abstract and highly generalized questions of epistemology, as if any significant developments in social science had to await a clear-cut solution to these.*

Giddens's argument appears to parallel that of American pragmatists such as Dewey, James, and Rorty. These philosophers have generally eschewed the search for "truth with a capital *T*," concluding that philosophical questions concerning the "True" nature of reality have little sway on our day-to-day lives (Rorty, 1982).

As referenced above, the paradigm debate has assumed political as well as philosophical dimensions. It is a fair criticism that much positivist-oriented, instrumentalist research is managerialist in orientation. It is a mistake, however, to conflate particular research paradigms with particular sets of political values. For example, if one wishes to pursue a critical research agenda, the identification of causal or structural relationships that could be manipulated consistent with one's emancipatory objectives would seem desirable. Conversely, my use of an interpretivist perspective served instrumental, even managerialist, objectives.

It is not necessary to adopt Giddens's theory of structuration or Rorty's pragmatic philosophy to conclude that, at least within the IS community, the paradigm debate should be depoliticized. Multi-paradigmatic research requires inevitable compromises with purist forms of positivist and non-positivist research traditions. Depoliticizing the debate allows the IS research community to focus its energies on the substantive costs and benefits of these compromises rather than on competing political values where reaching agreement is unlikely.

I do not mean to suggest that all researchers should adopt multi-paradigmatic research designs. Clearly, the research methods selected must be appropriate for the specific phenomenon of inquiry, and it is only logical that some phenomena of interest will align more closely with the subjective or objective dimensions of the social world. Multi-paradigmatic research is neither quick nor easy. High-quality multi-paradigmatic research likely requires a team effort, where the team is comprised of members knowledgeable of and committed to faithful execution of methods associated with the research paradigms employed. As an independent researcher, I must confess that I found conducting multi-paradigmatic research to be a mind-expanding (perhaps even mind-bending) experience. At times, I felt as if my intellectual energy were spread too thin, limiting the depth of analysis I could accomplish. Yet my experience as practitioner/ neophyte researcher suggests that the phenomena of most interest to the practitioner community are complex, necessitating examination of the subjective and objective dimensions of social life.

The IS community would do well to heed Hammersley's (1995) caution that social science researchers must be modest in their expectations regarding the development of instrumental knowledge. Research is rarely able to cover all considerations relevant to social phenomena. Yet, while IS researchers will continue to value knowledge for knowledge's sake and to seek to expand disciplinary knowledge, I believe most IS researchers would subscribe to this sentiment, expressed by British economist Pigou (1920), which calls for increasing research relevance:

> *When a man sets out upon any course of inquiry, the object of this search may be either light or fruit—either knowledge for its own sake or knowledge for the sake of the good things to which it leads. ... There will, I think, be general agreement that in sciences of human society, be their appeal as bearers of light ever so high, it is the promise of fruit and not light that chiefly merits our regard. (p. 34)*

Multi-paradigmatic research may improve our chances of producing both fruit and light.

REFERENCES

Applegate, L. M., & King, J. L. (1999, March). Rigor and relevance: Careers on the line. *MIS Quarterly, 23*(1), 3-16.

Beachboard, J. C. (1999). *Assessing the consequences of federal information technology management policies on federal agency practice.* Unpublished doctoral dissertation, Syracuse University, New York, USA.

Benbaset, I., & Zmud, R. W. (1999, March). Empirical research in information systems: The practice of relevance. *MIS Quarterly, 23*(1), 3-16.

Boynton, A. C., Jacobs, J. C., & Zmud, R. W. (1992). Whose responsibility is IT management? *Sloan Management Review, 33*(4), 32-38.

Boynton, A. C., Zmud, R. W., & Jacobs, G. C. (1994). The influence of IT management practice on IT use in large organizations. *MIS Quarterly, 18*(3), 299-318.

Broadbent, M., & Weill, P. (1997). Management by maxim: How business and IT managers can create IT infrastructures. *Sloan Management Review, 38*(3), 77-92.

Brown, C. V. (1997). Examining the emergence of hybrid IS governance solutions: Evidence from a single case site. *Information Systems Research, 8*(1), 69-94.

Brown, C. V., & Magill, S. L. (1994). Alignment of the IS functions within the enterprise: Toward a model of antecedents. *MIS Quarterly, 18*(4), 371-394.

Churchman, C. W. (1971). *Design of Inquiring Systems: Basic Concepts of Systems and Organizations.* New York: Basic Books.

Coffey, A., & Atkinson, P. (1996). *Making Sense of Qualitative Data.* Thousand Oaks, CA: SAGE.

Creswell, J. W. (1994). *Research Design: Qualitative and Quantitative Approaches.* Thousand Oaks, CA: SAGE.

Denzin, N. K., & Lincoln, Y. S. (1994). *Handbook of Qualitative Research.* Thousand Oaks, CA: SAGE.

DeSanctis, G., & Poole, M. S. (1994). Capturing the complexity in advanced technology use: Adaptive structuration theory. *Organization Science, 5*(2), 121-147.

Ein-Dor, P., & Segev, E. (1982). Organizational context and MIS structure: Some empirical evidence. *MIS Quarterly, 6*(3), 55-68.

Falconer, D. J., & Mackay, D. R. (2000). The myth of multiple methods. In H. M. Chung (Ed.), *Proceedings of the Americas Conference on Information Systems* (Vol. 2, pp. 1467-1473). Long Beach, CA.

Feeny, D. F., & Willcocks, L. (1998). Core IS capabilities for exploiting information technology. *Sloan Management Review, 39*(3), 9-21.

Gage, N. (1989). The paradigm wars and their aftermath: A "historical" research on teaching. *Educational Researcher, 18*, 4-10.

Giddens, A. (1984). *The Constitution of Society.* Berkeley, CA: University of California Press.

Golden, B. R. (1992). The past is the past—or is it? The use of retrospective accounts as indicators of past strategy. *Academy of Management Journal, 35*(4), 848-860.

Guba, E. G., & Lincoln, Y. S. (1994). Competing paradigms in qualitative research. In N. K. Denzin & Y. S. Lincoln (Eds.), *Handbook of Qualitative Research* (pp. 105-117). Thousand Oaks, CA: SAGE.

Hammersley, M. (1995). *The Politics of Social Research.* London: SAGE.

Hogarth, R. M. (1981). Beyond discrete biases: Functional and dysfunctional aspects of judgmental heuristics. *Psychological Bulletin, 92*(2), 197-217.

Huber, G. P., & Power, D. J. (1985). Retrospective reports of strategic-level managers: Guidelines for increasing their accuracy. *Strategic Management Journal, 6*, 171-180.

Jick, T. D. (1979). Mixing quantitative and qualitative methods: Triangulation in action. *Administrative Science Quarterly, 24*(4), 602-611.

Kaplan, B., & Duchon, D. (1988). Combining qualitative methods in information systems research: A case study. *MIS Quarterly, 12*(4), 571-586.

Keil, M. (1995). Pulling the plug: Software project management and the problem of project escalation. *MIS Quarterly, 19*(4), 421-448.

King, J. L. (1983). Centralized versus decentralized computing: Organizational considerations and management options. *Computing Surveys, 15*(4), 319-349.

Kirk, J., & Miller, M. L. (1986). *Reliability and Validity in Qualitative Research.* Newbury Park, CA: SAGE.

Klein, H. K., & Myers, M. D. (1999). A set of principles for conducting and evaluating interpretive field studies in information systems. *MIS Quarterly, 23*(1), 67-93.

Kleinmuntz, B. (1990). Why we still use our heads instead of formulas: Toward an integrative approach. *Psychological Bulletin, 107*(3), 269-310.

Lee, A. S. (1991). Integrating positivist and interpretive approaches to organizational research. *Organizational Science, 2*(4), 342-365.

Lewis, B. (1999). *IS Survival Guide.* Indianapolis, IN: Sams.

Miles, M. B., & Huberman, A. M. (1994). *Qualitative Data Analysis: An Expanded Sourcebook.* Thousand Oaks, CA: SAGE.

Miner, J. B. (1984). The validity and usefulness of theories in an emerging organizational science. *Academy of Management Review, 9*(2), 296-306.

Mingers, J. (2001, September). Combining IS research methods: Toward a pluralist methodology. *Information Systems Research,* 240-259.

Mitroff, I., & Pondy, L. R. (1978). Afterthoughts on the leadership conference. In M. W. J. McCall & M. M. Lombardo (Eds.), *Leadership: Where Else Can We Go?* (pp. 145-149). Durham, NC: Duke University Press.

Orlikowski, W. J. (1992). The duality of technology: Rethinking the concepts of technology in organizations. *Organization Science, 3*(3), 398-427.

Orlikowski, W. J., & Baroudi, J. J. (1991). Studying information technology in organizations: Research approaches and assumptions. *Information Systems Research, 2*(1), 1-28.

Orlikowski, W. J., & Robey, D. (1991). Information technology and the structuring of organizations. *Information Systems Research, 2*(2), 143-169.

Pigou, A. C. (1920). *The Economics of Welfare.* London: MacMillan Press.

Rockart, J. F., Earl, M. J., & Ross, J. W. (1996). Eight imperatives for the new IT organization. *Sloan Management Review, 37*(1), 43-55.

Rorty, R. (1982). *Consequences of pragmatism (Essays 1972-1980).* Minneapolis, MN: University of Minnesota Press.

Ross, J. W., Beath, C. M., & Goodhue, D. L. (1996). Develop long-term competitiveness through IT assets. *Sloan Management Review, 38*(1), 31-42.

Sambamurthy, V., & Zmud, R. W. (1992). *Managing IT for Success: The Empowering Business Partnership.* Morristown, NJ: Financial Executives Research Foundation.

Sambamurthy, V., & Zmud, R. W. (1994). *IT Management Competency Assessment: A Tool for Creating Business Value Through IT.* Morristown, NJ: Financial Executives Research Foundation.

Sambamurthy, V., & Zmud, R. W. (1999, June). Arrangements for information technology governance: A theory of multiple contingencies. *MIS Quarterly*, 261-290.

Sandstrom, A. R., & Sandstrom, P. E. (1995, April). The use and misuse of anthropological methods in library and information science research. *The Library Quarterly*, 161-199.

Schultze, U. (2000, March). A confessional account of an ethnography about knowledge work. *MIS Quarterly*, 3-41.

Schutz, A. (1973). Concept of theory formation in the social sciences. In M. Natanson (Ed.), *Collected Papers* (pp. 48-66). The Hague, The Netherlands: Martinus Nijhoff.

Silverman, D. (1993). *Interpreting Qualitative Data: Methods for Analyzing Talk, Test and Interaction*. London: SAGE.

Strassmann, P. A. (1995). *The Politics of Information Management: Policy Guidelines*. New Canaan, CT: Information Economics Press.

Strauss, A. L. (1987). *Qualitative Analysis for Social Scientists*. Cambridge, UK: Cambridge University Press.

Tavakolian, H. (1989, September). Linking the information technology structure with organizational competitive strategy: A survey. *MIS Quarterly*, 309-317.

Trauth, E. M., & Jessup, L. M. (2000). Understanding computer-mediated discussions: Positivist and interpretivist analysis of group support system use. *MIS Quarterly*, *24*(1), 43-79.

Turner, J. H. (1986). *The Structure of Sociological Theory*. Belmont, CA: Wadsworth.

Tversky, A., & Kahneman, D. (1974). Judgment under uncertainty: Heuristics and biases. *Science*, *185*, 1124-1131.

Van Maanen, J. (1988). *Tales of the Field: On Writing Ethnography*. Chicago, IL: University of Chicago Press.

Van Schaik, E. A. (1985). *A Management System for the Information Business*. Englewood Cliffs, NJ: Prentice Hall.

Walsham, G. (1995). The emergence of interpretivism in IS research. *Information Systems Research*, *6*(4), 376-394.

Wright, W. F. (1980). Cognitive information processing biases: Implications for producers and users of financial information. *Decision Sciences*, *11*, 284-298.

Zmud, R. W. (1984). An examination of "push-pull" theory applied to process innovation in knowledge work. *Management Science*, *30*, 727-738.

Zmud, R. W. (1996). Editor's comments: On rigor and relevance. *MIS Quarterly*, *20*(3), xxxvii-xxxix.

Zmud, R. W., Boynton, A. C., & Jacobs, G. C. (1989). An examination of managerial strategies for increasing information technology penetration in organizations. In J. I. DeGross, J. C. Henderson, & R. Konsynski (Eds.), *Proceedings of the Ninth International Conference on Information Systems* (pp. 24-44). Boston, MA.

ENDNOTES

[1]   Actually, the term *demise* may not be entirely correct. Within the Department of Defense, old projects rarely die. More often, contracts are cancelled, the acronym is changed, and a new approach is attempted.

2   I am using the term *non-positivist* as a shorthand means of referencing a range of research traditions including constructivism, critical theory, feminist theory, interpretivism, phenomenology, post-modernism, etc.

3   There were studies that, with respect to my interests, provided a better balance of rigor and relevance (Boynton, Zmud, & Jacobs, 1994; Keil, 1995; Sambamurthy & Zmud, 1992, 1994; Zmud, Boynton, & Jacobs, 1989).

4   While emotions may run high on both sides, I am not comfortable using the "war" metaphor to describe this debate.

5   The case concerns a practitioner-turned-researcher who was dissuaded from pursuing her true interests and encouraged to conduct more traditional research but found it difficult to get that traditional research published because of problems with her study sample and the topic's no longer being considered "hot."

6   Lee identifies this framework as being an elaboration on first- and second-level constructs proposed by Schutz (1973).

7   The validity of triangulation is highly contested. See Coffey and Atkinson (1996), Silverman (1993), and Falconer and Mackay (2000).

8   Key participants completed a short survey concerning the study findings generated from the structured surveys and qualitative data analysis. Using a 7-point scale in which a "1" indicated strong disagreement and a "7" indicated strong agreement, the participants indicated strong agreement (6.8) with the statement that the qualitative findings reported "represent issues significant enough to merit further consideration within the bureau" (Beachboard, 1999, p. 184).

SECTION III

VIRTUAL
RESEARCH ISSUES

Chapter IX

Updating Ethnography to Investigate Contemporary Organizational Forms

Julie Rennecker
Case Western Reserve University, USA

ABSTRACT

The emergence of innovative organizational configurations enabled by recent advances in information and communication technology represent new and expanding venues for information systems research. At the same time, the distributed, dynamic nature of these new work forms challenge the premises and practices of traditional information systems research approaches. In this chapter, I advocate ethnography as a somewhat counterintuitive but valuable approach to the study of virtual work groups or, more specifically, virtual project teams. While the speed, fluidity, and physical distribution of virtual project teams pose unique challenges to ethnographic inquiry, it is these very characteristics that beg for the in situ *scrutiny that only ethnography can provide. The mission of this chapter is three-fold: I intend to contribute to prior efforts to demystify ethnographic research generally, to illustrate its applicability to emerging venues of IS research, and to advocate for more ethnographic studies of virtual project teams as an essential step in understanding the socio-technical infrastructure needed to support them. Topics covered include the rationale for adopting an ethnographic approach to the study of virtual project groups, modifications to traditional practice, and the challenges, risks, and benefits one can expect to meet along the way. In addition, the chapter discusses different models for conducting multi-site studies and their advantages and limitations with respect to studying virtual project teams.*

INTRODUCTION

The growing prevalence of technology-mediated, geographically distributed work configurations in contemporary organizations challenges the premises and practices of many revered methods for studying organizational phenomena. Today's professionals may work more closely with coworkers they rarely see than with the occupant of an adjacent desk. Their daily activities may be paced by circumstances, demands, and events external to their own particular work location (Ruhleder, 2000) yet simultaneously influenced by local practical and social conditions undisclosed and invisible to remote collaborators (Cramton, 2001; Rennecker, 2001). As work bridges more, and more diverse, contexts, it becomes increasingly important to understand how the nature of these contexts shapes the work that results. In the case of distributed, technology-mediated work forms, comprehension of the work practices of either an individual worker or a technology-mediated collective requires methods that take into account both contextual levels—the material and the virtual (see chapter 10)—and the tensions between them (Boland, 2002; House, Rousseau, & Thomas-Hunt, 1995).

Using virtual teams as the focal example, this chapter illustrates the efficacy of ethnography, with minor modifications in practice, as a viable and valuable approach to the study of these technology-enabled work configurations. While the speed, fluidity, and physical distribution of virtual project teams pose unique challenges to ethnographic inquiry (Hine, 2000; see also chapter 10), it is these very characteristics that beg for the in situ scrutiny that only ethnography can provide (Jordan, 1996; Rennecker, 2001; Ruhleder, 2000).

The chapter begins with an explication of the features of virtual work arrangements that make them ripe candidates for ethnographic exploration. Then a sketch of the distinguishing features of traditional ethnographic practice serves as backdrop for describing the tactical modifications called for in the study of distributed work environments (Van Maanen, 1988; Hine, 2000). Examples from a 23-month participant-observation study of a multi-organizational virtual team in the automotive industry illustrate the unanticipated challenges, benefits, and inherent limitations of taking this approach. Next I outline alternative models for conducting multisite field research represented in the literature and discuss their advantages and limitations for ethnographic studies of virtual project teams. Finally, I close with words of both caution and optimism.

Despite the number of texts written on the subject, ethnographers, as a lot, are typically averse to providing procedural direction for doing ethnographic research (Hine, 2000). The ethnographic approach is characterized by an ethos of opportunism and openness to emergent circumstances. Though this chapter explores the challenges and opportunities of both macro and micro design choices in the study of virtual project teams, it is not intended as a recipe to replace researcher judgment, resourcefulness, or improvisation. Rather, I hope that it evokes continued thought, debate, and experimentation to further the extension and adaptation of ethnographic methods to contemporary social forms and questions.

VIRTUAL WORK CONFIGURATIONS

Two features distinguishing virtual work configurations from "traditional" ones and posing new challenges for traditional research methodologies are the participants' geographic distribution and their primary reliance on technology-mediated communication for task-related interaction (Hinds & Bailey, 2000; Jarvenpaa & Leidner, 1999; Maznevski & Chudoba, 2000; Saunders & Ahuja, 2000). One consequence of the members' physical dispersion that makes virtual work configurations both interesting and challenging from an ethnographic perspective is the members' practical and social embeddedness in multiple, disparate work contexts. Numerous studies have detailed the significance of context for both the enactment and the interpretation of social action (Barker, 1968; Barley, 1986; Garfinkel, 1967/1984; Goffman, 1959; Orlikowski, 2000; Suchman, 1987). According to these studies, social actors draw upon preexisting meaning systems, practice routines, and available resources to enact socially meaningful behavior—i.e., intelligible and appropriate—and to interpret the actions of others. In virtual work configurations, the members' situation in their respective work contexts results in proximity to, interaction with, and dependence upon colocated coworkers and local resources for the conduct of their work on virtual group tasks (Barrett, 2000; Klein & Barrett, 2000; Rennecker, 2001). In addition, each local world is characterized by locally particular activity cycles and heuristics for prioritizing projects that also influence a virtual group member's capacity to contribute to the collective effort.

Cramton (2001) used the term "hidden profile" to describe the ubiquity and potency of these local, often invisible influences on the nature and timing of virtual team members' project-related actions. Though Weisband (2002) found that conflict and coordination breakdowns stemming from contextual differences across sites could be minimized through contextual information exchange, other studies indicate that virtual team members' contribution to and participation in a virtual group is integrally shaped by their situation in their local contexts in ways that are often discursively unavailable to the participants themselves (Gluesing, 1995; Rennecker, 2001; Sole & Edmondson, 2001).

Ethnographic methods are particularly well-suited for investigating the constitution of these situated actions and their relationship to team-level phenomena. To date, experiments, surveys, and interviews analyzed by a variety of methods have contributed significantly to our understanding of virtual work practices. Yet, a great deal remains to be learned regarding the significance of virtual team members' unique situation in their respective local contexts for designing, managing, and participating in virtual collaborative work.

TRADITIONAL ETHNOGRAPHIC PRACTICE

The practice of ethnography represents a commitment to understanding, representing, and making intelligible to "outsiders" the actions of a studied group in terms of "cultural patterning" (Wolcott, 1990, p. 48). Students of culture work out of an ontological stance that socially constructed meanings inform human action and that these meaning systems represent locally particular and dynamic, yet enduring, sense-making responses to the exigencies of daily life. The methodological traditions reflect this ontological stance.

The sine qua non of ethnographic methods include the researcher's full-time *immersion in the field* for an extended period of time (Schwartzman, 1993; Stewart, 1998; Van Maanen, 1988), and data collection through *participant-observation*. The typical study begins with the researcher arriving at a strange location, "suitcase in hand, prepared for a long stay" (Van Maanen, 1995, 1997). During this stay, the researcher attempts to adopt a socially legitimate participant role in order to both diminish her salience as a "researcher" and to acquire tacit cultural knowledge through the socialization processes associated with the role. A role that allows the researcher to contribute to the studied group can help to compensate the group members in some small way for the inconvenience of her presence (Van Maanen, 1988; Van Maanen & Kolb, 1985).

Data collection efforts focus on *learning* about and *understanding* the world of the "foreign" others from the "native's point of view" (Agar, 1996; Geertz, 1973; Spradley, 1979;). This generally involves in situ observations and close interactions with the members of the studied group during their normal work activities (Van Maanen, 1988). Relying more on conversations than interviews, the ethnographer observes and asks questions in the context of ongoing action. When in situ questioning is too obtrusive, "primary informants" fill the void by providing ex post explanations as well as accuracy checks on the ethnographer's interpretations of her observations. The ethnographer also takes advantage of other emergent and elicited sources of data—activity logs, formal and informal documents circulated in the studied group, etc. Finally, the ethnographer acts as a cultural translator, producing a written representation of the studied culture in a language intelligible to the expected readers. Applying this approach to the study of a virtual work group poses several challenges.

ADAPTING ETHNOGRAPHY
FOR THE DISTRIBUTED "FIELD"

"People who write about methodology often forget that it is a matter of strategy, not of morals." (Homans, 1950, p. 330)

The model of the traditional ethnographic process sketched in the previous section poses a number of design and process dilemmas for the ethnographer studying a presumably "placeless" and "boundaryless" phenomenon. For instance, where is the "field" in which she is to immerse herself? How long should she stay once she arrives? What role shall she play? What should she "observe" if the participants never meet (Hine, 2000)?

In this section, I use my own 23-month participant-observation study of a multi-organizational virtual team in the automotive industry to illustrate one approach to reconciling the disparities between ethnographic practice standards and the practical demands of studying a distributed collective. Later, I consider alternative approaches to conducting multisite ethnographies, but here I assume a solo ethnographer, studying a distributed, transient phenomenon, challenged by her inability to be in more than one place at a time.

Going to the "Field"

After gaining access to one or more teams, the question confronting the ethnographer, "suitcase in hand" (Van Maanen, 1995), is Where is the field? With regard to organizational ethnographies, Van Maanen (1995, 1993) has said "the field resides in offices, in meetings rooms, in factories … in corridors, or *wherever work is done* [italics added]." Assuming work will be done within individual members' workspaces, in collective forums, and in conversations among members, a comprehensive definition of the field includes the combination of the members' local work sites, team meetings (whether face-to-face or technology-mediated), and extra-meeting communication. I address each arena in turn.

Site Visits

The scheduling puzzle: The first decisions with respect to making site visits are where to begin and how to sequence the visits thereafter. Despite the substantive, methodological, and symbolic significance of these choices, the researcher may find she has limited control over them. Virtual project teams offer an extreme scheduling challenge because they are generally time-bound and rapidly paced, with the "hub" of the project work shifting frequently among sites. The heuristics employed to make this decision should be informed by a combination of ethnographic principles and theory regarding the focal phenomenon. Nonetheless, constraints on the researcher's time, funds, or other resources, as well as team members' preferences and schedules, will undoubtedly influence her plans.

The emergence of my own visit schedule is telling. Though guided by several objectives, the schedule in practice represented a continuously negotiated achievement contingent on a number of factors over which I had no control. First, guided by traditional ethnographic practice, I wanted to stay long enough in each site during each visit to mitigate the novelty of my presence. Second, guided by research in team development, I wanted to visit each site both before and after the midpoint (Gersick, 1988) to minimize the risk of obtaining a distorted impression peculiar to the project phase. For similar reasons, I wanted to visit each organization at different times in the calendar year so that no single annual cycle (Ancona & Chong, 1997; McGrath, Kelly, & Machatka, 1984)— such as budget allocation processes—unduly shaped my interpretations. Finally, without compromising the other goals, I also wanted to schedule visits to each site to coincide with times when project activities would be at the forefront there. Additional and unanticipated factors came into play, however. Travel budget limits required that I visit all the European sites in sequence. Then the combination of scheduled face-to-face team meetings, holidays, and individual vacation schedules influenced the timing of that trip so that I first visited several sites after the midpoint had passed. In addition, three of the organizations reorganized during the first year of the study, changing several members' organizational roles. In one case, an organization announced a corporate-wide restructuring, significantly affecting everyone I was to observe, four days prior to my first visit.

Negotiating access—over and over and over again!: Gaining access to any work group generally requires significant patience, persistence, and diplomacy (Van Maanen, 1995). Increasing the number of sites only multiplies the challenges. Though a manager may approve access to a virtual group or team, access to each site will be negotiated separately. In addition, all field-workers know that formal and practical access are not one and the same. Once on site, "backstage" access (Goffman, 1959; Kunda, 1992) to the day-to-day activities comprising a team member's workday typically occurs through a gradual development of trust through ongoing contact with the participants. The "virtual ethnographer's" limited time in each site and movement between sites complicate this process.

In order to achieve more than superficial access in each site, the ethnographer needs to rapidly establish rapport with the members, then maintain contact between visits to continue building the relationship. For this reason, I suggest that the study design include a brief "get acquainted" visit to each site before the extended site visits begin, allowing the researcher to make contact with at least one member at each site willing to act as key informant when she is away. While not fully substituting for in-person observation and conversations, these between visit exchanges do contribute to researcher-participant relationship development, facilitating access when the researcher is on site.

Confidentiality: The development and maintenance of researcher-participant relationships hinges on the ethnographer's demonstrated trustworthiness and commitment to maintaining confidentiality. The virtual ethnographer must recognize and respect that the boundaries crossed in her travels among sites are not just geographical but also identity and power perimeters, only semipermeable to information. If the team is multi-organizational, the information that can be exchanged among sites may also be regulated by law, as in the United States, where competitors are restricted to the exchange of "pre-competitive" information. In addition, however, image and reputation play an important role in organizational strategy and interorganizational relationships. Organizations have a great deal at stake in being perceived as "competent," "cutting edge," "reliable," and so forth by other organizations in their field, both competitors and customers. Even in an intra-organizational team, participants exhibit a great degree of selectivity regarding what information to share with whom, when, and under what circumstances as matters of both personal and subunit strategy. The automotive team members' assurances to coworkers outside the project, "It's okay. She won't say anything," illustrated their attention to and maintenance of information boundaries.

Nonetheless, the participants will likely be curious about the other sites and see the ethnographer as a handy informant. Well-established relationships among individuals and subunits within an organization and among organizations within an industry, however, represent the complex achievements of years of interaction and negotiation. Consequently, it is important, both for the ethnographer's reputation and for the maintenance of the social system, to resist the urge to be "helpful" by sharing even seemingly benign information across sites. In the automotive study, the members occasionally posed what I believed to be innocent queries about the other sites, representing either sincere curiosity or a genuine information need. For instance, "How many people do they have working on this?" "Do they do this like we do?" and "Do you think Bill knows about this?" Artfully dodging these questions explicitly demonstrated commitment to maintaining confidentiality and avoided making inadvertent interventions in an established social order.

Confidentiality is an important consideration in all fieldwork. In the case of geographically distributed teams, these concerns are multiplied by the number of boundaries crossed. The ethnographer's demonstrated sensitivity to and regard for the participants' construction of their worlds through conscientious maintenance of confidentiality will go a long way to facilitating more rapid access to the "backstage" dimensions of their work.

Technology-Mediated Meetings

Virtual groups typically meet via a variety and combination of media. Many groups may initially or occasionally meet face-to-face, but, for the most part, these groups will, by necessity, meet via audio, video-, or computer conferencing.

Participating: Unlike a face-to-face meeting in a particular location, the virtual group ethnographer is confronted with a dilemma of *what* to observe and *how* to participate. A rule of thumb in any field setting is to do what a native in your position would do (Van Maanen, classroom discussion, Fall 1995). If the team consists of a collection of colocated subgroups, then the ethnographer could simply join one of them. If, on the other hand, the group is composed of dispersed individuals, the researcher might need to locate her own videoconferencing facilities or dial into either an audio or computer conference from her own work site. While this "remote" approach provides an opportunity for the ethnographer to experience team meetings from the "native point of view" (Geertz, 1973) of a solitary, remote team member, it can also be useful for the ethnographer to join one of the team members to observe her use of technology, nonverbal responses to meeting events, and how that member's context influences participation in the team meeting.

Observing team meetings from multiple vantage points will provide for the most comprehensive understanding of both the team dynamics and the contextual influences on virtual group interaction. For instance, I observed videoconference meetings from both a U.S. and a German conference room. By joining one of the subgroups rather than "dialing in" remotely, I observed the colocated members discussing the meanings of terms used by "the other side" and heard comments revealing hidden conflicts that were not audible on the meeting audiotape. In addition, being physically present allows access to the remotely inaccessible "meeting after the meeting" conversations among colocated coworkers.

Data quality: In the technology-mediated environment, data quality varies significantly between the ethnographer's multisensory observations of copresent others and her records of the audible and visible traces of their remote collaborators. The use of technology-mediated communication channels expands the "backstage" (Goffman, 1959) arena, allowing members to participate simultaneously in front stage and backstage interactions, such as when team members participate in a technology-mediated meeting and simultaneously communicate with colocated coworkers via means invisible and inaudible to their remote collaborators. Consequently, the ethnographer will gain a more complex view of any copresent participants than would be available in a face-to-face meeting, but a more partial view of the remote participants. Two tactics that will help to mitigate distortion include rotating among meeting observation sites, which may occur naturally during site visits, and following up with remote meeting participants via telephone after each meeting.

In geographically bounded social groups, the ethnographer can often rely on serendipity and contact redundancies to provide opportunities to fill gaps in understanding and to triangulate among data sources. The physical distribution of members all but eliminates such opportunities, so the ethnographer needs to create opportunities by maintaining regular contact with remote participants. In the case of team meetings, this is best done immediately after the meeting when the events of the meeting will be fresh in their minds.

Technology-Mediated Communication

The third component of the "field" as I have defined it here, technology-mediated communication outside team meetings, may pose either the greatest challenge or the greatest boon to the ethnographer's data collection efforts, depending upon the affordances of the technology employed and the members' use practices. While no ethnographer, even in geographically-bounded settings, can be omnipresent, the redundancies afforded by colocation mean that others' references to and recounting of missed conversations allow the ethnographer to track the progress of a project or decision and maintain awareness of the dynamics within a group. In distributed groups where e-mail and telephone conversations replace hallway chats, few such redundancies exist.

If the members of a virtual team work for the same organization or communicate via an application installed on a common server, the technology can archive the electronic exchanges among members. If the members work in different organizations or within different firewall-protected divisions within the same organization and do not use a common server, creating such an archive may be more difficult both technically and politically. If it is possible to create such an archive, electronic mail interaction is a boon to the ethnographer's data collection, providing access to more conversations than she could have possibly witnessed in person, even if the members were colocated. In the absence of a computer-generated archive, however, the ethnographer must depend upon the (variable) goodwill and mindfulness of the participants to include her in the distribution.

In the automotive study, the members were most conscientious about including me in their message distribution when I was visiting their own site but would eventually forget when they were no longer seeing me on a daily basis. Despite the partial nature of the resulting archive, it did include a series of exchanges that revealed an otherwise hidden conflict between two sites and another series of technical messages between two managers from different organizations that revealed a professional friendship explaining some of the intra-group dynamics observed in team meetings. So even a partial archive can be helpful.

Information and communication technologies provide a practical channel for collaborative work among physically and temporally dispersed workers, thus constituting an important dimension of the field. However, the unpredictable, invisible, and ephemeral nature of technology-mediated interactions makes them difficult to observe unless the technologies themselves archive these interactions.

Summary: The Field

The combination of geographic distribution and technology-mediated communication that characterizes virtual project teams results in a more complicated and fragmented "field" for the ethnographer to explore than in a traditional place-based study. Through the combination of site visits, team meeting participation, and monitoring of the team's extra-meeting interactions, she "immerses" herself in the project group and its activities rather than in any particular locale. In the end, the virtual team ethnographer's account, like all accounts, will be a partial one (Hine, 2000; Van Maanen, 1988), and she will likely come away with a more comprehensive understanding of the project as a whole than any of the other team members, but with a more limited perspective on each of the participating sites than its inhabitants.

ESTABLISHING A PARTICIPANT ROLE

Participation in the studied group complements the ethnographer's observation of in situ activities. Participation gives the ethnographer firsthand experience with the practical, emotional, and political tensions managed by the natives on a day-to-day basis to better understand their operating logics. The nature of the community of study will determine "legitimate" participant roles that allow the researcher to fit into the fabric of day-to-day life. The members' receptivity to outsiders, preconceptions of gender-appropriate activities, and practical task needs will all influence the roles they make available and the ones they withhold. In the absence of a designated role, the natives may assign her a de facto role such as "spy," "fly on the wall," or "therapist"—better to find a legitimate contributing identity.

By facilitating greater integration into the community of study, the participant role also helps the ethnographer to gain better access than would be granted a pure observer. The roles of "student" or "apprentice" (Van Maanen & Kolb, 1985) can be particularly effective. If the nature of the work or the study design precludes the apprentice role, any helpful but noninterventionist role will suffice, the more integrated with the workers' actual tasks, the better. For instance, during my time with the automotive team, my roles included writing the draft version of team meeting minutes, writing a literature review of the risks of human exposure to the new technology, doing impromptu clerical tasks, translating English for the international members, and generally being an "extra set of hands" as the occasion warranted.

The study design and team configuration both influence the degree of field fragmentation with which the ethnographer must contend in identifying participant roles. The solo researcher approach to the study of a multisite, time-bound virtual project team obviously represents an extreme case but one useful for foregrounding the range of challenges likely to be encountered in the ethnographic study of contemporary work configurations. For instance, a decision to visit multiple sites more than once in order to be present during different stages of a project and at different times of the calendar year means relatively short stays at any single site with longer periods between visits while observing at the other sites. Intermittent presence limits the researcher's role options to jobs that require little training, can be done intermittently, or can be done remotely as well as in person.

Adopting a local role at each site introduces another complication common in multisite studies: convergence of disharmonic personae (Marcus, 1995; Martin, 1992). As the researcher adapts herself to each environment, she occupies a certain position in the group relative to the other members—e.g., more or less intimate, higher or lower status, more or less active, etc. If the researcher comes into simultaneous face-to-face contact with participants from different sites, such as in a face-to-face meeting, or if a participant from one site initiates informal interaction with the ethnographer in a virtual forum, such as an audio or computer conference, contradictions between the personae evoked by the interaction and the one assumed by the other members may create tension for the ethnographer and skepticism for the members regarding her authenticity. For example, in face-to-face meetings in the automotive study, the participants tended to sit in their locational subgroups. At one meeting, each of the groups assumed I would sit next to them. Once the meeting began, the groups on either side included me in inside jokes about the other sites, creating an awkward situation for me of wanting to honor my relationships with both the instigator and the targets of the humor.

In sum, ethnographers are always challenged to find a socially appropriate role that allows them to participate in and observe the social group under study with minimal intrusiveness. The study of a geographically distributed team amplifies this challenge by multiplying the number of groups in which the ethnographer participates yet limiting the time spent with any single group, thus narrowing the available role options. In addition, the researcher only partially controls the roles she assumes, and the resulting portfolio of "characters" she plays may be rife with contradictions.

ALTERNATIVE RESEARCH DESIGNS

So far I have described the modifications to traditional ethnographic practice called for in the case of a solo ethnographer studying a time-bound virtual project team. In this section I outline alternative models for conducting multisite ethnographic studies generally and discuss their relative challenges and benefits for the study of virtual project teams. The models described include *single-cycle solo series, concurrent solo, multi-cycle solo/concurrent hybrid*, and *concurrent team* designs. I compare the models based on their implications for process loss, data quality, length of stay per visit, relational complexity, and analytic synergy. The comparisons are summarized in Table 1.

Single-cycle solo series model: In the single-cycle series model, the researcher visits each site once in series. This design has several advantages for the study of a virtual team. Because the researcher only visits each site once, she spends less time traveling between sites, scheduling visits, and transitioning in and out of sites. In addition, for a given study length, each site visit can be longer than if she were to visit each site multiple times, potentially enhancing her integration into each local community. Finally, this design involves lower relational complexity than ones that engage the researcher in multiple sites simultaneously. The "relational complexity" of a situation for a particular actor refers to the number of different people and different groups of people with whom the actor must interact (Brodt, DeSanctis, & Emery, 2002). In the single-cycle series model, the researcher's "participant" status is limited to the role she assumes at

Table 1. Comparison of Multisite Ethnographic Research Designs for Studying Virtual Project Teams.

Model	Description	Advantages	Challenges & Limitations	Examples
Single-cycle series—solo	Researcher visits sites once in series.	• low process loss • longer site visits[+] • low relational complexity	• single-stage access • no repeat observation opportunity • low analytic synergy in the field	Orlikowski (1988) Star and Ruhleder (1996)
Concurrent—solo	Study sites in sufficient proximity to allow visits to multiple sites during same calendar period (e.g., alternating days, split days, etc.).	• low process loss • longer site visits (calendar time) • access to multiple sites during same project stages • access to same site across multiple project stages • high analytic synergy	• persistent salience of researcher's involvement in other sites → integration difficult if inter-site relationships competitive (i.e., multi-org team) • high relational complexity	Barley (1986) Schultze (1999)
Multi-cycle series/concurrent hybrid—solo	Serial site visits coupled with ongoing communication with non-visit sites.	• access to same site in multiple project stages • contact with multiple sites during same project stage • high analytic synergy	• high process loss • shorter site visits • high relational complexity	Gluesing (1995) Barrett (2000) Rennecker (2001)
Concurrent—team	Multiple researchers, each conducts a single-site ethnography. Cross-site communication is among researchers.	• low *logistical* process losses • optimal site visit lengths • low relational complexity • access to same site in multiple project stages • indirect access to multiple sites in same project stages	• potential loss of data consistency due to researcher variation • higher *analysis* process costs • overwhelm team with researcher presence	Majchrzak et al. (2000)

[+] *Comparative advantages and limitations assume the same fixed time frame.*

the visit site and whatever team role she may have taken on, uncomplicated by the continuation of participant roles from previously visited sites. While team meetings provide ongoing contact with all team members, the researcher's direct responsibilities and interdependencies would be limited primarily to the current visit site.

The limitations of this model for studying virtual teams center on data quality and analytic synergy. Because the researcher visits each site only once, she loses the analytic synergy of revisiting each site with new sensitivities developed in the other sites. In addition, the single visit, by definition, constrains her data to a single project stage (depending upon the project pace) and a single portion of the calendar year. Besides the potential interpretive distortions regarding the data on any single site, this design also limits cross-site comparisons to those phenomena unaffected by project stage or calendar year, which may be difficult to discern in the absence of within site comparative data.

Examples of this model include Orlikowski's (1988) study of CASE tools implementation and Star and Ruhleder's (1996) study of the WORM community. This design would also be appropriate for the study of a serial phenomenon in which focal activities shift from one community to the next, with the researcher following the product, idea, issue, conflict, or process through these activity stages (Hine, 2000; Marcus, 1995). However, the single-cycle model poses significant threats to data quality for the investigation of many phenomena of interest in time-bound virtual project teams, such as technology use over time and the consequences of local change on team members' contributions to the virtual team.

Concurrent solo model: In the concurrent solo model, the researcher studies two or more sites in sufficient physical proximity that she is able to visit the sites during the same calendar period, for instance, by alternating days or weeks between sites over several months. This model would not be practical for widely distributed virtual teams, but for virtual teams with two or more sites within some reasonable distance that the researcher can move between them without significant loss of field time, this model offers several advantages.

First, this model entails minimal process losses. After arranging the logistics for the initial entry into each site, the available research time is spent being *in* the field rather than transitioning in and out of it. Besides saving time and minimizing distraction, this model is a boon to data quality because the researcher stays in each site over a longer period of time. Longer stays provide an opportunity for greater integration in the studied communities. In addition, this model enables her to observe *more than one* site during the *same* project stage and phases of the calendar year as well as observe *each site* in *more than one* project stage and more than one phase of the calendar year. Finally, alternating visits between sites in such close temporal proximity heightens the potential for analytic synergy, allowing sensitivities developed in one site to be immediately employed in her investigation of the other site(s).

For the study of a virtual team, this model has two main drawbacks. First, depending upon the nature of the interdependencies across sites, the participants may be sensitive to the ethnographer's concurrent "membership" in the "other" site, regarding her as one of "them," and, consequently, may be more reluctant to grant her backstage access. In addition, the simultaneous engagement at the "participant" level in multiple sites places a significant relational burden on the researcher. The greater the number of communities to which the researcher believes herself to be accountable, the greater the relational complexity.

Examples of the concurrent solo model include Barley's (1986) study of the social change "occasioned" by the implementation of CT scanners at two different hospitals and Schultze's (2000) study of outsourced systems administrators. Relative to the other models for multisite studies, this approach offers optimum data quality and minimal logistical hassles. Its usefulness for the study of virtual teams, however, will be determined by the team's physical distribution. For instance, a researcher might consider this design to study an automotive design team consisting of several team members or subgroups within a 20-minute drive of one another in the Detroit area.

Multi-cycle solo/concurrent hybrid model: Using this model, the researcher visits each site more than once in series while maintaining technology-mediated contact with key informants between visits. The bulk of this chapter has been devoted to elaborating this approach, but here I recap the advantages and disadvantages relative to the other multisite study designs.

In terms of data quality, this design offers the benefits of access to both the same site in different project stages and at different times in the calendar year and to multiple sites during the same project stage and time period. In addition, the researcher's return to each site at least once after having been to all the sites facilitates analytic synergy.

Nonetheless, these benefits come at significant cost relative to the concurrent model. First, the process losses are staggering. Time that more stationary researchers might spend writing up notes or resting, the traveling ethnographer will likely spend packing, unpacking, coordinating travel, shuttling between planes, trains, and automobiles, and finding her way to her new home, new site, new desk, new grocery, etc. Then reviewing her notes upon leaving the site, she will no doubt identify new questions that do not lend themselves to an e-mail exchange with her informant and that may no longer be easily answerable upon her return. Finally, the relational complexity can be daunting.

The solo researcher model is not for the faint of heart, body, or mind. It is physically and potentially emotionally taxing. Upon return from the first round of visits in the automotive study, a friend of mine observed, "It's like starting a new job every six weeks in a new city with no friends and no help." Though the second round of visits was easier, the challenges of mobility should be taken into consideration when planning such a study.

Concurrent team model: In the concurrent team model, multiple researchers, each conducting a single-site ethnography, integrate and triangulate their data across sites to develop a single portrait of the phenomenon of interest. In terms of data collection, this model offers the benefits of continuity and minimal process losses inherent in single-cycle or concurrent designs. In this approach, however, the members of a research team will expend extra time and energy interacting with one another across sites to make sense of their data and develop working theories to guide their ongoing data collection. In addition, the participation of multiple researchers in team meetings may prove overwhelming for the members, except in the case of very large teams or ones that only meet via nonvisual media, allowing less obtrusive researcher presence. Majchrzak, Rice,

Malhotra, King, and Ba's (2000) study of a multi-organizational virtual team is an example of the team design.

Summary

Multisite investigations pose numerous practical and philosophical challenges for ethnographic inquiry. The research designs described here offer a sketch of several possible approaches and the practical trade-offs involved in applying these designs to the study of virtual project teams with respect to data quality, analytic synergy, relational complexity, and process losses. In practice, a researcher will need to improvise as she goes, and the resulting design will likely be some hybrid of the approaches described here.

FUTURE TRENDS: CYBERANTHROPOLOGY AND VIRTUAL ETHNOGRAPHY

A challenge was created that continues to this day to find ways to describe and define ethnography, and to continue to adapt for contemporary settings in modern societies a research tradition developed for long and typically solo encounters among small groups of people with "exotic" customs. (Wolcott, 1990, p. 68)

Multisite ethnographic studies reflect one outcome of an ongoing conversation regarding ethnography's relevance for studying contemporary social phenomena. Specifically, the multisite ethnography represents a figure-ground shift in the focus of ethnographic studies from holistic portraits of bounded social groups to understanding the social mosaics comprising phenomena that span or traverse locale (Marcus, 1995; Martin, 1992). Most recently, scholars have exploited the interactive and archiving capabilities of communication and information technologies to study online social phenomena. These studies have been put forth as anthropological in nature and given labels such as "virtual ethnography" (Hine, 2000) and "cyberanthropology" (Paccagnella, 1997).

In her study of the use of the Internet with respect to a highly publicized criminal trial in the U.S., Hine (2000) advocates "virtual ethnography" and questions the necessity of physical immersion and copresence with studied subjects as an appropriate basis for the investigation of online phenomena, such as online communities and political activists' activities, where the members never meet. She argues that the researcher's online participation and observation provide an experience more true to that of the participants in that forum, who typically only know one another through their online contact. She suggests that conceptualizing ethnography as "an experientially-based way of knowing" (p. 10) opens it up for adaptation to explore phenomena defined by "connection rather than location" while remaining true to the "ethos of fidelity to the processes of meaning construction *in situ*" (p. 37).

In another approach labeled "cyberanthropology," Paccagnella (1997) describes the opportunities and benefits of using electronic traces left by technology-mediated conversations to do larger scale comparative studies of the communicative practices of virtual groups than would be possible if the researcher tried to study the groups in person. This approach offers the possibility of gathering data on multiple groups simultaneously regardless of their locations and to do cross-group, cross-industry, or cross-occupational comparisons impossible using traditional ethnographic practices.

Both of these approaches are well-suited for describing and comparing online interaction practices and patterns. With respect to virtual project teams, however, they risk interpretive distortion by focusing solely on the participants' virtual interaction without regard for how the members' physical and social situation shapes their online contributions. Hine (2000), herself, found that, in fact, "geography matters."

Over the next several years, we can expect the number of multisite ethnographies to grow, reflecting the continued globalization of work and corporate experimentation with new work designs, including contingent workforces and interorganizational alliances. These same trends in work design coupled with shrinking research budgets and increasingly sophisticated technologies suggest the likely proliferation of "cyberanthropological" studies as well. As always, the method should match the question and all research is shaped by a variety of practical contingencies. Nonetheless, only traditional ethnography, adapted to the distributed environment, allows for the development of empirically grounded theories regarding the interrelationships between individuals' contextually-particular work strategies and the work, communication, and participation patterns observed in a virtual collective.

CONCLUSION

The increasing dispersion, technology-mediation, and transience of contemporary organizational forms pose a variety of challenges to research methods implicitly premised on colocated work configurations, calling for adaptations to and refinement of these methods as well as the creation of new methods. This chapter has used the particular case of virtual project teams, an increasingly prevalent work configuration, to illustrate adaptations of traditional ethnographic practice that retain ethnography's fundamental ethos. Because time-bound virtual project teams represent the extreme case of contemporary organizational configurations for ethnographic study, the illustrated efficacy of ethnography to study a geographically-distributed, technology-mediated, transient population suggests its appropriateness for studying contemporary organizational forms and practices more generally.

REFERENCES

Agar, M. H. (1996). *The Professional Stranger: An Informal Introduction to Ethnography*. San Diego, CA: Academic Press.

Ancona, D. G., & Chong, C.-L. (1996). Entrainment: Pace, cycle, and rhythm in organizational behavior. In B. M. Staw & L. L. Cummings (Eds.), *Research in Organizational Behavior* (vol. 18), pp. 251-284. Greenwich, CT: JAI Press.

Barker, R. G. (1968). *Ecological Psychology: Concepts and Methods for Studying the Environment of Human Behavior*. Stanford, CA: Stanford University Press.

Barley, S. R. (1986). Technology as an occasion for structuring: Evidence from observation of CT scanners and the social order of radiology departments. *Administrative Science Quarterly, 33*, 24-60.

Barrett, B. J. (2000). *Factors influencing the performance effectiveness of globally-dispersed teams.* Unpublished doctoral dissertation, Michigan State University, Lansing, Michigan, USA.

Boland, R. J. J. (2002). *Position paper for the Workshop on Distributed Mediated Practices.* Unpublished manuscript.

Brodt, S. E., DeSanctis, G., & Emery, J. D. (2002). *Beyond messages: The effects of informational and relational complexity on e-communication overload.* Paper presented at the meeting of the Academy of Management, Denver, Colorado, USA.

Cramton, C. D. (2001). The mutual knowledge problem and its consequences for dispersed collaboration. *Organization Science, 12*(3), 346-371.

Garfinkel, H. (1967/1984). *Studies in Ethnomethodology.* Cambridge, UK: Polity Press.

Geertz, C. (1973). *The Interpretation of Cultures.* New York: Basic Books.

Gersick, C. J. (1988). Time and transition in work teams: Toward a new model of group development. *Academy of Management Journal, 31*, 9-41.

Gluesing, J. C. (1995). *Fragile alliances—Negotiating global teaming in a turbulent environment.* Unpublished doctoral dissertation, Wayne State University, Detroit, Michigan, USA.

Goffman, E. (1959). *The Presentation of Self in Everyday Life.* Garden City, NY: Anchor Books.

Hinds, P. J., & Bailey, D. E. (2000). *Virtual team performance: Modeling the impact of geographic and temporal virtuality.* Paper presented at the meeting of the Academy of Management, Toronto, Ontario, Canada.

Hine, C. (2000). *Virtual Ethnography.* London: SAGE.

Homans, G. C. (1950). *The Human Group.* New York: Harcourt, Brace.

House, R., Rousseau, D. M., & Thomas-Hunt, M. (1995). The meso paradigm: A framework for the integration of micro and macro organizational behavior. In B. M. Staw & L. L. Cummings (Eds.), *Research in Organizational Behavior* (Vol. 17, pp. 71-114). Greenwich, CT: JAI Press.

Jarvenpaa, S., & Leidner, D. (1999). Communication and trust in global virtual teams. *Organization Science, 10*(6), 791-815.

Jordan, B. (1996). Ethnographic workplace studies and CSCW. In D. Shapiro, M. Tauber, & R. Traunmuller (Eds.), *The Design of Computer Supported Cooperative Work and Groupware Systems* (12th ed., pp. 17-42). Amsterdam: Elsevier Science.

Klein, J. A., & Barrett, B. J. (2001). One foot in a global team, one foot at the local site: Making sense out of living in two worlds simultaneously. In M. Beyerlein (Ed.), *Advances in Interdisciplinary Studies of Work Teams* (Vol. 8), pp. 107-126. Rotterdam, The Netherlands: JAI Press.

Kunda, G. (1992). *Engineering Culture: Control and Commitment in a High-Tech Corporation.* Philadelphia, PA: Temple University Press.

Majchrzak, A., Rice, R. E., Malhotra, A., King, N., & Ba, S. (2000). Technology adaptation: The case of a computer-supported interorganizational virtual team. *MIS Quarterly, 24*(4), 569-599.

Marcus, G. E. (1995). Ethnography in/of the world system: The emergence of multi-sited ethnography. *Annual Review of Anthropology, 24*, 95-117.

Martin, J. (1992). *Cultures in Organizations: Three Perspectives*. New York: Oxford University Press.

Maznevski, M. L., & Chudoba, K. M. (2000). Bridging space over time: Global virtual team dynamics and effectiveness. *Organization Science, 11*(5), 473-492.

McGrath, J. E., Kelly, J. R., & Machatka, D. E. (1984). The social psychology of time: Entrainment of behavior in social and organizational settings. *Applied Social Psychology, 5*, 21-44.

Orlikowski, W. (1988). *Information Technology in Post-Industrial Organizations*. New York: New York University, Graduate School of Business Administration.

Orlikowski, W. (2000). Using technology and constituting structures: A practice lens for studying technology in organizations. *Organization Science, 11*(4), 404-428.

Paccagnella, L. (1997). Getting the seats of your pants dirty: Strategies for ethnographic research on virtual communities. *Journal of Computer-Mediated Communication, 3*(1), 18.

Rennecker, J. (2001). *The myth of spontaneous connection: An ethnographic study of the situated nature of virtual teamwork*. Unpublished doctoral dissertation, Massachusetts Institute of Technology, Cambridge, Massachusetts, USA.

Ruhleder, K. (2000). The virtual ethnographer: Fieldwork in distributed electronic environments. *Fieldwork, 12*(2), 3-17.

Saunders, C. S., & Ahuja, M. K. (2000). *A framework for understanding temporal issues in virtual teams*. Paper presented at the meeting of the Academy of Management, Toronto, Ontario, Canada.

Schultze, U. (2000). A confessional account of an ethnography about knowledge work. *MIS Quarterly, 24*(1), 3-41.

Schwartzman, H. B. (1993). *Ethnography in Organizations* (Vol. 27). Newbury Park, CA: SAGE.

Sole, D., & Edmondson, A. (2001). Situated knowledge and learning in dispersed teams. *British Journal of Management, 13*(S2), S17-S34.

Spradley, J. P. (1979). *The Ethnographic Interview*. New York: Holt, Rinehart, and Winston.

Star, S. L., & Ruhleder, K. (1996). Steps toward an ecology of infrastructure: Design and access for large information spaces. *Information Systems Research, 7*(1), 111-135.

Stewart, A. (1998). *The Ethnographer's Method* (Vol. 46). Thousand Oaks, CA: SAGE.

Suchman, L. (1987). *Plans and Situated Action: The Problem of Human-Machine Communication*. Cambridge, UK: Cambridge University Press.

Van Maanen, J. (1988). *Tales of the Field: On Writing Ethnography*. Chicago, IL: University of Chicago Press.

Van Maanen, J., & Kolb, D. (1985). The professional apprentice: Observations on fieldwork roles in two organizational settings. In S. B. Bacharach (Ed.), *Research in the Sociology of Organizations* (Vol. 4, pp. 1-33). Greenwich, CT: JAI Press.

Weisband, S. (2002). Maintaining awareness in distributed team collaboration. In S. Kiesler & P. J. Hinds (Eds.), *Distributed Work: New Research on Working Across Distance Using Technology*. Cambridge, MA: MIT Press.

Wolcott, H. F. (1990). *Writing Up Qualitative Research* (Vol. 20). Thousand Oaks, CA: SAGE.

Chapter X

Studying Virtual Work in Teams, Organizations and Communities

Daniel Robey
Georgia State University, USA

Leigh Jin
San Francisco State University, USA

ABSTRACT

This chapter addresses empirical methods for obtaining data on virtual teams, organizations and professional communities. We begin by reviewing different ways of defining virtual work. We then examine two epistemological paradoxes involved in empirical research on virtual work: (1) virtual work is simultaneously mobile *and* motionless, *and (2) virtual work is simultaneously* distributed *and* situated. *We address these paradoxes by identifying four data generation approaches that can be used separately or in combination: participant observation, computer logs, interview, and questionnaire. The chapter describes each of these methods and illustrates each with one or more exemplary studies. By studying virtual teams, organizations, and communities from various angles with different types of data, researchers can better inform the process of theorizing.*

INTRODUCTION

This chapter addresses empirical methods for obtaining data on virtual teams, organizations, and professional communities. Because virtual work settings are enabled by advanced information and communication technologies, IS researchers are often in an advantageous position to conduct rigorous studies on the design, development, implementation, use, and consequences of virtual work arrangements. Such studies are needed because work is increasingly mediated by technologies that potentially liberate workers from specific places and times. However, studies of virtual work face fundamental ontological and epistemological challenges that must be addressed before research findings can be considered valid and applicable. This chapter identifies these challenges and offers methodological guidance to researchers investigating virtual work in teams, organizations, and communities.

The chapter begins by emphasizing the importance of defining virtual work. Given the variety of definitions of virtuality in research, it is essential that researchers choose a definition that suits their purposes and allows comparison with other studies. Researchers' definitions comprise their ontological assumptions about virtual work. We review a range of definitions of virtual work, noting that all uses of the term *virtual* are not equal.

We then turn to two epistemological paradoxes involved in obtaining data for empirical research on virtual work. The first paradox is that virtual work is simultaneously *mobile* and *motionless*. That is, virtual workers are able to move freely from place to place, but their work activities require stationary attention to technology interfaces. The second paradox is that virtual work is simultaneously *distributed* and *situated*. That is, workers can connect with people in different places whom they may never meet in person, yet each individual is situated in a particular physical and social context. We address these paradoxes by identifying four data generation approaches that can be used separately or in combination: participant observation, computer logs, interview, and questionnaire (including Web-based surveys). The chapter describes each of these methods and illustrates each with one or more exemplary studies.

WHAT IS VIRTUAL WORK?

Taken literally, work described as *virtual* means work that exists "in effect or essence, although not in actual fact or name" (*Webster's New World Dictionary*). The literal meaning of *virtual* derives from its use in computer science to describe virtual machine environments and its use in science fiction, where concepts like virtual reality were born. In most contemporary research, the literal definition has been abandoned, allowing the term *virtual* to acquire many meanings. We briefly review the conventional assumptions about virtual work when applied to teams, organizations, and communities. Following this, we identify alternative conceptions of virtual work that researchers might usefully exploit.

In *teams*, virtuality has most often been used to describe work that is distributed across time and space (Saunders, 2000; Townsend, DeMarie, & Henrickson, 1998). Because distributed work is enabled by information and communication technologies, virtual teams have also been defined as teams that rely upon electronic communication to accomplish their work. Examples of research on virtual teams date back to the early uses of computer conferencing (Hiltz & Turoff, 1978). Two kinds of studies have become common in recent years: studies of student teams solving hypothetical problems devised by researchers (e.g., Cramton, 2001; Jarvenpaa & Leidner, 1999; Montoya-Weiss, Massey, & Song, 2001) and studies of teams working on real problems in field situations (e.g., Majchrzak, Rice, Malhotra, King, & Ba, 2000; Maznevski & Chudoba, 2000; Robey, Khoo, & Powers, 2000).

The concept of virtual *organization* is most commonly used to describe organizations that rely upon alliances with business partners (Davidow & Malone, 1992; Grenier & Metes, 1995). Thus, an organization positioned within a network of partners is considered to be virtual because many other organizations perform the functions necessary to service customers (Lucas, 1996). Virtual organizations are able to achieve such coordination through the enabling technologies that link partners together. Virtual organizations are also distributed because the location of alliance partners is immaterial as long as their activities can be coordinated with information technologies.

Although virtual *communities* have attracted less attention by information systems researchers, they share similar characteristics with virtual teams. That is, members are distributed in time and space and they interact primarily through electronic media. Virtual communities may be organized for professional purposes, or they may exist simply for entertainment value. Our focus in this chapter is on communities with professional interests, such as the open source software community (Raymond, 2001). Virtual communities are interesting because they rely upon voluntary and often unpaid contributions by community members (McClure Wasko & Faraj, 2000). As such, the vitality of virtual communities depends more upon social capital than upon the authoritative mechanisms that govern teams and organizations (Adler, 2001).

The treatments of virtuality described above appear to be achieving some consensus. However, it is premature to exclude other ways of defining virtual work. Schultze and Orlikowski (2001) reviewed the professional literature on virtual organizations to reveal a wide variety of definitions and their underlying metaphors. They identified five metaphors of virtual organizing: platform, space, bits, community, and network. Clearly, authors have not converged on a single metaphor or definition of virtuality.

For example, Mowshowitz (1997, 2002) defined virtual organization as the separation of work requirements from the ways in which requirements are met. Separating these elements allows organizations to switch from one way of meeting a requirement to others that may be more cost-effective. Switching requires "management activities that explore and track the abstract requirements needed to realize some objective while simultaneously, but independently, investigating and specifying the concrete means for satisfying the abstract requirements" (Mowshowitz, 1997, p. 33). In practice, this definition of virtual organization invites inquiries into the ways in which organizations contract with other organizations that can provide essential functions, such as order fulfillment, customer service, logistics, and others, without becoming part of the organization seeking to satisfy customer requirements.

A second alternative definition of virtuality is to treat work as consisting of two separate but interrelated layers of activity. For example, Turoff (1997) claimed that computers do not simply represent reality but rather provide a new reality that differs from other experience. Information technology's mediation of relationships among human actors allows reality to become "what we negotiate it to be" (Turoff, p. 41), potentially deviating from previous experience in organizations. Thus, transactions mediated by information technology in a virtual layer of reality may have material consequences in the physical world. In essence, virtual work becomes a new, alternative reality, an "imploded view" of an organization that "re-presents" reality in a qualitatively different way (Sotto, 1997). This dual-layer view of organizations draws attention to the relationships between virtual, technology-mediated work and material work. Virtual work may reinforce and complement physical work or even produce new synergies (Robey, Schwaig, & Jin, 2003).

Treating virtual work as a duality draws attention to the notions of time-space configuration and time-space edge, as formulated by Giddens (1984, 1990, 1991). While place connotes boundedness, localness, and particularity, space is more universal, generalizable, and abstract (Schultze & Boland, 2000). Because the social systems for organizing work increasingly engage both place and space, it is useful to conceive of them as time-space configurations. According to this view, work may be conceived as both transcendent of temporal and spatial barriers (the virtual layer) while also situated and anchored in local, physical reality (Cramton, 2001; Jin & Robey, 2002; Rennecker, 2002). Inevitably, work involving both layers depends upon the navigation of the edges between these two types of social systems. Giddens defined time-space edge as the "interconnections, and differentials of power, found between different societal types" (1984, p. 164). Time-space edges can exist in both virtual and material layers, and there may be significant costs associated with bridging time-space edges within and between layers (Jin & Robey, 2002).

In sum, definitions of virtual work do not need to conform to conventional uses. Researchers must carefully define what is meant by virtual. Researchers must also carefully distinguish between concepts of virtuality at the team, organization, and community levels of analysis. Although virtuality may have similar functions at all three levels of analysis, the functions may be represented quite differently at each level (Morgeson & Hofmann, 1999).

PARADOXES OF STUDYING VIRTUAL WORK

In this section we explore two apparent paradoxes that affect research on virtual work. First, we consider virtual work to be both *mobile* and *motionless*. Virtual work is mobile to the extent that ubiquitous, pervasive computing devices allow workers to move in time and space rather than being confined to particular times and places. The spread of ubiquitous computing and communication technologies enables such mobility, making it difficult for the researcher to investigate the phenomenon of work in virtual teams or organizations (Lyytinen & Yoo, 2002). The challenge that mobility poses for the researcher is that it creates a moving target. If virtual work settings can occur anywhere, anytime, how can they be studied? Clearly, research on any phenomenon that is mobile poses challenges that research on more stationary work does not.

But virtual work is also motionless. Like other knowledge work, virtual work is comprised of manipulating, reading, and interpreting symbols on a two-dimensional screen. So, even though the worker may be 30,000 feet in the air traveling at 600 miles per hour, the work itself is not exciting to watch. While much is occurring in the head and the hard drive, not much is visibly apparent to the observer.

This paradox is common to most studies of knowledge work, where the work itself involves processing information instead of transforming or transporting physical materials or performing other physical activity. Although virtual work requires physical interaction with information technologies, the work itself is unlike the study of industrial work. There is often little of apparent interest to observe when workers interact with information technologies. A virtual organization also may have relatively little physical presence if it is comprised primarily of alliances with other organizations. The virtual organization may consist largely of computer technology: servers to process and control transactions involving business partners and customers. Getting at the social essence of knowledge work in virtual organizations is therefore difficult.

The second paradox is that virtual work is both *distributed* and *situated*. As our review of definitions and conceptions of virtuality indicates, most researchers consider virtual work to be distributed spatially, operating somewhat independently of space and time. Distribution poses a challenge similar to the challenge posed by mobility of virtual workers: it makes the study of people in multiple locations difficult.

But virtual work is also situated. Although members of a virtual team may relate to each other using electronic communication, each member is necessarily situated in a physical and social place. Many virtual teams also include colocated subgroups who might meet frequently face-to-face while seeing their counterparts in distant locations much less frequently. Even where distance is a factor, most teams are not designed to prevent face-to-face interaction or prohibit business travel between sites. Thus, we cannot assume that all virtual work occurs strictly through processes that are mediated by technology. Because virtual work is both distributed and situated, it is more complex and more challenging for the researcher to understand.

These paradoxes can be resolved by resourceful researchers. In the following section, we describe four conventional approaches to collecting data on virtual teams, organizations, and communities. Although the methods themselves are not novel, their application to the study of virtual work requires special care on the part of the researcher. For example, participant observation may not make immediate sense as a method for gathering data about motionless work that is distributed and mobile. Yet, uses of this methodology can be quite effective in the study of virtual work. By contrast, the widely accepted methodology of survey questionnaires has enjoyed infrequent use in studies of virtual teams and organizations. Questionnaires more often supplement other forms of data collection. Our hope is to guide researchers toward informed choices of methods for collecting data by discussing the variety of options available and by illustrating each method with exemplary cases.

METHODS FOR STUDYING VIRTUAL WORK

Participant Observation

Despite the challenge of observing work that is dispersed and largely mediated by information technologies, participant observation can be a valuable source of data.

Participant observation is a data generation method that has been widely adopted in various qualitative research traditions, including phenomenology, grounded theory, ethnography, and case study (Creswell, 1997). Traditionally, the roles of participant and observer have been considered as different in research, and combining them poses challenges. Researchers who participate and observe must wear two hats simultaneously. In practice, researchers may find ways to separate the functions of participating and observing. Creswell noted that researchers may range from the extremes of conducting an observation as a participant and as an observer. In addition, the researcher may gather field notes first by observing as an "outsider" and then moving into the setting and observing as an "insider." Three studies exemplify the range of participant-observer roles.

Pentland's (1992) study of software hot line operators in two organizations illustrates the "observation" end of the participant-observation continuum. Pentland observed operators engaged in telephone conversations by sitting near them, observing their behaviors, monitoring their conversations with customers, and asking them questions about each call. This method allowed him to gather data involving remote communication from one side of the conversation, leading to the theoretical conclusion that organizational knowledge is situated in performance and embodied in "organizing moves" involving multiple actors.

Although primarily an observer, Pentland (1992) reported that, over the three months of the study, his presence came to be expected and he was given some work to do.

> *Given the technical nature of the work, my role was predominantly that of observer, although I was sometimes asked to help with simple tasks such as copying, looking things up in manuals, or running down the hall to get help. Occasionally, I was invited to observe a situation that an informant felt might be especially interesting (for example, when a particularly vexing problem came up). Although the engineering and software development areas were essentially off-limits at each site, I had free run of the support area, and it wasn't long before everyone knew me and expected me to be around. (Pentland, 1992, p. 535)*

Pentland's acceptance as a limited participant thus moved him away from the role of strict observer of the software hot line operators. Acceptance typically increases the researcher's rapport with other participants, leading to more candid answers to questions and greater ability to interpret the actions and language. However, the researcher who is primarily an observer still lacks the experience of doing the work that is being studied.

Jin's (2002) study of a virtual organization (iTalk) illustrates the practice of initially observing as an outsider and moving into the setting as a true participant. Although employed by the company as an intern, Jin's view of most iTalk workers was blocked by cubicle walls or secured working areas. These barriers made the majority of job-related activities invisible to the researcher. Assigned to a separate office, she was unable to observe people and events when she wanted to. As Jin became a more central participant in a project team, she gained greater access to activities that were worth recording in field notes. Interestingly, the participation and observer roles can facilitate and conflict with each other at the same time. On the one hand, Jin sometimes missed opportunities to observe because of her own intense work on projects with deadlines. On the other hand, she was able to develop rapport and trust with software developers within the engineering department through project-related meetings and discussions.

Although physical confinement made direct observations relatively difficult, Jin found alternative ways to conduct "virtual" observations by tracking e-mail communications among iTalk employees. In addition to e-mail, the source code itself provided opportunities for the researcher to observe. At iTalk, the software development code libraries were centrally managed by a source control system to enable the codevelopment of software applications among multiple developers. Before developers could modify the code, they needed to check out a software module under their own name. After making the necessary changes, developers checked the modified version back into the library. By tracking the source control system and reading the detailed comments made by developers in the source code, Jin was able to identify the core developers who coded the main system architecture.

Participant observation in a virtual community is illustrated by Raymond's (2001) research on the open source software community. Claiming to be an observer/participant anthropologist in the Internet hacker culture, Raymond has been actively involved in the open source community for more than 20 years. His collected essays (Raymond, 2001) not only reveal insights about the open source community culture over a long period of time but also share his experience in organizing one open source project in detail. His research has helped to explain the effectiveness of the decentralized open source model of software development in the evolution of Linux and the Internet.

Raymond's participation in the open source project was essential to his research purpose. To have his observations and research findings accepted within the community and incorporated into future action depended upon his credibility as an open source developer. In a recent interview, E. Raymond (personal communication, September 6, 2002) explained:

> *I feel my credibility, my authenticity, as a person who describes and analyzes that culture comes from the fact that I participate in its core activity. I write a lot of code. I actually had quite a reputation as a programmer in the culture. ... Also I observe behaviors, keeping track of what is going on. I observe other people's behavior, and I observe my own behavior. When I think I see patterns, I look through the mailing lists and archives, I think back on my experiences, which is substantial at this point—over a quarter of a century. I ask myself if those observations confirm the patterns I have seen.*

The credibility of Raymond's essays is established through a virtual "peer-review" process involving members of the open source community. The evolving documents were originally published on the Internet and subjected to continuous reviews from many open source developers over 10 years. Raymond's first essay, "A Brief History of Hackerdom," was first published on the Internet in 1992, and the book version incorporates the comments, feedback, and suggestions from contributors within the community.

In this sense, Raymond's research methods involve not only his own participation and observation, but the participation of other members of the community.

Computer Logs

Because virtual work requires members to exchange information via electronic communication media, much of the activity that researchers are interested in can be retrieved from the various storage areas connected to the media. Teams, for example, may share communication in discussion forums on groupware systems. Experimental studies are typically designed to capitalize on this source of data. However, field researchers may also gain permission to access such data.

In other cases, field researchers may ask members to provide documents, such as electronic mail messages, for analysis. To the extent that these documents are forwarded electronically, later analysis is facilitated. Clearly, it is more convenient for the researcher to have full access, but (just as clearly) it is also necessary for the privacy of data subjects to be preserved in an ethical manner. Participants may also be asked to keep logs of their regular activities, recording for research purposes their work practices and/or reactions to events experienced as workers. Participant activity logs can be used to supplement other data collection methods (e.g., Majchrzak et al., 2000), but they are rarely used as a sole source of data.

Cramton's (2001) study of global student teams relied upon archival data gathered over the course of a seven-week project. Teams of six students from three participating universities were given an assignment to complete using a variety of communication technologies, including electronic mail, Internet chat room facilities and voting tools, fax, and telephone. The data generated by the 13 teams studied included 1,649 electronic mail messages, printouts of chat room contributions, logs completed by team members, and papers written by the students analyzing the virtual team experience. Given the preponderance of electronic mail conversations, Cramton's analysis focused on the conflicts, frustrations, and confusion that arose as groups struggled to forge the "mutual knowledge" necessary to accomplish their tasks. The study illustrates the value of studying virtual teamwork by examining the tangible traces of electronically mediated communication.

Computer logs contain data that is usually "time-stamped" because the exact timing of entries to the logs is recorded automatically. This affords the capability to study longitudinal development of the variables of interest, such as the development of trust in a virtual team over time. Where researchers are interested in the performance of virtual teams, it may also be possible to derive dependent variable measurement from computer logs. Especially in experimental studies, performance metrics can be obtained if assigned tasks (e.g., group reports, solutions to problems) are created and stored electronically, for example, in a Lotus Notes forum (Montoya-Weiss et al., 2001).

Depending upon the researcher's ontological assumptions, it may be essential to exploit data that exist in computer logs. Electronically stored e-mails, discussions, Web archives, and even software code can be treated as evidence of activity occurring in the virtual layer of an organization while direct observation of human workers may be treated as evidence of the physical layer. As noted above, participation in virtual work can facilitate access to both computer logs and direct observation.

Interview

The problem of studying virtual teams that are spatially distributed can be addressed if researchers have the ability to travel to each of the sites where team members work. In interview studies, it is important not to rely upon one group of informants to provide data on other participants because such answers may be inaccurate and not representative of the interests and experiences of all groups. For example, Robey et al. (2000) studied virtual teams that were distributed over two primary locations: a major Northeastern U.S. city and a small town in the Southern United States. Traveling to both sites to conduct interviews permitted the researchers to understand the perspectives of most team members, while also acquainting themselves with the differences in geographical and cultural settings where team members worked. Moreover, geographic differences were associated with functional differences, as design and sales were located in the Northeast whereas production and customer service were located in the South. Interviews compensate for the inherent difficulties in observing work that is "motionless," that is, performed at the computer terminal. As workers talk about their relationships with team members in distant locations, including coordination and communication experiences, one may also learn about the subtle ways in which adjustments can be made. Robey and his colleagues (2000) considered such adjustments to be evidence of situated learning in cross-functional virtual teams.

Avery and Baker (2002) illustrate another approach to interviewing in their study of "infomated" households. Since many workers in virtual teams work out of their homes, Avery and Baker sought to examine the effects of technology-intensive households on the social life of the household itself. Treating households as workplaces brought the researchers into 10 purposively selected households in Sydney, Australia, to conduct group interviews with members of each household. Respondents were encouraged to tell stories about the way that they used various technologies in their work and how technologies allowed household members to manage their domestic schedules as well. This method allowed the researchers to create profiles of technology use and to analyze the contradictory effects of technologies in households. From a methodological point of view, the interview strategy brought all members of the social unit being studied into one place at one time to participate in the interview.

One aspect of interviewing methodology is the advantage of multiple interviews. Especially in cases where tape-recording is not permitted or used (e.g., Maznevski & Chudoba, 2000), interview teams comprised of two or three members can relieve the pressure that a single interviewer often experiences. Because the demands of interviewing are considerable (Mason, 1996), multiple interviewers can divide the functions among them. For example, a primary questioner may need help from a partner who can ask follow-up questions or ask for clarification. The partner can also keep a checklist of areas covered during the interview, allowing for completeness without inducing an artificial structure to the sequence of questions. Interview partners can also share notes following interviews and stimulate each other for interpretations, particularly of nonverbal communications, which may be difficult for a single interviewer to notice.

Questionnaire

Although questionnaire measurement offers the potential to reach respondents in an efficient manner, studies of virtual teams, organizations, and communities have not relied primarily upon survey methods. More typically, questionnaires are used in a supportive manner to measure particular variables in experimental research (e.g., Montoya-Weiss et al., 2001) or to provide descriptive information in support of observations or interviews (e.g., Majchrjak et al., 2000; Maznevski and Chudoba, 2000). Montoya-Weiss and her colleagues studied the relationship between conflict management and performance in 35 five-person student teams. The researchers took advantage of the prior development of questionnaire measures for five conflict management constructs (Rahim, 1983) and used an adapted version of those scales to measure their independent variables. Dependent variables, reflecting performance, were generated by expert raters who evaluated the range, organization, and depth of teams' rationales supporting their decision. The researchers also manipulated the presence of a temporal coordination mechanism provided to half of the teams (the experimental groups) but not to the other half (the control groups). The results of the experiment showed that the coordination mechanisms interacted with conflict management to affect team effectiveness. Questionnaires alone, however, provide limited information about the context of virtual work.

Where researchers are interested in the effects of virtual work on individuals and not teamwork per se, survey methods are more appropriate. For example, Ahuja, Chudoba, and Robert (2002) surveyed 171 "virtual associates" who worked for a health systems consulting company. Because the researchers' interest was in individual perceptions of social identity, their survey questionnaire served their purpose. However, questionnaires more often play a supportive role in research where entire teams are identified or created experimentally.

Ahuja et al.'s (2002) questionnaire was deployed via the Internet rather than sent through postal mail. Given the distributed, computer-mediated nature of most virtual work, Internet surveys are an appealing and an increasingly popular option. Verma (2001) examined the benefits and drawbacks of using the Internet as a survey vehicle. Benefits include: (1) online questionnaires are available in the same medium where virtual work is performed, which is particularly suited to the population of the research; (2) cost savings for data collection via the Internet are substantial, approximately 15% of the cost of mail surveys (Comley, 1996); (3) a quicker response, for example, Mehta and Sivadas (1995) received about 50% of their responses within three days compared to three weeks for postal surveys; and (4) ability to reach a global audience and gather international data more easily (Mehta & Sivadas, 1995). In sum, the combined benefit of quick responses, low cost, easy access, global reach, and automated coding of data make Web and e-mail based data collection methods an attractive alternative (Verma, 2001).

However, Internet surveys are also subject to potential drawbacks: (1) loss of researcher control over sample structure and composition due to respondent self-selection (Bonchek, Hurwitz, & Mallery, 1996); (2) difficulty in identifying the actual respondent due to the quasi-anonymous nature of the Internet; and (3) added care needed to prevent potential violations of respondent privacy. Although each of these drawbacks can be addressed with appropriate methodological adjustments (Verma, 2001), researchers should not assume that Internet questionnaires are the same as postal mail questionnaires simply delivered by an alternate medium.

Multiple Methods

Increasingly, studies of virtual teams employ more than one of the data generation methods discussed above. In this way, the strengths of one type of data might compensate for the weaknesses of others. Multiple methods permit triangulation of evidence on a phenomenon (Jick, 1979), thereby ensuring the researchers' confidence in interpreting and analyzing data. For example, it may be hard for a researcher examining hundreds of electronic mail messages to catch the essence of a conflict. An interview with a participant may be able to provide a simple explanation in a few words of response to a direct question.

Using multiple methods, however, increases the research demands in two important ways. First, more data take more resources to collect. If interviews are to be supplemented by observation of archived material generated by a virtual team, this data needs to be collected. Observation studies are particularly demanding on researcher time. Such demands might be met by using a larger research team (e.g., the five researchers contributing to Majchrzak et al.'s, 2000, study). The second demand is upon data analysis. It is often difficult for researchers to reconcile discrepancies, for example, between what they read in formal documents and hear in interviews. Mechanics of analysis also vary for different types of data, which again places demands on a research team to be expert, for example, in both qualitative and quantitative data analysis. Where such data are longitudinal, even greater demands are placed on the analysis process.

Two exemplary studies of virtual teams using multiple data sources are Maznevski and Chudoba's (2000) study of three global virtual teams and Majchrzak and colleagues' (2000) study of a single team involving members from multiple organizations. Maznevski and Chudoba generated data over 21 months, including semi-structured interviews (not recorded), observations of face-to-face meetings, listening in on conference calls, logs of electronic communications taken over a typical week for each team, questionnaires, and documents (copies of faxes, e-mails, and letters given to the researchers and formal documents). Analyzing this large data set to make sense of team dynamics over time led the authors to see the intricate connections between teams' tasks and their communication patterns, including the identification of deep rhythms related to the timing of teams' face-to-face encounters.

Majchrzak and her colleagues (2000) examined a similarly daunting variety of data to study the performance of one team over 10 months. The data set was comprised of private interviews with each of the eight team members, entries to the coordinating groupware technology, direct observations of team members during 89 audio conferences, attendance at four face-to-face team meetings, a weekly questionnaire completed by team members, and a final questionnaire to assess team effectiveness. The five contributing authors played different roles, combining their resources to capture a highly detailed portrait of team activity over time. Like Maznevski and Chudoba (2000), Majchrzak and colleagues provided valuable insights into the modification of team practices over time, for example, the introduction of audio conferences to supplement the groupware technology.

DISCUSSION AND CONCLUSION

Each of the methods and approaches to data collection described in the previous section allow the researcher to "see" teams, organizations, or communities in different ways. When employed by researchers, these methods (alone or in combination) overcome the challenges of studying work that is paradoxically mobile and motionless, and distributed and situated. The paradoxes are resolved if researchers go to where the work is performed, observe closely, participate to the extent possible, examine computer logs, conduct interviews, and supplement these methods with questionnaires. We have focused on the methodological challenges of gathering data about virtual work because this appears to offer the greatest challenge. Once gathered, data should be subjected to the standard guidelines for analysis discussed elsewhere in this book.

By studying virtual teams, organizations, and communities from various angles with different types of data, researchers can better inform the process of theorizing. For example, rather than settling on conventional theories about teamwork that is geographically distributed, researchers may focus on issues such as the intertwining between physical and virtual representations of work (Sotto, 1997). In this sense, a greater variety of data can enrich theory building. The advantage of richer theory is, ultimately, a richer view toward practice. A focus on the relationship between physical and virtual representations of work, for example, may inform practical methods for coordinating work across those two representations, or layers (Robey et al., 2003).

Participant observation, in particular, places the researcher in a position to obtain intimate knowledge and insights that have practical value. In most cases, the participant observer already affects practice during the research process. For example, E. Raymond (personal communication, September 6, 2002) explained that his research goes beyond identifying and articulating the best practices within successful open source projects like Linux. The real intention was to influence the open source community as a whole so that other, less successful open source projects could benefit from those best practices. As a participant, E. Raymond (personal communication, September 6, 2002) was intimately involved in the community practices: "We are the people who help create this culture partly by the process of our participation, and partly by the process of our observation and articulation of its values."

Practical guidance is frequently enhanced by research employing multiple approaches to generating data. More "objective" methods such as interviews and examination of computer logs may help to compensate for an extreme insider view of the participant observer. Multiple methods and multiple team members may offer challenges to the insider's interpretation based on participation in the virtual team, organization, or community. These outsider interpretations provide additional validity to research findings and make them more relevant to practice.

Although collecting data from multiple sources is beneficial, it poses potential problems for analysis. Researchers need analysis tools to help manage the resulting heterogeneous data set drawn from multiple sources: field notes, surveys, e-mails, interviews, mailing lists, Web archives, and software codes across both time and space dimensions. Ideally, the researcher could cross-reference between specific sources of data stored in a manner to facilitate retrieval, comparison with other data, interpretation, and the drawing of conclusions. Developing such supporting tools would not only help the researcher to analyze data already collected but also to guide ongoing data collection. A principle of qualitative data analysis is to conduct analysis during data collection, so that early interpretations may generate "strategies for collecting new, often better, data" (Miles & Huberman, 1994, p. 50). As the analysis continues, cross-referencing capabilities are needed to help the researcher triangulate sources of evidence to produce more plausible interpretations of the research phenomenon. The ability to cross-reference heterogeneous data from both time and space dimensions is particularly advantageous to researchers who study virtual work as time-space configurations.

In conclusion, research on virtual teams, organizations, and communities potentially offers valuable new insights into contemporary work practices. Although such work poses specific challenges to researchers, those challenges can be met by judicious consideration of multiple methods of data collection. Before proceeding with data collection, researchers should carefully consider their ontological assumptions about virtual work. Most researchers conventionally assume that virtual work is like any other work, except that it is geographically distributed. Alternative conceptions of virtuality have been proposed, and they may reveal more novel insights into contemporary and future work arrangements.

REFERENCES

Adler, P. S. (2001). Market, hierarchy, and trust: The knowledge economy and the future of capitalism. *Organization Science, 12*(2), 215-234.

Ahuja, M., Chudoba, K., & Robert, L. (2002). *Identity formation among virtual workers.* Paper presented to the *62nd Annual Meeting of the Academy of Management,* August 9-14, Denver, Colorado.

Avery, G. C., & Baker, E. (2002). Reframing the infomated household-workplace. *Information and Organization, 12*(2), 109-134.

Bonchek, M. S., Hurwitz, R., & Mallery, J. (1996). Will the Web democratize or polarize the political process? *World Wide Web Journal, 1*(3), Summer 1996. Retrieved from: http://www.w3j.com/3/s3.bonchek.html.

Comley, P. (1996). *The use of the Internet as a data collection method.* November 1996. Retrieved from: http://www.virtualsurveys.com.

Cramton, C. D. (2001). The mutual knowledge problem and its consequences for dispersed collaboration. *Organization Science, 12*(3), 346-371.

Creswell, J. W. (1997). *Qualitative inquiry and research design.* Thousand Oaks, CA: SAGE.

Davidow, W. H., & Malone, M. S. (1992). *The Virtual Corporation: Structuring and Revitalizing the Corporation for the 21st Century.* New York: Harper Business.

Giddens, A. (1984). *The Constitution of Society, Outline of the Theory of Structuration.* Berkeley, CA: University of California Press.

Giddens, A. (1990). *The Consequences of Modernity.* Stanford, CA: Stanford University Press.

Giddens, A. (1991). *Modernity and Self-Identity: Self and Society in the Late Modern Age.* Stanford, CA: Stanford University Press.

Grenier, R., & Metes, G. (1995). *Going Virtual: Moving your Organization into the 21st Century.* Upper Saddle River, NJ: Prentice Hall.

Hiltz, S. R., & Turoff, M. (1978). *The Network Nation: Human Communication via Computer.* Reading, MA: Addison-Wesley.

Jarvenpaa, S. L., & Leidner, D. E. (1999). Communication and trust in global virtual teams. *Organization Science, 10*(6), 791-815.

Jick, T. (1979). Mixing qualitative and quantitative methods: Triangulation in action. *Administrative Science Quarterly*, *24*(4), 602-611.

Jin, L. (2002). *An interpretive analysis of the relationship between virtual and material representations in an e-business company: A participant observation study*. Doctoral dissertation, Georgia State University, Atlanta, GA, USA.

Jin, L., & Robey, D. (2002). *Bridging time and space: An interpretive analysis of a virtual organization*. Paper presented to the *62nd Annual Meeting of the Academy of Management*, August 9-14, Denver, Colorado.

Lucas, H. C., Jr. (1996). *The T-Form Organization*. San Francisco, CA: Jossey-Bass.

Lyytinen, K., & Yoo, Y. (2002). The next wave of nomadic computing. *Information Systems Research 13*(4), 377-388.

Majchrzak, A., Rice, R. E., Malhotra, A., King, N., & Ba, S. (2000). Technology adaptation: The case of a computer-supported inter-organizational virtual team. *MIS Quarterly*, *24*(4), 569-600.

Mason, J. (1996). *Qualitative Researching*. Thousand Oaks, CA: SAGE.

Maznevski, M. L., & Chudoba, K. M. (2000). Bridging space over time: Global virtual team dynamics and effectiveness. *Organization Science, 11*(5), 473-492.

McLure Wasko, M., & Faraj, S. (2000). It is what one does: Why people participate and help others in electronic communities of practice. *Journal of Strategic Information Systems, 9*, 155-173.

Mehta, R., & Sivadas, E. (1995). Comparing response rates and response content in mail versus electronic mail surveys. *Journal of the Market Research Society, 37*(4), 429-446.

Miles, M. B., & Huberman, A. M. (1994). *Qualitative Data Analysis*. Thousand Oaks, CA: SAGE.

Montoya-Weiss, M. M., Massey, A. P., & Song, M. (2001). Getting it together: Temporal coordination and conflict management in global virtual teams. *Academy of Management Journal, 44*(6), 1251-1262.

Morgeson, F. P., & Hofmann, D. A. (1999). The structure and function of collective constructs: Implications for multilevel research and theory development. *Academy of Management Review, 24*, 249-265.

Mowshowitz, A. (1997). Virtual organization. *Communications of the ACM, 40*(9), 30-37.

Mowshowitz, A. (2002). *Virtual Organization*. Westport, CT: Praeger.

Pentland, B. T. (1992). Organizing moves: Software support hot lines. *Administrative Science Quarterly, 37*, 527-548.

Rahim, M. A. (1983). A measure of styles of handling interpersonal conflict. *Academy of Management Journal, 26*, 368-376.

Raymond, E. (2001). *The Cathedral and the Bazaar: Musings on Linux and Open Source by an Accidental Revolutionary* (Rev. ed.). Sebastopol, CA: O'Reilly.

Rennecker, J. (2002). *The situated nature of virtual teamwork: Using "place" and "space" to understand the local-global dynamics of a virtual team*. Paper presented to the *62nd Annual Meeting of the Academy of Management*, August 9-14, Denver, Colorado.

Robey, D., Khoo, H. M., & Powers, C. (2000). Situated learning in cross-functional virtual teams. *IEEE Transactions on Professional Communication, 43*(1), 51-66.

Robey, D., Schwaig, K., & Jin, L. (2003). Intertwining material and virtual work. *Information and Organization, 13*(2), 111-129.

Saunders, C. S. (2000). Virtual teams: Piecing together the puzzle. In R. W. Zmud (Ed.), *Framing the Domains of IT Management: Projecting the Future ... Through the Past* (pp. 29-50). Cincinnati, OH: Pinnaflex.

Schultze, U., & Boland, R. J. (2000). Place, space and knowledge work: A study of outsourced computer systems administrators. *Accounting, Management, and Information Technologies, 10,* 187-219.

Schultze, U., & Orlikowski, W. J. (2001). Metaphors of virtuality: Shaping an emergent reality. *Information and Organization, 11*(1), 45-77.

Sotto, R. (1997). The virtual organization. *Accounting, Management, and Information Technologies, 7*(1), 37-51.

Townsend, A. M., DeMarie, S. M., & Henrickson, A. R. (1998). Virtual teams: Technology and the workplace of the future. *Academy of Management Executive, 12*(3), 17-29.

Turoff, M. (1997). Virtuality. *Communications of the ACM, 40*(9), 38-43.

Verma, S. (2001). *Diffusion and adoption of multicasting: Role of implicit versus explicit communication methods.* Doctoral dissertation, Georgia State University, Atlanta, GA, USA.

SECTION IV

GLOBAL ISSUES

Chapter XI

Methodological Issues in MIS Cross-Cultural Research

Elena Karahanna
University of Georgia, USA

Roberto Evaristo
University of Illinois, Chicago, USA

Mark Srite
University of Wisconsin-Milwaukee, USA

ABSTRACT

This chapter presents a discussion of methodological issues that are relevant and idiosyncratic to cross-cultural research. One characteristic that typifies cross-cultural studies is their comparative nature, i.e., they involve a comparison across two separate cultures on a focal phenomenon. When differences across cultures are observed, the question arises as to whether the results are true cultural differences or merely measurement artifacts. Methodological considerations in cross-cultural research focus on ruling out alternative explanations for these differences and thus enhancing the interpretability of the results. The chapter presents an overview of key methodological issues in cross-cultural research and reviews methods of preventing or detecting methodological problems.

INTRODUCTION

Globalization of business has highlighted the need to understand the management of organizations that span different nations and cultures. In these multinational and transcultural organizations, there is a growing need to utilize information technology (IT) to achieve efficiencies, coordination, and communication. However, cultural differences between countries may have an impact on the effectiveness and efficiency of IT deployment. Despite its importance, the effect of cultural factors has received limited attention from information systems (IS) researchers.

Cross-cultural information systems research, in general, remains relatively undeveloped. Although several important research endeavors have been recently published in the better IS journals, the overall number of cross-cultural articles is fairly low considering the number of practical and theoretical questions that remain unanswered. This incongruence can be partly explained by methodological and resource difficulties inherent in cross-cultural research as well as the long time horizon required to complete and conduct these types of studies.

This chapter focuses on these difficulties. Methodological considerations are of the utmost importance to cross-cultural studies since valid comparisons require cross-culturally equivalent research instruments, data collection procedures, research sites, and respondents. Ensuring equivalency is an essential element of cross-cultural studies and is necessary to avoid confounds and contaminating effects of various extraneous elements.

In the next section, we provide a brief discussion of key methodological issues in cross-cultural research, presenting both threats to making valid cross-cultural comparisons as well as methods of preventing or detecting potential problems. Next, sampling considerations and guidelines for instrument wording and translation are presented. The chapter concludes with a summary discussion of the issues.

METHODOLOGICAL ISSUES

Cross-cultural research has some unique methodological idiosyncrasies that are not pertinent to intracultural research. One characteristic that typifies cross-cultural studies is their comparative nature, i.e., they involve a comparison across two or more separate cultures on a focal phenomenon. Any observed differences across cultures give rise to many alternative explanations. Particularly when results are different than expected (e.g., no statistical significance, factor analysis items do not load as expected, or reliability assessment is low), researchers may question whether results are true differences due to culture or merely measurement artifacts (Mullen, 1995).

Methodological considerations in carrying out cross-cultural research attempt to rule out alternative explanations for these differences and enhance the interpretability of results (van de Vijver & Leung, 1997). Clearly, the choice and appropriateness of methodology can make a difference in any research endeavor. In cross-cultural research, however, one could go to the extreme of classifying this as one of the most critical decisions. In this section, we briefly review such cross-cultural methodological considerations. Specifically, this section will address equivalence (Hui & Triandis, 1985; Mullen, 1995; Poortinga, 1989) and bias (Poortinga & van de Vijver, 1987; van de Vijver

& Leung; van de Vijver & Poortinga, 1997) as key methodological concerns inherent in cross-cultural research. Then sampling, wording, and translation are discussed as important means of overcoming some identified biases.

Equivalence

Achieving cross-cultural equivalence is an essential prerequisite in ensuring valid cross-cultural comparisons. Equivalence *cannot* be assumed a priori. Each cross-cultural study needs to establish cross-cultural equivalence. As such, equivalence has been extensively discussed in cross-cultural research, albeit using different terms to describe the phenomenon. For instance, Mullen (1995) uses the term measurement equivalency and describes its three key aspects: translation equivalence, metric equivalence, and calibration equivalence. He then defines metric equivalence to imply that subjects across cultures respond to measurement scales in the same way. Furthermore, he views scalar inequivalence and inconsistent scoring across populations as two major threats to metric equivalence. Poortinga's (1989) categorization of equivalence distinguishes between equivalence at the construct level (termed identical and nonidentical domains of generalization) and measurement scale equivalence. The latter includes equivalence at the following hierarchy of levels: same scale origin and same metric, same metric, and same metric after linear transformation.

To alleviate confusion created by the multiplicity of concepts and terms used to describe different but somewhat overlapping aspects of equivalence, Hui and Triandis (1985) have integrated prior research into a summary framework that consists of four levels of equivalence: conceptual/functional equivalence, equivalence in construct operationalization, item equivalence, and scalar equivalence. Van de Vijver and Leung (1997) use a similar typology: construct inequivalence, construct equivalence (also called structural equivalence), measurement unit equivalence, and scalar equivalence. Even though each level of equivalence is a prerequisite for the subsequent levels, in practice the distinction between adjacent levels of equivalence often becomes blurry. Nonetheless, the objective in cross-cultural research is to achieve all four types of equivalence. Hui and Triandis' four levels of equivalence are discussed next.

Conceptual/functional equivalence is the first requirement for cross-cultural comparisons and refers to whether a given construct has similar meaning across cultures. Furthermore, to be functionally equivalent, the construct should be embedded in the same nomological network of antecedents, consequents, and correlates across cultures. For instance, workers from different cultures may rate "supervisor is considerate" as a very important characteristic; however, the meaning of "considerate" may vary considerably across cultures (Hoecklin, 1994).

Equivalence in construct operationalization refers to whether a construct is manifested and operationalized the same way across cultures. Not only should the construct be operationalized using the same procedure across cultures, but the operationalization should also be equally meaningful.

Item equivalence refers to whether identical instruments are used to measure the constructs across cultures. This is necessary if the cultures are to be numerically compared.

Finally, *scalar equivalence* (or full score comparability; van de Vijver & Leung, 1997) occurs if the instrument has achieved all prior levels of equivalence and the construct is measured on the same metric. This implies that "a numerical value on the scale refers to same degree, intensity, or magnitude of the construct regardless of the population of which the respondent is a member" (Hui & Triandis, 1985, p.135).

Bias: Sources, Detection, and Prevention

To achieve equivalence, one has to first identify and understand factors that may introduce biases in cross-cultural comparisons. Van de Vijner and Poortinga (1997) describe three different types of biases: construct bias, method bias, and item bias.

Construct bias occurs when a construct measured is not equivalent across cultures both at a conceptual and at an operational level. This can result from different definitions of the construct across cultures, lack of overlap in the behaviors associated with a construct (e.g., behaviors associated with being a good son or daughter [filial piety] vary across cultures; van de Vijver & Leung, 1997), poor sampling of relevant behaviors to be represented by items on instruments, and incomplete coverage of the construct (van de Vijver & Leung). Construct bias can lead to lack of conceptual/functional equivalence and lack of equivalence in construct operationalization.

There are a number of techniques used to detect the presence of construct bias. First, informants in each culture should be asked to describe the construct and associated behaviors (Serpell, 1993) to ascertain that the construct is not only identical across cultures, but that it also encompasses similar behaviors. Second, internal structure congruence techniques can be used to assess the anatomy of the construct across cultures (Hui & Triandis, 1985). These include techniques such as factor analysis, which can be used to examine the factor structures of an instrument across cultures (Hui & Triandis; van de Vijver & Leung, 1997). Differences in factor structures point to possible construct bias. Other internal structure congruence techniques include multidimensional scaling (Hui & Triandis), "Simultaneous Factor Analysis in Several Populations" (which relies on confirmatory factor analysis using structural equation modeling tools such as LISREL), and comparison of correlation matrices (Hui & Triandis). Finally, construct bias may be detected by embedding the construct in a nomological set of relationships (Hui & Triandis). If the construct antecedents and consequents differ across cultures, then construct bias may be suspected.

Method bias refers to bias in the scores on an instrument that can arise from characteristics of an instrument or its administration (van de Vijver & Leung, 1997) which result in subjects across cultures not responding to measurement scales in the same manner (Mullen, 1995). Method bias gives rise to concerns about the internal validity of the study. One source of method bias is sample inequivalency in terms of demographics, educational experience, organizational position, etc. Other method bias concerns relate to differential social desirability of responses (Ross & Mirowsky, 1984) and inconsistent scoring across populations (termed selection-instrumentation effects by Cook & Campbell, 1979). For instance, on Likert scales Koreans tend to avoid extremes and prefer to respond using the midpoints on the scales (Lee & Green, 1991), while Hispanics tend to choose extremes (Hui & Triandis, 1985). Differential scoring methods may also arise if respondents from a particular culture or country are not familiar with the type of instrument being used.

Other biases include differences in physical conditions of administering the instrument (such as noise and lighting); communication problems between interviewer and interviewee, particularly when the language used in the study is not the native language of the interviewer/interviewee; differential response procedures; and differential familiarity with the stimuli used in the study. Method bias can influence both conceptual/functional equivalence, equivalence of operationalization, and item equivalence.

Before attributing a significant main effect for culture to true cultural differences, method bias needs to be ruled out. To detect method bias, van de Vijver and Leung (1997) suggest administering the same instrument to the different cultures repeatedly and examining differential changes in scores. If these changes are dissimilar then method bias is present. Furthermore, method triangulation can also be used to assess method bias (Lipson & Meleis, 1989).

Method bias can be reduced if careful attention is devoted to sampling and administration of the instrument. Sampling equivalence can be achieved if the cross-cultural groups are matched on key demographic, educational, and socioeconomic characteristics. Furthermore, identical administration procedures should be followed across cultures (i.e., a detailed instruction manual should be developed that anticipates contingencies), including the physical environment within which the instrument is administered. Familiarity of respondents across cultures with the testing techniques, item formats, test conventions, and procedures should also be assessed, and only those that are appropriate across cultures should be employed. In addition, communication between the interviewer and respondent is enhanced when the two have similar cultural backgrounds.

Item bias refers to measurement artifacts. These can arise from poor item translation, complex wording of items, or items inappropriate for a cultural context. Consequently, item bias is best prevented through careful attention to these issues. Like method bias, item bias can influence both conceptual/functional equivalence, equivalence of operationalization, and item equivalence.

Item bias can be detected via a number of statistical techniques known collectively as item bias or differential item functioning techniques (see Hui & Triandis, 1985, and van de Vijver & Leung, 1997, for a comprehensive review and Berk, 1982, for a set of articles). These techniques are based on the premise that irrespective of culture, individuals of the same standing on the construct should have the same expected average score on the construct. Differential item functioning techniques include regression methods (Poortinga, 1971, 1975), analysis of variance (Clauser, Mazor, & Hambleton, 1994; Cleary & Hilton, 1968), item response theory (Lord, 1980; Lord & Novick, 1968; Shepard, Camilli, & Averill, 1981; Thiesen, Steinberg, & Wainer, 1993), response pattern methods such as Delta plots (Angoff, 1982), standardized p-difference (Dorans & Kulick, 1986), the Mantel-Haenszel procedure (Dorans & Holland, 1993; Holland & Thayer, 1988), alternating least squares optimal scaling, and multiple-group LISREL (Mullen, 1995).

However, use of these techniques is not without its drawbacks. The most significant concerns in using differential item functioning techniques to detect item bias are: (a) the frequent lack of convergence of bias statistics among the different techniques (Devine & Raju, 1982; Ironson & Subkoviak, 1979; Reise, Widaman, & Pugh, 1993; Rudner, Getson, & Knight, 1980; Shepard et al., 1981); (b) the poor stability of item bias statistics in test-retest studies (Hoover & Kolen, 1984; Skaggs & Lissitz, 1992); and (c) the low agreement between statistical methods and experts' subjective judgments about item bias (Englehard, Hansche, & Rutledge, 1990; Plake, 1980).

Table 1 presents a summary of how the three types of bias can be prevented or detected. The next section discusses three important methods of bias prevention: sampling, and wording and translation. The chapter concludes by presenting a set of cross-cultural methodological guidelines derived by a committee of international scholars.

Sampling

Sampling decisions in cross-cultural studies involve two distinct levels: sampling of cultures and sampling of subjects (van de Vijver & Leung, 1997). Sampling of cultures involves decisions associated with selecting the cultures to be compared in the study. Many studies involve a convenience sample of cultures, typically ones where the researcher has preestablished contacts. Even though this strategy reduces the considerable costs of conducting cross-cultural research, it may hinder interpretability of results, particularly when no differences are observed across cultures (van de Vijver & Leung). Systematic sampling of cultures, on the other hand, identifies cultures based on theoretical considerations. Typically, this involves selecting cultures that are at different points along a theoretical continuum such as a cultural dimension. Random sampling of cultures involves selection of a large number of cultures randomly and allows wider generalizability of results.

Table 1. Types of Bias, Prevention and Detection.

	Detection	Prevention
Construct Bias (focus: Constructs)	• Informants describe construct and associated behaviors • Factor analysis • Multidimensional scaling • Simultaneous confirmatory factor analysis in several populations • Comparison of correlation matrices • Nomological network	• Informants describe construct and associated behaviors in each culture
Method Bias (focus: Administration Procedures)	• Repeated administration of instrument • Method triangulation • Monomethod-multitrait matrix	• Sampling (matching, statistical controls) • Identical physical conditions of administering the instrument • Unambiguous communication between interviewer and interviewee • Ensure familiarity with the stimuli used in the study
Item Bias (focus: Operationalizations)	• Analysis of variance • Item response theory • Delta plots • Standardized p-difference • Mantel-Haenszel procedure • Alternating least squares optimal scaling • Multiple-group LISREL	• Wording • Translation

Most cross-cultural studies discussing sampling considerations, however, refer to sampling of subjects. Ensuring sample equivalency is an important methodological consideration in cross-cultural research, and it refers to the inclusion of subjects that are similar on demographic, educational, and socioeconomic characteristics. Sample equivalency can be achieved by either the matching of subjects across groups based on these background variables or statistically controlling for the differences by including such demographic variables as covariates in the cross-cultural comparisons (van de Vijver & Leung, 1997).

Many studies choose students as subjects both for convenience reasons and also because these students provide an ideal matched sample in terms of their demographic characteristics. Students are readily available, are normally cooperative, and follow instructions well, and the experimenter can even claim that she is improving the students' educational experience (Hampton, 1979). Moreover, with the internationalization of education, sometimes one does not even have to go to another country to find a sizable sample. In the United States, many universities have a large body of foreign students. Several researchers, however, have taken exception, or at least presented cautionary notes, with the use of students as subjects (Khera & Benson, 1970; Shuptine, 1975). Hampton found that in nine of the 10 studies reviewed in international marketing, students had been used as subjects. His own analysis was inconclusive, suggesting that although the use of students may be acceptable in some cases, external validity of studies would be enhanced by choosing an appropriate sample. For instance, Englehard et al. (1990), when describing the international meaning of work (MOW) project, mention that their samples were matched across countries on occupation, a way to reach equivalence.

In the choice of an appropriate sample for cross-cultural survey research, a distinction is made between representativeness and scope of the sample. Representativeness is critical when the objective is to demonstrate differences between nations, whereas for other specific needs—such as studying the effect of education on citizenship participation—representativeness is not enough (Brislin & Thorndike, 1973), and stratified sampling becomes relevant. A special sampling design may be needed depending on the question asked. A common sampling problem, however, encountered in many cross-cultural studies is the lack of (or limited) existence of lists from which to draw samples, or the fact that many existing lists contain many errors.

In deciding on the nature of the sampling frame, Brislin and Thorndike (1973) suggest that several questions need to be answered, some similar to questions pertinent to non-cross-cultural research: (a) Should a national sample be attempted, given the goals of a specific project, the adequacy of national lists, and the possibility of different response rates from country to country? (b) How many callbacks to not-at-home people should be attempted? (c) What replacement procedures should be used? (d) On what basis, if any, can respondents be self-selected? (the answers to points b, c, and d should be included in the final description of the sample); and (e) How good is the sampling frame? Are there different sets of information in existence to check the adequacy of the frame?

Finally, in surveys administered personally, the choice of interviewers is critical since unambiguous communication between interviewer and respondent is crucial in reducing method bias. Interviewers should, to the extent possible, belong to the same socio-economic-cultural strata as the interviewees. They should also be appropriately trained and assigned to specific tasks and areas, and their work checked to avoid nightmares such as fabricated data.

Wording and Translation

This is one of the key problems in cross-cultural methods, since in most cases different cultures also have different languages. Even in cases when subjects from different countries are conversant with English, they may miss the nuances of the intended meanings in questionnaire items (e.g., British, Canadian, and American English all have unique terms). Researchers should ensure that measurement instruments keep the same meaning after translation. Moreover, a given latent construct should be measured by the same questionnaire items in different populations. In fact, researchers such as Irvine and Carrol (1980) made a convincing case to use factor matching procedures to test for invariance of factor structures across groups before any quantitative analysis is performed.

To translate correctly, there is a need to translate to the target language—which needs to be performed by a native speaker of the target language—and then back translate to the original language, this time by a different native speaker of the original language. Brislin (1986) provides fairly complete guidelines about this process. He starts by suggesting that the original instrument should be written with an eye toward translation. Therefore, he recommends that the original instrument should: (a) use short simple sentences of less than 16 words; (b) use the active rather than the passive voice; (c) repeat nouns instead of using pronouns, which may not be translatable; (d) avoid colloquialisms and metaphors; (e) avoid the subjunctive such as could, would, or should; (f) add short sentences to add context; (g) avoid adverbs and propositions; (h) avoid possessives; (i) use specific rather than general terms; (j) avoid vagueness; (k) use wording that is familiar to translators; and (l) avoid sentences with two different verbs.

Similarly, when modifying items, one should: (a) attempt to retain functional equivalency; (b) use knowledge about the target culture to improve translation; and (c) keep in mind the translation problems when evaluating the results. To develop new items, adequate pretesting with the correct bilingual population should be performed, perhaps in collaboration with colleagues from other cultures.

Implications of Methodological Issues

Judging by the issues described above, achieving cross-cultural equivalence is all but straightforward. However, it is also clear that many precautions can be taken to prevent construct, method, and item bias and thus increase the level of equivalence. These range from sampling, wording, and translation to careful attention to administration procedures across cultures. A number of guidelines for cross-cultural research have been put forth by an international committee of scholars (Hambleton, 1994; van de Vijver & Hambleton, 1996). Even though the primary focus of these is on research on psychological and educational issues, these guidelines easily generalize to MIS research. These guidelines, taken from van de Vijver and Leung (1997), are shown in Appendix A.

In addition to prevention, various statistical tools can assist in the detection of the various types of biases. In summary, similar patterns of functional relationships among variables need to be shown (Triandis, 1976). Moreover, multimethod measurement not only can avoid the confound between the interaction of the method and groups studied but also is unlikely to share the same statistical underlying assumptions or even require strong conceptualization ability (Hui & Triandis, 1985). This idea is similar to the notions of multiple operationism and conceptual replication (Campbell & Fiske, 1959). Hui and Triandis claim that this may not be as difficult as one may think, as long as there is prior planning of research. As an example they mention that an instrument may be improved by proper translation techniques, and "then establish conceptual/functional equivalence as well as instrument equivalence by the nomological network method and by examination of internal structure congruence. After that, the response pattern method and regressional methods can be used to test item equivalence and scalar equivalence" (p. 149).

The major implication of methodological problems is complications in making valid inferences from cross-cultural data. Clearly, there are many problems with correctly inferring from data in a cross-cultural research project and attributing results to true cross-cultural differences. To do so, alternative explanations need to be ruled out. Establishing (and not merely assuming) the four levels of cross-cultural equivalence previously discussed in this chapter is a major step in this direction.

CONCLUSION

Initial attempts at reviews of cross-cultural research in MIS (Evaristo, Karahanna, & Srite, 2000) show that for the most part MIS studies have refrained from testing theories across cultures, and when comparisons are made they are often post hoc comparisons utilizing data from prior published studies in other countries. Clearly, this provides some insights into differences across cultures but suffers from a number of methodological shortcomings. In fact, the conclusions of those authors were:

> *In summary, we suggest that there are mainly three points where the MIS cross-cultural research is lacking: lack of theory base (testing or building); inclusion of culture as antecedents of constructs; and general improvement in methodologies used.*

All three points are related, although to different extents, to methodological issues. The conclusion is that, to reach the same level of sophistication and quality already attained by mainstream MIS research, cross-cultural MIS research needs to seriously attend to cross-cultural methodological issues. The current paper is a step ahead in this direction.

REFERENCES

Angoff, W. H. (1982). Use of difficulty and discrimination indices for detecting item bias. In R. A. Beck (Ed.), *Handbook of Methods for Detecting Item Bias* (pp. 96-116). Baltimore, MD: Johns Hopkins University Press.

Berk, R. A. (ed.) (1982). *Handbook of Methods for Detecting Item Bias*. Baltimore, MD: John Hopkins University Press.

Brislin, R. W. (1986). The wording and translation of research instruments. In W. J. Lonner & J. Berry (Eds.), *Field Methods in Cross-Cultural Research,* Thousand Oaks, CA: Sage Publications.

Brislin, R. W., Lonner, W. J. & Thorndike, R. M. (1973). *Cross-Cultural Research Methods*, New York, NY: John Wiley & Sons.

Campbell, D. T., & Fiske, D. W. (1959). Convergent and discriminant validation by the multitrait-multimethod matrix. *Psychological Bulletin, 56,* 81-105.

Clauser, B. E., Mazor, K. M., & Hambleton, R. K. (1994). The effect of score group width on the Mantel-Haenszel procedure. *Journal of Educational Measurement, 31,* 67-78.

Cleary, T. A., & Hilton, T. L. (1968). An investigation of item bias. *Educational and Psychological Measurement, 28,* 61-75.

Cook, T., & Campbell, D. (1979). *Quasi-Experimentation: Design and Analysis Issues for Field Settings.* Boston, MA: Houghton Mifflin.

Devine, P. J., & Raju, N. S. (1982). Extent of overlap among four item bias methods. *Educational and Psychological Measurement, 42,* 1049-1066.

Dorans, N. J., & Holland, P.W. (1993). DIF detection and description: Mantel-Haenszel and standardization. In P. W. Holland & H. Wainer (Eds.), *Differential Item Functioning* (pp. 35-66). Hillsdale, NJ: Lawrence Erlbaum.

Dorans, N. J., & Kulick, E. (1986). Demonstrating the utility of the standardization approach to assessing unexpected differential item performance on the Scholastic Aptitude Test. *Journal of Educational Measurement, 23,* 355-368.

Englehard, G., Hansche, L., & Rutledge, K. E. (1990). Accuracy of bias review judges in identifying differential item functioning on teacher certification tests. *Applied Measurement in Education, 3,* 347-360.

Evaristo, J. R., Karahanna, E., & Srite, M. (2000). *Cross-Cultural Research in MIS: A Review.* Paper Presented at the *Global Information Technology Management Conference*, Memphis, TN.

Hambleton, R. K. (1994). Guidelines for adapting educational and psychological tests: A progress report. *European Journal of Psychological Assessment, 10,* 229-244.

Hampton, G. (1979). Students as subjects in international behavioral studies. *Journal of International Business Studies, 10*(2), 94-96.

Hoecklin, L. (1994). *Managing Cultural Differences — Strategies for Competitive Advantage.* Workingham, UK: Addison-Wesley.

Holland, P. W., & Thayer, D. T. (1988). Differential item performance and the Mantel-Haenszel procedure. In H. Wainer & H. I. Braun (Eds.), *Test Validity* (pp. 129-145). Hillsdale, NJ: Lawrence Erlbaum.

Hoover, H. D., & Kolen, M. J. (1984). The reliability of six item bias indices. *Applied Psychological Measurement, 8,* 173-181.

Hui, H., & Triandis, H. (1985). Measurement in cross-cultural psychology. *Journal of Cross-Cultural Psychology, 16*(2), 131-152.

Ironson, G. H., & Subkoviak, M. J. (1979). A comparison of several methods of assessing item bias. *Journal of Educational Measurement, 16,* 209-225.

Irvine, S., & Carrol, W. (1980). Testing and assessment across cultures: Issues in methodology and theory. In H. C. Triandis & W. Lonner (Eds.), *Handbook of Cross-Cultural Psychology: Methodology* (pp. 181-244). Boston, MA: Allyn & Bacon.

Khera, I. P., & Benson, J. D. (1970, November). Are students really poor substitutes for businessmen in behavioral research? *Journal of Marketing* (November), 529-532.

Lee, C., & Green, R. (1991). Cross-cultural examination of the Fishbein behavioral intentions model. *Journal of International Business Studies, 22*(2), 289-305.

Lipson, J. G., & Meleis, A. I. (1989). Methodological issues in research with immigrants. *Medical Anthropology, 12*, 103-115.

Lord, F. M. (1980). *Applications of Item Response Theory to Practical Testing Problems.* Hillsdale, NJ: Lawrence Erlbaum.

Lord, F. M., & Novick, M. R. (1968). *Statistical Theories of Mental Test Scores.* Reading, MA: Addison-Wesley.

Mullen, M. (1995, 3rd Quarter). Diagnosing measurement equivalence in cross-national research. *Journal of International Business Studies, 26*(3), 573-596.

Plake, B. S. (1980). A comparison of a statistical and subjective procedure to ascertain item validity: One step in the test validation process. *Educational and Psychological Measurement, 40*, 397-404.

Poortinga, Y. H. (1971). Cross-cultural comparisons of maximum performance tests: Some methodological aspects and some experiments with simple auditory and visual stimuli. *Psychologia Africana Monograph Supplement, 6*.

Poortinga, Y. H. (1975). Some implications of three different approaches to inter-cultural comparison. In J. W. Berry & W. J. Lonner (Eds.), *Applied Cross-Cultural Psychology* (pp. 329-332). Amsterdam: Swets & Zeitlinger.

Poortinga, Y. H. (1989). Equivalence in cross-cultural data: An overview of basic issues. *International Journal of Psychology, 24*(6), 737-756.

Poortinga, Y. H., & van de Vijver, F. (1987). Explaining cross-cultural differences: Bias analysis and beyond. *Journal of Cross-Cultural Psychology, 18*(3), 259-282.

Reise, S. P., Widaman, K. F., & Pugh, R. H. (1993). Confirmatory factor analysis and item response theory: Two approaches for exploring measurement invariance. *Psychological Bulletin, 114*, 552-566.

Ross, C. E., & Mirowsky, J. (1984). Socially-desirable response and acquiescence in cross-cultural survey of mental health. *Journal of Health and Social Behavior, 25*, 189-197.

Rudner, L. M., Getson, P. R., & Knight, D. L. (1980). A Monte Carlo comparison of seven biased item detection techniques. *Journal of Educational Measurement, 17*, 1-10.

Serpell, R. (1993). *The Significance of Schooling: Life Journeys in an African Society.* Cambridge, UK: Cambridge University Press.

Shepard, L., Camilli, G., & Averill, M. (1981). Comparison of six procedures for detecting test item bias using both internal and external ability criteria. *Journal of Educational Statistics, 6*, 317-375.

Shuptine, K. (1975, July). On the validity of using students as subjects in consumer behavior expectations. *Journal of Business*, 383-390.

Skaggs, G., & Lissitz, R. W. (1992). The consistency of detecting item bias across different test administrations: Implications of another failure. *Journal of Educational Measurement, 29*, 227-242.

Thiesen, D., Steinberg, L., & Wainer, H. (1993). Detection of differential item functioning using the parameters of item response models. In P. W. Holland & H. Wainer (Eds.), *Differential Item Functioning* (pp. 67-113). Hillsdale, NJ: Lawrence Erlbaum.

Triandis, H. (1976). Methodological problems of comparative research. *International Journal of Psychology, 11*(3), 155-159.

van de Vijver, F., & Hambleton, R. K. (1996). Translating tests: Some practical guidelines. *European Psychologist, 1*, 89-99.

van de Vijver, F., & Leung, K. (1997). *Methods and Data Analysis for Cross-Cultural Research*. Thousand Oaks, CA: SAGE.

van de Vijver, F., & Poortinga, Y. H. (1997). Towards an integrated analysis of bias in cross-cultural assessment. *European Journal of Psychological Assessment, 13*, 21-29.

APPENDIX A

Guidelines for Translating and Adapting Instruments for Cross-Cultural Research (Source: Hambleton, 1994; van de Vijver & Hambleton, 1996; van de Vijver & Leung, 1997)

Context (defining the general background)

1. Effects of cultural differences that are not relevant or important to the main purposes of the study should be minimized to the extent possible.
2. The amount of overlap in the constructs in the population of interest should be assessed.

Instrument Development, Translation, and Adaptation

3. Instrument developers should ensure that the translation/adaptation process takes full account of linguistic and cultural differences among the populations for whom the translated/adapted versions of the instrument are intended.
4. Instrument developers should provide evidence that the language used in the directions, rubrics, and items themselves as well as in the handbook are appropriate for all cultural and language populations for whom the instrument is intended.
5. Instrument developers should provide evidence that the testing techniques, item formats, test conventions, and procedures are familiar to all intended populations.
6. Instrument developers should provide evidence that item content and stimulus material are familiar to all intended populations.
7. Instrument developers should implement systematic judgmental evidence, both linguistic and psychological, to improve the accuracy of the translation/adaptation process and compile evidence on the equivalence of all language versions.
8. Instrument developers should ensure that the data collection design permits the use of appropriate statistical techniques to establish item equivalence between the different language versions of the instrument.
9. Instrument developers should apply appropriate statistical techniques to (a) establish the equivalence of different versions of the instrument and (b) identify problematic components or aspects of the instrument which may be inadequate to one or more of the intended populations.
10. Instrument developers should provide information on the evaluation of validity in all target populations for whom the translated/adapted versions are intended.
11. Instrument developers should provide statistical evidence of the equivalence of questions for all intended populations.
12. Nonequivalent questions between versions intended for different populations should *not* be used in preparing a common scale or in comparing these populations. However, they may be useful in enhancing content validity of scores reported for each population separately.

Administration Procedures

13. Instrument developers and administrators should try to anticipate the types of problems that can be expected and take appropriate actions to remedy these problems through the preparation of appropriate materials and instructions.

14. Instrument administrators should be sensitive to a number of factors related to the stimulus materials, administration procedures, and response modes that can moderate the validity of the inferences drawn from the scores.

15. Those aspects of the environment that influence the administration of an instrument should be made as similar as possible across populations for whom the instrument is intended.

16. Instrument administration instructions should be in the source and target languages to minimize the influence of unwanted sources of variation across populations.

17. The instrument manual should specify all aspects of the instrument and its administration that require scrutiny in the application of the instrument in a new cultural context.

18. The administration should be unobtrusive, and the examiner-examinee interaction should be minimized. Explicit rules that are described in the manual for the instrument should be followed.

Documentation/Score Interpretations

19. When an instrument is translated/adapted for use in another population, documentation of the changes should be provided, along with evidence of the equivalence.

20. Score differences among samples of populations administered the instrument should not be taken at face value. The researcher has the responsibility to substantiate the differences with other empirical evidence.

21. Comparisons across populations can only be made at the level of invariance that has been established for the scale on which scores are reported.

22. The instrument developer should provide specific information on the ways in which the sociocultural and ecological contexts of the populations might affect performance of the instrument and should suggest procedures to account for these effects in the interpretation of results.

Chapter XII

Global Information Management Research: Current Status and Future Directions

Felix B. Tan
Auckland University of Technology, New Zealand

R. Brent Gallupe
Queen's University, Canada

ABSTRACT

A growing body of knowledge is being accumulated in the area of global information management (GIM). Research in this area has grown significantly in the 1990s. Not only are established IS journals publishing an increasing amount in this area, but there are now specific journals devoted to the major issues in the development, use, and management of global information systems. However, much of this research has been limited to isolated survey studies or case studies into particular aspects of GIM. This has resulted in a rather disjointed and ad hoc development of this literature that now needs some structure to further its development. The purpose of this chapter is to provide a framework for research into GIM. It hopes to set a future direction for research in this area by challenging IS researchers to consider studying a number of potentially productive subareas of GIM that the framework has identified as being unstudied or understudied. This research framework builds on the general IS framework of Ives, Hamilton, and Davis (1980) and surveys the GIM published literature between 1990 and 2000. The application of this literature to the Ives, Hamilton, and Davis framework indicates where much GIM research has been conducted and where further research needs to be done.

INTRODUCTION

Research in the field of global information management (GIM) is an area of information systems research that has grown tremendously in the 1990s (Palvia, 1998a). A large number of research studies have been published that have examined issues relating to the development, use, and management of information systems in a global context. In general, most of these studies have either been key issues studies[1] (where the researcher(s) surveys IS practitioners to determine what they feel are the key issues in this area) or they have been anecdotal studies that have described a particular development of an information system (Dutta & Doz, 1995; Neumann & Zviran, 1997; Shore, 1996). A survey of the literature in this area indicates that no systematic framework is guiding GIM research. It appears that current GIM research is being driven by temporal, "hot" issues in the field and not by a structured approach to knowledge accumulation. In our view, this seems to be leading to research that may have little enduring value, that possibly duplicates itself, and that does not stretch the boundaries of what we know.

What is needed is a general framework for research into GIM that aids in categorizing research that has already been done and that helps to identify where important research is still to be done. This framework is intended to help guide GIM research and challenge GIM researchers to look at their field from a broad perspective. It will help set future directions for GIM research by identifying those areas that have been understudied and beginning to find ways to examine those areas that have not been studied at all.

Research frameworks have been used in a number of fields to guide research in those areas (Shaw, Gardner, & Thomas, 1997; Snow & Thomas, 1994; Thomas & Dewitt, 1996). This is particularly true of information systems. The information systems field has used research frameworks for the past 20 to 30 years in order to identify where research was being done and where research was not being done (Dickson, Senn, & Chervany, 1977; Gorry & Scott Morton, 1971; Ives et al., 1980; Mason & Mitroff, 1973; Nolan & Wetherbe, 1981). Indeed, one of the main benefits of these frameworks has been to identify the "gaps" in the knowledge that has been accumulating in that field. A good research framework provides an overall perspective for the researcher that may point to potentially important and productive research areas that have been understudied.

The purpose of this paper is to provide a research framework that will help identify the "gaps" in GIM research. It is appropriate at this time to propose such a framework because enough GIM research has now been conducted and published that areas of research strength and weakness can be identified. We survey and analyze all the relevant published studies in journals that focus on the management of global information resources and apply them to the framework. The chapter proceeds as follows. First, GIM is defined and a review of previous GIM frameworks is described, indicating the appropriate application of those frameworks and why a broad research framework is needed. Next, the "model for global information management research" is described and the GIM studies are assigned to the framework. Finally, the model is discussed, which highlights areas where GIM research needs to be done and provides a "call to action" for GIM researchers worldwide.

GIM RESEARCH FRAMEWORKS

No formal definition of global information management could be found in the IS literature. Deans and Ricks (1991) refer to issues at the "interface of MIS and international business" (p. 58). Palvia (1997) refers to "global IT research" and describes a model to "assess the strategic impact of IT on a global organization engaged in international business" (p. 230). For this chapter, we define global information management as the development, use, and management of information systems in a global/international context. By *global* we mean those information systems that have impacts beyond a single country or country of origin. The term *global* is used in a general sense since no firm or information system is found in every country in the world. Global information management deals with management, technological, and cultural issues such as differing national communications infrastructures, differing IS quality standards, IS development in different cultures, and many others. GIM research is the rigorous and systematic study of the development, use, and operations/management of a global information system(s) in a multicountry organizational environment. At the same time, traditional GIM research includes numerous single country studies focusing on the management of the information resource in a domestic context. According to Palvia (1998a), these "first generation" studies have laid the foundation and helped define global IT. This paper has therefore included single country studies in the analysis.

Most of the published literature in GIM that provides some kind of guide to research in the field has concentrated on identifying the "key issues" in the global management of information resources (Badri, 1992; Deans & Ricks, 1991; Ives & Jarvenpaa, 1991; Palvia, 1998b; Watson et al., 1997). These publications survey various stakeholders involved in the research and practice of GIM and are useful in that they attempt to capture what these people think are the critical issues in the field.

Very few papers propose frameworks or models that will help guide comprehensive research in this area. One exception is the work of Deans and Ricks (1991), who identify key issues and develop a research model based on Nolan and Wetherbe's (1981) IS research model and Skinner's (1964) work on international dimensions. This model views research as a set of subsystems that places management information systems (or GIM) at the center of the set. Skinner's international dimensions (social/cultural, economic, technological, political/legal) are overlaid on this framework to show the scope of the issues involved in GIM. This model is useful in a general sense but does not appear to help in showing where previous research fits or in guiding future research.

Another exception is Palvia (1997). In this paper, a model that attempts to measure the strategic impact of IT on the global firm is proposed. This model is useful in that it identifies a number of strategic factors that should be considered in studying global IT.

However, this model does not identify key areas for future research in GIM and was not developed specifically to guide comprehensive research in the field.

Other preliminary frameworks with a focus on culture might also be considered GIM research frameworks. Ein-Dor, Segev, and Orgad (1993), in their model, contend that culture as a variable consists of three major dimensions—economic, demographic, and psycho-sociological. The authors argue that any research into global IT should consider these cultural dimensions. Nelson and Clark (1994) propose a model describing the effect of multicultural environments on IT development and use. However, both of these models are too narrow in their scope and do not provide a broad framework to guide research in GIM.

What appears to be missing at this point is an overall research model, similar to the early IS research models, which will help guide future research into GIM and help organize and categorize research previously done. According to Palvia (1998a), such a framework has yet to be developed.

A MODEL FOR GLOBAL INFORMATION MANAGEMENT RESEARCH

Ives, Hamilton, and Davis General IS Research Model

The research model for GIM that is developed in this paper is based on an early IS research model described by Ives et al. (1980). Palvia (1998a) argues that "for a framework to be useful and gain acceptance, it needs to be comprehensive yet parsimonious, and at the same time should have gone through some form of validation" (p. 8). He further added that the framework must clearly define the dependent variable(s) and the independent variable(s). The Ives, Hamilton, and Davis model (see Figure 1) meets this criteria in that it is comprehensive, has been validated by the authors, and clearly identifies variables to be researched. In addition, it provides a broad view of the IS field and has been widely cited in the IS literature.

Ives et al. (1980) sought to develop a comprehensive framework for research in management information systems (MIS). They reviewed the frameworks that had guided MIS research up to that point and found them lacking. Their intent was to provide a broad enough framework so that all MIS research could be categorized within it. They used a basic systems approach to identify the major components of their model.

According to Ives et al. (1980), the three categories of information systems environment (user, IS development, and IS operations), information systems processes, and information systems characteristics exist within an organizational environment and an external environment. Their environmental variable group consists of five classes—external, organizational, user, IS development, and IS operations. The characteristics within each class act as resources or constraints to the scope and form of each information system. These environmental classes are represented by rectangles in Figure 1. The information systems process variable group is made up of performance or outcome measures—development process, operations process, and use process. These process classes are portrayed in Figure 1 by ellipses. The third variable group, information

Figure 1. A Model for Information Systems Research (Ives, Hamilton, & Davis, 1980).

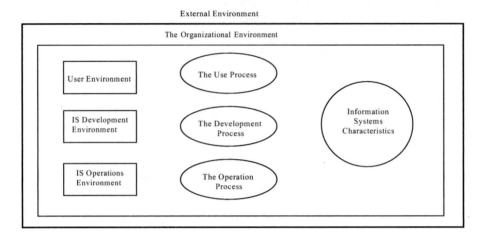

systems characteristics, describes the features and functionalities in the information system. This is depicted in Figure 1 as a circle. The authors provide a comprehensive description of each variable group and the classes delineated in their model.

Global Information Management Research Model

In the global information management context, this model extends beyond a single system in a single location or organizational context to multiple systems with diverse users in a global environment (see Figure 2). The external environment consists of the political, economic, and social conditions in the countries where the information systems operate. The organizational environment includes the structure, composition, and management processes of the organization or organizations that the systems function in. The user environment consists of all the different types of users and their character-istics that would interface with the system. The IS development environment includes the characteristics of the hardware and software and people in the locations where the global systems are developed and tested. The IS operations environment consists of the network and computing infrastructures that support a global IT environment.

In terms of the global information systems process variable group, the use process consists of measures of how diverse users use a global system. The development process includes measures of practices and procedures used to develop information systems in possibly widely dispersed locations. The operations process consists of measures of network and computing performance for systems that operate in many countries.

Finally, the global information systems characteristics variable group lists the functions and features of the specific global system or systems under study. These would include such characteristics as data structure, logic structure, security factors, as well as other attributes.

Figure 2. A Model for Global Information Management Research (Adapted Ives, Hamilton, & Davis).

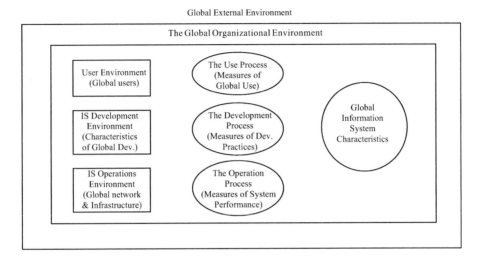

CATEGORIES OF GLOBAL INFORMATION MANAGEMENT RESEARCH

Together the three variable groups identified by Ives et al. (1980), and extended in Figure 2, can provide a number of different perspectives for research in GIM. Researchers can examine one or more variables within the same variable group or between variable groups. This chapter contends that GIM research can also be classified into five different categories as depicted in Figure 3.

Type I research involves variables within a single category—global IS environment, global IS processes, or global IS characteristics. An example of this category of GIM research is a study of the global IS development processes for a single company. Type II research explores the relationship between one or more variables from the process category and one or more from the environment category. An example of this type of GIM research might be a study of end-user satisfaction for a system that is used in a number of countries. Type III research examines the relationship between the IS characteristics and IS process variables. An example of this research might be a case study that examines the way information is presented to users and how they use the system in a variety of countries. Type IV research investigates the relationship between environmental resources and constraints and IS characteristics. This type of research might look at the content of an EDI system and its effect on organizational planning tasks. Type V research studies the relationship between one or more variables from each of the three categories. An example of this research might be a comprehensive study of the impact of national culture on the characteristics and use of a global EIS application.

Figure 3. Five Categories of Global Information Management Research.

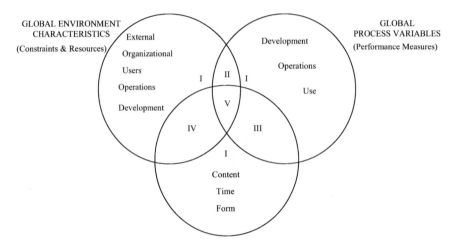

APPLICATION OF THE
GIM RESEARCH MODEL

The application of the GIM literature to the GIM research model can provide for a better understanding of the state of GIM research. An analysis of a representative sample of journal publications relevant to the field was conducted. The main purposes of this analysis are to establish the types of GIM research that have been done in the past and identify the gaps in the field for future work.

Method and Sample

The following approach was taken.

a.   A search for relevant GIM publications was the first step. It was felt that conceptual and empirical GIM research is more likely to be found in journals rather than other forms of publication such as books. Conference proceedings were not examined because it was assumed that high quality GIM research papers would be published in journals. As such the following journals were referenced:

•   Established IS journals where GIM-related research has been consistently published (i.e., *MIS Quarterly, Information Systems Research, Journal of Management Information Systems*, and *Information & Management*).

•   Niche journals that focus on publishing GIM research (i.e., the *Journal of Global Information Management, International Information Systems, Journal of Strategic Information Systems, Journal of Global Information Technology Management*, and *Journal of International Information Management*).

Table 1. Number of Publications in the Five Categories of GIM Research.

Research Type	Description	Count	Percent
Type I	A single variable group	323	80.1
Type II	Relationship between process and environment variable groups	68	16.9
Type III	Relationship between process and IS characteristics variable groups	6	1.5
Type IV	Relationship between environment and IS characteristics variable groups	4	1.0
Type V	Relationship between environment, process and IS characteristics variable groups	2	0.5
	Total Number of Publications	403	100%

- Regional IS journals from around the globe (i.e., *European Journal of Information Systems*, *Scandinavian Journal of Information Systems*, *Australian Journal of Information Systems*, and the *Asia Pacific Journal of Information Management*).
- Societal/Culture-oriented IS journals which publish research dealing primarily with socioeconomic issues and cross-cultural dimensions of societies across the globe (i.e., *Information Technology & People* and *The Information Society*).

An examination of these journals is expected to provide a representative sample of the research done in the field. The period covered in the analysis is 1990-2000.

b. Based on the full text of the paper (and sometimes on the abstract if the study was clearly described), the authors independently categorized the publications into the five research categories. This was determined by identifying the variables and variable groups examined in each article.

c. The authors also independently identified the research strategy employed in each article and categorized these.

d. In the final step, the authors independently identified distinct GIM research themes and categorized each article accordingly.

e. Disagreements between the authors were discussed and a classification was agreed upon.

Results of Analysis

The search process identified 403 GIM-related articles. These articles were categorized into the five types of research as summarized in Table 1. The research strategy employed was categorized using the same approach taken by Ives et al. (1980). Each of the five research types and the types of research strategy used are described next.

Type I Research: A Single Variable Group

This category of GIM research involves variables within a single variable group—environment, process, or IS characteristics. Three research subtypes can be identified:

Table 2. Breakdown of Type I GIM Research.

Variable Group Examined	Variable Class Examined	Type Ia	Type Ib	Type Ic
	External	82	}	
	Organization	29	}	
Environment	Development	28	} 30	NA
	Operations	30	}	
	User	4	}	
	Development	16	}	
Process	Operations	16	} 0	NA
	Use	32	}	
Characteristics	Information System	3	0	53
	Total Type I GIM Research	240	30	53
	Percent of Total Publications	59.6	7.4	13
	NA = Not Applicable			1

- Type Ia. Conceptual or methodological studies of a single variable or class of variables
- Type Ib. Analysis of the relationship between two or more variables from the same variable group
- Type Ic. Conceptualization or description of the characteristics a specific information system

The 323 Type I GIM research publications can in turn be broken down to the three subtypes. Table 2 illustrates the distribution.

Research classified as Type Ia tends to be highly descriptive or prescriptive in nature. These conceptual or methodological studies do not use any dependent or independent variables nor test any hypotheses. Of the 403 publications surveyed, 240 (59.6%) can be categorized as Type Ia. Eighty-two of the 240 Type Ia publications examine variables in the external environment. These involve cultural, political, legal, economic, educational, and trade variables. For example, Wan and Lu (1997) provided an overview of computer crime and related legislation in the People's Republic of China (legal environment). Robichaux and Cooper (1998) examined GSS participation in different cultural settings (cultural environment). Mehta and Darier (1998) reported on electronic governmentality in the new wired world (political environment). Dutta (1992) considered the rural coverage of telecommunication infrastructure in developing nations (economic environment). Forer, Goldstone, and Tan (1998) reviewed developments in utilizing geographic information technology to create a flexible IT-rich learning environment (educational environment).

Research involving variables from the development, operations, and organization environment is also popular. Studies in the development environment tend to focus on comparing IS development characteristics between different countries. For example, Foley, Meyer, and Sorensen (1996) compared U.S., Japanese and European software development practices and methods. Couger, Halttunen, and Lyytinen (1991) compared the motivation environment for programmers/analysts in Finland and the United States. Examples of research on operations environment include Ramanujan and Lou (1997), who discussed the issues involved in selective outsourcing of maintenance operations from an offshore location; and Niederman (1993), who considered the issues facing information systems professionals as expatriates. Research on the organization environment is highly varied. For example, Jarvenpaa and Ives (1994) discussed the opportunities and challenges facing the global network organization of the future. Smits and van der Poel (1996) examined the practice of information strategy in six information-intensive organizations in the Netherlands. Pervan (1997) explored the key issues in IS management in Australasia. Mehta and Shah (1997) investigated the impact of IT on the global workforce. Slaughter and Ang (1995) compared the IS employment structures between the United States and Singapore. A total of four Type Ia publications investigated variables in the user environment. An example is Ishman's (1998) paper on Latvian attitude toward IT.

In comparison, there is relatively little Type Ia research involving the IS process and IS characteristics variable groups. Within the process group, 32 publications can be classified as research examining the use process. For example, Lebre La Rovere (1998) explored the diffusion of IT in Brazilian small and medium-sized enterprises. Coakes and Merchant (1996) examined the use of expert systems in UK businesses. Mahmood, Gemoets, and Goslar (1995) reported on the use of IT in Mexico. Andersen and Kraemer (1994) compared the use of IT in the public sector in the United States and Scandinavia. Harrison, Farn, and Coakley (1992) compared user satisfaction with MIS across two cultures. There appears to be relatively little research investigating the development and operations process classes. According to Ives et al. (1980), development measures include participation, support, and satisfaction with the development effort whilst operations measures encompass resource use, service to users, and satisfaction of end users. Examples of these include: Lai and Reeh (1995), who compared ISDN implementation in the United States and Germany; Cross, Earl, and Sampler (1997), who reported on the transformation of the IT function at British Petroleum; and Yusof and Rahim (1994), who gave a Malaysian perspective on problems in computer-based IS development.

Of the 403 GIM publications reviewed, only 30 (7.4%) can be classified as Type Ib research. Studies in this category explore the link between two or more variables from the same variable group. There is a good mix of variables examined, with just under half focusing on the relationship between external/organizational environments and IS development/operations characteristics. For example, Dologite, Fang, Chen, Mockler, and Chao (1997) examined the impact of organizational characteristics on IS planning, support, and management in Chinese state-owned enterprises. Tractinsky and Jarvenpaa (1995) explored IS design decisions in global and domestic contexts. Walczuch, Singh, and Palmer (1995) analyzed the cultural motivations for transborder data flow legislation.

Type Ic research conceptualizes or describes the characteristics of a specific information system. Fifty-three (13.1%) of the 403 articles fall into this category. Most of the 53 articles describe the features and functionalities of a particular system in a selected country or region. For example, Lockett and Holland (1996) outlined the international payment system at Barclays Bank in the UK. Matsuda (1994) gave an account of IT in the agricultural commodity markets in Japan. Cats-Baril and Jelassi (1994) described the development of Minitel, the French national videotex system. Campbell-Kelly (1996) explored the changes in IT within the British Census.

Type II Research: Relationship Between Process and Environment Variable Groups

This category of GIM research explores the impact of one or more variables from the environment variable group on the process variable group measures—development, operations, and use. Sixty-eight (16.9%) of the publications analyzed can be grouped as Type II research. The emphasis of publications in this category appears to be on the relationships between the external/organizational characteristics and the use process class—36 (52.9%) of the 68 analyzed. Most of the research studying the external environment has used cultural characteristics as the independent variable. This supports the argument by authors in the field that national culture is an important factor in GIM research (Ein-Dor et al., 1993; Nelson & Clark, 1994; Palvia, 1998b). For example, Hill, Loch, Straub, and El-Sheshai (1998) reported on a qualitative assessment of the Arab culture and IT transfer. Marchewka and Wu (1997) explored the link between culture and IT diffusion in the People's Republic of China. Mejias, Shepherd, Vogel, and Lazaneo (1997) investigated the effects of U.S. and Mexican culture on perceived satisfaction levels. Table 3 summarizes the 68 Type II research articles into the classes according to the relationships examined.

Type III Research: Relationship Between Process and IS Characteristics Variable Groups

This category of GIM research focuses on the influence of IS characteristics on the variable classes in the process variable group. A review of the 403 publications indicates that only six (1.5%) articles fall into this category. All six research articles studied the impact of IS characteristics on the use process variable. For instance, Raymond and Bergeron (1997) examined the effect of a global distribution system on the use of the technology in the travel industry in Canada and Belgium. Jansen (1995) assessed the impact of various IT projects on the diffusion and use of IT in rural Norway. Peffers and Tuunainen (1998) investigated the effect of an online banking application on the business value of a global bank in Hong Kong. Others considered the impact of group support systems on planning effectiveness and group productivity (Aiken, Hwang, Paolillo, Kim, & Lu, 1994; Splettstoesser & Splettstoesser, 1998). None of the publications analyzed examined the relationship between IS characteristics and the IS development and IS operations process classes.

Type IV Research: Relationship Between Environment and IS Characteristics Variable Groups

This category of GIM research examines the relationship between environmental characteristics and IS characteristics. Only four (1%) of the 403 articles reviewed can be classified in this category. All four publications examined the effect of a particular type

Table 3. Breakdown of Type II GIM Research.

Process	Classes of Variables in Environment Group				
Group	External	Organization	Development	Operations	User
Development Process	4	3	3	0	2
Operations Process	3	6	1	4	1
Use Process	17	19	1	1	3
Total Type II GIM Research = 68					

of IS on various environmental variables. For instance, Cox and Ghoneim (1996) compared the effects of EDI on seven U.K. industry sectors. Reekers and Smithson (1996) assessed the impact of EDI on the trading relationships between manufacturers and suppliers in the German and U.K. automotive industries. Jonas and Laios (1992) explored the effect of an expert system on managerial planning tasks in Greek small to medium-sized enterprises. None of the research in this category examined the impact of environment variables on the characteristics of IS.

Type V Research: Relationship Among All Variable Groups

This category of GIM research explores the relationships between variables from all three variable groups—environment, process, and IS characteristics. Of the 403 articles analyzed, only two (0.5%) can be classified in this category. Both articles explored the effect of variables in the environment and IS characteristics variable groups on the use process variable. One article examined the characteristics of the Norwegian's army culture and its IT system on successful adoption of IT (Tolsby, 1998). The other investigated the fit between managerial decision tasks and types of systems and its impact on the amount of IT use between Greek and U.S. managers (Ferratt & Vlahos, 1998).

Research Strategies

The other objective of the analysis of the 403 GIM publications is to determine the research strategies employed. This was done using the same classification scheme as Ives et al. (1980). Ives et al. used Van Horn's (1973) taxonomy of MIS research methods—case studies, field studies, field tests, and laboratory studies. They added a "non-data" classification to refer to studies that "relied primarily on secondary sources or concep-tual work" (p. 927). We have slightly modified this classification scheme by including action research and other qualitative research strategies in the "case study" category. Field studies include both survey and interview research strategies.

Table 4 presents the breakdown of the publications by research strategies used against the five categories of GIM research types. The cells shaded dark grey represent the research strategies that have not been used in the publications surveyed. The light grey shading identifies the research strategies underemployed.

Table 4. Research Strategies by GIM Research Types.

	Research Type	Publications Count	In GIM Percent	Case Study	Field Study	Field Test	Laboratory Study	Non-Data
Type I:	A Single Variable Group							
Ia:	A Specific Variable	240	59.5	61	91	1	0	97
Ib:	Relationship between variables with a Group	30	7.5	5	18	2	0	5
Ic:	Characteristics of a Specific IS	53	13.1	30	4	1	0	18
Type II	Relationship Between Environment & Process Variable Groups	68	16.9	17	47	3	1	0
Type III	Relationship Between IS Characteristics & Process Variable Groups	6	1.5	2	2	0	1	1
Type IV	Relationship Between Environment & IS Characteristics Variable Groups	4	1.0	2	1	0	1	0
Type V	Relationship Among All Variable Groups	2	0.5	1	1	0	0	0
Total		403		118	154	7	3	121
Percent		100%	100%	29.3%	38.2%	1.7%	0.8%	30.0%

The analysis presented in Table 4 suggests that GIM research is normally under-taken with field studies (38.2%), case studies (29.3%), and non-data (30.0%) research strategies. Research strategies used in each of the GIM research categories are summarized below.

- A good number of *Type Ia* research articles are descriptive or prescriptive in nature and involve conceptual work. Non-data research strategy is the dominant approach used in these conceptual works. Empirical Type Ia studies tend to employ case studies and field studies to examine a specific variable.
- Eighteen out of the 30 *Type Ib* research articles use field study to explore the relationship between two or more variables from the same variable group.
- Research in the *Type Ic* category mostly employs case study and non-data research strategies to examine the characteristics of specific information systems in domestic and global contexts.
- Field study is the preferred approach taken by *Type II* studies. The case study approach is also a popular strategy used to examine the link between the external/organizational environment and the IS use process.
- *Type III* research generally utilizes a wide range of strategies—from case study to laboratory experiments—to examine the effect of IS characteristics on the IS use process variable.
- Only case and field study research strategies are employed in *Type IV and Type V* research categories.

A large majority of the field studies are considered quantitative in nature. These are evidenced by formal propositions, quantifiable measures of variables, and hypothesis testing. Qualitative field studies have also been published. For example, Hill et al. (1998) reported on a qualitative field study of the Arab culture and IT transfer. Sheffield and Gallupe (1994) used qualitative techniques to analyze the long-term impacts of electronic meetings in New Zealand. The most common qualitative approach in GIM research is case study. Case study research can be positivist or interpretive (Myers, 1997). Interpretive case study as opposed to positivist does not predefine dependent and independent variables. Examples of these include Barrett and Walsham (1995), who used an interpretive case study method to evaluate issues of culture, learning, and leadership in the management of IT in a Jamaican insurance company; and Harvey (1997), who conducted an ethnographic case study of national culture differences in IT theory and practice between Germany and the U.S. Whereas, Dologite et al. (1997) examined the impact of changes in the Chinese economy (independent variable) on IS planning, support, and management (dependent variables) in four state-owned enterprises using a positivistic case study approach.

INTEGRATING THE RESEARCH MODEL WITH GIM KEY ISSUES

Although the field of GIM has a number of similarities with the study of IS as framed by Ives et al. (1980), there are a number of distinct themes which differentiate GIM research from the traditional scope of IS investigations. A content analysis of the 403 publications sampled reveal six distinct GIM research *themes*. Table 5 presents these themes and their descriptions.

As part of the analysis, the 403 GIM publications surveyed are categorized into these themes. Table 6 presents the results of this analysis.

By combining the GIM research model with the key research themes identified, a three-dimensional framework for GIM research can be developed (see Figure 4). The global information management research framework is intended to highlight the main research categories, strategies, and themes in the field. We contend that it is not sufficient to only consider just research categories and strategies. To ensure that the appropriate GIM issue is addressed, researchers must also reflect on a third dimension—the key GIM research themes. Through the three-dimensional GIM research framework, it is possible to consider individual cells in the framework to identify potentially important research projects or areas that have been understudied.

The remainder of this section describes the application of this three-dimensional GIM research framework, where all three aspects of research category, strategy, and theme are integrated.

Single country "domestic" type studies dominate GIM research. Of the 403 publications analyzed, 189 (46.9%) can be considered single country studies. All of these studies focus on different aspects of managing information resources in a domestic context. Most of these studies are Type Ia and Ic research using the case study or non-data research strategies. For instance, Kautz and McMaster (1994) presented a case study of an attempt to take a structured development method into use in the IT unit of a UK public sector organization. Wan and Lu (1997) provided an overview of computer crime and related legislation in the People's Republic of China using a non-data research strategy.

Table 5. Research Themes Distinct to GIM Research.

Research Themes In GIM Research	Description
Single Country Studies	The development, operations, management and use of IT in a domestic context. Does not include the management of information resources in a global context. For example, the adoption of IT in rural China.
Comparative Study of Nations	The comparison of IT development, operations, management and use between two or more countries. Culture is not a variable in these studies. For example, comparing the skills of systems analyst in Canada, New Zealand and Singapore.
Culture / Socio-economic Issues	The effect of national culture on IT development, operations, management and use. These are regarded as "pure" cross-cultural studies as opposed to those merely comparing nations. For example, exploring the effect of complex cultural dimensions on the level of IT transfer in Arab and East European nations. Also includes socio-economic issues relating to IT like government policy, legislation and economic factors.
Research Frameworks and Issues	Conceptual research offering frameworks, theory and research agendas on various aspects of global information management. Key issues studies in IS management from around the globe are included.
Global Information Resources Management	The development, operations, management and use of IT in a global context. Includes the management of information resources in a regional but not domestic context. For example, managing global IT outsourcing; motivating global IT development teams; and managing the introduction of telecommunications technology in Latin America.
Global Enterprise Management	Functional management of enterprises across national boundaries using IT. Includes the management of multinational and trans-national corporations. For example, the impact of IT on global supply chains, global distribution or global marketing.

Table 6. Research Themes Distinct to GIM Research.

Research Themes Distinct to GIM	Research Themes Count	Research Themes Percent
Single Country	189	46.9
Comparative Study of Nations	57	14.1
Culture	24	5.9
Socio-economic Issues	25	6.2
Research Concepts & Issues	25	6.2
Global Information Resources Management	61	15.2
Global Enterprise Management	22	5.5
Total GIM Publications	403	100

Figure 4. A Global Information Management Research Framework.

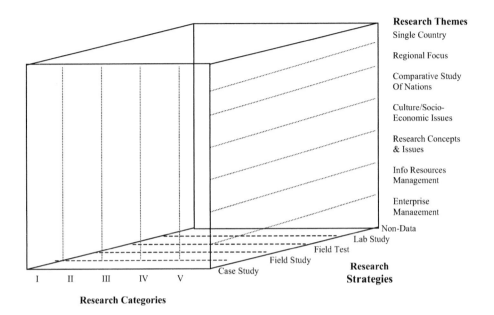

Studies comparing two or more nations prove to be another fruitful area of work. Fifty-seven (14.1%) can be classified into this group. The majority of these articles fall under the Type Ib and Type II categories. Three of the 6 Type III research articles are also comparative studies of nations. Several of these studies have compared the United States to countries from Europe, Asia, and the Middle East. For example, Abdul-Gader and Kozar (1995) examined the impact of computer alienation on IT investment decisions between the U.S and Saudi Arabia. Straub, Keil, and Brenner (1997) tested the technology acceptance model across three countries—Japan, Switzerland, and the United States. Others have compared two or more countries in the same region. For instance, Simon and Middleton (1998) analyzed the human resource management best practices in IS departments in Singapore, Hong Kong, Malaysia, and the People's Republic of China. Tam (1998) examined the impact of IT investments on firm performance and evaluation in four newly industrialized economies in Asia. In all of these instances, field study research strategy was used.

The "global information resources management" research theme accounts for 61 (15.2%) articles of the sample surveyed. Research in this category considers the development, operations, management, and use of IT in a global context. It includes the management of information resources in a regional but not domestic context. Most of the research in the global context is Type Ia and Ic using either case study, field study, or non-data research strategies. Examples of these are Ramanujan and Lou (1997), who conducted a field study on the issues involved in selective outsourcing of maintenance operations from an offshore location; Gibson and McGuire (1996), who discussed quality control for global software development using non-data research strategy; and Trauth and Thomas (1993), who called for a global standards policy for EDI.

The articles focusing on regions are primarily Type Ia research employing non-data research strategy. These articles describe IT-related issues in a given region or prescribe guidelines for IT diffusion and transfer in developing countries. These publications are not studies comparing countries within the region. For example, a paper by Gibson (1998) identifies important developmental factors in the relationship between IT diffusion and economic development in Latin America. Loh, Marshall, and Meadows (1998) discuss the ethical appropriateness of information and communication technologies for developing nations.

The "culture/socioeconomic issues" research themes account for 5.9% and 6.2% (respectively) of the 403 articles surveyed. What was surprising though is that only 24 (5.9%) articles of the total sample surveyed are what we considered "pure" cross-cultural research, as opposed to studies merely comparing two or more nations, but label themselves as multicultural studies. All of these publications are considered Type II GIM research, and field study is the predominant research strategy used. These 24 articles deal with and address the cultural dimensions and elements that are inherent in the countries studied. For instance, Hill et al. (1998) focuses on the complex sociocultural constructs (beliefs and values) which can influence the level of IT transfer in Arab nations. Straub (1994) investigated the effect of culture on the use of e-mail and fax technologies in Japan and the U.S. Harvey (1997) conducted an ethnographic study of national culture differences in IT theory and practice between Germany and the U.S. using Hofstede's (1980) framework. Hasan and Ditsa (1999) explored the impact of culture on the adoption of IT in three regions—Australia, West Africa, and the Middle East. Most of the publications dealing with the socioeconomic issues are considered Type Ia GIM research which primarily employ non-data research strategy. An example of this is the article by Mehta and Darier (1998), who discussed electronic government via the Internet.

The remaining two themes—"research concepts and issues" and "global enterprise management"—together account for less than 12% of the research surveyed . Conceptual research offering frameworks, theory, and research agendas on various aspects of GIM is categorized into the former group. For example, Nelson and Clark (1994) propose a research framework for cross-cultural issues in IS research. Martinsons and Westwood (1997) developed an explanatory theory of MIS in Chinese business culture. Deans and Ricks (1993) suggest an agenda for research linking IS and international business. Studies of key issues in GIM practice and research are also included in this grouping (Burn & Ma, 1993; Mata & Fuerst, 1997; Watson et al., 1997; Yang, 1996). The "global enterprise management" grouping focuses on research dealing with the management of different aspects of the enterprise across national boundaries using IT. The published research surveyed used both field and case study methodologies and primarily falls under Type I and Type II categories. The bulk of the research which falls in this grouping is publications on multinational companies. For instance, Chidambaram and Chismar (1994) examined the use and investment patterns in U.S. multinational corporations. Cummings and Guynes (1994) compared the IS activities in U.S. and non-U.S. subsidiaries of transnational corporations. There is, however, a dearth of studies dealing with IT and global supply chain, human resource, marketing, manufacturing, and distribution management. Exceptions are studies by Niederman (1993) and Sankar and Liu (1998).

DISCUSSION AND CALL TO ACTION

The application of the published research studies in GIM to the three-dimensional GIM research framework indicates a number of obvious gaps in the research that has been conducted to date. This section discusses the findings of the analysis of 403 GIM research publications and presents a call to action to GIM scholars. GIM research categories, research strategies, and research themes and their call to action are discussed in turn.

GIM Research Categories

What is immediately apparent is that most GIM research has been essentially single variable studies, and most of these have focused on environmental variables. This is not too surprising due to the nature of GIM research, but the lack of research across variable groups is interesting and may be leading to "one-dimensional" research that does not consider a variety of factors that make GIM so interesting and challenging.

It may be that the single variable group studies are the simplest and easiest to conduct. In the global context, this is an important consideration when "simple research" may involve multiple trips to different countries to complete the research. It may also be that single variable research provides the sharpest focus for research in this area and that conducting research across multiple variable groups leads to a level of complexity that is difficult to handle for both researchers and readers. Finally, the current scope and boundary of the field as perceived by its researchers may be somewhat "narrow." The lack of an overall research framework guiding GIM research may have contributed to this perception.

Call to action: We therefore encourage GIM researchers to move beyond the current single variable focus. Starting with the GIM research framework presented in Figure 4 and the findings of this paper, researchers should begin considering the dependent and independent variables to be studied. For instance, studies of environment variables should now include a measure of impact on a process variable— development, operations, and/or use—or a measure of impact on the characteristics of the global system being investigated. Research including variables from each of the three variable groups in the GIM research model (Figure 2) can lead to a more comprehensive understanding of the field. An example of this research might be a comprehensive study of the impact of national culture on the characteristics and use of a global EIS application.

GIM Research Strategies

In terms of research strategies, the predominant methods have been case and field studies as well as what we term "non-data" studies. Virtually no studies have been conducted using field tests and laboratory studies. This extensive use of qualitative techniques may be giving the impression that GIM research cannot be conducted using more quantitative techniques. We don't believe this is the case. Certainly the use of qualitative strategies has added to the field, and more quality studies of this type need to be conducted, perhaps using a variety of qualitative techniques from wider disciplines (Myers, 1997). In addition, we believe that there is also a need to conduct rigorous GIM research using quantitative techniques such as experiments. The balance between qualitative and quantitative approaches seems to be lacking in this area. We believe that conducting more quantitative studies where more variables are controlled and measured will provide the field with research that is testable and replicable.

Call to action: We agree with Palvia (1998a) that what is required is the building of a cumulative tradition in GIM research—a model-based approach developed a priori with clear research questions and/or propositions to be investigated. As presented earlier, the GIM field is an extension of the traditional IS field—beyond a single system in a single location to multiple systems with diverse users in a global environment. We argue that models developed and validated in the traditional IS field can be and should be applied to and validated within the global context. We are beginning to see some of this occurring in the more recent publications. For instance, Rose and Straub (1998) applied the technology acceptance model to the Arabic world, and Straub, Keil, and Brenner (1997) tested the technology acceptance model across three countries—Japan, Switzerland, and the U.S. However, there is an issue researchers must be alerted to as they consider variables to be included in their study. It is not as straightforward to operationalize many of these variables in a global setting. For example, does user satisfaction have the same meaning in countries with different cultures? Researchers are therefore warned to be very cautious when using measures validated in one global setting in another global setting.

Interviewing is the dominant technique employed by qualitative strategies surveyed in this paper. There are very few researchers who break out of the traditional mould and conduct studies using techniques like ethnography, interpretive epistemology, or grounded theory. Examples of recent studies employing these approaches are Harvey (1997), who conducted an ethnographic study of national culture differences in IT theory and practice between Germany and the U.S.; and Montealegre (1998), who explored Internet adoption in four Latin American countries using interpretive epistemology. We therefore challenge GIM scholars to consider using alternative qualitative techniques in GIM research.

GIM Research Themes

Single country "domestic" studies have been the predominant research theme. This type of research can be mostly classified as Type Ia and Ic categories of GIM research. They tend to be descriptive and exploratory. According to Palvia (1998a), these "first generation" studies are important, especially during the early years of GIM research. "They have been useful in defining the global IT field ... [and have] ... given us a reasonably good grasp of global IT" (p. 7).

Call to action: We believe that single country studies are as important today as they have been in the early years of GIM research, provided these studies include some insights for GIM practice and research. For instance, a study of the influence of government policy on the adoption of global neural networks in Latvia is only useful if it includes discussion on the implications of the study findings to GIM practice (i.e., to international companies planning to do business in the country) and research. Opportunities also abound for research on themes relating to national culture and global enterprise management. Surprisingly, there is comparatively little published research in journals examining national culture. It is generally accepted that differences in national culture may explain variations in IS in different cultures (Deans & Ricks, 1991; Ein-Dor et al., 1993; Shore & Venkatachalam, 1995, 1996). We therefore call for more research exploring how national culture can impact on the global IS process measures and to better understand the characteristics of IS developed and used in various cultural settings. There is also very little published research into aspects of global enterprise management. Organizations which span national boundaries are required to operate rather differently from those in a domestic context. How can IT be used to best support and enhance the international competitiveness of these enterprises? We urge our GIM research colleagues to embark on more investigations into the impact of IT on the global supply chain, human resource, marketing, manufacturing, and distribution management. This aspect of GIM research may not be within the traditional scope of IS research, but we believe it is equally compelling as organizations grapple with the management of their functional operations as they establish and compete globally.

CONCLUSION

This chapter proposes a three-dimensional GIM research framework which takes into account three important aspects of GIM research—research categories, research strategies, and research themes. The application of past and current research to the GIM research framework indicates that much work needs to be done in some areas and that some research areas may be reaching saturation. By describing this research framework we hope to guide future GIM research into productive areas that will facilitate the accumulation of knowledge in a systematic and comprehensive way.

REFERENCES

Abdul-Gader, A. H., & Kozar, K. A. (1995). The impact of computer alienation on information technology investment decisions: An exploratory cross-national analysis. *MIS Quarterly, 19*(4), 535-559.

Aiken, M., Hwang, C., Paolillo, J., Kim, D., & Lu, L.-C. (1994). A group decision support system for the Asian Pacific Rim. *Journal of International Information Management, 3*(2), 1-14.

Andersen, K. V., & Kraemer, K. L. (1994). Information technology and transition in the public service: A comparison of Scandinavia and the United States. *Scandinavian Journal of Information Systems, 6*(1), 3-24.

Badri, M. A. (1992). Critical issues in information systems management: An international perspective. *International Journal of Information Management, 12*, 179-191.

Barrett, M., & Walsham, G. (1995). Managing IT for business innovation: Issues of culture, learning, and leadership in a Jamaican insurance company. *Journal of Global Information Management, 3*(3), 25-33.

Burn, J., & Ma, L. (1993). Critical issues of IS management in Hong Kong. *Journal of Global Information Management, 1*(4), 28-37.

Campbell-Kelly, M. (1996). Information technology and organizational change in the British Census, 1801-1911. *Information Systems Research, 7*(1), 22-36.

Cats-Baril, W., & Jelassi, T. (1994). The French videotex system Minitel: A successful implementation of a national information technology infrastructure. *MIS Quarterly, 18*(1), 1-20.

Chidambaram, K., & Chismar, W. G. (1994). Telecommunication technologies: Use and investment patterns in U.S. multinational corporations. *Journal of Global Information Management, 2*(4), 5-18.

Coakes, E., & Merchant, K. (1996). Expert systems: A survey of their use in UK business. *Information & Management, 30*(5), 223-230.

Couger, J. D., Halttunen, V., & Lyytinen, K. (1991). Evaluating the motivating environment in Finland compared to the United States - A survey. *European Journal of Information Systems, 1*(2), 107-112.

Cox, B., & Ghoneim, S. (1996). Drivers and barriers to adopting EDI: A sector analysis of UK industry. *European Journal of Information Systems, 5*(1), 24-33.

Cross, J., Earl, M. J., & Sampler, J. L. (1997). Transformation of the IT function at British Petroleum. *MIS Quarterly, 21*(4), 401-424.

Cummings, M. L., & Guynes, J. G. (1994). Information system activities in transnational corporations: A comparison of U.S. and non-U.S. subsidiaries. *Journal of Global Information Management, 2*(1), 12-27.

Deans, P. C., & Ricks, D. A. (1991). MIS research: A model for incorporating the international dimension. *Journal of High Technology Management Research, 2*(1), 57-81.

Deans, P. C., & Ricks, D. A. (1993). An agenda for research linking information systems and international business: Theory, methodology and application. *Journal of Global Information Management, 1*(1), 6-19.

Dickson, R. W., Senn, J. A., & Chervany, N. L. (1977). A program for research in MIS. *Management Science, 23*(9), 913-923.

Dologite, D. G., Fang, M. Q., Chen, Y., Mockler, R. J., & Chao, C.-n. (1997). Information systems in Chinese state-owned enterprises: An evolving strategic perspective. *Journal of Global Information Management, 5*(4), 10-22.

Dutta, A. (1992). Telecommunications infrastructure in developing nations: Rural coverage. *International Information Systems, 1*(3), 31-54.

Dutta, S., & Doz, Y. (1995). Linking information technology to business strategy at Banco Comercial Portugues. *Journal of Strategic Information Systems, 4*(1), 89-110.

Ein-Dor, P., Segev, E., & Orgad, M. (1993). The effect of national culture on IS: Implications for international information systems. *Journal of Global Information Management, 1*(1), 33-44.

Ferratt, T. W., & Vlahos, G. E. (1998). An investigation of task technology fit for managers in Greece and the US. *European Journal of Information Systems, 7*(2), 123-136.

Foley, K., Meyer, M. H., & Sorensen, E. V. (1996). A comparison of U.S., Japanese and European software development practices and processes. *Journal of Global Information Management, 4*(3), 18-26.

Forer, P., Goldstone, M., & Tan, F. B. (1998). Implementing flexible learning in GIS education: Experiments using a spatial analysis facility. *Journal of Global Information Management, 6*(1), 33-40.

Gibson, R. (1998). Informatics diffusion in South American developing economies. *Journal of Global Information Management, 6*(2), 35-42.

Gibson, R., & McGuire, E.G. (1996). Quality control for global software development. *Journal of Global Information Management, 4*(4), 16-22.

Gorry, G. A., & Scott Morton, M. S. (1971). A framework for management information systems. *Sloan Management Review, 13*(1), 55-70.

Harrison, W. L., Farn, C.-K., & Coakley, J. R. (1992). A comparison of user satisfaction with MIS across two cultures. *International Information Systems*, *1*(4), 89-98.

Harvey, F. (1997). National cultural differences in theory and practice: Evaluating Hofstede's national cultural framework. *Information Technology & People*, *10*(2), 132-146.

Hasan, H., & Ditsa, G. (1999). The impact of culture on the adoption of IT: An interpretive study. *Journal of Global Information Management*, *7*(1), 5-15.

Hill, C. E., Loch, K. D., Straub, D. W., & El-Sheshai, K. (1998). A qualitative assessment of Arab culture and information technology transfer. *Journal of Global Information Management*, *6*(3), 29-38.

Hofstede, G. (1980). *Cultural Consequences: International Differences in Work Related Values*. Beverly Hills, CA: SAGE.

Ishman, M. (1998). Soviet influences on Latvian attitude to information technology. *Journal of Global Information Management*, *6*(4), 15-22.

Ives, B., & Jarvenpaa, S. L. (1991). Applications of global information technology: Key issues for management. *MIS Quarterly*, *15*(1), 32-49.

Ives, B., Hamilton, S., & Davis, G. B. (1980). A framework for research in computer-based management information systems. *Management Science*, *26*(9), 910-933.

Jansen, A. (1995). Rural development through diffusion of information technology. *Scandinavian Journal of Information Systems*, *7*(1), 99-120.

Jarvenpaa, S. L., & Ives, B. (1994). The global network organization of the future: Information management opportunities and challenges. *Journal of Management Information Systems*, *10*(4), 25-57.

Jonas, S., & Laios, L. (1992). Knowledge acquisition and integration tools to support managerial planning in Greek SMEs. *European Journal of Information Systems*, *2*(2), 103-116.

Kautz, K., & McMaster, T. (1994). Introducing structure methods: An undelivered promise? — A case study. *Scandinavian Journal of Information Systems*, *6*(2), 59-78.

Lai, V. S., & Reeh, B. (1995). ISDN implementation in the United States and Germany: A cross-country assessment. *Information & Management*, *29*(3), 131-140.

Lebre La Rovere, R. (1998). Diffusion of information technologies and changes in the telecommunications sector: The case of Brazilian small- and medium-sized enterprises. *Information Technology & People*, *11*(3), 194-206.

Lockett, A. G., & Holland, C. P. (1996). The formation of a virtual global bank. *European Journal of Information Systems*, *5*(2), 131-142.

Loh, P., Marshall, C., & Meadows, C. J. (1998). High-tech/low-tech: Appropriate technologies for developing nations. *Journal of Global Information Management*, *6*(2), 5-13.

Mahmood, M. A., Gemoets, L. A., & Gosler, M. D. (1995). Information technology transfer and diffusion to Mexico: A preliminary analysis. *Journal of Global Information Management*, *3*(4), 5-15.

Marchewka, J. T., & Wu, Q. (1997). The cultural and political influences on IT diffusion in the People's Republic of China. *Journal of International Information Management*, *6*(2), 41-50.

Martinsons, M. G., & Westwood, R. I. (1997). Management information systems in the Chinese business culture: An explanatory theory. *Information & Management, 32*(5), 215-228.

Mason, R. O., & Mitroff, I. I. (1973). A program for research in management information systems. *Management Science, 19*(5), 475-485.

Mata, F. J., & Fuerst, W. L. (1997). Information systems management issues in Central America: A multinational and comparative study. *Journal of Strategic Information Systems, 6*(3), 173-202.

Matsuda, Y. (1994). The use of information technology to achieve accurate pricing in agricultural commodity markets in Japan. *Information Technology & People, 7*(3), 37-49.

Mehta, K. T., & Shah, V. (1997). Information revolution: Impact of technology on global workforce. *Journal of International Information Management, 6*(2), 85-94.

Mehta, M. D., & Darier, E. (1998). Virtual control and disciplining on the Internet: Electronic governmentality in the new wired world. *Information Society, 14*(2), 107-116.

Mejias, R. J., Shepherd, M. M., Vogel, D. R., & Lazaneo, L. (1997). Consensus and perceived satisfaction levels: A cross-cultural comparison of GSS and non-GSS outcomes within and between the United States and Mexico. *Journal of Management Information Systems, 13*(3), 137-161.

Montealegre, R. (1998). Waves of change in adopting the Internet: Lessons from four Latin American countries. *Information Technology & People, 11*(3), 235-260.

Myers, M. D. (1997, May 20). Qualitative research in information systems. *MIS Quarterly, 21*(2). www.misq.org/misqd961/isworld/. *MISQ Discovery* updated version, last modified. Retrieved from: http://www.qualauckland.ac.nz.

Nelson, K. G., & Clark, T. D. J. (1994). Cross-cultural issues in information systems research: A research program. *Journal of Global Information Management, 2*(4), 19-29.

Neumann, S., & Zviran, M. (1997). Tel Aviv City Hall - The computerization revolution. *Journal of Strategic Information Systems, 6*(2), 149-167.

Niederman, F. (1993). Information systems personnel as expatriates: A review of the literature and identification of key issues. *Journal of Strategic Information Systems, 2*(2), 153-170.

Nolan, R. L., & Wetherbe, J. (1981). Toward a comprehensive framework for MIS research. *MIS Quarterly, 4*(2), 1-19.

Palvia, P. (1997). Developing a model of the global and strategic impact of information technology. *Information and Management, 32*(5), 229-244.

Palvia, P. (1998a). Global information technology research: Past, present and future. *Journal of Global Information Technology Management, 1*(2), 3-14.

Palvia, P. (1998b). Research issues in global information technology management. *Information Resources Management Journal, 11*(2), 27-36.

Peffers, K., & Tuunainen, V. K. (1998). Expectations and impacts of a global information system: The case of a global bank from Hong Kong. *Journal of Global Information Technology Management, 1*(4), 17-37.

Pervan, G. (1997). Information systems management: An Australasian view of key issues - 1996. *Australian Journal of Information Systems, 5*(1), 55-68.

Ramanujan, S., & Lou, H. (1997). Outsourcing maintenance operations to off-shore vendors: Some lessons from the field. *Journal of Global Information Management, 5*(2), 5-15.

Raymond, L., & Bergeron, F. (1997). Global distribution systems: A field study of their use and advantages in travel agencies. *Journal of Global Information Management, 5*(4), 23-32.

Reekers, N., & Smithson, S. (1996). The role of EDI in inter-organizational coordination in the European automotive industry. *European Journal of Information Systems, 5*(2), 120-130.

Robichaux, B. P., & Cooper, R. B. (1998). GSS participation: A cultural examination. *Information & Management, 33*(6), 287-300.

Rose, G. & Straub, D. (1998). Predicting general IT use: Applying TAM to the Arabic world. *Journal of Global Information Management, 6*(3), 39-46.

Sankar, C. S., & Liu, L. (1998). Study of job characteristics and organizational progressiveness posture in Singapore and Chinese companies. *Journal of Global Information Technology Management, 1*(3), 27-42.

Shaw, M. J., Gardner, D. M., & Thomas, H. (1997). Research opportunities in electronic commerce. *Decision Support Systems, 21*, 149-156.

Sheffield, J., & Gallupe, R. B. (1994). Using group support systems to improve the New Zealand economy, part II: Followup results. *Journal of Management Information Systems, 11*(3), 135-153.

Shore, B. (1996). Using information technology to coordinate transnational service operations: A case study in the European Union. *Journal of Global Information Management, 4*(2), 5-14.

Shore, B., & Venkatachalam, A. R. (1995). The role of national culture in systems analysis and design. *Journal of Global Information Management, 3*(3), 5-14.

Shore, B., & Venkatachalam, A. R. (1996). The role of national culture in the transfer of information technology. *Journal of Strategic Information Systems, 5*(1), 19-36.

Simon, S. J., & Middleton, K. L. (1998). Asia's pending labor crunch: An analysis of human resource management best practices in IS departments. *Journal of Global Information Technology Management, 1*(3), 9-26.

Skinner, W. C. (1964). Management of international production. *Harvard Business Review, 42*(5), 125-136.

Slaughter, S., & Ang, S. (1995). Information systems employment structures in the USA and Singapore: A cross-cultural comparison. *Information Technology & People, 8*(2), 17-36.

Smits, M. T., & van der Poel, K. G. (1996). The practice of information strategy in six information intensive organizations in the Netherlands. *Journal of Strategic Information Systems, 5*(2), 93-110.

Snow, C. C., & Thomas, J. B. (1994). Field research methods in strategic management: Contributions to theory building and testing. *Journal of Management Studies, 31*(4), 457-480.

Splettstoesser, D., & Splettstoesser, M. (1998). GSS-based environmental planning in Tanzania. *Journal of Global Information Management, 6*(2), 26-34.

Straub, D. (1994). The effect of culture on IT diffusion: E-mail and FAX in Japan and the U.S. *Information Systems Research, 5*(1), 23-47.

Straub, D., Keil, M., & Brenner, W. (1997). Testing the technology acceptance model across cultures: A three country study. *Information & Management, 33*(1), 1-11.

Tam, K. Y. (1998). The impact of information technology investments on firm performance and evaluation: Evidence from newly industrialized economies. *Information Systems Research, 9*(1), 85-98.

Thomas, J. B., & Dewitt, R. (1996). Strategic alignment research and practice: A review and research agenda. In J. N. Luftman (Ed.), *Competing in the Information Age: Strategic Alignment in Practice* (pp. 385-403). New York: Oxford University Press.

Tolsby, J. (1998). Effects of organizational culture on a large scale IT introduction effort: A case of the Norwegian army's EDBLF project. *European Journal of Information Systems, 7*(2), 108-114.

Tractinsky, N., & Jarvenpaa, S. L. (1995). Information systems design decisions in a global versus domestic context. *MIS Quarterly, 16*(4), 507-534.

Trauth, E. M. & Thomas, R. S. (1993). Electronic data interchange: A new frontier for global standards policy. *Journal of Global Information Management, 1*(4), 6-16.

Van Horn, R. L. (1973). Empirical studies in management information systems. *Database, 5*(2), 172-180.

Walczuch, R. M., Singh, S. K., & Palmer, T. S. (1995). An analysis of the cultural motivations for transborder data flow legislation. *Information Technology & People, 8*(2), 37-58.

Wan, H. A., & Lu, M.-t. (1997). An analysis of Chinese laws against computer crimes. *Journal of Global Information Management, 5*(2), 16-21.

Watson, R. T., Kelly, G. G., Galliers, R. D., & Brancheau, J. C. (1997). Key issues in information systems management: An international perspective. *Journal of Management Information Systems, 13*(4), 91-115.

Yang, H. (1996). Key information management issues in Taiwan and the US. *Information & Management, 30*(5), 251-267.

Yusof, M., & Rahim, M. M. (1994). Problems in computer-based information systems development: Malaysian perspective. *Asia Pacific Journal of Information Management, 2*, 17-30.

ENDNOTE

[1]   Refer to Watson, Kelly, Galliers, and Brancheau (1997) for a summary of the "key-issues" studies around the globe.

SECTION V

EMERGING ISSUES

Chapter XIII

Structuration Theory in Information Systems Research: Methods and Controversies

Marshall Scott Poole
Texas A&M University, USA

Gerardine DeSanctis
Duke University, USA

ABSTRACT

Numerous scholars in the information systems field have formulated variants of structuration theory in order to extend some of its basic constructs to information-technology-related phenomena and contexts. Along with this theoretical formulation has grown an extensive empirical literature. Here we take stock of the empirical research on structuration in IS to consider the requirements and options inherent to rigorous IS research that employs a structuration lens. The conceptual relationships presented in structuration theories of IS imply a set of seven requirements for a full-blown program of empirical study; we outline these requirements. We identify five sets of choices that researchers have as they design specific studies and the options available within these choice sets. We then summarize the empirical work in IS to date in terms of major methods that have been applied—case studies, direct observation, experiments, and surveys. We evaluate the relative strength of these methods in light of the requirements and options outlined earlier. We discuss important methodological controversies and directions and emphasize the potential power of adopting an interlocking, comprehensive set of research approaches when studying structuration in IS.

INTRODUCTION

Of the many theoretical paradigms influencing information systems research over the past decade or more, structuration theory has been one of the most influential—and the most controversial. A recent review by Pozzebon and Pinsonneault (2002) of IS-related articles identified 116 articles published between 1985 and 2000 that referenced structuration theory. Structuration theory has influenced theorizing about phenomena as far-reaching as systems development (Newman & Robey, 1992; Stein & Vandenbosch, 1996), systems failure (McCartt & Rohrbaugh, 1995), virtual teams (Boczkowski, 1999; Majchrzak, Rice, Malhotra, King, & Ba, 2000), online relationships (Chidambaram, 1996), technology mediation (Miranda & Bostrom, 1999; Orlikowski, Yates, Okamura, & Fujimoto, 1995), and implementation of new information systems (Brooks, 1997; Karsten, 1995; Orlikowski, 1993; Robey & Sahay, 1996; Volkoff, 1999).

Structuration theory has been popular in the broader field of organization studies as well, attracting attention for its ability to yield insight into group decision making (Poole, Seibold, & McPhee, 1985), organizational communication (Fulk, 1993; Heracleous & Hendry, 2000), social network formation (Sydow & Windeler, 1998), organizational learning and knowledge management (Browning, Sitkin, & Sutcliffe, 1998; Hargadon & Fanelli, 2002), organizational change (e.g., Barley, 1986; Beckert, 1999; Sarason, 1995), industry cooperation (Browning, Beyer, & Shetler, 1995), entrepreneurship (Sarason, Dillard, & Dean, 2002), and the evolution of institutions and organizational fields (Barley & Tolbert, 1997; DiMaggio, 1991; Scott, 1995).[1]

In the overlap of research on information systems and organizations, structuration theory has been the theoretical lens of choice for most scholars during the past decade. It provides a major theoretical pillar, though it specifies no detailed theorems or formal hypotheses; and it offers little methodological guidance. Associated with the seminal work of Anthony Giddens (1979, 1984), structuration is more a guiding philosophy of social scientific inquiry than a theory per se. It offers a grand formulation—a way of viewing the world—that is so general and encompassing that it cannot be falsified. Competing formulations include phenomenology, functionalism, hermeneutics, critical theory, and positivism (Thompson, 1981). Sometimes referred to as a "meta-theory," structuration offers a set of value choices or sensitizing devices, not a set of propositions or hypotheses (Orlikowski & Robey, 1991; Walsham & Han, 1991). The theory requires researchers within a domain to specify whatever premises are appropriate to phenomena and contexts of interest. Similarly, structuration theory leaves decisions about research settings, procedures, measurements, and analytic tools to the researchers themselves. It offers no more than general strategies for research conduct.

Historical Perspective—The Appeal of Structuration Theory for IS

Structuration theory concerns the nature of social systems and does not include consideration of technology or the influence of technology on social life.[2] Nonetheless, its appeal to IS lies in its focus on structure and on the processes by which structures are used and modified over time. The IS field has a deep-seated concern with analysis and design of structures for decision making and human-computer interaction (Davis, 1974; Dickson, Senn, & Chervany, 1977; Keen & Scott Morton, 1978; Sprague & Watson, 1979; Wynne & Dickson, 1975). The structuring properties of IT were the focus of much of the early empirical work in IS and fueled the growth and maturity of the discipline (e.g., Benbasat & Dexter, 1985; Benbasat & Nault, 1990; Daft & Lengel, 1986; Dhaliwal & Benbasat, 1996; Gerrity, 1971; Hiltz & Turoff, 1985; Huber, 1984; Ives, Hamilton, & Davis, 1980; Jarvenpaa, Rao, & Huber, 1988; Rice, 1982; Silver, 1991).

As information technology has advanced to become more communication based and collaborative, the field's concern with the structuring properties of technology has persisted (e.g., Dennis, Valacich, Connolly, & Wynne, 1996; DeSanctis & Gallupe, 1987; Gray & Olfman, 1989; Griffith, 1999; Huber, 1984; Nunamaker, Dennis, Valacich, & Vogel, 1991; Olson & Olson, 1991). But the focus of study has broadened considerably. No longer are IS researchers solely interested in structure as a property of technology. Our scope has extended to include structure as a property of work groups, organizations, and other social entities that use IT (e.g., Contractor & Seibold, 1993; Cramton, 2001; Finholt & Sproull, 1990; Gutek, 1990; Webster, 1998). It is here that the IS field adjoins research on groups, organizations, and society—fields of study that have long histories of concern with social structure and the design of procedures for improving interpersonal relationships and decision making.[3] But unlike research in those fields, IS research is not squarely interested in the structure of social life per se. Our concern is the interplay of people with technology—the structure of human-computer interaction, the structure of systems design and use, and the possibilities for somehow improving the human condition through applications of information technology to society. It is here that structuration theory has gained its appeal, for it attends to structure as an interactive process. Furthermore, structuration is a highly dynamic theory; it concerns the evolution of social structure through the ongoing interaction of people with one another and the social institutions of which they are a part.

In sum, the contributions of structuration theory to IS must be understood in historical context. Structuration theory does not include technology; nonetheless, its concern with the development and use of structure in social interaction makes it appealing to IS scholars. Technology can be viewed as a potential contributor to the process of structuring human interaction.

Purpose and Scope of this Chapter

Since structuration theory does not incorporate consideration of the structuring properties of technology, numerous scholars in the IS field have formulated variants of structuration theory in order to apply some of its basic constructs to specific IT-related phenomena and contexts (for example, Barrett & Walsham, 1999; Coombs, Knights, &

Willmott, 1992; DeSanctis & Poole, 1994; Fulk, 1993; Nyerges & Jankowski, 1997; Orlikowski, 1992, 2000; Orlikowski & Robey, 1991; Poole & DeSanctis, 1990; Rosenbaum, 1993; Sahay, 1997; Yates & Orlikowski, 1992). Such attempts have been roundly criticized by some social theorists, who argue that structuration theory cannot be expanded to include technology as a source of structure for social life (Jones, 1999).[4] There is further debate within the IS field as to which version of structuration theory is "the best," or the most true to Giddens's original formulation, or the most empirically sound (Pozzebon & Pinsonneault, 2002). We leave theorizing and theoretical debate aside for the moment to focus instead on the practicalities of doing empirical research on structuration in IS.

Relatively little attention has been devoted to the question of how to conduct empirical study of structuration in IS. Measurement scales, coding schemes, and the like can be found in the literature (e.g., Chin, Gopal, & Salisbury, 1998; Poole & DeSanctis, 1992). In addition, several authors have put forth suggestions for empirical study based on reviews of empirical work in the area (Contractor & Seibold, 1993; Fulk & Boyd, 1991; Pozzebon & Pinsonneault, 2002). General guidelines for the conduct of non-positivist studies in IS, including structuration theory, also are available (Lee, 1999a; Lee, Liebenau, & Degross, 1997; Robey & Boudreau, 1999). In this chapter our objective is to build on these discussions of method to provide a more thorough explication of the requirements and options inherent to rigorous IS research that employs a structuration lens.

We begin by briefly summarizing the concepts of structuration theory that IS researchers have most frequently embraced. We argue that the conceptual relationships presented in structuration theory imply a set of seven requirements for a full-blown program of empirical study in IS; we outline these requirements. Next, we identify five sets of choices that researchers have as they design specific studies and the options available within these choice sets. We then summarize the empirical work in IS to date in terms of major methods that have been applied using a structuration lens—case studies, direct observation, experiments, and surveys. We evaluate the relative power of these methods in light of the requirements and options outlined earlier. We conclude by noting important method controversies and directions, and we emphasize the value of adopting a comprehensive set of research approaches when applying structuration theory to IS research.

STRUCTURATION: CONCEPTS AND ISSUES

The core argument of structuration theory is that social structure exists in the actions of human agents as they use existing structures and create new ones in the course of everyday life. Structuration theory bridges two philosophical extremes that tradition-ally have been viewed as incompatible: *functionalism*, which holds that social structures are independent of people (they exist in institutions, organizations, technologies, or other entities) and can directly influence human behavior; and *interpretivism,* which holds that social structures exist only in the minds of people and hold no meaning outside of the social constructions that people create. The functionalist view holds that the consequences of structures explain their existence and persistence; causal arguments prevail. The interpretivist view holds that structures are cognitively formed through experience; social constructionist arguments prevail. Functionalists give more weight to the power of structure, whereas interpretivists give more weight to the power of human agency, especially knowledge and social scripts (Scott, 1995; Walsham & Han, 1991). Giddens (1979, 1984) bridges these views by stating that structures are neither inherent to institutions nor inherent to people; they are rooted in both and occur in the actions people take, especially as they interact with one another.[5] Thus, *structures* exist as *actors* apply them; they are the medium and outcome of human interaction. This is called the duality of structure.

Structuration is the process of putting structures into action. Structuration is "the structuring of social relations across time and space, in virtue of the duality of structure" (Giddens, 1984, p. 376). As Scott (1995, p. 113) notes, Giddens uses the verb *structuration* to stress that "structures are systems of ongoing action, being continuously produced and reproduced through time. The concept also emphasizes the "duality of structure: the mutual dependence of structure and agency" (Giddens, 1979, pp. 69-79). Structuration occurs as actors move to invoke existing structures or to create new ones, *producing* and *reproducing* the structures and the associated social system. Structures include *resources* (command over people or material goods) and *rules* (recipes for action), which operate to provide a social *system* with power (structures of domination), norms/routines (structures of legitimation), and meaning (structures of signification). In this way, the social order of a system is maintained over time (*stability*) and yet has the capacity to adapt (*change*) as actors modify structures in the course of their interactions with one another. The routine of everyday structuration constitutes the social order of a system.

As Jones (1999) points out, it is important to note that the concept of system in structuration theory differs from the traditional IS use of the term or its use by systems theorists. Within structuration theory, systems are generated as the rules and resources of a structure are produced and reproduced in the interactions of actors. As structures are repeatedly reproduced, systems tend toward stability. As people produce new structures, systems tend toward change (Giddens, 1984). Traditionally, information technology has been treated more like a physical system—with predictability based on inputs, processes, and feedback loops. The attractiveness of structuration theory to IS scholars is its action-oriented, social view; it makes human agents part of the system itself and thus can account for the interplay between people and technology, as well as the less than full predictability of IT use in groups and organizations (Fulk, 1993).[6]

Quandaries for IS Research

There are at least two aspects of structuration theory that are not developed by Giddens but are essential to address in order for empirical study of structuration to proceed for IS. These concern the role of technology in structuration and the application of deterministic reasoning within the recursive logic of the theoretical arguments.

Technology. Giddens holds that structures are "traces in the mind" instantiated only through action (Giddens, 1984, p. 17). He does not separate structure from action and actor. But analytically it is useful to do so, especially as we begin to think about empirical study of structuration. Most IS structuration theorists view technology as a potential source of the structures that people employ in the course of performing some task. Technology is an "occasion for structuring" (Barley, 1986)—a structural potential (DeSanctis & Poole, 1994) that may or may not find its way into the unfolding interaction of the everyday workplace of which it is a part (Orlikowski, 2000). The resources and rules of technology become the resources and rules of structuration only when drawn upon in the production or reproduction of structure in human interaction—that is, when actors *move* to use them (DeSanctis & Poole, 1994). Some scholars have argued that the province of IS research on structuration should *only* include a focus on human action; the logic is that we only have to study structuring moves and not technology itself, since technology has no independent meaning or force outside of its use (Jones, 1999). However, most technologists find the disregard of technology as artifact—even in the study of structuration—to be too limiting. Instead, technology is seen as one source of social structures (i.e., sets of rules and resources), which are embedded in technology by designers during development and then dynamically changed as users interact with technology. The argument is similar to Latour's (1992), which is that technology is society made durable. Further, the structural set available to technology users is not "fixed" but instead produced and reproduced in the context of use. This is an "ensemble" view of technology (Orlikowski & Iacono, 2001). It assumes that technology and user behavior coevolve as a structurational process during the course of human-computer interaction. (For an example of a theoretical exposition on technology as structuring artifact, see Masino & Zamarian, in press.)

Determinism. Within Giddens's formulation of structuration theory there is no accommodation for the deterministic impacts of structure on action. The theory is recursive in its logic, not causal. Structuration is an ongoing process, not a sequence of events. Therefore, the theory does not explain variance in behavior or predict outcomes; it is not normative. For some aspects of IS research this is not problematic. However, other analyses require IS researchers to decompose the structuration process, attending to one or more operative sequences within the actor-structure relationship. This is especially true in studies of technology design and impacts. In these instances, causal logic becomes embedded within a larger program of study that is recursive and examines the duality of structure. Some argue that deterministic thinking has no place inside structuration models (e.g., Jones, 1999). We disagree. Just as positivist and interpretative research, though opposing, can be integrated (Lee, 1999a), so too can deterministic reasoning be used to decompose and study a recursive model. The inclusion of deterministic logic allows the IS research agenda to be not only reflective but also anticipatory. This is important because IS scholarship is interested not only in describing the unfolding of human-technology interaction but also in anticipating the consequences of technology adoption and its use and in providing systems development advice where possible. Structuration theory can help the IS field to move beyond purely deterministic views of technology, but it does not demand that we abandon causal logic altogether.

Analytic Necessity

Testable theory. Beyond specific concerns for IS, the importance of empirical study of structuration deserves emphasis. Decomposition and analysis of the structuration process, followed by data gathering and interpretation, are necessary for the theory to be scientifically and practically useful as a general matter of course. Structuration theory is pliable and can become self-sealing. It is easy to imagine how the cognitively complex mind of the researcher might readily interpret any phenomenon in structurational terms—seeing production and reproduction, the mutual entailment of action and structure, and so on in everything. But reading structuration into phenomena does not really advance our understanding very much. It is akin to applying one of those other great, seductive social theories, exchange theory (Homans, 1961). There is the danger that everything becomes an exchange, and the circular exchange theory formula is applied too readily and without insight:

> *Research question: Why did X do Y?*
> *Theoretical account:*
> *Because of the exchange: X got something X valued, or X avoided something noxious.*
> *How do you know an exchange took place (or was meaningful to X)?*
> *Because X did Y.*
> *(Or you can start at the bottom and work up; it's circular!)*

In such cases the theory is not actually tested but applied as an article of faith. For understanding of structuration to advance, it is important to have rigorous and critical specification of how structuration happens and applications of the framework subjected to empirical study.

Comparative analyses. A strength of structuration theory is its ability to accommodate the study of change. IS researchers often are interested in change, whether engineering change, as in introducing new forms or functions within technology, or observing change, as in monitoring individual or organizational behavior following introduction of a change in technology. Researchers recognize that multiple technology designs are possible, as are multiple outcomes following introduction of change. Further, there are interlinkages in the change process among technology components, individual actions, groups, organizations, and larger social activities. Structuration theory can accommodate these multiple perspectives, possibilities, and levels of analysis. For example:

> *Research question: How did change take place?*
> *Empirical account:*
> *Structures X and Y were produced.*
> *Structure X was reproduced. Structure Y was not reproduced.*
> *Over time, structure X became a structure of domination in the institution.*

The empirical account is useful as a general frame. But comparative accounts, sequential logic, and statistical analyses (e.g., probability estimation of outcomes) will be helpful if the researcher is interested in related questions, such as: Why were X and Y produced and not Z? Were X and Y equally likely to have been reproduced or not? What would have been the outcome of X had Y not been produced? How might the reproduction of X be thwarted in favor of Y? What might be done to disrupt the reproduction of X in the future? If Z is introduced along with X and Y, what is the likely outcome? For IS researchers, these kinds of comparative questions and scenarios are important. They can be investigated within structuration theory, so long as the research agenda is comprehensive and systematic. Sequential analysis should accompany recursive analysis.

Probability estimation should accompany descriptive analysis. Controlled studies should accompany passive studies. In sum, the research should not favor one method over another so much as it should incorporate multiple methods and analytic techniques. The thick description of ethnography will be most powerful if accompanied by manipulation, control, comparison, and estimation of probabilities. For the story to yield a comprehensive perspective on the dynamics of X and Y, a systematic set of interlocking studies is required.

We now turn to articulation of the requirements and options for empirical research on structuration in IS.

REQUIREMENTS AND OPTIONS FOR EMPIRICAL RESEARCH

Figure 1 presents a visual representation of the structuration process that can serve as a general model for empirical analysis. At the center of this analysis are the perspectives of actor and system, representing two frames of the same phenomenon. Giddens (1984) acknowledges the value of decomposing structuration in his articulation of two alternative strategies for research: the analysis of strategic conduct and institutional analysis. The *analysis of strategic conduct* takes institutions as a backdrop and focuses on how actors draw on and reproduce the structures of the system in social practices. The *analysis of institutions* (systems) assumes that strategic conduct is going on but focuses on the structural characteristics of institutions and their long-term development. Each approach brackets, or frames, a certain part of the structuration process and uses the rest as an unanalyzed ground for its object of interest. Giddens notes that this bracketing artificially segments structuration, but he argues that it is necessary for methodological purposes. In short, it is not only legitimate but necessary to parse the coevolving aspects of structure and action, focusing first on one and then on the other.

Seven Requirements for Study

How can the researcher proceed to examine the complex and multifaceted process of structuration? We propose an analytic approach that examines the relationships of Figure 1 in cumulative fashion. The full-blown analysis of structuration should address the following set of interlocking problems:

1. It must identify the array of relevant **structures** that are used to constitute the system. This may involve identification of both potential (e.g., within technology) and active (i.e., in use) structures; it may include identification of structures in other systems that make up the context in which the focal system operates. (For example, structures operating in the organization or larger society may be relevant to analysis of the structures within a group system that is being studied.) All such identifications are, of course, reifications that "freeze" the modalities of structuration for purposes of analysis.

2. It should also clarify **relationships among structures**, including complementarities and contradictions between structures, or how one structure supports another or conflicts with another.

Figure 1.   Components of the Study of Structuration that Correspond to Seven Interlocking Requirements for Empirical Study.

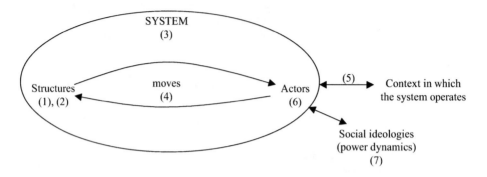

3.   It must develop a description of how the social **system** works. This analysis defines the general field in which structuration occurs and its "surface" indicants. By implication, this requires identification of actions that characterize the system's operation and actors' interpretive maps. It also requires determining what features of the context influence structuration.

4.   It must identify **moves** or activities by which agents produce and reproduce structures. Referring to the institutional level of analysis, Giddens (1979) labeled these as *modalities*. At a more concrete level of interpersonal interaction, Ollman (1971) referred to these as *appropriations*—the immediate, visible actions that evidence deeper structuration processes (DeSanctis & Poole, 1994; Poole & DeSanctis, 1992). The impacts of context on structuring moves should be included in the analysis.

5.   It ultimately should shed light on how social **context** is reproduced or shaped by the process in question. This is the larger set of institutional forces in which the system operates and turns the context issue on its head: How does structuration influence the context itself?

6.   The **actors** themselves are produced and reproduced in structuration (Poole et al., 1985). Actors are the intelligent agents in the system who choose to produce and reproduce structures. Hence we have to account for the roles of human actors in the social system—their positions relative to one another and the expectations and contextual demands on their actions.

7.   It must also undertake critical inquiry into the **power** dynamics underlying the structuration process and possible relations of dominance among different classes of actors. Giddens (1984) emphasizes that power imbalances, covered by societal ideologies of rationality or equality, can strongly shape structuration, creating relative advantage for certain parties at the expense of other parties and perpetuating preexisting biases in social institutions.

These are not a set of stages for research. Instead they are the components that make up a fully realized empirical agenda. Working on any single component can produce insights on others. For example, characterizing the structuring moves in microlevel interaction may lead to identification of additional structures and also to insights as to how the system operates. Insights into how structuration shapes social institutions may shed light on structuring moves through illuminating constraints. Ideally, a mature research agenda on structuration would incorporate these multiple and multilayered analyses into a complex, but coherent, whole.

For IS scholars, these seven interlocking requirements offer multiple perspectives on structuration in IS. For example, studies that focus on identification of structures and their mediation can take the view of technology as "occasion for structuring" (Barley, 1986, p. 78) or as having structural potential (DeSanctis & Poole, 1994). In isolation, such a perspective can be criticized as too akin to a functional, technology-as-artifact view. But when coupled with research on IS as a system of actor-structure interaction (Orlikowski, 2000), as the process of technology use (Poole & DeSanctis, 1992), as an organizational dynamic (Coombs et al., 1992), and as a process of social governance (Han & Walsham, 1989), a more comprehensive view of IS emerges. Structuration opens up multiple facets and layers of analysis for IS research. This is the marvel of structuration theory. (See Table 1.)

Required Modes of Analysis

Social systems can be described and explained from both the exterior perspective (the viewpoint of the analyst who seeks to understand what causes actions and what makes action effective) and from the interior perspective (in terms of the actions, cognitions, interpretations, feelings, and intentions of the actors). *Functional analysis* looks at systems from the outside, from the perspective of the observer interested in understanding the factors that cause system behavior and that yield outcomes. *Consti-*

Table 1. Seven Interlocking Requirements for a Structuration Research Agent and Seven Corresponding Perspectives on the Structuration Process for IS Research.

	Interlocking Requirements	Perspectives for IS Research
(1)	Identification of structures	IS as structure or sets of structure
(2)	Relationship of structures and their contradictions	
(3)	Analysis of the system, including effects of context	IS as system of actor-structure interaction
(4)	Identification of structuring moves: production and reproduction of structures	IS as use of structure
(5)	Effects of process on context	IS as organizational dynamic
(6)	Analysis of actors and their roles	IS as social governance
(7)	Analysis of power dynamics and social ideologies	

tutive analysis attempts to get more of an inside perspective on the system, to study the interpretations that give meaning to events and the actions and interactions that constitute the system, its processes, and actor responses to exogenous influences. Constitutive analysis aims to elucidate the processes that constitute the variables, causes, and effects that the functional analysis identifies. Each mode of analysis involves a different, complementary approach to the study of structuration. Table 2 outlines these modes of analysis, both of which are required for empirical study of structuration.

Functional analysis focuses on the system itself and depicts it as a network of causal, moderating, and correlational relationships among abstract variables. Exogenous influences, structures, actor moves, and outcomes are decomposed into well-defined variables. These variables may be part of the actors' life world, but they are defined and operationalized by researchers; they reflect the scientist's perspective and are subjected to analysis of reliability and validity. The validity of a functional analysis depends on its ability to stand up to empirical evaluation. Relationships between variables are relevant only insofar as they can be investigated in the laboratory or field. Traditionally, most research on social systems relies on functional analyses. Hence, most of what we

Table 2. Comparison of Functional and Constitutive Modes of Analysis.

	Functional Analysis	**Constitutive Analysis**
Explanation	Causal explanation	Causal explanation combined with interpretive explanation
Sample size	Substantial samples possible	Relatively small samples
View of constructs and relationships	Takes variables and relationships as "givens" and nonproblematic	Regards constructs and relationships as problematic; concerned with constitution of variables and relationships
Measurement	Focuses on variables; uses measurement theory	Concerned with faithful representation of participants' viewpoints and meanings
Validation of theory	Validity of theory depends on empirical test	Validity of theory depends on coherency, empirical consistency, and heuristic value
Relation to other mode of analysis	Can indicate the practical importance of a constitutive process or factor or its constraints	Captures the processes by which the variables and relationships in functional analysis are realized in the social world
Strengths	Enables rigorous, structured research	Emphasizes the role of agency in social effects
Weaknesses	Oversimplification. Omits role of agency	How to test, falsify, or replicate constitutive analyses is not clear. The analysis can be idiosyncratic to the study or researcher.

know about social systems is stated in causal terms. As just one example, Poole and Roth (1989) found that task complexity was inversely related to the complexity of group decision paths. Systems of variables can also be modeled, as this explanation advanced by Homans (1950) and Schacter (1968) illustrates: Increased liking among actors causes an increase in communication; increased communication causes an increase in perceived similarity among actors; an increase in perceived similarity causes increased liking (which completes a deviation-amplifying causal loop). Functional analyses need not be quantitative. Qualitative methods can be used to derive generalizations about behavioral systems. And interpretive insights can be used to generate functional theories; Lindesmith's (1947) study of addicts and Glaser and Strauss's (Strauss, 1987) numerous grounded theories are illustrative. Of course, qualitative and quantitative modes of analysis can be combined in functional research, as Weber's (1958) analysis of the Protestant ethic illustrates. Functional analysis is useful because it permits both explanation and prediction of behavior. It also employs an explanatory scheme that is amenable to the application of powerful measurement and statistical methods to test theories.

Constitutive analysis is necessary to discover how social systems and the variables and relationships that compose them are constructed through human interaction. Constitutive analyses reveal the interpretive processes that figure in the operation of causal relationships. For example, task is commonly used as a causal variable in systemic studies of work. However, it may not be task per se, but *actors' interpretations* of work tasks that influence organizational processes. These interpretations may be included in a functional analysis as "perceived task," but this transforms an interpretive process into a static variable. It does not fully capture the role of interpretation in the actors' approach to their work. Underlying every variable and relationship in a causal analysis is a process of social construction responsible for making it an active force in the social system. A constitutive analysis takes the functional analysis as a starting point, shows how the system operates in terms of actor-structure interaction, and then adds additional rich detail from the actors' viewpoints about these processes. A constitutive analysis is a useful supplement to functional analysis because it reveals the "whole picture" behind seemingly deterministic facts. A constitutive analysis can often help by resolving inconsistencies in causal relations and showing why expected causal relationships do not hold. As an example, an early hypothesis was that word processing systems would enhance office productivity. However, only a weak relationship between word processing and productivity was found. Johnson and Rice (1985) showed that different offices "reinvented" word processing technology in different ways and that each of four different reinvention types had different effects on productivity. Social processes involved in technology implementation resulted in different reinventions of the same technology in different offices that, in turn, produced different outcomes.

Constitutive analysis is also valuable because some social processes are simply too complex to be "variabilized" and reduced to causal maps. As an example, Bormann (1996) describes the symbolic convergence process, whereby groups develop shared meanings that inspire them to greater effort and movement to coordinate activities; symbolic convergence may occur in many different ways and defies analysis in terms of tidy variables and causal explanations. Similarly, many IS researchers have found that the process of implementing and adapting technology to specific organizations or social settings cannot be captured via clean specification of variables (e.g., Orlikowski, 1993; Prasad, 1992). Although certain aspects of IT implementation can be captured via functional analysis, the unique adaptations and the give-and-take of interaction are generally best understood using constitutive analyses (see Lee, 1999a, 1999b).

In sum, functional and constitutive analyses complement and buttress one another to provide a comprehensive picture of structuration processes. Looking back to the seven requirements outlined in Figure 1, functional analysis can lead in the first three components, understanding how the system works and the key structures involved. For example, studies by Chudoba and George (1995), Jankowski and Nyerges (2001b), and Miranda and Bostrom (1993-1994) illustrate in small group systems how functional analyses can be used to successfully identify what variables really make a difference in the structuration of IS. Constitutive analysis then can clarify how the various factors fit together and how actions of actors influence them. Studies by Jankowski and Nyerges (2001a) and Poole, Kirsch, Jackson, and DeSanctis (1998) are illustrative. Constitutive analysis generally takes the lead in study of Components 4 through 7 because these research requirements concern how the system is produced and reproduced over time. Functional analyses can be useful in the study of these components as well: Functional analysis is important to critical inquiry (Fay, 1987) so it also plays an important role in study of Component 7. Functional analyses also can play a role in study of Components 4 through 6—to explore and test implications of the findings of constitutive studies. As an example, suppose a constitutive analysis suggested that managers' interpretations of an IT system prejudiced worker views of a system. This conjecture and its importance in the organizational system could be put to a test with a survey. The survey might gather data on typical dimensions of managerial interpretations identified in the constitutive analysis and determine their relationship to worker attitudes toward the IT.

Three important implications of the discussion thus far deserve emphasis. First, it is important not to assume identification of functional analyses with causal models or identification of constitutive analysis with process models. Although they may be associated in current social scientific practice, in conception they are independent of one another. Both functional and constitutive analyses can, and do, incorporate causal logic. Causal and process approaches represent two different types of *explanations*, whereas functional and constitutive inquiries pose two different sets of modes, or questions, that can be asked about any phenomenon.

Second, a structuration research agenda must include longitudinal studies. The only sure way to determine the nature of a structuring process is to study it as it unfolds, either through direct observation or through analysis of reliable archival data that preserves time ordering of events. Ultimately, structuration research is process research, as defined by Mohr (1982) and, more recently, Poole, Van de Ven, Dooley, and Holmes (2000). Process research is longitudinal by definition, as it explains the order in which things occur and the stage in the process at which they occur. Longitudinal studies provide insight into development and change, and so they are ideal for research on structuration.

Thirdly, all studies of structuration do not have to be ethnographic or even qualitative. Some social theorists, including Giddens, have argued that structuration researchers must include ethnography in their programs. Others go further to say that only an ethnographic approach to the study of structuration will do (e.g., Banks & Riley, 1993; Jones, 1999). Our view reflects the more mainstream view of the IS field, which is that insider views of a social system can be captured by means other than ethnography, including interviews or surveys. The review of literature in the next section reports a number of non-ethnographic studies of structuration in IS. There is no single methodological path to the discovery of valid insights into structuration. As Giddens (1984, p. xxx) concedes, "I do not try to wield a methodological scalpel. ... I do not believe there is anything in either the logic or substance of structuration theory which would somehow prohibit the use of some specific research technique." Giddens further notes that quantitative methods can be useful in the study of the system level because they permit the testing of models to determine which relationships are likely candidates for structurational analysis. Quantitative approaches are also useful for the study of structuring moves where many observations or cases are available for analysis and when indicators of structuring moves can be developed. Studies by Barley (1986) and Poole and DeSanctis (1992) illustrate the use of quantitative models in structuration research. Historical studies of structuration are also important, as Giddens's work illustrates. Historical accounts rely on archival data to reconstruct the structuration of IT using all the tools of the historian—colligation, interpretation, multiple readings, and dense interconnections of elements of the social process being studied.

Having outlined the requirements of a research agenda on structuration, we now turn to the choices and options researchers have in an empirical program of study.

Choices in Structuration Research

At least five choices are involved in designing a study of structuration in IS. These are summarized in Table 3 and described below.

Level of Analysis

The structuration process as summarized in Figure 1 can be studied from at least three general levels (DeSanctis & Poole, 1994). Figuratively speaking, these correspond to the closeness of the microscope held by the researcher while examining a social system. *Microlevel analysis* attends to the immediate, visible indicators of structures in use. The analysis is based on the specific, visible actions that take place as structures are produced or reproduced by actors. Depending on the system of interest, microanalysis might take place at the level of a dyadic communication, of a specific meeting, of memos or messages exchanged, or of other specific events or activities. The system is examined from the lowest level feasible given the phenomenon of interest. As examples, for researchers interested in groups or teams, meetings or e-mail exchanges provide a good source of microlevel study. For researchers interested in organizational systems, announcements, annual reports, and general protocols for writing memos, holding meetings, or conducting business are appropriate. For researchers interested in interorganizational systems, the specific moves of key leaders or the unfolding of interorganizational projects or transactions might be examined. Microlevel analysis seeks to examine production and reproduction of structure in an immediate, visible venue(s) within the system of interest.

Next is the *global level* of analysis, which pulls the microscope away from immediate evidence of human action to examine more persistent production and reproduction of structures across venues. Here, a series of memos or meetings might be studied, or collections of project team activities; or significant cross-organizational transactions

Table 3. Important Choices and Options for Researchers Studying Structuration

Choices	Optional Approaches
System level of analysis	Institutional
	Global
	Micro
Structural focus	Related structure(s)
	Diverse structures
Framing	Structure view: influence of structure on action
	Actor view: actors' structural moves
	Alternating: structure and actor views
Dynamics	System change
	System stability
Stance	Positive
	Skeptical
	Critical

might be tracked for a period of time. Finally, the *institutional level* looks at deeply embedded structuration—systems as they occur "in the large"—over extensive venues and time periods. As examples, researchers interested in group systems might study top management team members over a period of decades to understand their actions and interactions with information technology. Researchers interested in interorganizational systems might examine persistence in patterns of industry investment in IT, comparing instances of mimetic behavior with instances of coalition behavior to dominate other firms via technology.

Any individual researcher has the option to choose a level of analysis that is most relevant to the phenomenon and research question of interest. Research on structuration benefits from studies within levels and across levels of analysis. As illustrations: Poole and DeSanctis (1992) provide an example of microlevel analysis of IT use in a small group setting; they also study group use of the same IT at a global level (Poole et al., 1998). Orlikowski and colleagues (1995) provide a global analysis of IT implementation for an organizational system. DiMaggio and Powell (1983) and Scott (1995) discuss how structuration can be examined at the institutional level. Studies at the different levels can build on one another. Where to begin? DeSanctis and Poole (1994) advise that the most logical sequence for studies of small group use of IT is to start at the microlevel, then move to the global level, and finally to the institutional level of analysis, progressively investigating more and more strata of the technology's role in organizational change. However, different sequences also are feasible, and one can imagine a rich program of research that stays within a given level of analysis.

Structural Focus

A second important choice is the focus of the study: Will it concentrate on a *set of related structures*, i.e., one or more structures that have rules or resources in common, or will it consider the interrelationship among a *diverse set of structures*? Structures may complement one another, or they may oppose one another. Some studies primarily focus on a limited set of structures of one type. For example, Chudoba and George (1995) analyzed the procedural structures within a group support system (GSS) and the extent to which they worked together to yield structures of participation in group tasks. Other studies explicitly focus on how two or more distinctive sets of structures influence one another. For example, Yates and Orlikowski (1992) advanced a model of how the practice of memo writing evolved over time as a function of the interrelationship between the genre of the memo in practice and the set of genres of organizational communication.

The choice of structural focus is critical in IS research since IS researchers tend to be keenly interested in the structuring potential of technology. For this reason, theorists have devised ways to define and operationalize commonalities and differences in structural sets. For example, DeSanctis, Snyder, and Poole (1994) provide schemes for characterizing the "features" (individual structures) and "spirit" (structural sets) of group decision support systems.[7] They further articulate a way of examining diverse sets of structures in action, in terms of "faithful" versus "ironic" appropriation of IT structures (Poole & DeSanctis, 1990). Similarly, Orlikowski and Yates (1994, p. 543) define a communication "genre" as a "distinctive type of communication action, characterized by a socially recognized communication purpose and common aspects of form. ... The communication purpose of a genre is not rooted in a single individual's motive for communicating, but in a purpose that is constructed, recognized, and reinforced within a community." Examples include the business letter, shareholders' meeting, or report. Other IS researchers have followed suit in terms of defining structures and structural sets. Chin et al. (1998) and Nyerges and colleagues (Nyerges, Moore, Montejano, & Compton, 1998) have developed survey and coding methods for identifying commonalities and differences in actors' appropriation of groupware structures. Still other researchers use more traditional constructs—such as norms, knowledge frames, and interpretive scripts—to describe and operationalize the structures they are studying (e.g., Browning et al., 1998; Han & Walsham, 1989).

Framing

This choice hinges on the ratio of action to structure that the investigator posits. On the one hand, there may be a strong emphasis on *structural influence* on action. In such a study the researcher presumes that structure is the lead player; the focus is on how structure shapes and constrains actions. Studies of how IT structures influence decision outcomes exemplify this approach (e.g., Watson, DeSanctis, & Poole, 1988). Other types of studies emphasize the role of *agency* in the operation of structures. The Poole and DeSanctis (1992) study of microlevel structuration in the use of GSSs is an example of the second approach, though it is not radically constructive and offers a rather conservative design.

Structuration framing relates to the two general strategies for research on structuration described earlier: the analysis of strategic conduct and institutional analysis. Giddens (1984) argues that these are the two possible frames for structuration research. Although we agree that parts of any structuration process must serve as "ground" against which to discern the "figure," we do not agree that structuration studies must be limited to these two frames. An alternative is to shift back and forth between action and institutional levels during an analysis, hoping that the "whole" will convey the nature of structuration. As illustration, studies by Smith (1983) and Brewer (1988) do this in a single report, as do studies by Barley (1986) and Orlikowski (1991). So, the researcher has three options with regard to research framing: (a) structure view, (b) actor view, and (c) alternating structure and actor views.

Dynamics

This choice concerns the ratio of production to reproduction that the study incorporates. Some studies focus primarily on *change* due to structuration. Blomberg's (1986) study of changes in work design due to implementation of IT provides an example. The alternative is to focus on *stability*, or how structuring processes are contributing to the stabilization of technology or other structures. As an example, implementation of IT is sometimes argued to favor reigning managerial values (Dutton, 1999), and so a study of the structuring of IT could explore how technology further embeds existing values into an organization. Of course, it is possible to consider both change and stability in the same study, giving one or the other primacy.

In structuration research, dynamics are often the object of study—analogous to the dependent variable in variance-oriented research. For example, structuration researchers may study the degree of change or stability in a system within a given period. They might identify evolutionary stages that reflect patterns of change or formation of routines of interaction following a change in, for example, a new technology. Alternative structural sets might be contrasted for the degree of change or stability they yield in a social system, either in one period or over a longer time horizon. Dynamics are usually studied over time, in longitudinal fashion, but sometimes researchers assess dynamics at precise points in time, as indicators of possible longer-term change or stability.

Stance

Researchers also take different attitudinal positions on the research enterprise. In structuration research there are three important stances. The *positive* stance takes the existence of structuration as a given and seeks to explore how it occurs and how it influences use of IT and outcomes for the system. Most of the research on structuration in IS to date takes on a positive stance. The *critical* stance presumes that power inequalities and ideologies drive structuring processes and seeks to uncover these. Giddens (1984) takes a critical stance toward structuration. The *skeptical* stance is taken by those who believe the utility of structuration as a model is still open for each case. They wish to interrogate each situation in order to determine the utility of the structuration model. Contractor and Seibold (1993) elucidate a skeptical stance for some types of structuration research in IS.

These five choices enable a mapping of the terrain of structuration research in IS, to which we will now turn.

LESSONS FROM THE EMPIRICAL LEGACY

Research to date on structuration in IS can be divided into four categories on the basis of methodology: case studies, observational studies, experiments, and surveys. Case studies rely on information gleaned from documents, historical records, and/or actors to reflect on structuration that has occurred in the recent or distant past or may take place in the future. Observational studies capture structuration in practice—in the actions and interactions of people during the course of everyday life; videotapes, e-mail conversations, or ethnographic notes are typical sources of data. Experiments occur when there is deliberate manipulation of some aspect of the structuration process and the effects are then compared; per Figure 1, researchers may attempt to manipulate the structural set associated with IT or the context, the types of actors involved, or the type of system or ideology surrounding structuration. Survey studies attempt to capture components of the structuration process through self-reports gathered in the form of questionnaires. In surveys, the study of large numbers of structuring instances becomes possible.

Although many studies of structuration use multiple methods, most rely on a single, dominant method as the foundation for the research design. We classified studies based on the dominant method reported by the researcher in the published report but noted mixed methods where they occurred. Here we summarize the work for each category in terms of how research is typically conducted, the strengths of each method, major challenges, and how the work of each category contributes to filling out a structuration research agenda for the field. Note that while our summary tables highlight research design, structural focus, and dynamics, we consider all of the research requirements and choices discussed earlier in our review of each method.

Case Studies

The most common empirical method used by structuration researchers is the case study, whether in IS or other domains. Giddens's (1977) reinterpretation of Durkheim's study of suicide is one of the first case studies. A wonderful example of a case study is Barthes's *S/Z* (1974), which defines interwoven threads of signification that wind through a short story and explores how the reader is situated by the text as it constructs itself through being read. Case studies have particular advantages for research on structuration: (1) They enable researchers to look at a phenomenon in depth, which is necessary to unearth the multiple layers of action involved in structuration. (2) The time horizon for the study is longitudinal, typically over a period of months or years. (3) The use of one or a few cases allows researchers the luxury of looking at multiple perspectives of the structuration process; this is especially useful for tracing the effects of context on structuration in IS (and vice versa). Since context is quite complex and there are likely to be many effects, an in-depth view is important.

But there are also challenges that case studies must surmount: (1) Only a small sample of cases can be examined in a given study. Small sample sizes make it difficult to determine whether findings are generalizable or peculiar to the case. As more and more studies are conducted, they can cumulate (to the extent that they focus on the same aspects of structuration), which mitigates this problem somewhat. (2) A by-product of the publication process is a tendency for case studies to focus on the novel aspects of phenomena, especially the changes brought about by new IT implementation. Novelty is "news," whereas report of no change brought on by technology or repetition of previous findings (whether reporting change or stability in dynamics) is much less likely to get journal space. Replication across cases is downplayed, which further exacerbates the problem noted in Point (1). (3) Most cases are reconstructions based on interviews and whatever records were deemed appropriate to preserve. Researchers may make site visits to observe meetings or actors' interactions with technology, but such visits tend to be limited in duration and the resulting data is descriptive (rather than ethnographic). In case studies scholars have not enjoyed direct access to the unfolding process of structuration and so may be giving an inauthentic view. The other side on this point would argue that the salient features of the process are being reported in interviews or historical records, or they are visible during a researcher's visit to the case site, and so there is an advantageous presorting of dross from gold.

Table 4 summarizes case study research on structuration in IS. This survey suggests that most studies have attempted a holistic account of the structuration process, including identification of IT, task, contextual, and organizational structures relevant to structuration (Components 1 and 2 of the structuration agenda presented in Figure 1) and description of structuring moves (Component 3) and of the effects of organizational and other contextual forces on the structuration process (Component 5). Most studies have included at least some analysis of actors and their roles (Component 6) and an accounting of the relationship between system and action levels of analysis (Component 3). Commonalities among structures usually have been highlighted, and diversity of structures—especially in the form of new IT—have been set in contrast to preexisting commonalities.

Structures within case studies have been conceptualized as fairly encompassing rule or norm sets, as genres, or as archetypes. A few case studies (Han & Walsham, 1989; Yates & Orlikowski, 1992) have focused on how institutions are reproduced in structuration, but most are confined to the study of how IT structures have been shaped by the social interactions of teams, departments, or firms or the obverse—how introduction of new IT has changed group or organizational interaction patterns. In other words, the usual level of analysis is global (as opposed to micro or institutional). Most studies have framed structuration as an alternation between action and structural influences (see the figures that accompany some of these studies). With regard to dynamics, the cases seem to document both stability and change, but they give change something of an edge in the ratio in that the changes are portrayed as occurring against a background of preestablished structures. This may be a by-product of the types of data available to case studies, as noted earlier. The stance of the majority of case studies of IT structuration has been positive. Structuration of IS is assumed to have occurred, and critical or skeptical aspects of structuration have not been much considered.

Constitutive analyses have been the dominant analytic mode in case studies, but it is notable that case study researchers have incorporated functional modes as well, especially in more recent years. Researchers increasingly use comparative case study methods and larger sample sizes beyond the single case; and surveys sometimes accompany interviews and document reviews, allowing for specification and measurement of discrete variables. Overall, case studies aim for comprehensive analysis, allowing a view of "the big picture" of structuration in IS.

Table 4. Case Studies of Structuration in Information Systems.

Studies	Design and Data Sources	Structural Focus	Research Question and Dynamics
Blomberg (1986)	Single-case study of technology implementation; studied two design groups, one before and one after technology implementation	Meaning of software Task design	1. Difference in task design before and after implementation. Contrast between the two design groups. 2. Changes in power
Han & Walsham, (1989)	Historical single-case study based on records and histories	Norms Interpretive schemes Facilities	How different types of computer systems were shaped by and reshaped government policy
Yates & Orlikowski (1992)	Single-case historical study of memo form	Genres, defined by situation, form, level of abstraction, normative scope	1. Change in genre over time 2. Relation of change in genre to historical context
Dubinskas (1993)	Six case studies of implementation of a computer conferencing system, based on interviews and site visits	Existing organization structures; Power moves by managers; Modification of organizational structures by IT users; Social interpretations of technology	How existing organization structures were either reproduced or modified as new technology was implemented, depending on managerial domination and user actions and interpretations
Karsten (1995)	Implementation of Lotus Notes in a consulting firm; interviews, review of documents (minutes of meetings, invoices, memos); transcript of one important meeting	Structures of signification, domination, and legitimation Social interpretations of technology	Interaction processes that brought about the decision to implement Lotus Notes; tracking of firm's decision path; a focus on change
Zack & McKenney (1995)	Comparative case study of editorial groups of two daily newspapers; questionnaires, interviews, direct observations of meetings and e-mail	Contextual structures: communication climate and management philosophy; Group interaction patterns: perceptions and usage rules and practices	How social context promoted stability in appropriation of communication media
Scheepers & Damsgaard (1997)	Comparative case study of four intranet implementations in large organizations	Structures of signification, legitimation, and domination	How do these structures enable and constrain implementation of IT; interaction among the three structures

Observational Studies

Social action is at the center of structuration theory, so studies that examine social action firsthand, rather than through retrospective or filtered accounts, deserve special consideration. Whereas traditional discussions of research method subsume observa-

Table 4. (continued) Case Studies of Structuration in Information Systems.

Studies	Design and Data Sources	Structural Focus	Research Question and Dynamics
Maznevski & Chudoba (2000)	Comparative analysis of 3 global virtual teams over 21 months based on interviews, observation, survey, and communication logs	Team and task structural properties; Technology appropriation; Decision processes; Rhythms of interaction	Effectiveness of team interaction and outcomes based on rhythms of interaction incidents; including media use
Dedeke (2001)	Implementation of new IT in two sites of the same company; Interviews, surveys, document review	Technology properties; Implementation process (rules, norms, communication and decision structures) Institutional and contextual structures	System-wide explanation of structuration; how organizational change was brought about as part of IT implementation
de Vaujany (2001)	Four case-studies of French firms to verify a structurational model of Intranet implementation; common interview used in the four firms	Technological archetypes (neutral, regenerative, disruptive); Appropriation trajectories (balancing point, improvisational)	Use of IT to reproduce, disrupt, or produce new social structures; different types of technology archetypes promote different social structural effects
Hettinga (2002)	Implementation of videoconferencing for oncology consultations in three hospitals; observation of meetings, interviews, document review, and participant survey	Breakdowns (interruption of routines) Appropriation of social structures, task structures, and technical structures	Evolutionary perspective: Change in technical, social and task structures as IT was adopted
Peters (2002)	Case study of project teams within large multi-national firm; interviews, observation, and document review	Structural features Spirit of technology	Comparison of email, groupware, web, and traditional media (letters, phone, meetings) for control of interpersonal contact and value for teams
Masino & Zamarian (in press)	Comparison of software design and use in a car rental firm and an engineering firm, based on interviews and site visits	Design choices: IT as repository of social structure (1) (2) Use choices: IT as artifact in use (4)	How design choices and use decisions were structured by and structured work processes

tional methods within case or other methods, here we isolate observational studies due to their unique and important focus on actors' behavior and discourse. For the study of structuration in IS, observations typically consist of videotapes of users interacting with technology, stored logs of human-computer interaction, or records of speech acts made in meetings, documents, or other venues in which IT is discussed. In a sense, observational studies are the purest form of structuration research; they are true ethnographic accounts. Whether conducted in the field or laboratory, observational studies have the potential to capture social structure in action, as people are observed in situ. This is not to say that observational studies are ideal, however; like other research methods, they

Table 5. Observational Studies of Structuration in Information Systems.

Studies	Design	Structural Focus	Research Question and Dynamics
Orlikowski (1991)	Study of single firm, ethnography, interviews, document review	Forms of control: personal, technology, social structure, culture, professional	1. Shift in forms of control due to IT 2. Dialectic of control, whereby IT is used to resist control by organization
DeSanctis, Poole, Dickson, & Jackson (1993)	Coded videotapes of four groups using GSS in the field over six-month period. Supplemented with qualitative analysis of the meetings and post-meeting surveys of participants	GSS structures (tools to support procedures, general organization of system, nature of output); Faithful vs. ironic appropriation	1. Group differences in GSS appropriation in terms of extent of use and functions (see previous entry) 2. Relationship of appropriation to team effectiveness
Poole & DeSanctis (1992)	Coded videotapes of 18 groups in the lab using GSS. Supplemented with qualitative analysis	Structural features, and spirit of IT Appropriation moves (faithfulness, instrumental uses, consensus on appropriation)	1. Between group differences in IT appropriation patterns 2. Change in appropriations over time and how they occurred (continuously versus intermittently)
Orlikowski & Yates (1994)	Study of e-mail archive in one organization supplemented by interviews	Genres - defined by situation, form, level of abstraction, normative scope	1. Types of genres that appeared 2. Change in genres over time
Saunders, Robey, & Vaverek (1994)	Study of computer-conferencing (CC); CC-mediated course with physician, administrator, and nurse participants. Bales' IPA coding system used to code e-message archive	External status structure (preexisting); Emergent status structure; Interaction patterns; Situational norms for interaction	1. How external structure influenced emergent structures in CC 2. How status structures influenced interaction patterns 3. Impact of interaction norms on group system 4. Evolution of stability of interaction patterns over time

have both strengths and weaknesses for filling out a complete research agenda. Table 5 summarizes observational research on structuration in IS.

In general, observation studies seem to have the following advantages for those who study structuration: (1) Given favorable observational access, they enable the development and testing of true process theories of structuration, which meets an important requirement of structuration research. The time horizon of an observational study can be brief (e.g., an hour-long meeting), but analysis still takes on a decidedly

Table 5. (continued) Observational Studies of Structuration in Information Systems.

Studies	Design	Structural Focus	Research Question and Dynamics
Chudoba & George (1995)	Coding of appropriation of GSS by laboratory groups	GSS structure (support for tasks; participation equalization) Faithful vs. ironic appropriation	1. Impact of faithful appropriation on sequence of activities, appropriate use of software, and outcomes 2. Effect of dominant actor on appropriation
Poole, Kirsch, Jackson, & DeSanctis (1998)	Analysis of videotapes of eight groups using GSS in the field; global appropriation coding system. Longitudinal multiple- meeting design supplemented with interview data.	GSS structures (tools to support procedures, general organization of system, nature of output). Task structure; Appropriation of IT	1. Dominant appropriation patterns across groups 2. Alignment of technology and task, and group system in appropriation of GSS
Scott, Quinn, Timmerman, & Garrett (1998)	Analysis of interviews and transcripts of 26 student groups that used a GSS	GSS structures (anonymity, equality); Spirit vs. feature levels; Appropriation–ironic vs. faithful	1.Ironic appropriations of GSSs 2. Variations of ironic use
Faber, Raesfeld Meijer, & Wognum (1999)	Used micro-level coding scheme to examine appropriation of IT by geographically dispersed R&D teams	Appropriation (direct, substitution, combination, enlargement, contrast, constraint, affirmation, negation, neutrality)	Appropriation patterns over time; similarities and variations across teams and relation to team's coordination effectiveness
Yates, Orlikowski, & Okamura (1999)	Use of a new IT system by an R&D group in a Japanese firm; coding of messages posted on the news-system over 15 months	Genres of communication; Explicit and implicit structuring of interaction; Institutionalized norms, knowledge and authority relations	How explicit and implicit attempts to structure interaction via new IT served to both reinforce and change social interaction; comparison of subgroup versus wider community influences and outcomes
Majchrzak, Rice, Malhotra, King, & Ba (2000)	Observation of a virtual, inter-organizational product development team over 10 months; electronic log files, observations of weekly meetings, interviews, surveys	Alignments and mis-alignments among organizational environment, group, and technology structures	Structural stability, modification, and creation of new structures over time; mutual adaptation of structures

process-oriented approach. (2) Again, subject to constraints on access, observational studies do not restrict the constructs that scholars can utilize as much as interviews or archives, which by their very nature represent selections. Although there are likely some restrictions on what can be preserved, the "right" kinds of information are more likely to be preserved since it is the investigator who is collecting the data rather than a possibly self-interested participant or archivist. (3) Presuming the videotapes, computer log files, field notes, or other data are kept for repeated review, then deeply layered analyses are possible.

But there are challenges as well: (1) Observation alone does not enable the researcher to completely capture the meaning of events for the participants. The observer must deduce what participants must be thinking or feeling in order to make claims about meaning or interpretations. In view of well-established attributional biases, these deductions seem unlikely to be entirely accurate. Several observational studies have attempted to address this drawback by conducting interviews or surveys of actors. It is also possible to have participants read and comment on any reports or conclusions. (2) There is a tendency for observational studies to focus on microlevel aspects of structuration, making it more difficult to see macrolevel or global dynamics. Few observational studies span multiple levels of analysis (for an exception, see Yates, Orlikowski, & Okamura, 1999). (3) While observational studies typically have larger sample sizes than case studies, they still employ somewhat restrictive samples compared to experiments or surveys. An important concern is selection of cases and observations so that they are representative of the phenomenon of interest. The intensive nature of observational studies—which tends to make them intrusive as well—may result in selective sampling only of more cooperative sites or groups.

Referring to the structuration agenda in Figure 1, though there are exceptions, most observational studies pay close attention to the nature of the system (Component 3), identification of important structures relevant to the system (Components 1 and 2), and— most importantly—careful tracking of structuring moves over time (Component 4). Two observational studies (Orlikowski, 1991; Orlikowski & Yates, 1994) have also considered the obverse relationship in Component 5 and focused on how structuring processes remake institutions. Overall, observational studies have made little contribution to our understanding of how institutions are reproduced (Component 5) or how actors are positioned/reproduced (Component 6). Nor have they advanced critical analysis of structuration of IT (Component 7).

The primary analytic mode of observational studies is constitutive, though an impressive number of studies have incorporated functional analyses as well. The latter are more likely when sample sizes are relatively large so that the researcher can build and compare causal models linking structuration to specific events, such as evaluation of a team's decision effectiveness. Some observational studies have focused on single structures or sets of structures, but most have considered the interrelationships among structures, especially the structural potential of IT and the norms or social routines within the group using the IT. Action tends to dominate framing of observational studies, with context serving as a backdrop. Change and stability are both considered in characterizing dynamics, but change is the larger component in the ratio since it is easier to identify change in direct observation than to sort out continuities. In terms of types of structures studied, observational studies have usually singled out specific rules and resources as they figure in sets—such as in electronic communication systems or group decision support systems. As with case studies, the majority of observational studies of IT structuration have been positive in stance.

Experiments

Experiments offer several advantages for the study of structuration: (1) They allow direct comparison of the effects of diverse IT structures on social interaction. (2) They utilize larger samples than case studies or observational studies and therefore consider more replications of the phenomenon under study than the previous two designs. (3) They control factors that might offer competing explanations for the role of IT in social processes, thereby leading to "cleaner" analyses. For IS researchers, experimental studies are vital to a vibrant research agenda if the structuring power of technology is to ever be understood. But experiments also bring research challenges: (1) Subjects in an experiment are in a controlling situation, so there is the possibility that they may respond more readily and strongly to structural manipulations than they would under normal circumstances. (2) Since experiments control so many extraneous factors, they eliminate the full body of contextual effects and thus provide an impoverished view of the role of context in structuration. Even the most careful attempts to create a realistic experimental situation still omit many elements of real-life situations; to gain an authentic view of everyday social life requires creativity on the part of the experimenter.

Table 6 summarizes the experimental research on structuration in IS. Most have been based on some version of adaptive structuration theory (AST; DeSanctis & Poole, 1994; Poole & DeSanctis, 1990). AST attempts to give sufficiently clear construct definitions so that researchers can variabilize the structural potential of technology, system-level attributes, work tasks, context, and action at micro and global levels of analysis. Further, the theory links structuration processes to decision making and other outcomes of interest to IS scholars. For these reasons, the theory lends itself to theoretical test via experimental design. At least two types of experimental studies of structuration may be distinguished. First are studies that operationalize structuration indirectly through some variable that is an outcome or concomitant of structuration; these studies have employed structuration theory as part of their theoretical rationale, specifying an IT manipulation or actor behavior in structuration terms, but they do not directly study structuration per se. Component 3 of the structuration agenda is inferred but not directly examined. Many of the studies listed in Table 6 are illustrative. The second type of study directly incorporates structuration-related measures, such as direct appropriation, attitudes toward appropriation, or faithfulness of appropriation.

Experimental studies of structuration have increased in scope and sophistication over the years. The research has moved from simple comparison of computerized and noncomputerized structures (e.g., baseline versus manual versus GSS) to comparison of various levels of computerized support for social processes (e.g., communication versus decision modeling technologies). Researchers increasingly have incorporated longitudinal designs, whereby participants are observed at multiple points in time so that routines of social interaction are more likely to form, and process models of group development and change can be tested. Research designs have become more complex, incorporating more variables and measurement approaches in an attempt to get at the subtleties of structuration. Finally, experiments increasingly occur in the field and/or include live groups working on their everyday work problems in controlled settings. Recent studies by Dennis and Garfield (2001) and Jankowski and Nyerges (2001b) reflect these trends.

Dennis, Wixom, and Vandenberg (2001) published a meta-analysis exploring the effect of appropriations of GSS structures on several group outcomes. They identified 61 studies with treatment and control groups in which they could identify the type of technology-based structuring provided (communication support and information processing support) and the fit between GSS tools and the group's task. Their analysis

Table 6. Experimental Studies of Structuration of Information Systems*.

Studies	Design	Structural Focus	Research Question and Dynamics
*Watson, DeSanctis, & Poole (1988)	Groups given access to GSS structures compared to groups given non-computerized (manual) structures or no (baseline) group decision support Consensus decision task	GSS structures (tools to support group communication)	Not a direct study of structuration, but generates evidence on whether structures affect outcomes
*Zigurs, Poole, & DeSanctis (1988)	Groups given access to GSS structures compared to groups given non-computerized (manual) structures or no (baseline) group decision support Social judgment task	GSS structures (tools to support group communication)	Not a direct study of structuration, but generates evidence on whether structures affect outcomes and group interaction
*DeSanctis, D'Onofrio, Sambamurthy, & Poole (1989)	Restrictiveness of the group's use of technology manipulated (open vs. constrained); task comprehensiveness also varied (high vs. low)	GSS structures (varied in terms of restrictiveness and comprehensiveness);	Effects on group interaction patterns and attitudes toward appropriation
Sambamurthy & Poole (1992)	Groups given access to GSS with communication support (level 1) compared to groups also given information processing support (level 2) and groups given non-computerized structures	Degree of sophistication in group decision support structures provided to the group	Effects on conflict management, consensus and attitudes toward the group process and outcomes
Gopal, Bostrom, & Chin (1992-1993)	Groups given one of two different GSS software systems; Task also varied to yield a two by two design	GSS structures (tools to support group communication); Control of faithfulness of appropriation	1. How different GSS structures affected attitudes toward appropriation of technology 2. Shifts in relationships among variables over time.
Sambamurthy, Poole, & Kelly, (1993)	Secondary analysis of data from Sambamurthy & Poole (1992) (see above)	Degree of sophistication in group decision support structures provided to the group	Effects on group task interaction patterns; relationship between group task interaction and outcomes (consensus and attitudes)

* Indicates a study that used structuration as a general lens, or manipulated IT structures per predictions made by adaptive structuration theory, but did not otherwise examine structuration processes. These studies consider only components (1) and (2) of the structuration agenda shown in Figure 1.

Table 6. (continued) Experimental Studies of Structuration of Information Systems*.

Studies	Design	Structural Focus	Research Question and Dynamics
*Wheeler, Menneck, & Scudder (1993)	Group use of GSS in which actors' preferences for structural sets varied (high vs. low preference for procedural order); and restrictiveness of group's use of technology was manipulated (high versus low)	GSS structures (varied in terms of restrictiveness)	To determine whether accounting for actor preferences could influence technology use and outcomes; to determine whether restrictiveness could direct use and outcomes
*Miranda & Bostrom (1993-1994)	GSS vs. baseline groups. Studied conflict management over time; Multi-trial study	GSS structures (tools to support group communication)	Effects of GSS on conflict management over time
Anson, Bostrom, & Wynne (1995)	Two (presence versus absence of facilitation) by two (GSS vs. baseline) design	GSS appropriation; Facilitation as mediating appropriation of IT	To assess if facilitation improved impacts of GSS on appropriation and resulting effects on outcomes
Wheeler & Valacich (1996)	Two (presence versus absence of facilitation by two (level 1 vs. level 2 GSS) by two (training vs. none)	Degree of sophistication in group decision support structures provided to the group; Facilitation as mediating appropriation of IT	1. Impact of facilitation, training, and level of support on appropriation 2. Impact of faithfulness of technology use on outcomes
Contractor, Seibold, & Heller (1996)	Four (baseline vs. manual vs. GSS identified vs. GSS anonymous) conditions	Perceptions of structures-in-use	Temporal shifts in perceptions due to network influence
*Kahai, Sosik, & Avolio (1997)	Two (participative vs. directive leadership) by two (fairly vs. moderately structured problem)	Leadership as mediating appropriation of IT	Impact of leadership style and problem type on outcomes of IT use

suggested support for the dual contingency model (DeSanctis & Poole, 1994) in which positive outcomes depend on (a) provision of appropriation support and (b) fit between task and GSS features. However, Dennis et al. (2001) were not able to measure structuration processes directly and so did not directly test the impact of appropriation on outcomes.

Experiments have tended to focus on structuration in IS as it occurs in small groups, as opposed to dyads or larger social systems. To some extent this is historical accident—GSS technology for work groups emerged about the same time that structuration theory entered the consciousness of the IS field. But there are also practicalities—larger social systems, or networks of groups and teams, have not been feasible to study within experimental designs. Possibly, the advent of the Internet will make experimental studies of larger social systems more likely in future.

Table 6. (continued) Experimental Studies of Structuration of Information Systems*.

Studies	Design	Structural Focus	Research Question and Dynamics
Salisbury, Chin, Gopal, Newsted, & Reeves (1999)	High vs. low restrictive GSS	Appropriation; interpretation of appropriation	The impact of common understanding of and agreement on appropriation and perceived technology efficacy on satisfaction
Limayem & DeSanctis (2000)	Presence or absence of decisional guidance within multicriteria decision modeling software; group use of GSS for consensus task	User understanding of decision models; Faithful versus ironic appropriation	To determine whether software-embedded facilitation would affect group understanding of decision models and IT appropriation
Jankowski & Nyerges (2001b)	Manipulated task complexity, cognitive conflict, and access to geographic information system (GIS) technology; relationship of these to appropriation; 22 groups of citizens addressed the problem of selecting a site for habitat restoration; five decision sessions over five weeks	GIS appropriation - direct appropriation moves	Impact of task and other context variables on appropriation patterns and use of GIS components (e.g., maps versus multicriteria decision models); relationship of moves to group conflict and consensus
Dennis & Garfield (2001)	Field experiment of six medical project teams; half used a GSS and half used their traditional team processes; Observations of meetings, interviews, transcripts, & questionnaires	GSS spirit and structural features; Faithful versus ironic appropriation	Effects of GSS use on leadership and participation processes, team attitudes, meeting processes and outcomes, and project outcomes

With regard to the larger structuration agenda (Figure 1), experiments have explored the nature of the system by identifying and manipulating social structures associated with technology, task, or context (Components 1 and 2) and key factors that affect group interaction (Component 3). Coding of group interaction in some experiments has helped to characterize the structuring process, and many studies have tested the counterfactual that IT structures do not impact interaction and outcomes (Component 4). Some studies have manipulated the roles of actors in the social system, especially the relative positions of facilitators, leaders, and intelligent agents within the software (Component 6). Thus far, experiments have not had much bearing on Components 5 and 7 of the structuration agenda.

Experiments are resoundingly functional in their analytic mode, although many studies have surveyed user attitudes in attempt to capture actor views of the structuration process (e.g., DeSanctis, D'Onofrio, Sambamurthy, & Poole, 1989; Gopal, Bostrom, &

234 Poole & DeSanctis

Table 7. Survey Studies of Structuration in Information Systems.

Studies	Design	Structural Focus	Research Question and Dynamics
Ruel (1999)	Developed survey based on DeSanctis & Poole's AST constructs of spirit and appropriation to measure five aspects of appropriation; administered to 44 workers in a Dutch financial services firm adopting a new IT	Spirit of IT

Appropriation moves, faithfulness, attitudes and consensus

Task-oriented and explorative use of IT | How changes in work context moderate the relationship between spirit of IT and appropriation moves, faithfulness, etc. (4, 5) |
| DeSanctis, Poole, & Dickson (2000) | Survey of appropriation and groupware (e-mail, GSS, etc.) use by 47 teams in an energy company over a three-year period; supplemented with interviews and site visits | Direct appropriation, attitudes toward appropriation (respect, comfort, challenge, understanding), consensus on appropriation | To determine how team structural attributes, work tasks, and interaction patterns affected appropriation of IT over time |
| Ruel (2002) | Administered survey developed by Ruel (1999) to 159 workers in four Dutch service firms using new office technologies | Spirit of IT

Appropriation moves, faithfulness, instrumental uses, consensus on appropriation | How clarity of IT spirit affects appropriation moves and faithfulness, instrumental uses, and consensus of IT appropriation; influence of agent characteristics |
| Salisbury, Chin, Gopal, & Newsted (2002) | Survey of 236 undergraduate student participants in experiments of using GSS technology | Faithfulness of appropriation; Consensus on appropriation Restrictive vs. nonrestrictive use of technology | Comparison of three measurement models of AST constructs, followed by a causal model analysis of relationship between appropriation and satisfaction |

Chin, 1992-1993; Sambamurthy & Poole, 1992). Dennis and Garfield (2001) are unique in their attempts to complement functional with constitutional analyses. In terms of design choices, all experiments have included microlevel analyses, and some have included global-level analyses as well (i.e., those that examine groups over time). Manipulations generally contrast diverse structures for group interaction, as opposed to studying related social structures. The studies typically are framed as examining the influence of structure on action. In terms of dynamics, most experiments attempt to cast change against stability in the social system via comparison of treatment to control conditions. The stance of experimental reports is more skeptical than in other research methods. The use of control and contrast allows for the possibility that structuration of IS is not occurring at all or makes relatively small contributions to the effect. In the same way, experiments are not biased toward detection of change in dynamics due to IT. Stability (in the form of no difference between treatments and control conditions) can readily be

Table 8. Comparison of Research Requirements and Options for Four Methods of Study of Structuration in IS.

	Case Study	Direct Observation	Experiment	Survey
Requirements				
Dominant perspective on structuration[1]	(4), (5) and (6)	(3), (4)	(1) and (2)	(4)
Major analytic mode[2]	constitutive	constitutive	functional	functional
Options[3]				
Primary level of analysis	global	micro	micro	global
Structural focus	related (primary) diverse (secondary)	related (primary) diverse (secondary)	diverse (primary) related (secondary)	related (primary) diverse (secondary)
Framing	alternating	actors' structural moves	influence of structure on action	actors' structural moves
Dynamics	change (primary) stability (secondary)	change (primary) stability (secondary)	stability (primary) change (secondary)	stability (primary) change (secondary)
Stance	positive	positive	skeptical	positive

[1] *Numbers correspond to the components displayed in Figure 1 and explained in Table 1.*
[2] *See Table 2 for explanation of each mode.*
[3] *See Table 3 for a listing of options associated with each of the five choices.*

detected. A final limitation of experiments is that they typically run for such a short time that longer-term structuring processes cannot be studied. While important processes of microstructuration can occur during an hour or two, longer-term dynamics will be missed by experimental sessions of this length.

Surveys

Several sets of questionnaires have been developed to measure structuration constructs. Ruel (1999) developed a questionnaire based on adaptive structuration theory that he used in two field studies of IT adoption. Poole and colleagues (DeSanctis, Poole, & Dickson, 2000) developed an instrument that taps seven dimensions of work-group perceptions of appropriation of advanced IT: respect for the IT; comfort with the IT; degree to which the team has adapted the IT; degree of understanding of the IT; extent to which the IT has been used to include actors in decision making; extent to which the IT has been used to manipulate the group; and consensus on appropriation. Finally, a group based at the University of Calgary (Chin et al., 1998; Salisbury, Gopal, & Chin, 1996) has developed instruments to measure perceptions of faithfulness and consensus on appropriation. These have been carefully developed and validated in several studies. Table 7 summarizes survey studies of structuration in IS.

The hallmark of survey studies is their near or complete reliance on the survey as data for the research. Surveys bring a potential advantage to the structuration agenda in their focus on actor views of their actions within the social system under study. Unlike much of behavioral research that uses survey measures as surrogates for another behavior of interest, structuration theory is directly concerned with cognition—i.e., with actor views of their roles as social agents and with the influence of structure on their actions. To the extent that surveys can provide valid insight into actors' cognitions, they can make an important contribution to the study of structuration in IS. Surveys are also advantageous for structuration research because they tap larger and more diverse samples than are possible with any other research method. Of course, survey studies are limited in that they do not tap the process of use per se but rather subjects' summary recollections and interpretations of it. It is a premise of structuration theory that actors, though knowledgeable and reflective, are able to act on their knowledge more fully than they can articulate (Giddens, 1984). For this reason surveys may be best used as complements to case, observational, and experimental studies.

Survey studies to date have addressed Component 6 in the structuration agenda and, in a more limited way, Component 4. By their nature, surveys are functional in analytic mode, though they incorporate a constitutive approach to measurement in that they are concerned with gleaning a faithful representation of actors' viewpoints and meanings. They gather information at a global level of the system rather than the microlevel. They can be focused on both singular structures and relationships among structures but generally capture information about related structures (e.g., multiple types of groupware and group decision technologies that are similar). Surveys typically frame research to emphasize actors' structural moves, and they emphasize stability over change dynamics (although longitudinal surveys can capture change to some extent). If the survey asks respondents to contrast their use of different technologies or other structures, or if the survey is given to people with different types of IT access or in distinctly different social settings, then framing to emphasize the influence of structure on action and the dynamics of system change becomes possible. To date, though, we know of no study that has proceeded in this fashion. Thus far, survey studies have adopted a positive stance toward structuration.

Trends in Structuration Methodology

Reviewing the landscape of research on structuration in IS, it is notable that while early studies largely adopted a single type of methodology, more recent work has crossed the four types. There has been some movement over time on the part of case study researchers, on the one hand, and experimental researchers, on the other, to add observational methods to their studies. Survey methods rarely stand alone and increasingly appear as add-ons to studies in the other method categories. Multimethod studies have become the norm in all methodological categories. Further, within each method type there has been progression of sophistication; studies build on one another and increasingly incorporate larger samples and comparative data sets. Nonetheless, few programs of study cross all four method lines. Each method type has its biases, and researchers tend to gravitate toward one style of work or another and stay there as they build the discipline. Case study researchers, for example, favor the study of genres, norms, and other "big picture" views of structure; they are biased in terms of a view of IS as an organizational dynamic. Experimental researchers, at the other extreme, favor the study of appropriation and the decomposition of structural potential within different types of IT. Experimentalists are biased in the view of IS as structure, or sets of structures, for interaction. Both camps agree that IS as actor-structure interaction is also important, as evident when each migrates to use of observational methods. But even here the researchers tend to stay within the analytic mode (constitutive or functional) of the case or experiment and to focus on the pieces of the structuration agenda that each tends to favor. Since survey studies are relatively new, it is hard to say where they will migrate long run, but they appear to have grown more out of the experimental tradition than the case study or observational tradition. Table 8 summarizes the four research methods in terms of their biases and contributions to the overall study of structuration in IS.

Researchers and research streams would do well in the future to operate more in synchrony with one another rather than in parallel. The different method types have the potential to complement one another since each attends to somewhat different issues and has unique strengths and weaknesses. Within each approach, there seem to be active efforts to take the results of other similar researchers into account. There is a sense of cumulative tradition. The same accumulation is needed at the field level so that a more complete view of structuration in IS can emerge.

Finally, our analysis of the literature suggests that two issues in particular appear to be rather neglected up to this point in time. Very few studies consider IS as a social context for the formation of individuals and their identities or IS as a context for dominance of participants and reproduction of the existing social order (Components 6 and 7 of the structuration agenda). There is also less attention as to how IS as institutions are produced and reproduced than would be optimal; there are several theoretical analyses but few empirical studies of this dynamic. Most studies focus instead on groups and organizational systems. Despite large lacunae in our knowledge on the other issues, at least research seems to be addressing them.

CONCLUSION

The study of structuration in IS has made significant contribution to the discipline over the past 20 years. Structuration theory blossomed into popularity at about the same time that IS scholars were seeking theoretical models that included human behavior along with the technology and that accommodated group interaction with technology, not just individual human-computer interaction. At a time when researchers were perplexed by inconsistent and contradictory effects of new, advanced information technologies such as e-mail, group decision tools, and the like, structuration theory offered a ready base of explanation. The infusion of structurational thinking has helped to move the IS field from the study of technology to the study of action, from predicting direct affects of technology on people to exploring recursive shaping of technology and people over time. The agency emphasis of structuration theory has fulfilled a call for greater attention to the study of social forces influencing technologies and their use. Over time, hardware and software have drifted to the background of the research psyche, and in their place have come groups, organizations, and institutions.[8]

Recently, Orlikowski and Iacono (2001) lamented a general drift away from focus on IT within the IS field. They plead for a refocus by scholars on IT as artifact. Looking ahead, will structuration theory continue to meet the needs of the discipline? As discussed at the start of this paper, a danger of the structuration perspective is that it can remove technology from the picture altogether. But our review also has emphasized that structuration theory can accommodate modeling and empirical testing of IT as artifact; numerous scholars have demonstrated this to be the case, especially (but not only) in experimental settings. We believe that there is more that structuration theory can contribute than has been brought to the fore by IS scholars to date. In other words, the usefulness of structuration theory to the discipline has not yet run its course. To move ahead, we believe that much greater specificity and quantification are needed, both with regard to the structural potential of IT and the social processes in which IT operates. The most valuable embarkation at this juncture is to articulate structuration models that provide more detailed accounts of the constructs and relationships presented in our Figure 1, that accommodate both functional and constitutive analyses, that can be put to the test using multiple methods, and that lead to accumulation of clear thinking about IT design, use, and outcomes.

Several promising ventures lie ahead. We mention just a few here. First are programs of research that embed related areas of IS study inside of structuration models. For example, Salisbury, Chin, Gopal, and Newsted (2002) embed the theory of reasoned action and theory of planned behavior inside a model of appropriation behavior. The result is a more powerful explanation of group use of an IT and a model that is highly specified and subject to critical review. Similarly, Dennis and Garfield (2001) specify and examine the role of leadership and participation processes within a study of faithful versus ironic appropriation of a GSS. Research of this sort is conceptually rich and detailed, and it shows how structuration processes relate to other important social processes, such as decision making, social influence, and attitude formation.

Second are programs of research that—like those just described—embed other relevant theory within a structuration framework *and* are both micro and institutional in applicability. Such programs of research are able to build large-scale models of social/ institutional change, all the while remaining rich in detail and specificity. We attempted such an approach in our earlier work, some of which has been referred to in this manuscript. But a more recent and impressive illustration lies in the efforts of Jankowski and Nyerges (2001a, 2001b), who have developed a modified version of adaptive structuration theory which they call EAST ("enhanced" AST). Gradually they are building what they call a participatory, geographic information science that has structuration theory as its core. Their five-year program of theory testing and grounded theory development has produced an increasingly specified research model for the study of community discourse and decision making surrounding high-risk social change, including health-care management, transportation improvement, and habitat restoration. Their focus is on the application of geographic information systems to groups, organizations, and communities involved in these change initiatives. Their research occurs at micro, global, and institutional levels and incorporates many of the methods that have been described in this chapter.

Finally, programs of study that penetrate the complexities of the structure-action relationship over time are promising ventures for the IS field. Orlikowski's (2002) recent work on knowledge enactment and organizational learning is illustrative, as is a program of research at the Telematica Instituut (see Hettinga, 2002) which takes an evolutionary view of structuration in IS. Related areas of study with high potential for IS scholars include the structuration of online communities, global learning processes, and collective knowledge systems.

The theory of structuration is fascinating, its constructs captivating, its language at once clarifying and bewildering. Our analysis has highlighted the range of possibilities for empirical study that can be driven by this powerful theoretical paradigm. We have outlined important requirements and shown how scholars can build a cumulative research agenda. We hope our review will further progress in this vibrant area of study.

REFERENCES

Anson, R., Bostrom, R., & Wynne, B. (1995). An experiment assessing group support system and facilitator effects on meeting outcomes. *Management Science, 41*, 189-208.

Archer, M. (1990). Human agency and social structure: A critique of Giddens. In J. Clarke, C. Modgil, & J. Modgil (Eds.), *Anthony Giddens: Consensus and Controversy* (pp. 73-84). Brighton, UK: Falmer Press.

Banks, S., & Riley, P. (1993). Structuration theory as an ontology for communication research. In S. A. Deetz (Ed.), *Communication Yearbook 17* (pp. 167-196). Newbury Park, CA: SAGE.

Barbalet, J. M. (1987). Power, structural resources and agency. *Current Perspectives in Social Theory, 8*, 1-24.

Barley, S. R. (1986). Technology as an occasion for structuring: Evidence from observations of CT scanners and the social order of radiology departments. *Administrative Science Quarterly, 31*, 78-108.

Barley, S. R., & Tolbert, P. S. (1997). Institutionalization and structuration: Studying the links between action and institution. *Organization Studies, 18*(1), 93-117.

Barrett, M., & Walsham, G. (1999). Electronic trading and work transformation in the London insurance market. *Information Systems Research, 10*(1), 1-22.

Barthes, R. (1974). *S/Z*. New York: Hill & Wang.

Beckert, J. (1999). Agency, entrepreneurs, and institutional change: The role of strategic choice and institutionalized practices in organizations. *Organization Studies*, *20*(5), 777-799.

Benbasat, I., & Dexter, A. S. (1985). An experimental evaluation of graphical and color-enhanced information presentation. *Management Science*, 31, 1348-1363.

Benbasat, I. & Nault, B. R. (1990). An evaluation of empirical research in managerial support systems. *Decision Support Systems*, *6*, 203-226.

Blomberg, J. L. (1986). The variable impact of computer technologies on the organization of work activities. In *Proceedings of the Conference on Computer-Supported Cooperative Work* (pp. 35-42). Austin, Texas, USA. New York: Association for Computing Machinery.

Boczkowski, P. J. (1999). Mutual shaping of users and technologies in a national virtual community. *Journal of Communication*, *49*(2) 86-111.

Bormann, E. G. (1996). Symbolic convergence theory and communication. In R. Y. Hirokawa & M. S. Poole (Eds.), *Communication and Group Decision Making* (pp. 81-113). Thousand Oaks, CA: SAGE.

Brewer, J. D. (1988). Micro-sociology and "the duality of structure." In N. Fielding (Ed.), *Action and Structure* (pp. 144-166). Thousand Oaks, CA: SAGE.

Brooks, L. (1997). Structuration theory and new technology: Analysing organizationally situated computer-aided design (CAD). *Information Systems Journal*, *7*(2), 133-151.

Browning, L. D., Beyer, J. M., & Shetler, J. C. (1995). Building cooperation in a competitive industry: SEMATCH and the semicondctor industry. *Academy of Management Journal*, *38*(1), 113-151.

Browning, L. D., Sitkin, S. B., & Sutcliffe, K. M. (1998, July). *A structuration analysis of control and learning in TQM using organizations: The presence of feature and spirit in the reports of the use of procedures*. Paper presented at the annual meeting of the International Communication Association, Jerusalem, Israel.

Chidambaram, L. (1996). Relational development in computer-supported groups. *MIS Quarterly*, *20*(2), 143-165.

Chin, W. W., Gopal, A., & Salisbury, W. D. (1998). Advancing the theory of adaptive structuration: The development of a scale to measure faithfulness of appropriation. *Information Systems Research*, 8, 342-367.

Chudoba, K. M., & George, J. F. (1995, August). *Use of a group support system over time: An empirical investigation with small groups*. Paper presented at Academy of Management Conference, Vancouver, British Columbia, Canada.

Contractor, N. S., & Seibold, D. R. (1993). Theoretical frameworks for the study of structuring processes in group decision support systems: Adaptive structuration theory and self-organizing systems theory. *Human Communication Research*, *19*, 528-563.

Contractor, N. S., Seibold, D. R., & Heller, M. A. (1996). Interactional influence in the structuring of media use in groups: Influence in members' perceptions of group decision support system use. *Human Communication Research, 22*, 451-481.

Coombs, R., Knights, D., & Willmott, H. C. (1992). Culture, control and competition: Towards a conceptual framework for the study of information technology in organizations. *Organization Studies, 13* 51-72.

Cramton, C. D. (2001). The mutual knowledge problem and its consequences for dispersed collaboration. *Organization Science, 12*(3), 346-372.

Currie, W., & Galliers, B. (eds.) (1999). *Rethinking Management Information Systems: An Interdisciplinary Perspective.* New York: Oxford University.

Daft, R. L., & Lengel, R. H. (1986). Organizational information requirements, media richness, and structural determinants. *Management Science, 32,* 554-571.

Davis, G. (1974). *Management Information Systems.* New York: McGraw-Hill.

Davis, J. H. (1973). Group decision and social interaction: A theory of social decision schemes. *Psychological Review, 80*(2), 97-125.

Dedeke, A. (2001). *A structurational model for understanding technology implementation.* Unpublished working paper, Suffolk University, Sawyer School of Management, Computer Information Systems Department, Boston, Massachusetts, USA.

Dennis, A. R., & Garfield, M. J. (2001). *Breaking structures: The adoption and use of GSS in project teams.* Unpublished working paper, Indiana University, Kelly School of Business, Bloomington, USA.

Dennis, A. R., Valacich, J. S., Connolly, T., & Wynne, B. E. (1996). Process structuring in electronic brainstorming. *Information Systems Research, 7*(2), 268-277.

Dennis, A. R., Wixom, B. H., & Vandenberg, R. J. (2001). Understanding fit and appropriation effects in group support systems via meta-analysis. *MIS Quarterly, 25,* 167-193.

DeSanctis, G., & Gallupe, R. B. (1987). A foundation for the study of group decision support systems. *Management Science, 33*(5), 589-609.

DeSanctis, G., & Poole, M. S. (1994). Capturing the complexity in advanced technology use: Adaptive structuration theory. *Organization Science, 5,* 121-147.

DeSanctis, G., D'Onofrio, M. J., Sambamurthy, V., & Poole, M. S. (1989). Comprehensiveness and restrictiveness in group decision heuristics: Effects of computer support on consensus decision-making. In J. I. DeGross, J. C. Henderson, & B. R. Konsynski (Eds.), *Proceedings of the Tenth International Conference on Information Systems* (pp. 131-140). New York: ACM Press.

DeSanctis, G., Poole, M. S., & Dickson, G. W. (2000). Teams and technology: Interactions over time. In T. L. Griffith & E. A. Mannix (Eds.), *Research on Managing Groups and Teams: Technology* (Vol. 3, pp. 1-27). Stamford, CT: JAI Press.

DeSanctis, G., Poole, M. S., Dickson, G. W., & Jackson, B. M. (1993). An interpretive analysis of team use of group technologies. *Journal of Organizational Computing, 3,* 1-31.

DeSanctis, G., Snyder, J. R., & Poole, M. S. (1994). The meaning of the interface: A functional and holistic evaluation of a meeting software system. *Decision Support Systems: The International Journal, 11,* 319-335.

De Vaujany, F.-X. (2001, September). *Grasping the social dynamic of IT use: Illustration of a structurational approach.* Paper presented at Communication a la Conference ECITE (European Conference on Information Technology Evaluation), Oxford, Oriel College.

Dhaliwal, J. S., & Benbasat, I. (1996). The use and effects of knowledge-based system explanations: Theoretical foundations and a framework for empirical evaluation. *Information Systems Research, 7*(3), 342-362.

Dickson, G. W., Senn, J., & Chervany, N. (1977). Research in MIS: The Minnesota experiments. *Management Science, 23,* 913-924.

DiMaggio, P. (1991). Constructing an organizational field as a professional project: U.S. art museums, 1920-1940. In W. W. Powell & P. J. DiMaggio (Eds.), *The New Institutionalism in Organizational Analysis* (pp. 267-292). Chicago, IL: University of Chicago Press.

DiMaggio, P. J., & Powell, W. W. (1983). The iron cage revisited: Institutional isomorphism and collective rationality in organizational fields. *American Sociological Review, 48*, 147-160.

Dubinskas, F. A. (1993). Virtual organizations: Computer conferencing and organizational design. *Journal of Organizational Computing, 3*(4), 389-416.

Dutton, W. H. (1999). *Society on the Line: Information Politics in the Digital Age.* New York: Oxford University Press.

Faber, E., Raesfeld, M. A., & Wognum N. (1999, May). *Studying structuration processes of collaboration between geographically dispersed R&D teams.* Paper presented at the Second International Workshop on Organization of the Future in the "Information Society": Managing Change, Human Resources, and Structure, Cadiz, Spain.

Fay, B. (1987). *Critical Social Science.* Ithaca, NY: Cornell University Press.

Finholt, T., & Sproull, L. (1990). Electronic groups at work. *Organization Science, 1*(1), 41-64.

Fisher, B. A. (1975). *Small Group Decision Making.* New York: McGraw-Hill.

Fulk, J. (1993). Social construction of communication technology. *Academy of Management Review, 36*(5), 921-950.

Fulk, J., & Boyd, B. (1991). Emerging theories of communication in organizations. *Journal of Management, 17*(2), 407-446.

Gerrity, T. P. (1971, Winter). Design of man-machine decision systems: An application to portfolio management. *Sloan Management Review, 12*(2), 59-76.

Giddens, A. (1977). *Studies in Social and Political Theory.* London: Hutchinson.

Giddens, A. (1979). *Central Problems in Social Theory: Action, Structure, and Contradiction in Social Analysis.* Berkley, CA: University of California Press.

Giddens, A. (1984). *The Constitution of Society: Outline of the Theory of Structuration.* Cambridge, UK: Polity.

Giddens, A. (1990). *The Consequences of Modernity.* Cambridge, UK: Polity.

Giddens, A. (1997). The globalization of modernity. In A. Sreberny-Mohammadi, D. Winseck, J. McKenna, & O. Boyd-Barrett (Eds.), *Media in Global Context: A Reader* (pp. 19-26). London: Arnold.

Gopal, A., Bostrom, R. P., & Chin, W. W. (1992-1993). Applying adaptive structuration theory to investigate the process of group support systems use. *Journal of Management Information Systems, 9*, 45-69.

Gray, P., & Olfman, L. (1989). The user interface in group decision support systems. *Decision Support Systems, 5*(2), 119-137.

Griffith, T. L. (1999). Technology features as triggers for sensemaking. *Academy of Management Review, 24*(3), 472-488.

Gutek, B. A. (1990). Work group structure and information technology: A structural contingency approach. In J. Galegher, R. E. Kraut, & C. Egido (Eds.), *Intellectual Teamwork: Social and Technological Bases for Cooperative Work.* Hillsdale, NJ: Lawrence Erlbaum.

Han, C. K., & Walsham, G. (1989). *Public Policy and Information Systems in Government: A Mixed Level Analysis of Computerisation* (Management Studies Research Paper No. 3/89).Cambridge University. Cambridge, UK: Department of Engineering.

Hargadon, A., & Fanelli, A. (2002). Action and possibility: Reconciling dual perspectives of knowledge in organizations. *Organization Science, 13*(3), 290-302.

Heracleous, L., & Hendry, J. (2000). Discourse and the study of organization: Toward a structurational perspective. *Human Relations, 53*(10), 1251-1286.

Hettinga, M. (2002). *Understanding evolutionary use of groupware*. Working paper. Telematica Instituut Fundamental Research Series, No. 007, Enschede, The Netherlands: Telematica Instituut. Retrieved from http://www.telin.nl/publicaties/frs.htm.

Hiltz, S. R., & Turoff, M. (1985). Structuring computer-mediated communication systems to avoid information overload. *Communications of the ACM, 28*(7), 680-689.

Holloman, C. R., & Hendrick, H. W. (1972). Adequacy of group decisions as a function of the decision-making process. *Academy of Management Journal, 15*, 175-184.

Homans, G. C. (1950). *The Human Group*. New York: Harcourt Brace.

Homans, G. C. (1961). *Social Behavior: Its Elementary Forms*. New York: Harcourt, Brace, & World.

Huber, G. P. (1984). Issues in the design of group decision support systems. *MIS Quarterly, 8*(3), 195-204.

Ives, B., Hamilton, S., & Davis, G. B. (1980). A framework for research in computer-based management information systems. *Management Science, 26*(9), 910-934.

Jankowski, P., & Nyerges, T. (2001a). *Geographic Information Systems for Group Decision Making: Towards a Participatory, Geographic Information Science*. New York: Taylor & Francis.

Jankowski, P., & Nyerges, T. (2001b). GIS-supported collaborative decision making: Results of an experiment. *Annals of the Association of American Geographers, 91*(1), 48-70.

Jarvenpaa, S. L., Rao, V. S., & Huber, G. P. (1988). Computer support for meetings of groups working on unstructured problems: A field experiment. *MIS Quarterly, 12*(4), 645-666.

Johnson, B., & Rice, R. (1985). Reinvention in the innovation process: The case of word processing. In R. Rice (Ed.), *The New Media: Communication, Research, and Technology* (pp. 157-184). Beverly Hills, CA: SAGE.

Jones, M. (1999). Structuration theory. In W. Currie & B. Galliers (Eds.), *Rethinking Management Information Systems* (pp. 104-135). New York: Oxford University Press.

Kahai, S. S., Sosik, J. J., & Avolio, B. J. (1997). Effects of leadership style and problem structure on work group process and outcomes in an electronic meeting system environment. *Personnel Psychology, 50*, 121-146.

Karsten, H. (1995). Converging paths to Notes: In search of computer-based information systems in a networked company. *Information Technology & People, 8*(1), 7-34.

Keen, P. G. W., & Scott Morton, M. S. (1978). *Decision Support Systems*. Reading, MA: Addison-Wesley.

Kelley, H. H., & Thibaut, J. W. (1969). Group problem solving. In G. Lindsey & E. Aronson (Eds.), *The Handbook of Social Psychology* (2nd ed., chap. 29). Reading, MA: Addison-Wesley.

Latour, B. (1992). Technology is society made durable. In J. Law (Ed.), *Sociology of Monsters: Essays on Power, Technology and Domination* (pp. 103-131). London: Routledge.

Layder, D. (1985). Power, structure and agency. *Journal for the Theory of Social Behavior, 15*, 131-149.

Lee, A. S. (1999a). Rigor and relevance in MIS research: Beyond the approach of positivism alone. *MIS Quarterly, 23*(1) 29-33.

Lee, A. S. (1999b). Researching MIS. In W. Currie & B. Galliers (Eds.), *Rethinking Management Information Systems* (pp. 7-27). New York: Oxford University Press.

Lee, A. S., Liebenau, J., & Degross, J. I. (eds.) (1997). *Information Systems and Qualitative Research*. London: Chapman & Hall.

Limayem, M., & DeSanctis, G. (2000). Providing decisional guidance for multicriteria decision making in groups. *Information Systems Research, 11*(4), 386-401.

Lindesmith, A. (1947). *Opiate Addiction*. Bloomington, IN: Principia Press.

Majchrzak, A., Rice, R., Malhotra, A., King, N., & Ba, S. (2000). Technology adaptation: The case of a computer-supported inter-organizational virtual team. *MIS Quarterly, 24*(4), 569-601.

Masino, G., & Zamarian, M. (in press). Information technology artifacts as structuring devices in organizations: Design, appropriation and use issues. *Interacting With Computers*.

Maznevski, M. L., & Chudoba, K. M. (2000). Bridging space over time: Global virtual team dynamics and effectiveness. *Organization Science, 11*(5), 473-492.

McCartt, A. T., & Rohrbaugh, J. (1995). Managerial openness to change and the introduction of GDSS: Explaining initial success and failure in decision conferencing. *Organization Science, 6*(5), 569-584.

Miranda, S. M., & Bostrom, R. P. (1993-1994). The impact of group support systems on group conflict and conflict management. *Journal of Management Information Systems, 10*, 63-95.

Miranda, S. M., & Bostrom, R. P. (1999). Meeting facilitation: Process versus content interventions. *Journal of Management Information Systems, 15*(4) 89-114.

Mohr, L. (1982). *Explaining Organizational Behavior*. San Francisco, CA: Jossey-Bass.

Nelson, R., & Winter, S. (1982). *An Evolutionary Theory of Economic Change*. Cambridge, MA: Harvard University Press.

Newman, M., & Robey, D. (1992). A social process model of user-analyst relationships. *MIS Quarterly, 16*(2) 249-266.

Nunamaker, J. F., Jr., Dennis, A. R., Valacich, J. S., & Vogel, D. R. (1991). Information technology for negotiating groups: Generating options for mutual gain. *Management Science, 37*(10), 1325-1346.

Nyerges, T., Moore, T. J., Montejano, R., & Compton, M. (1998). Developing and using interaction coding systems for studying groupware use. *Human-Computer Interaction, 13*, 127-165.

Nyerges, T. L., & Jankowski, P. (1997). Enhanced adaptive structuration theory: A theory of GIS-supported collaborative decision making. *Geographical Systems, 4*(3), 225-259.

Ollman, B. (1971). *Alienation: Marx's Conception of Man in Capitalist Society*. Cambridge, UK: Cambridge University Press.

Olson, G. M., & Olson, J. S. (1991). User-centered design of collaboration technology. *Journal of Organizational Computing, 1*(1), 41-60.

Orlikowski, W. J. (1991). Integrated information environment or matrix of control? The contradictory implications of information technology. *Accounting, Management, and Information Technology, 1*, 9-42.

Orlikowski, W. J. (1992). The duality of technology: Rethinking the concept of technology in organizations. *Organization Science, 3*(3) 398-427.

Orlikowski, W. J. (1993). Learning from Notes: Organizational issues in groupware implementation. *Information Society, 9*(3), 237-250.

Orlikowski, W. J. (2000). Using technology and constituting structures: A practice lens for studying technology in organizations. *Organization Science, 11*(4), 404-428.

Orlikowski, W. J. (2002). Knowing in practice: Enhancing a collective capability in distributed organizing. *Organization Science, 13*(3), 249-273.

Orlikowski, W. J., & Iacono, C. S. (2001). Research commentary: Desperately seeking the "IT" in IT research—A call to theorizing the IT artifact. *Information Systems Research, 12*(2), 121-134.

Orlikowski, W. J., & Robey, D. (1991). Information technology and the structuring of organizations. *Information Systems Research, 2*(2), 143-169.

Orlikowski, W. J., & Yates, J. (1994). Genre repertoire: The structuring of communicative practices in organizations. *Administrative Science Quarterly, 39*, 541-574.

Orlikowski, W. J., Yates, J., Okamura, K., & Fujimoto, M. (1995). Shaping electronic communication: The metastructuring of technology in the context of use. *Organization Science, 6*(4), 423-445.

Peters, L. (2002). *Conceptualising technology: Structure and spirit in CMC media.* Unpublished working paper, University of East Anglia, School of Management, Norwich, UK.

Poole, M. S., & DeSanctis, G. (1990). Understanding the use of group decision support systems: The theory of adaptive structuration. In J. Fulk & C. Steinfield (Eds.), *Organizations and Communication Technology* (pp. 175-195). Newbury Park, CA: SAGE.

Poole, M. S., & DeSanctis, G. (1992). Microlevel structuration in computer-supported group decision-making. *Human Communication Research, 19*, 5-49.

Poole, M. S., & Roth, J. (1989). Decision development in small groups IV: A typology of group decision paths. *Human Communication Research, 15*, 323-356.

Poole, M. S., Kirsch, L., Jackson, M., & DeSanctis, G. (1998). Alignment of system and structure in the implementation of group decision support systems. In S. J. Havlovic (Ed.), *Conference Best Paper Proceedings, Academy of Management* [CD-ROM]. Briarcliff Manor, NY: Academy of Management.

Poole, M. S., Seibold, D. R., & McPhee, R. D. (1985). Group decision-making as a structurational process. *Quarterly Journal of Speech, 71*, 74-102.

Poole, M. S., Van de Ven, A. H., Dooley, K., & Holmes, M. E. (2000). *Organizational Change and Innovation Processes: Theory and Methods for Research.* New York: Oxford University Press.

Pozzebon, M., & Pinsonneault, A. (2002). *Using structuration theory to study information technology and organization: An epistemological and methodological assessment.* Unpublished working paper, McGill University, Montreal, Quebec, Canada.

Prasad, P. (1992). Symbolic processes in the implementation of technological change: A symbolic interactionist study of work computerization. *Academy of Management Journal, 36*(6), 1400-1429.

Rice, R. (1982). Communication networking in computer-conferencing systems: A longitudinal study of group roles and system structure. In M. Burgoon (Ed.), *Communications Yearbook* (pp. 925-944). Beverly Hills, CA: SAGE.

Robey, D., & Boudreau, M.-C. (1999). Accounting for the contradictory organizational consequences of information technology: Theoretical directions and methodological implications. *Information Systems Research, 19*(2), 167-185.

Robey, D., & Sahay, S. (1996). Transforming work through information technology: A comparative case study of geographic information systems in county government. *Information System Research, 7*(1), 93-110.

Rosenbaum, H. (1993). Information use environments and structuration—Towards an integration of Taylor and Giddens. *Proceedings of the ASIS Annual Meeting, 30*, 235-245.

Ruel, H. (1999). Spirit of ICT: What difference does it make for ICT appropriation? Unpublished paper, University of Twente, School of Management Studies, Enschede, The Netherlands.

Ruel, H. J. M. (2002). The non-technical side of office technology: Managing the clarity of the spirit and of the appropriation of office technology. In *The Human Side of IT*. Hershey, PA: Idea Group.

Sahay, S. (1997). Implementation of information technology: A time-space perspective. *Organization Studies, 18*(2) 229-260.

Salisbury, W. D., Chin, W. W., Gopal, A., & Newsted, P. R. (2002). Better theory through measurement—Developing a scale to capture consensus on appropriation. *Information Systems Research, 13*(1), 91-103.

Salisbury, W. D., Chin, W. W., Gopal, A., Newsted, P. R., & Reeves, W. J. (1999). *Extending adaptive structuration theory: Regarding advanced information technology appropriation as meaning creation*. Mississippi State: Mississippi State University, Management and Information Systems Department, USA.

Salisbury, W. D., Gopal, A., & Chin, W. W. (1996). Are we all working from the same script? Developing an instrument to measure consensus on the appropriation of an electronic meeting system. In J. F. Nunamaker, Jr. & R. H. Sprague, Jr. (Eds.), *Proceedings of the 29th Annual Hawaii International Conference on System Sciences* (Vol. 3, pp. 13-23). Los Alamitos, CA: IEEE Computer Society Press.

Sambamurthy, V. & Poole, M. S. (1992). The effects of variations in capabilities of GDSS design on management of cognitive conflict in groups. *Information Systems Research, 3*, 224-251.

Sambamurthy, V., Poole, M. S., & Kelly, J. (1993). Effects of level of sophistication of a group decision support system on group decision-making processes. *Small Group Research, 24*, 523-546.

Sarason, Y. (1995). A model of organizational transformation: The incorporation of organizational identity into a structuration theory framework. In D. P. Moore (Ed.), *Academy of Management Best Papers Proceedings* (pp. 47-51). Madison, WI: Omnipress.

Sarason, Y., Dillard, J. F., & Dean, T. (2002, August). *Structuration theory as a framework for exploring the entrepreneurship domain.* Paper presented at the Academy of Management meeting, Denver, Colorado, USA.

Saunders, C. S., Robey, D., & Vaverek, K. A. (1994). The persistence of status differentials in computer conferencing. *Human Communication Research, 20*(4), 443-472.

Schacter, S. (1968). Deviation, rejection, and communication. In D. Cartwright & A. Zander (Eds.), *Group Dynamics* (3rd ed., pp. 165-181). New York: Harper & Row.

Scheepers, R., & Damsgaard, J. (1997). Using Internet technology within the organization: A structurational analysis of intranets. In S. C. Hayne & W. Prinz (Eds.), *Group 97: The Integration Challenge* (pp. 9-18). New York: ACM Press.

Scott, C. R., Quinn, L., Timmerman, C. E., & Garrett, D. M. (1998, March). *Ironic uses of group communication technology: Evidence from meeting transcripts and interviews with group decision support system users.* Paper presented to the Western States Communication Association Convention, Denver, Colorado, USA.

Scott, W. R. (1995). *Institutions and Organizations.* Thousand Oaks, CA: SAGE.

Silver, M. S. (1991). *Systems that Support Decision Makers: Description and analysis.* New York: John Wiley & Sons.

Simon, H. A. (1960). *The New Science of Management Decision.* New York: Harper & Row.

Smith, C. W. (1983). A case study of structuration: The pure-bred beef business. *Journal for the Theory of Social Behavior, 13*, 19-43.

Sprague, R. H., & Watson, H. (1979). Bit by bit: Toward decision support systems. *California Management Review, 22*(1), 61-68.

Stein, E. W., & Vandenbosch, B. (1996). Organizational learning during advanced system development: Opportunities and obstacles. *Journal of Management Information Systems, 13*(2) 115-136.

Strauss, A. (1987). *Qualitative Analysis for Social Scientists.* Cambridge, UK: Cambridge University Press.

Sydow, J., & Windeler, A. (1998). Organizing and evaluating interfirm networks: A structurationist perspective on network processes and effectiveness. *Organization Science, 9*(3), 265-284.

Thompson, J. B. (Ed.). (1981). *Paul Ricoeur: Hermeneutics and the Human Sciences.* London: Cambridge University Press.

Van de Ven, A. H., & Delbecq, A. L. (1971). Nominal versus interacting group processes for committee decision making. *Academy of Management Journal, 14*, 203-213.

Volkoff, O. (1999). Using the structural model of technology to analyze an ERP implementation. *Proceedings of the Fifth Conference on Information Systems, 1*, 235-237.

Walsham, G., & Han, C.-W. (1991). Structuration theory and information systems research. *Journal of Applied Systems Analysis, 17*, 77-85.

Watson, R. W., DeSanctis, G., & Poole, M. S. (1988). Using a GDSS to facilitate group consensus: Some intended and unintended consequences. *MIS Quarterly, 12*, 463-480.

Weber, M. (1958). *The Protestant Ethic and the Spirit of Capitalism.* New York: Charles Scribner's Sons.

Webster, J. (1998). Desktop videoconferencing: Experiences of complete users, wary users, and non-users. *MIS Quarterly, 22*(3), 257-286.

Wheeler, B. C., & Valacich, J. S. (1996). Facilitation, GSS, and training as sources of process restrictiveness and guidance for structured group decision making: An empirical assessment. *Information Systems Research*, 7(4), 429-450.

Wheeler, B. C., Mennecke, B. E., & Scudder, J. N. (1993). Restrictive group support systems as a source of process structure for high and low procedural order groups. *Small Group Research*, 24, 504-522.

White, S. E., Dittrich, J. E., & Lang, J. R. (1980). The effects of group decision making process and problem situation complexity on implementation attempts. *Administrative Sciences Quarterly*, 25(3), 428-440.

Wynne, B., & Dickson, G. W. (1975). Experienced managers' performance in experimental man-machine decision systems. *Academy of Management Journal*, 18, 52-41.

Yates, J., & Orlikowski, W. J. (1992). Genres of organizational communication: A structurational approach to studying communication and media. *Academy of Management Review*, 17, 299-326.

Yates, J., Orlikowski, W. J., & Okamura, K. (1999). Explicit and implicit structuring of genres in electronic communication: Reinforcement and change of social interaction. *Organization Science*, 19(1), 83-103.

Zack, M. H., & McKenney, J. L. (1995). Social context and interaction in ongoing computer-supported management groups. *Organization Science*, 6(4), 394-422.

Zigurs, I., Poole, M. S., & DeSanctis, G. (1988). A study of influence in computer-mediated group decision making. *MIS Quarterly*, 12, 625-644.

ENDNOTES

[1]   The studies listed in this section are provided as examples and are not a thorough listing of structuration studies in the IS or organization sciences. For extensive reviews of the literature on structuration in IS research, see Walsham and Han (1991), Contractor and Seibold (1993), Jones (1999), and Pozzebon and Pinsonneault (2002).

[2]   An important exception is Giddens' (1990, 1997) concern with time-space distanciation in modern life and the process of "lifting out" of social relations and their reproduction from specific contexts. As several writers have noted (e.g., Jones, 1999; Walsham & Han, 1991), these concepts would seem to be of interest to IS scholars, but they have yet to be wholeheartedly pursued.

[3]   As illustrations of the focus on structure within social psychology, management, and organization studies, the reader is referred to classic works by Davis (1973), Fisher (1975), Holloman and Hendrick (1972), Kelley and Thibaut (1969), Van de Ven and Delbecq (1971), White, Dittrich, and Lang (1980), and Simon (1960).

[4]   It is important to point out that the debate as to whether structuration theory can incorporate technology as a source of structure extends beyond the IS field. Giddens has been criticized among social theorists for not acknowledging that material artifacts (such as information technologies) have structuring potential and for his complete rejection of a sequential relationship between external constraint and human actions (e.g., Archer, 1990; Barbalet, 1987; Layder, 1985).

[5]   Note that Giddens is not alone in seeking this middle ground. For example, in the realm of institutional theories Scott (1995) provides an overview of theories that incorporate functional, constructionist, and combined perspectives. Similarly, Nelson and Winter (1982) emphasize action over structure or agency in their articulation of an evolutionary theory of organizations.

[6]   For further explication of structuration theory and its application to IS research, readers are referred to Walsham and Han (1991), Orlikowski and Robey (1991), and Jones (1999).

[7]   Poole and DeSanctis (1990) provide theoretical exposition of *features* versus *spirit* of IT structures and *faithful* versus *ironic* appropriation of IT by users.

[8]   For a sense of the extent to which the IS field has drifted away from the study of technology, the reader is referred to a recent text by Currie and Galliers (1999).

An earlier version of this paper was presented at the Organization Science *Winter Conference, Winter Park, CO, February 6, 2000. Comments welcome. Please do not cite without permission.*

Chapter XIV

Simulation in IS Research: Technique Underrepresented in the Field

Theresa M. Vitolo
Gannon University, USA

Chris Coulston
Pennsylvania State University, USA

ABSTRACT

Simulation has been a fundamental research approach in the social and physical sciences. Through the modeling, experimentation, and analysis processes of simulation, the functional dependencies in systems can be probed statistically. The approach has enabled social and physical science researchers to examine dynamically complex systems. Even though information systems (IS) can fall into both of categories of social or physical systems—depending upon the aspect of the system being analyzed – IS researchers have not embraced the paradigm. The reasons for simulation not being more common in IS research can be attributed to four points: the structure of IS curriculums, the level of modeling sophistication driving the research, the separation of the field's IS developments from the physical reality of the usage of the systems, and the level of maturity with the field. The chapter presents the basic concepts for the construction and use of simulation, the need and potential for simulation in IS research, the reasons why IS research has not utilized simulation, and the way IS research can embrace simulation in the future.

INTRODUCTION

Simulation has become a standard research technique of the natural sciences, social sciences, and engineering disciplines. The paradigm of simulation provides an accepted mode of development, validation, and verification by which complex, highly dynamic interactions can be probed and analyzed. The approach enables researchers to phrase experiments in a controlled environment where the concepts, variables, and relationships of the domain can be manipulated. Unfortunately, to date, simulation has not become a general paradigm in IS research even though many problems can be viewed from a simulation perspective. The following example shows how simulation can be applied to an IS research problem.

Consider the problem of determining the appropriate sourcing policies for software project development. The analysts for a global manufacturing and software development corporation wish to examine the correct mix of domestic and offshore developers over the different components of an application's development. Numerous connections relate sourcing, contracts, distribution, and costs to quality, security, and acceptance. If the question were viewed from an operations management perspective, then an optimization problem may be feasible. However, the aspects of quality, security, and acceptance push this question into the realm of IS research and often out of the realm of optimization solutions. In such a situation, simulation offers another formal framework for examining the behavior of complex, dynamic systems.

In order to insure validity, the examination of quality, security, and acceptance from a simulation perspective requires a standard framework. For instance, analysts need to know the characteristics of the past and current development project, of their sourcing pools, of their contract options, and of their development processes. Relationships are expressed, connecting the current task to historical characteristics. The analysts build these relationships into the simulation model using them to investigate a variety of system-specific questions as they relate to the statistically parameterized simulation.

By defining and employing the experimental framework that is simulation, researchers can benefit in a variety of ways. First, in order to construct a simulation, the underlying system and its relationships need to be understood and characterized. The researcher benefits by formalizing the phenomena of the system into the structure of a simulation, thus formalizing the underlying assumptions of the system. Next, the development of the simulation requires a statement about inputs and outputs. The researcher benefits by acknowledging the observable and manipulable aspects of the systems in question. Third, a developed simulation provides an ongoing, readily accessible platform for a variety of interaction questions. The researcher benefits by gaining a validated model through which current and future hypotheses can be examined. Overall, the researcher is able to apply the scientific method to highly complex and dynamic systems which may not offer themselves to normal modes of controlled experimentation.

IS research has not taken advantage of simulation to examine complex situations as other domains have. A variety of reasons exist for the limited use of simulation in IS research.

- The field is relatively young compared to the other domains using simulation. As such, IS researchers have not had simulation presented to them as a potential technique.

- The formalization of the problems and systems within the IS field has not reached the level of maturity and understanding existing in other domains. For example, research in meteorology typically employs simulation for weather prediction. In IS research, the focus has been on capturing and describing the phenomena. Simulation will enable researchers to take the next step, prediction.
- The technical competencies to develop a valid and verified simulation are not standard components of IS curriculums. IS curriculums do not provide the mathematical and analytical emphasis required to construct a robust simulation. IS curriculums stress the technical competencies to plan, to build, and to deploy systems but not to predict the ramifications of incorporating new processes into an organization from a scientific perspective.

As IS research moves into supporting strategic initiatives and into providing efficient renovations of main-line-of-business IS infrastructures, the need for simulation will become paramount. Currently, researchers are able to make statements about observed tendencies and statistical commonalities. By employing simulation, tendencies and commonalities can be expressed into a simulation framework. The framework can be individualized for a particular organization and its IS infrastructures. The unique, but still complex, questions of the particular organization can be phrased and examined. Then, the researchers will be able to make assertions about the modeled systems as they exist within their set of comparable systems. Returning to the outsourcing example presented in the introduction, researchers examine the differences between outsourcing policies for global software development corporations as opposed to nationally based software development corporations. Consequently, simulation provides a resilient mechanism for inductive and deductive reasoning about complex phenomena.

The following sections of the chapter present the general paradigm of simulation modeling and analysis, a framework for using simulation in order to enhance IS research, the current conceptual and academic limitations for employing simulation in IS research, and the changes required to build acceptance and utilization of simulation in the field.

BACKGROUND

Simulation is historically connected with the development of computers and the representation of models within a computing environment. Prior to the advent of the computer, the concept of simulation was regulated to the manipulation of physical models in controlled environments such as wind tunnels or cockpit mock-ups. As scientists and engineers gained the ability to program computers with mathematical relationships, the ability to describe complex systems in computer programs enabled them to examine the systems' interactions and behaviors. The fields of operations research and management science gained recognition as they employed the concepts of statistics, modeling, and simulation to solve difficult planning, logistics, operations, and control problems.

Models, long a standard of research and engineering, are an abstraction of the significant features and relationships of a system. This abstraction, as described by the researcher in the model, enables the system to be studied for the purpose of prediction or comparison.

Generally, models may be represented as linguistic, iconic, or physical representations. The choice depends upon how the modeler expresses the fundamental relationships of the target behavior. Examples of each of these are as follows:

1. A mathematical model of a business's inventory-supply interactions requires equations—a model based on the language of mathematics.
2. A process model of an organization's network configuration requires diagrams of nodes and connections—a model capturing behavior possibilities by icons.
3. A construction model of a company's proposed new headquarters facility requires an architectural layout of objects of buildings and land—a model showing components' interactions based on physical scale.

With computers, however, models can be realized and manipulated along one or more of these dimensions. For instance, each component of a factory may behave in predictable, mathematical manner while the components as a whole interact according to a node-arc diagram. The notion of a "simulation model" is the combination of the system's features and behaviors abstracted into a computer-realizable program. The computer-realizable program is often expressed by a software package designed to do simulations.

To date, however, the field of information systems research has not joined the other technical disciplines using simulation. For the most part, when simulation is used in conjunction with questions of information systems, the work is germane to the field of management science (for example, Arundhati, Ow, & Prietula, 1993; Baligh, Burton, & Obel, 1996; Ballou, Wang, & Pazer, 1998). For examples where simulation is used to support the main line of questioning for other business-related domains, see Baranoff, Sager, and Shively (2000), with Bettman, Luce, and Payne (1998) and with Koch (1981). Boland and Tenkari (1994), Burton and Obel (1988), and Pattinson (2000) offer examples of the potential for simulation in IS research. However, even with state-of-the-art developments in IS such as multi-agent systems, the prevalence of an operations-management perspective to the writing is seen (Seredynski, 1997).

IS RESEARCH ENHANCED WITH SIMULATION

The general paradigm of a simulation stems from the perspective that one is constructing a controlled experiment over a highly complex, possibly dynamic system whose underlying relationships and tendencies can be described mathematically or probabilistically. Although a variety of texts present simulation, classic coverage of the topic can be found in Banks and Carson (1984), Law and Kelton (2000), Winston (1987), and Zeigler (1976). Pegden, Shannon, and Sadowski (1990, pp. 12-13) identify the simulation process as a set of 12 steps. These steps cover the project management aspects of the simulation study as well as the conceptual management of the experiment.

1. *Problem definition:* Identifying the goal and purpose to the simulation
2. *Project planning:* Identifying and coordinating the hardware, software, staff, and management resources required
3. *System definition:* Identifying the system to be studied—in classical general systems analysis terms

4. *Conceptual model formulation:* Extending the system definition to incorporate formally variables, relationships, and interaction logic
5. *Preliminary experimental design:* Identifying an experimental framework by which to assess the study, that is, control variables, output variables, or factors to vary
6. *Input data preparation:* Identifying and collecting data to configure parameters and probability distributions
7. *Model translation:* Representing the system and experiment in the language of a software application designed for simulation
8. *Verification and validation:* Confirming the accuracy, integrity, and credibility of the model's parameters, distributions, and output
9. *Final experimental design:* Finalizing the structure of the experiment to test a specific stated hypothesis
10. *Experimentation:* Executing the simulation according to the experimental design
11. *Analysis and interpretation:* Examining the output of the simulation study in light of the hypothesis of the experiment
12. *Implementation and documentation:* Using the results of the analysis to drive action as a consequence of study

The following section continues the example in the introduction (analysts trying to understand sourcing relationships for a development project) in light of the 12 steps above.
1. *Problem definition:* The goal of the simulation is to understand the system generating sourcing decisions. The purpose is to examine how different sourcing decisions affect the quality, security, and acceptance of the final development. The researcher has conceived of the hypothesis that different sourcing arrangements express different ranges of quality, security, and acceptance in the final development and wishes to probe the relationships in a more methodical manner.
2. *Project planning:* A valid simulation requires resources in the form of adequate facilities, data, and statistical modeling support. The researcher secures the commitment of the resources, identifying the platform for the simulation effort.
3. *System definition:* The researcher identifies what constitutes the system as opposed to its environment, the boundaries, and other external interacting systems. In this step, the analysts identify previous situations where the sourcing decisions had been made in the past and identify what were the resultant ranges of quality, security, and acceptance produced given different sourcing arrangements, different contract provisions, different sections of the development distributed to different sources, and different costs.

While the amount of information at this point seems immense, the predictive influence of such an immense amount of information is being enabled by assembling the associations. The analysts are identifying how the sourcing decision is realized within the organization, identifying the components or subprocesses contributing to the final specification.
4. *Conceptual model formulation:* The researcher describes the sourcing-decision system in terms of its input variables, output variables, parameters, and logic. The

representation of the formulation can be done graphically, in pseudo-code, or in logic blocks fitting a simulation package.

5. *Preliminary experimental design:* The researcher reviews the set of output variables and identifies those associated with quality, security, and acceptance. If these measures are implicit and not explicitly given, then the associations with explicit output variables are stated. For instance, system acceptance may not be an explicit variable but may need to be deduced from other output variables such as the number of calls to the help desk in a six-month duration following installation. For such an association to be valid, the researcher needs to include the six months after installation into the time frame about the sourcing-decision system and has identified the need to collect data about calls to the help desk in such a time frame when developing the system definition in Step 3.

6. *Input data preparation:* The model of the sourcing-decision system must be represented—and, hence, supported—by data sets described functionally or probabilistically. The researcher coalesces the data from previous sourcing decisions in order to obtain summary measures to set the parameters of the model. For instance, if the researcher identifies high-quality systems occurring whenever the decision is made by a senior-level analyst, then what fraction (S) of the time does a senior-level analyst make such a decision? If a component of the model constituted a professional responsible for enacting the decision, then the level of the professional could be parameterized by the fraction S for the behavior of the model.

7. *Model translation:* In Step 2, the researcher identified a simulation platform of hardware, software and data capabilities. In Step 7, the researcher moves the conceptualization of the research problem into the language conventions of the selected platform.

8. *Verification and validation:* The researcher ensures accuracy by running the simulation with input variables known to have been in place for previous sourcing decisions. The output behavior of the simulation model should conform to the output generated by the actual sourcing decision. If the behavior does not correspond, then the researcher debugs the simulation model until historical sourcing behavior is mimicked by the simulation.

9. *Final experimental design:* Once the simulation model validly mimics reality, then the experiment can be developed. The researcher sets the variations to be manipulated over the input variables. These variations will give resultant output variables to be summarized statistically. In this step, the scientific understanding of producing experiments is shown.

10. *Experimentation:* The researcher conducts the experiment he/she has planned in Step 9.

11. *Analysis and interpretation:* The output in its statistically summarized format is analyzed in light of the original hypothesis. At this point, the researcher is able to state whether the set of input variables, system components, and process logic formulated as the simulation model actually does produce a statistically significant effect on the output variables. The simulation model will produce—have effect— on the output variables. What is being sought is whether the effect is statistically significant, that is, truthful, about the association of the input variables on the output variables. Step 11 requires an understanding of statistical analysis over an experimental design and its output.

12. *Implementation and documentation:* The researcher now has a valid tool to examine the sourcing-decision system. The degree of association between the development source, the contract, the development components, and the costs upon the quality, security, and acceptance of the development has been established. The researcher can now perform sensitivity analysis on the system. For instance, the question, How inferior is the quality of the system when a junior analyst makes the decision as opposed to a senior-level analyst? can be probed.

In review, then, once the project aspects of a simulation study are confirmed (Steps 1-2), a researcher doing simulation constructs a model of the target system. The target system is represented as connected components and the connections express potential dynamic interaction among the components (Steps 3-4). The parameters governing the behavior of the model statistically represent the regularly observed nature of the behavior. Behavior is elicited from the model by the generation of initial conditions and driving inputs into the simulation model. A researcher needs to formulate these dynamic assertions into the model (Steps 5-6).

The long-term behavior of the system is the focus of the simulation study. Ballistic, one-shot behavior reveals nothing of statistical importance to a researcher. Just as the nature of a single rain drop reveals nothing about the weather condition of an area, the nature of a single simulated occurrence of behavior within a model reveals nothing about the underlying system. To examine the long-term behavior, the model must be incorporated into a simulation language and software package (Steps 7, 8, and 9). As the simulation generates statistically significant cycles of simulated behaviors, the inherent nature of the underlying system is described by statistical measures (Steps 10-11). Finally, as a consequence of the simulation study, the researcher is able to recommend a decision, a course of action, and assertion that is supported by the study (Step 12). This final step is the realization of the goal of the simulation study.

SIMULATION IN IS EDUCATION

IS researchers could benefit from deploying simulations, but they have not embraced the technique yet. Several reasons can be given for this lack, namely:

- The academic preparation of the IS researcher;
- The modeling sophistication to envision simulation opportunities;
- The separation of IS development from its physical use and evaluation; and
- The field's maturity to rely upon simulation.

Each of these reasons can be addressed once their influence on IS research is understood.

Academic Preparation: Within management science, operations management, and industrial engineering curriculums, simulation is taught as a technique for examining complex situations, to be used when appropriate—much as chemists are taught different chemical analyses to be applied when appropriate. As such, simulation is incorporated into the experimental framework of researchers in these applied analysis disciplines.

More so, the conceptual processes and techniques required to develop, assess, and reason about simulations are a standard part of these curriculums. These conceptual foundations are captured in statistical, mathematical, and programming courses.

For the most part, the typical IS curriculum does not develop these foundations with the appropriate emphasis except for the programming aspect. However, in the applied analysis disciplines, the conceptual foundations become the base for explicit instruction in the art and science of simulation, either as a course or as a major topic within a course. Since IS curriculums and IS model curriculums do not include simulation, IS researchers rarely are prepared to formulate a simulation model, let alone conceive of using the technique to address a research question.

Modeling Sophistication: For a simulation model to be accurately developed, the regularity and stability of its corresponding system's components and relationships must be stated in mathematical and probabilistic terms. Researchers require data collection and assessment to support the parameters and variables of the model. For instance, if a researcher is investigating usability aspects of a new voting application for group decision support systems, does the researcher have data on past usability aspects of other voting applications, probability assessments of the characteristics of the user population, and performance parameters on the execution of the voting application under various usage scenarios? If IS research is to move into the realm of prediction and analytically supported improvement of systems, then it needs to move away from the concept that development of new systems comprises IS research. Rather, development opportunities and new systems' needs would be identified as a consequence of simulating a current or a proposed application and its use.

The Separation of IS Development from Use: In the IS field, the physical domain—how is it used, who used it, and where is it used—of an application influences the development process during the requirements-gathering phase. Once the system is launched, the physical reality in which the IS resides dictates the environment for the application. However, the character of the usage side of IS does not trickle into the development of IS; the two are kept separate. For instance, consider a management information system (MIS) reviewing enrollments for a registrar of a university. Once it is deployed, how often is its efficiency and effectiveness assessed *after* it is launched? In the requirements-gathering stage of the MIS's development, the needs for efficiency and effectiveness may have been stated. However, the usage and demand profile of the MIS is not analyzed in order to proactively declare the need and the nature of a renovation of the MIS. The MIS's usage profile is not examined because it cannot be examined—appropriate data has not been collected. From the IS researchers' perspective, the organization's characteristics are used to forecast the time to institute the renovation. Rather than waiting for the crunch of diminished services within an organization, IS research could describe for the organization the parameters that would configure the crunch-point.

The Field's Maturity: To date, the IS field has focused on generating a critical mass of applications and involvement in organizations' strategic, tactical, and operational infrastructures. The entire field has been an emerging technology since its inception, compared to many other scientific and technical disciplines. As such, IS has had limited opportunities to employ scientific management techniques to what it does and to what it develops. Extending the previous example of the MIS for a registrar's need to examine enrollments shows a simulation opportunity. A research hypothesis is proposed that as usage of the MIS reveals certain regularity patterns, the registrar and enrollment processes would benefit by using a decision support system (DSS), and hence, a DSS should be planned and developed. Researchers could experiment through simulation with the usage profile of the MIS to ask whether the usage indicates a tendency for the organization to seek a decision support system to analyze enrollments. Behind such an experiment, the IS field would need to own the maturity in its research hypotheses that such development connections exist and could be analyzed.

While these four points are inhibiting the use of simulation in IS research, the situation need not be enduring. The restrictions are systemic to the way IS research and IS development have been done in the past. Consequently, the restrictions can be reduced by practitioners seeking more robust analysis and predicative techniques. Each of the four restrictions may be attenuated, as expressed in the following sections.

Academic Preparation: IS curriculums will need to offer courses in the scientific management of IS operations. IS operations comprise basic facility operations from security protection measures to strategic market analysis. Courses in project management and software quality introduce IS students to aspects of scientific management but not sufficiently enough to develop an ability to formulate simulation models to assess the efficiency and effectiveness of designed or deployed systems.

Ironically, researchers in operations management simulate IS operations as an application domain of operations management, but IS researchers have not studied their own operations using the same perspective.

Modeling Sophistication: As the academic scene begins to support simulation and analytical techniques, IS researchers would begin to pose hypotheses to be tested by simulation and hence they would gather the appropriate data. Researchers would express system relationships in terms amenable to simulation modeling through mathematical and probabilistic constructions. For example, information congruency of an e-commerce site could be examined. The site and its components could be expressed analytically in terms of information density, "clicks from the top," and relative importance to neighboring pages. Then the traffic over the site could be gathered in terms of timing and duration of retrievals. Researchers could predict the traffic patterns over a particular e-commerce site as a function of the correspondence of the particular site relative to the simulated behavior. Simulation would open ways to examine with precision correspondences hypothesized.

The Separation of Development from Use: As the hypotheses researchers propose change, so will the nature of IS development change. At one time in civil engineering, bridges may have been built for a particular site without any wisdom from other bridges' constructions and usage and without any wisdom about the statics and dynamics of the bridges. A modern civil engineer would not consider such an effort rational. In due time, IS researchers would be able to provide the static and dynamic relationships of IS in order to connect previous developments and use to proposed ones.

The Field's Maturity: This restriction will naturally change as the IS field does mature. Its maturity level will be a function of the type of research it supports. Are the research questions seeking to reveal fundamental relationships spanning types of IS? As the research questions become more mature, the techniques will have to support the questions, and the field will advance.

FUTURE TRENDS

The study of IS will significantly change as it is driven by IS research. Historically, IS developed to serve the agendas of accounting. Over time, IS development led to a variety of domain-specific applications such health-care monitoring systems and geographic information systems, of general-purpose applications such as network analysis programs, and of niche applications such as fuzzy-logic programs or expert systems. As IS groups seek to understand growth and viability of IS within organizations, researchers will need to employ techniques such as simulation in order to express the regular and repeated patterns shown by the field.

IS researchers have the immense benefit of owning the paradigm The world is composed of systems and subsystems. With this perspective, researchers can represent the problems of the field in models, which can be extended into simulation models. The missing component is the mathematical and numeric correspondences to drive the static models of the field into dynamic models. As researchers become familiar with the potential of simulation, the data required to express the correspondences for the simulations will be captured by the researchers doing "field studies" of IS.

The software packages designed for simulation are not a limitation to IS researchers. In fact, most of the packages support visual modeling and representation, which blend naturally with the diagramming conventions already embraced by the IS field. The visual representations can be easily manipulated and executed by the software. What would limit IS researchers from adequately using the packages is their understanding of the simulation paradigm. The situation is analogous to the understanding of spreadsheet software. Use of spreadsheet software is a literacy skill; formulating an appropriate system within a spreadsheet requires a conceptual skill. Similarly, the simulation paradigm can be taught; the creative questioning of the field for the intent of simulation must come from the researchers.

Eventually, IS research would give to IS planners and managers an analytical framework for examining the use, need, and character of IS at the strategic, tactical, and operational level of analysis. The analytical framework would be well-defined simulation models for reviewing the efficiency and effectiveness of proposed and operational systems. The simulation results could provide comparisons between proposals or explanations of problematic events.

CONCLUSION

IS research is a burgeoning field, reaching for new ways to probe and to understand the complexity of information systems. Simulation has been a hallmark technique for examining complexity in many analytical and applied scientific disciplines. Many of these scientific disciplines are intimately related to IS research and development. Yet this reliable technique has not been incorporated into the IS field.

The reasons for simulation not being more common in IS research can be attributed to four points: the structure of IS curriculums, the level of modeling sophistication driving the research, the separation of the field's IS developments from the physical reality of the usage of the systems, and the level of maturity with the field. The limitations each of these reasons impose upon IS research and its relation to the use of simulation can be reduced.

IS researchers have vastly intricate and multifaceted systems to study. With their training in systems thinking, systems analysis, and programming, IS researchers could tap a greater understanding of their domain by adding simulation to their repertoire of techniques. More so, the software applications for conducting simulation are not as daunting. Simulations can be constructed in software quite easily by an analyst. The limitation at this time is in the ability of IS researchers to phrase appropriate hypotheses and to formulate valid simulations.

REFERENCES

Arundhati, K., Ow, P. S., & Prietula, M. J. (1993). Organizational simulation and information systems design: An operations level example. *Management Science, 39*(2), 218-240.

Baligh, H. H., Burton, R. M., & Obel, B. (1996). Organizational consultant: Creating a useable theory for organizational design. *Management Science, 42*(12), 1648-1662.

Ballou, D., Wang, R., & Pazer, H. (1998). Modeling information manufacturing systems to determine information product quality. *Management Science, 44*(4), 462-484.

Banks, J., & Carson, J. (1984). *Discrete-Event System Simulation*. Englewood Cliffs, NJ: Prentice Hall.

Baranoff, E., Sager, T. W., & Shively, T. S. (2000). A semiparametric stochastic spline model as a managerial tool for potential insolvency. *Journal of Risk & Insurance, 67*(3), 369-396.

Bettman, J. R., Luce, M. F., & Payne, J. W. (1998). Constructive consumer choice processes. *Journal of Consumer Research, 25*(3), 187-217.

Boland, R. J., Jr., & Tenkari, D. (1994). Designing information technology to support distributed cognition. *Organizational Science, 5*(3), 456-475.

Burton, R. M., & Obel, B. (1988). *Designing Efficient Organizations: Modeling and Experimentation*. Amsterdam: North-Holland.

Koch, H. S. (1981). Online computer auditing through continuous and intermittent simulation. *MIS Quarterly, 5*(1), 29-41.

Law, A. M., & Kelton, W. D. (2000). *Simulation Modeling and Analysis* (3rd ed.). New York: McGraw-Hill.

Pattinson, C. (2000). A simulated network management information base. *Journal of Network & Computer Applications, 23*(2), 93-107.

Pegden, C. D., Shannon, R. E., & Sadowski, R. P. (1990). *Introduction to Simulation Using SIMAN*. New York: McGraw-Hill.

Seredynski, F. (1997). Competitive coevolutionary multi-agent systems: The application to mapping and scheduling problems. *Journal of Parallel & Distributed Computing, 47*(1), 39-57.

Winston, W. (1987). *Operations Research: Applications and Algorithms*. Boston, MA: PWS-Kent.

Zeigler, B. P. (1976). *Theory of Modelling and Simulation*. New York: John Wiley & Sons.

Chapter XV

Cognitive Research in Information Systems Using the Repertory Grid Technique

Felix B. Tan
Auckland University of Technology, New Zealand

M. Gordon Hunter
University of Lethbridge, Canada

ABSTRACT

This chapter discusses the design and application of a cognitive mapping methodology known as the repertory grid. Grounded in personal construct theory (Kelly, 1955), the repertory grid is an extremely flexible technique to conduct both qualitative and/or quantitative research and, in organizational research, is the preferred methodology for mapping the content and structure of cognition. The aim of this chapter is to expound upon the potential of this technique to information systems researchers by considering the variety of ways the repertory grid may be employed. This application is illustrated by examining published studies in both the information systems and the broader management fields.

INTRODUCTION

The existence and significance of cognition in organizations and its influence on patterns of behaviour in organizations and organizational outcomes are increasingly accepted in information systems (IS) research (Barley, 1986; DeSanctis & Poole, 1994; Griffith, 1999; Griffith & Northcraft, 1996; Orlikowski & Gash, 1992, 1994). However, assessing the commonality and individuality in cognition and eliciting the subjective understanding of research participants either as individuals or as groups of individuals remain a challenge to IS researchers (Orlikowski & Gash, 1994). Various methods for studying cognition in organizations have been offered—for example, clinical interviewing (Schein, 1987), focus groups (Krueger, 1988), and discourse-based interviewing (Odell, Goswami, & Herrington, 1983). This article proposes that cognition applied to making sense of IT in organizations can also be explored using Kelly's (1955) personal construct theory and its methodological extension, the repertory grid (RepGrid). The RepGrid can be used in IS research for uncovering the constructs research participants use to structure and interpret events relating to the development, implementation, use, and management of IS in organizations.

In the context of this chapter, cognition is considered to be synonymous with subjective understanding, "the everyday common sense and everyday meanings with which the observed human subjects see themselves and which gives rise to the behaviour that they manifest in socially constructed settings" (Lee, 1991, p. 351). Research into cognition in organizations investigates the subjective understanding of individual members within the organization and the similarities and differences in the understandings among groups of individuals (Daniels, Johnson, & de Chernatony, 1994; Jelinek & Litterer, 1994; Porac & Thomas, 1989). In IS research, it is the personal constructs managers, users, and IS professionals use to interpret and make sense of information technology (IT) and its role in organizations.

In this chapter, we discuss the personal construct theory (Kelly, 1955) and in particular the myriad of ways the RepGrid can be employed to address specific research objectives relating to subjective understanding and cognition in organizations. It illustrates, from a variety of published studies in IS and management, the flexibility of the RepGrid to support both qualitative and/or quantitative analyses of the subjective understandings of research participants. We hope that this will initiate further discussions and responses to calls for more cognitive emphasis in organizational research (Langfield-Smith, 1992; Stubbart, 1989; Swan, 1997).

We are not implying in this chapter that the personal construct theory and the RepGrid are the best or the only theory and method available to the IS researcher in the study of cognition in organizational settings. There are certainly other cognitive theories and mapping methods applied in organizational research (Huff, 1990; Sims, Gioia, & Associates, 1986). These produce different types of cognitive maps capable of depicting different perspectives of cognition. Our focus is on the subjective understandings of organizational members—that is, personal constructs applied to everyday sense-making. Kelly's (1955) theory and method are widely accepted in the study of cognitive constructs and understandings of individuals in fields from psychology to management.

The primary audience is IS researchers who are interested in investigating the cognitive perspective in the development, implementation, use, and management of IS in organizations. It is anticipated that by examining the subjective understandings in organizations, researchers will better understand the interplay of various cognitive dimensions in the organizational context.

The chapter continues with an elaboration of Kelly's (1955) personal construct theory and the relevance of this theory and its method to IS research and practice. The basics of the repertory grid—its components, various design decisions, and its implications—are then discussed. This discussion is followed by considering how the repertory grid is used in a variety of published studies in the IS and management fields. These examples illustrate the flexibility of the technique to support both qualitative and/or quantitative approaches as related to the specific research objectives. Finally, the chapter concludes with the suggestion that IS researchers consider the adoption of the repertory grid as an appropriate technique in addressing investigations into cognition—the subjective understandings of individuals in organizations.

PERSONAL CONSTRUCT THEORY AND RELEVANCE TO INFORMATION SYSTEMS

Kelly (1955) argues that individuals use their own personal constructs to interpret and understand events that occur around them and that these constructs are tempered by the individual's personal experiences. "Man looks at his world through transparent templets which he creates and then attempts to fit over the realities of which the world is composed" (pp. 8-9). Thus, individuals come to understand the world which they live in by erecting a personally organized system of interpretation or constructs of experienced events. The system is personal in that each individual makes his own interpretations of his experiences. But, the individual can share a view and appreciate another individual's interpretation or construction of events. Kelly's supposition, known as personal construct theory, is formally presented in a fundamental postulate and 11 corollaries. These corollaries are extensions of the basic tenet and elaborate the postulate in different directions.

Constructive Alternativism

Underlying Kelly's (1955) fundamental postulate and 11 corollaries is a philosophical assumption—that the events an individual faces are subject to a great variety of constructions. He calls this philosophical position constructive alternativism, an assumption that all events are subject to as many alternative interpretations as the individual can contrive. Constructive alternativism stresses the importance of events and the meaning individuals assign to these events. According to Kelly (1970):

Whatever the world may be, man can come to grips with it only by placing his own interpretations upon what he sees. ... None of this is a denial that men customarily share each other's insights and prejudices. Our ingenuity in devising alternative constructions is limited to our feeble wits and our timid reliance upon what is familiar. So we usually do things the way we have done them before or the way others appear to do them. ... Events do not tell us what to do, nor do they carry their meanings engraved on their

*backs for us to discover ... we ourselves create the only meanings. ... Thus
in constructive alternativism events are crucial, but only man can devise a
meaning for them. (pp. 2-4)*

Kelly's philosophy of constructive alternativism allows the individual to propose a reality but contends that no interpretation of reality is absolute and irrevocable. Alternative ways of construing an event may be offered.

Fundamental Postulate and Corollaries

Kelly's (1955) fundamental postulate is that individual understanding is "psychologically channelized" (p. 46) by the way in which events are anticipated. The assumption of constructive alternativism is embedded in this basic postulate. According to this tenet, all of an individual's representations are anticipatory in nature, that is, the function of an individual's personal constructs is to anticipate events. An individual interprets his or her own environment through a system of personal constructs that provide a framework for assessing events as they occur. Kelly further argues that an individual's system of constructs are not constant but will change as a result of experience. Thus the individual both creates and is created by the world within which he or she operates.

In support of the theory's fundamental postulate, Kelly presented 11 corollaries. These corollaries operationalize the theory. Appendix A lists and describes the 11 corollaries. Of these, the individuality and commonality corollaries are of the most significance to the interpretation of the subjective understandings of individuals or groups of individuals. Mancuso and Adams-Webber (1982) provide more details on the basic tenets of Kelly's theory.

Relevance to Information Systems Research and Practice

Recently, it has been shown that personal construct theory and in particular its repertory grid technique have implications for fields beyond psychology. "An obvious happening is the taking up of personal construct themes and methods by people working in very diverse fields" (Bannister & Fransella, 1980, p. 7). Our intention in this chapter is to describe the application of this theory and technique to individuals in IS research and practice. The reliability and validity of the repertory grid as a research tool is beyond the scope of this chapter. There exists research attesting to its psychometric rigor (Bannister & Mair, 1968; Ginsberg, 1989; Swan, 1997). Instead, we focus on how the theory and method can be best applied to IS.

A consideration which encourages the application of the repertory grid to the IS field is the proven value of the theory and method to IS research and practice. Hunter (1997) used the repertory grid technique to elicit the personal construct themes or qualities relating to "excellent" systems analysts. After reviewing alternative research approaches, Hunter selected the repertory grid as the most suitable method to determine what constitutes the qualities of an "excellent" systems analyst as perceived and understood by various research participants. The qualities identified can then be used in managing a systems analyst's job description, recruitment/selection, work allocation, project team selection/risk assessment, performance appraisals, career planning, and training needs. Similarly, the repertory grid technique was employed to identify the situational factors that IS project managers take into account when planning new projects for new customers (Moynihan, 1996). The personal constructs elicited reflected most of the contingency variables and risk-drivers in the IS development literature but also included some situational characteristics not accounted for in this literature. The study also concluded that the personal construct elicitation technique has a valuable role to play in IS development research. In another study, Latta and Swigger (1992) lend support for the use of the personal construct theory and the repertory grid to the design of information storage and retrieval systems.

A common objective of management research that uses the repertory grid is to improve organizational action. Some researchers intervene directly at the organizational level, examining differences in collective maps of groups, while others prefer to achieve this indirectly by exploring differences in individual maps. In addition, mapping permits the researcher to observe changes in the cognitive infrastructures of individuals and groups over time. The threefold utility of cognitive maps, in essence, allows researchers to inquire into the organizations' theories-in-use. IS research and practice can benefit from these emancipatory qualities of the repertory grid by supporting individual diagnosis and management/organizational intervention. As an example, consider the recent study on the factors influencing the social dimension of alignment between business and IT objectives (Reich & Benbasat, 2000). The study's research model, based on the theory of absorptive capacity (Cohen & Levinthal, 1990), postulated that communication between line and IT managers is important to achieving mutual understanding between line and IT managers. Communication over time leads individual managers to converge or diverge in their subjective understanding of the problem domain. Permitting line and IT managers to participate in various cross-functional roles will improve the communication process. The concepts mentioned in this study are consistent with three corollaries in Kelly's (1955) theory: (1) line and IT managers converge in their understandings—commonality corollary; (2) line and IT managers diverge in their understandings—individuality corollary; and (3) cross-functional contacts encourage line and IT communications—sociality corollary. From a construct theory perspective, the application of the repertory grid can provide insights into the quality of the mutual understanding between line and IT managers. The cognitive maps produced can display the understandings held in common by the managers as a whole. Furthermore, the maps can also reveal the differences in constructs between individuals and between line and IT management groups. These maps can provide the platform upon which the overall group can collectively diagnose disagreements. Individual managers can gain greater awareness of what the issue looks like from the other's standpoint through cross-level absorbing (Eden, Jones, Sims, & Smithin, 1981). This is where individual-level maps absorb characteristics of common-level maps, and conversely, common-level maps absorb more individuality. This can provide a basis for increasing mutual understanding through collective diagnosis and management of disagreements. The construct theory and method can assist individual managers in the subjective analysis of their own understanding, leading the individual to modify this understanding, if necessary.

THE REPERTORY GRID

The repertory grid is a flexible group of procedures for uncovering the constructs which individuals use to structure and understand their environments. The repertory grid is both a structured interview *process*, in which respondents classify and evaluate elements on a numerical scale according to their own personal constructs, and a grid of elements by constructs that is the *product* of these procedures (Ginsberg, 1989). In the management field, repertory grid has been the preferred methodology for mapping the cognitive constructs of individuals (Brown, 1992; Daniels, de Chernatony, & Johnson, 1995; Dutton, Walton, & Abrahamson, 1989; Hunter, 1997; Reger, 1990).

Basics of the Repertory Grid

There are three components to a repertory grid—elements, constructs, and links (Easterby-Smith, 1980). Elements are the subject within the domain of the investigation. They define the material upon which the grid is based. For instance, Hunter (1997) explored the similarities and differences between systems analysts in order to ascertain the qualities that can lead to an "excellent" systems analyst. The elements Hunter used are the systems analysts in each of the organizations he studied. Constructs are the ways that the individual differentiates between the elements. In the case of Hunter, the constructs are the attributes the participants employ to differentiate between systems analysts. An example of the grid produced by a single participant in Hunter's study is portrayed in Figure 1.

On the left of the example are the constructs or qualities employed by an individual participant to differentiate between the systems analyst (labelled A-F) s/he has associated with in his/her organization. Each analyst is then rated along each elicited construct.

Simply, elements are the objects of people's thoughts, and constructs are the qualities that people attribute to those objects. Constructs are bipolar in nature. They describe how some elements are alike and yet different from others. To illustrate, one of the constructs (i.e., qualities) elicited in Hunter (1997) describes systems analysts to be either "delegator—does work himself." Using this bipolar construct, the systems

Figure 1. Example of a Repertory Grid (Adapted from Hunter, 1997).

CONSTRUCTS	ELEMENTS					
	A	B	C	D	E	F
1. Delegator - Does work himself	7	2	5	4	2	6
2. Informs everyone - Keeps to himself	8	2	3	3	8	6
3. Good user rapport - No user rapport	5	2	4	2	4	2
4. Regular feedback - Inappropriate feedback	6	1	5	3	5	3
5. Knows details - Confused	2	1	4	3	5	1
6. Estimates based on staff-Estimates based on himself	8	3	4	6	4	6
7. User involvement - lack of user involvement	6	2	5	5	3	3

Note: Elements A to F represent the individual systems analyst.

analysts can then be differentiated or grouped. This brings us to the third component of a repertory grid—the links between elements and constructs. These links show how each element is being assessed on each construct. The links reveal the similarities and differences between the elements and between constructs. The rating employed in the example in Figure 3 is a 1 to 9 scale. This rating is the linking mechanism between the systems analysts (elements) and their qualities (constructs elicited from the research participant).

Repertory Grid Design Decisions

There are several ways to generate elements, elicit constructs, and link elements and constructs. There are also a variety of approaches to analyze grids. The design of the research using the repertory grid technique depends on the objectives of research—that is, whether the study focuses on the idiographic characteristics of personal construct systems or compares the similarities and differences in the construct systems of groups of individuals. This section discusses the design alternatives facing the IS researcher and how the research objectives affect the operationalization of the repertory grid technique.

Element Selection

As highlighted in the previous section, the repertory grid technique is a way of showing how an individual thought about aspects considered important within a specific domain of discourse. The elements represent these aspects. Elements may be people or objects, such as systems analysts (Hunter, 1997) or organizations (Reger & Huff, 1993). Elements have a dual purpose in constructing cognitive maps using the repertory grid technique (Reger, 1990). Firstly, the elements are used to elicit the constructs or dimensions the participant uses to interpret the issue. Secondly, the participant provides perceptions concerning how these elements and the constructs are categorized and related to each other (i.e., differentiated). Therefore, how elements are selected is an important issue.

There are two basic ways in selecting elements. One way is for the researcher to provide the elements (commonly referred to as supplied elements). The other way is to ask the participant to provide them (elicited elements). A number of reasons have been proposed to support the researcher supplying the elements (Reger, 1990). Firstly, researchers may choose to provide the elements if they are interested in learning more about a given set of elements. Secondly, researchers may wish to let an existing theory guide element choice. Finally, researchers may also be interested in comparing responses of a number of respondents given a standard set of elements. The final reason is especially important if the researcher desires to compare the results within a homogeneous group of individuals or across different groups. Alternatively, researchers may choose to request the participant to provide his/her own elements to ensure that the elements are relevant to the participant. This can be done in a variety of ways (Easterby-Smith, 1980):

- Researcher can provide role or situation descriptions—for example, specifying roles of people in the organization or types of experiences in the organization.

Participants are then asked to provide their own specific examples to fit these general categories.

- Researcher can define a "pool"—for example, participants are asked to "name five subordinates," to "name three effective and three ineffective managers," or to "list six leisure activities that you have indulged in."
- Researcher can elicit through discussion—in this case, the investigator and participant discuss the topic of interest, and a list of elements is drawn up jointly.

Whether the elements are supplied or elicited, there are a number of rules for selecting elements. Firstly, elements must be discrete (Stewart & Stewart, 1981). For example, commonly used elements in organizational research are people, objects, events, and activities—in other words, nouns and verbs. Researchers need to be very precise when selecting elements—specific nouns and specific verbs. Using the example in Figure 2, specific makes and models of cars should be used as elements and not their descriptions, e.g., Mitsubishi Lancer or Toyota Corolla and not four-door or economical. The latter should really appear as constructs. Secondly, elements must be homogeneous (Easterby-Smith, 1980). That is, elements should be drawn from the same sample. For example, people and objects must not be mixed. The reason for this is that constructs that are generated from elements in one category are not likely to be applicable to those in another category. Thirdly, elements must not be evaluative (Stewart & Stewart, 1981). For example, in order to elicit the qualities of successful managers, evaluative words like motivation, leadership, knowledge, and communication can be often mistakenly used. Instead, names of different managers should be used. This relates to the discrete nature of elements. Finally, elements should be representative of the area to be investigated (Beail, 1985; Easterby-Smith, 1980). Using the example of the qualities of successful managers, researchers must ensure that all participants can relate to the managers selected as elements. In addition, it is recommended to incorporate positive and negative—e.g., successful as well as unsuccessful managers.

Construct Elicitation

The repertory grid technique allows for several different methods of eliciting constructs. In some of these methods, researchers can apply minor variations and combinations (Beail, 1985; Easterby-Smith, 1980; Reger, 1990).

Firstly, the researcher can provide the constructs (supplied constructs). In this instance, the participant is not asked to contribute his/her own interpretation of the elements but is asked to rate the elements against constructs provided by the researcher. By supplying constructs, the researcher can make direct comparisons across groups of participants. In addition, supplying constructs can enable assessment of specific aspects of the issue at hand.

Secondly, the constructs may be elicited from triads (minimum context form). This method is considered the classical approach to generating constructs and is known as the triadic sort method. The minimum context form involves the random selection of three elements (triads) at a time from the repertory of elements for each elicitation. The participant is asked to identify (and label) some way in which two elements are similar and different from the third relative to the domain of discourse. The researcher may leave the issue of similarities and differences open-ended, allowing the participant to choose any labels that are relevant to him or her. Alternatively, researchers may provide contextual cues that focus the participant's attention on a specific research issue. For example, in Hunter (1997), participants were asked to differentiate between systems analysts (elicited elements) in terms of the qualities that constitute the research participants' interpretation of an "excellent" systems analyst. This procedure of identifying similarities and differences is intended to produce contrasting poles for the construct (i.e., the bipolar nature of constructs discussed in the previous section). This process is then repeated until the researcher is satisfied that all relevant constructs have been identified. Previous research suggests that seven to 10 triads are sufficient in most domains to elicit all of the participant's constructs in the domain (Reger, 1990). A variation of this procedure is the sequential form, where triads of elements are also presented and the same questions are asked of the participant. The difference is that instead of randomly selecting the elements, the researcher systematically substitutes the triads. Using the example in Figure 2, the first triad contains Car A, B, and C; the second contains Car B, C, and D; the third, Car C, D, and E; and so on until all elements in the sample have been presented. Other variants on the triadic process include combining supplied and elicited constructs (Easterby-Smith, 1980); eliciting constructs from dyads—i.e., presenting two elements at a time (Keen & Bell, 1980); using only a sample of the full repertory of elements elicited to generate constructs (Dutton et al., 1989); and asking participants for the opposite label instead of asking how the third element differed from the other two in the triad (Epting, Suchman, & Nickeson, 1971).

The third eliciting technique is the "full context form." It involves presenting the full repertory of elements and requesting the participant to sort the repertory into any number of discrete piles based on whatever similarity criteria the individual chooses to apply. Once the sorting is completed, the executive will be asked to provide a two- to three-word descriptive title for each pile of elements. This procedure is used to elicit the similarity judgements. A matrix can be built up which enables element relationships to be examined using statistical methods. The full context form is used primarily for understanding cognitive groupings (Reger, 1990).

The final approach is group construct elicitation (Stewart & Stewart, 1981). In this method, all participants involved in the study are gathered together with the researcher facilitating the group "workshop." The researcher can either ask each participant to name the elements on cards or to call out the elements. All participants are then required to collectively agree on the elements in the repertory grid—this is to ensure that all participants are comfortable with the elements used to elicit constructs. Using the minimum context elicitation technique, individual participants are then asked to identify how two elements are same and yet different from the third, thereby eliciting bipolar constructs. Triads may contain elements randomly selected by the individual, or the researcher can determine the sequence in which triads are to be administered. When the construct elicitation phase is completed, the researcher will facilitate the rating of the elements along each of the constructs identified by all individuals. Constructs are gathered from all participants and randomly selected in this process. The open discussion that ensues allows all participants to give information to and extract information from others. Group construct elicitation serves two purposes. The first is data collection—it is a highly economical and less time-consuming way of eliciting constructs. The second is that of team building—it allows each participant to see the different perceptions other participants have and come to understand and appreciate different viewpoints within the group.

A method employed to determine the research participant's interpretations of elicited constructs is known as "laddering" (Stewart & Stewart, 1981). This is normally used in conjunction with one of the other methods above. The participant is asked to look more closely at a construct after a few have been elicited. Laddering permits the researcher to better understand the participant A series of why and how questions prompts the participant to provide more detail. In this way, a series of new more detailed constructs can be generated from any of the original constructs. Researchers can therefore "drill down" and understand the underlying beliefs held by the participant.

Linking Elements to Constructs

Once the researcher has elicited the constructs considered important by the participant, the next step is to place the elements along these constructs. This is an important step in the repertory grid procedure. The way each construct is used in relation to the elements indicates the meaning of the labels given to each pole (Easterby-Smith, 1980). There are three methods of linking elements to constructs—dichotomising, ranking, and rating. Figure 4 illustrates the three ways of completing the repertory grid.

In dichotomising, a tick is placed in the relevant box in which the element is closest to the left pole of the construct. If it is closest to the right pole, a cross is placed in that box. This method of linking is like a simple sort routine or a rating scale with only two points. Dichotomising has the advantage of being easier to analyze without a computer. Today, this advantage is no longer relevant due to the wide range of statistical packages available. In addition, this method does not allow for shades of grey (Beail, 1985). Participants have to select one pole or the other. There may be instances in which somewhere in between is preferred. Another problem is that it can potentially produce skewed distribution (Easterby-Smith, 1980). To avoid skewed distributions, participants are sometimes instructed to make sure that the elements are divided equally between ticks and crosses on each construct. This may not always be possible.

Ranking elements was originally used as an alternative to dichotomising as it removed the problem of skewed distribution (Beail, 1985). Ranking simply involves placing the elements in an order between the two contrasting poles. In Figure 2, rank ordering is done using a 7-point scale, where no scores can be repeated. Ranking provides much greater discrimination than dichotomising, but it may force participants to indicate differences between elements where really no difference exists. There is also a tendency when ranking to judge the element in terms of one pole of the construct without giving full consideration to the other pole.

The most popular method of linking elements and constructs is by rating. This method allows the participant greater freedom when sorting the elements and does not force the participant to make discriminations that do not exist. Rating scales of 5, 7, 9, or 11 points have been used. An odd-numbered scale results in a midpoint that supports participant decisions about element location on the scale. Participant rating freedom is maximized when the range of rating values is greater than the number of elements. Others argue that the discrepancies between retest reliabilities for those participants who had the freedom to choose the rating scales and those who have a rating scale imposed was

Figure 2. Ways of Completing a Grid.

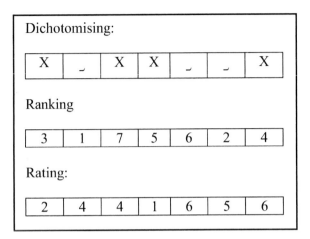

least for the 5-point category rating (Bell, 1990). It has been suggested that a 7-point scale approaches most participants' limits of discrimination and that anything much above five points is very difficult to examine visually (Stewart & Stewart, 1981).

Analyzing Individual RepGrids

Each repertory grid yields a geometric and quantitative representation of the participant's system of interpretation. A completed grid consists of m number of elements and n number of constructs. This means that there are $[n+m.2(poles)+n.m]$ pieces of information to consider in looking at a grid (Bell, 1990). For example, a grid with five elements and seven constructs will present 35 entries in the grid, five elements and seven pairs of constructs. This gives a total of 52 pieces of information to be analyzed. A number of questions can be asked of such a grid:

- How do the elements relate to each other?
- How do the constructs relate to each other?
- How do the elements relate to the constructs?

In the above example, there will be five elements to be compared to each other, giving 10 unique comparisons of element relationships. Likewise, for the construct relationships, there will be 21 unique comparisons between seven constructs. To relate elements and constructs, 35 pieces of data will have to be considered.

In order to adequately analyze an individual repertory grid, data can be reduced, while retaining the salient features, to the point where the above questions can be effectively answered. There are several approaches to reorganizing the raw grid data published in the repertory grid literature (Beail, 1985; Bell, 1990; Easterby-Smith, 1980;

Gaines & Shaw, 1980; Leach, 1980; Stewart & Stewart, 1981). These approaches allow the researcher to examine the relationship amongst elements and amongst constructs as well as between elements and constructs. These approaches are discussed in detail in this section.

Content Analysis: This can be a simple frequency count analysis, in which the researcher counts the number of times particular elements or constructs are mentioned. This method is used to examine the data for common trends amongst the business and IS executives interviewed. Alternatively, the researcher can select a series of categories into which constructs fall and then assign the constructs to categories (Stewart & Stewart, 1981).

Rearranging the Grid: This method of analyzing a grid is simply to rearrange the grid by changing the order of elements and constructs. The rows and columns are shuffled so that similar constructs are positioned close to each other and consequently similar elements are placed in proximity of each other (Bell, 1990; Easterby-Smith, 1980). This reordering of rows and columns can reveal similarities and differences among constructs and elements. This may also involve reversing the construct poles in order to easily highlight patterns in the grid. This process of rearranging the grid is known as visual focusing. An extended illustration of visual focusing is provided by Stewart and Stewart (1981).

Transforming the Grid: This method of analyzing a grid relates to the three questions raised earlier in this section. By transforming the grid, the researcher can better understand how elements are related to each other, how constructs are related to each other, and how elements are related to constructs. Correlation matrices can be obtained for both elements and constructs simply by counting the number of matches in pairs of elements and constructs. Correlations can also be obtained using cluster analysis. Cluster analysis can be applied to the grid data to identify patterns and major groupings of constructs and hence elements. A technique called FOCUS, introduced by Shaw and Thomas (1978), uses hierarchical cluster analysis to transform the grid. The grid when analyzed using cluster analysis appears with constructs and elements rearranged (i.e., an electronic form of visual focusing). The distances showing the correlation between elements are called an element tree and those linking the attributes elicited are known as a construct tree. An element tree is generated by taking into account the distances or dissimilarities between all pairs of elements (i.e., initially by developing an element distance matrix). Similarly, a measure of the distance between pairs of constructs is portrayed as the construct tree.

Decomposing the Grid: This method of analyzing the grid simplifies the grid data by breaking it down into fundamental structures. In this instance, the tool to apply is the principal components analysis. Factor analysis of repertory grid is a very popular method of analyzing grids (Bell, 1990; Easterby-Smith, 1980; Leach, 1980). According to Bell, most grids can be satisfactorily approximated by two or three factors (i.e., have more than 80% of the variance explained). As such, elements and/or constructs can be plotted in two- or three-dimensional pictures to reveal the basic structure of the grid. Figure 2 illustrates the product of a principal component analysis on a repertory grid of cars and their attributes. Economy and power account for most of the variance and most cars are differentiated on the first factor.

Analyzing Content and Structure: The repertory grid technique yields measures of cognitive content and structure of an individual's construct system. These indices of content and structure can be compared across individuals.

Cognitive content can be described in three ways: element distance, construct centrality, and element preference. These content descriptions were first proposed by Kelly (1955) and widely reviewed in the personal construct theory literature (Dunn, Cahill, Dukes, & Ginsberg, 1986; Fransella & Bannister, 1977; Slater, 1977).

- *Element distance* refers to the distance between elements and measures the perceived similarity among elements. Elements that are considered similar are elements that are rated similar on all constructs. Those that are rated differently on all dimensions are perceived to be different. In this study, element distance describes the differences in the meanings of the elements (i.e., dimensions of factors) as perceived by participants. Element distance can be calculated by conducting a vertical analysis of the grid. For example, computing inter-element distance statistics (Dunn et al., 1986) or using cluster analysis (Reger, 1990). Elements which are close together in meaning will have low inter-element distance values, while those which are far apart will have high inter-element values.

- *Construct centrality* refers to the importance of a construct in relation to all other constructs. Kelly (1955) theorised that certain constructs may be central to all individuals' systems of constructs. Constructs with high centrality are those that are highly correlated to every other construct. These correlations can be obtained by conducting a horizontal analysis of the grid. Correlation values can be acquired directly from a correlation matrix or indirectly from a factor analysis (Reger, 1990).

- *Element preference* is the perceived desirability of each element in relation to all other elements. An element which is more preferred is one which has a higher average score than another element, as measured by column means in the repertory grid.

Cognitive structure can be described and compared in three ways: cognitive differentiation, cognitive complexity, and cognitive integration. Univariate indices of all three measures of grid structure have been reviewed widely (Dunn et al., 1986; Fransella & Bannister, 1977; Slater, 1977). Multivariate analysis, such as factor analysis, may be used to explore two aspects of grid structure—complexity and integration (Reger, 1990).

- *Cognitive differentiation* refers to the number of constructs used to compare and contrast elements. A highly differentiated system of interpretation has many constructs, while one with low differentiation has few constructs. Cognitive differentiation can be measured by simply counting the number of constructs elicited.

- *Cognitive complexity* is the degree to which each construct is different in meaning from every other construct. It is measured by conducting a horizontal analysis of the grid (i.e., by examining the correlations among the constructs). A highly complex system of interpretation has low correlations among constructs, and thus each construct is used independently to add additional information about the elements. A system of interpretation with low complexity is one in which all constructs are highly correlated, and thus each adds little information about the elements. One measure of complexity is the index of frame complexity (Dunn et al., 1986). Alternatively, complexity can be measured using multivariate methods, which simultaneously consider correlations among all pairs of constructs.

- *Cognitive integration* refers to the degree of linkage between constructs. It is the flip side of complexity and is measured by conducting a horizontal analysis of the grid (i.e., by examining the correlations among the constructs). A highly integrated system of interpretation is characterised by high correlations, while one with low integration has low correlations.

Analyzing Commonality and Collectivity

The above discussion focuses on different methods of analyzing individual grids. Similarities in cognition between individuals and groups of individuals can be measured using three different approaches (Ginsberg, 1989).

Firstly, linguistic analysis can be used to classify groups of common constructs. This method was used in a study to classify descriptions into construct categories of financial terms (Walton, 1986). Linguistic analysis is a cumbersome procedure, but it focuses on the participant's own expressions, thereby minimising researchers' bias in interpreting descriptions.

Secondly, mapping techniques such as Q-type factor analysis and multidimensional scaling (MDS) can also be used to map collective meanings amongst individuals or groups of individuals. In the former technique, distance scores are first correlated across individuals. The resulting correlation matrix is then subjected to Q-factor analysis that yields clusters of individuals in terms of the best linear combination of distance scores for all pairs of elements. MDS was developed to help understand people's subjective judgements of similarities and differences between members of a set of objects. The aim of MDS is to determine the configuration of elements in multidimensional space. Points are arranged in this space such that pairs of elements which are more frequently judged similar appear closer together. The resulting normative map represents a best fit distribution of points based on the judgements of all the participants who provided ratings of element similarities.

Thirdly, multivariate techniques such as analysis of variance, regression analysis, and discriminant analysis can be used to analyze the pooled results of individual grid structures. This approach aims to identify groups of individuals with similar levels of cognitive structure. This permits the traditional testing of hypotheses.

In addition, indices of cognitive content and structure can be used to explore the collective understandings of groups within an organization. Several alternatives are available for examining collective content and structure (Dunn & Ginsberg, 1986). One approach is to conduct a construct inventory by listing constructs named by a group of participants and plotting their relative frequencies. Another option is to identify the set of constructs held by most members.

A third approach is by systematically constructing and analyzing a who-to-whom matrix of participants within an organization. In this approach, measures of cognitive content and structure are gathered for each individual (as discussed in the previous section). Convergency scores are then entered for these values onto a who-to-whom matrix, where converging measures are coded as 1 and diverging measures are coded as 0. Figure 3 illustrates the properties of the collective cognitive content of a group of executives in a hypothetical company.

A similar analysis can also be conducted to examine the collective cognitive structure of research participants.

Sample Size

The time-intensive nature of the repertory grid procedure often leads to a relatively small sample size—for example, a sample of 30 owners of independent retail stores (Jenkins & Johnson, 1997); 56 graduates entering different functions of a large UK company (Fournier, 1996); 29 full-time employees of the Port Authority of New York and

Figure 3. Collective Cognitive Content.

Element Distance

	A	B	C	D	E
Executive A	--	1	0	1	1
Executive B		--	1	0	0
Executive C			--	1	1
Executive D				--	1
Executive E					--

Construct Centrality

	A	B	C	D	E
Executive A	--	0	1	1	1
Executive B		--	1	1	0
Executive C			--	1	1
Executive D				--	0
Executive E					--

Element Preference

	A	B	C	D	E
Executive A	--	1	1	0	0
Executive B		--	1	1	1
Executive C			--	1	1
Executive D				--	1
Executive E					1

New Jersey (Dutton et al., 1989); 27 employees of a Canadian grain handling company and 26 employees of a Canadian insurance company (Hunter, 1997); 16 executives from a Canadian professional association (Swan & Newell, 1994); and 42 managers dealing with pumps supplied to the North Sea offshore oil industry (Daniels et al., 1995). It seems a small sample size is all that is required to successfully examine the cognitive maps of individuals. A sample size of 15 to 25 within a population will frequently generate enough constructs to approximate the "universe of meaning" regarding a given organizational context (Dunn et al., 1986; Ginsberg, 1989). That is, no new constructs are normally added even if the sample size is increased. For instance, in Dunn et al., 17 respondents generated a total of 23 unique constructs. These constructs were completely generated after the 10th interview. The last seven interviews added no new constructs.

EXAMPLES OF RESEARCH USING THE REPERTORY GRID

To further elaborate on how the repertory grid technique can be applied to IS research, a number of published examples in both the IS and management fields are discussed. These examples have successfully used the approach to investigate a variety of topics and issues. They have employed the technique using a standard variation or a combination of these variations discussed earlier in the repertory grid design section. Just as Lee (1991) used an exemplar to illustrate a framework integrating positivist and interpretive approaches and just as Klein and Myers (1999) demonstrated the usefulness of a set of principles for interpretive field studies in IS by evaluating three examples, so this chapter will employ a similar approach by analyzing articles which clearly illustrate the application of the repertory grid technique to explore subjective understandings in organizations. A summary of these examples is listed in Table 1.

We propose to use a framework to facilitate this discussion (see Figure 4). The framework presents a two-dimensional view of the types of research using the repertory grid. The examples in Table 1 are mapped along these two dimensions.

Figure 4. Distinguishing Research Using the Repertory Grid.

	Qualitative	Quantitative
Theory-Focused	Hunter (1997) [†]	Latta and Swigger (1992) [†] Simpson and Wilson (1999) [*]
Method-focused	Moynihan (1996) [*] Dutton et al. (1989) [*]	Daniels et al. (1994) [*] Phythian and King (1992) [†]

[*] Idiographic (i.e., individual interpretations – unique grids)
[†] Nomothetic (i.e., group interpretations – common grids)

Table 1: Examples of Research Using the Repertory Grid.

	Hunter (1997)	Moynihan (1996)	Phythian & King (1992)	Latta & Swigger (1992)	Simpson & Wilson (1999)	Daniels et al. (1994)	Dutton et al. (1989)
Research Field	Information Systems	Information Systems	Information Systems	Information Systems	Management	Management	Management
Research Objectives	Explore the qualities of 'excellent' systems analysts	Identify the situational factors considered in the planning/running of new systems development projects	Develop rules for an expert system to support customer tender evaluations	Validate the repertory grid in modelling communal knowledge regarding design of system interfaces	Explore shared meanings in organizations	Test the homogeneity of managerial cognition	Identify the important dimensions decision makers use to sort strategic issues
Research Perspective	Qualitative	Qualitative	Quantitative	Quantitative	Quantitative	Quantitative	Qualitative
Focus	Theory	Method	Method	Theory	Theory	Method	Method
Key Findings	Several themes considered as qualities of 'excellent' systems analysts	Identified themes over and above literature. Differences in project managers' construction of project contexts	Identified key factors and rules influencing tender decisions. Expert system improved consistency	Commonality of constructions support the use of the repertory grid to model group knowledge	Cognitive maps provided insights into the quality of shared meaning within companies	Managers' mental models are diverse and differs between companies and functions	Identified dimensions over and above literature. Organization contexts affect cognition

Table 1: (continued) Examples of Research Using the Repertory Grid.

Research Design:	Hunter (1997)	Moynihan (1996)	Phythian & King (1992)	Latta & Swigger (1992)	Simpson & Wilson (1999)	Daniels et al. (1994)	Dutton et al. (1989)
Element Selection	Systems analysts participant has interacted with	Systems development projects participant has worked on	Previous customer tender enquiries	Components of online bibliographic retrieval systems	Factors to be taken into account in forming strategies	Companies competing in North Sea off-shore pump industry	Set of strategic issues facing the organization in the study
Construct Elicitation	Minimum context form (triadic sort) and laddering	Minimum context form (triadic sort)	Minimum context form (triadic sort) and laddering	Minimum context form and supplied elements/ constructs	Full and minimum context forms (full and triadic sorts).	Minimum context form (triadic sort). Also visual card sort	Minimum context form (triadic sort)
Linking	Rating	None	Rating (Grid) Ranking (Elements)	Rating	Rating (Grid) Ranking (Elements)	Rating	None
Grid Analysis	Content analysis Visual focusing COPE and VISA	Content Analysis	Cluster analysis (FOCUS), correlation, mathematical modelling	Cluster analysis correlation	Multidimension al scaling, Content analysis, Correlation	Cochran Q test Helmert contrasts ANOVA	Linguistic Analyses
Sample and Size	53 from two insurance companies	14 systems development project managers	two manager-experts involved in assessing tender enquiries	Instructor and students who completed an 'information search and retrieval' course	12 members of strategic team in two research institutes	24 from North Sea off-shore pump industry	29 members of the New York/New Jersey Port Authority

Theory-Focused vs. Method-Focused

On one dimension, we distinguish research that applies Kelly's (1955) personal construct theory (theory-focused) from those applying the repertory grid method without delving into the conceptual underpinnings of the theory (method-focused). When introduced some 45 years ago, the repertory grid technique served as the methodological extension of the personal construct theory. It operationalizes key aspects of Kelly's fundamental postulate and corollaries. IS researchers interested in the subjective understandings of individuals will find the repertory grid a powerful tool that permits the study of the individual's construct system and are encouraged to take heed of the central tenets of the theory to provide richer cognitive insights to their findings. For example, in a study of strategic teams presented in Table 1, the authors defined shared meaning as cognition held in common (i.e., commonality corollary) and cognition which is distributed (i.e., individuality corollary) amongst team members (Simpson & Wilson, 1999). Both the commonality and individuality corollaries are key aspects of Kelly's personal construct theory. Similarly, Latta and Swigger (1992) validated the use of the repertory grid for representing commonality of construing among participants regarding the design of intelligent user interfaces. The study lent strong support to the commonality corollary in grids, which can be confidently used to represent a consensus of knowledge around a problem domain. Hunter (1997) used the laddering technique to elicit what Kelly termed as superordinate constructs—constructs that are core to the individual's system of interpretation.

In contrast, there is research that has accepted Kelly's theory and employed the repertory grid solely as a data gathering technique. These works have employed the utility of the technique purely for its methodological strengths. Stewart and Stewart (1981) suggest "At its simplest, Grids provide a way of doing research into problems— any problems—in a more precise, less biased way than any other research method" (p. vii). These authors further contend that the repertory grid "enables one to interview someone in detail, extracting a good deal of information ... and to do this in such a way that the input from the observer is reduced to zero" (p. 5). Others have asserted the psychometric properties of the repertory grid technique and have suggested the grid products to be reliable and stable over time (Pervin, 1989) as well as a valid measure of the individual's construct system (Daniels et al., 1995; Swan, 1997). Furthermore, the repertory grid technique does not constrain participant responses (unlike other methods that employ a priori assumptions about the phenomenon studied; Dutton et al., 1989; Moynihan, 1996), generates more quantifiable and reproducible results (Ginsberg, 1989), and is efficient and systematic in that it requires only a reasonably small number of respondents (15 to 25) to "generate enough constructs to approximate the 'universe of meaning' surrounding a given organizational context" (Ginsberg, p. 434). A number of the examples in Table 1 have taken the method-focused approach to the use of the repertory grid technique. For instance, both Moynihan (1996) and Dutton et al. (1989) were purely interested in using the repertory grid technique to collect data and to compare the results with the extant literature. These authors argue that the free-ranging responses resulting from the non-prohibitive nature of the technique permitted the participants to apply the "theories-of-action" (theories individuals use to guide their actions) they employ daily—resulting in the identification of themes and issues over and above the extant literature. In the studies by Phythian and King (1992) and Daniels, Johnson, et al. (1994), the repertory grid was used to explore the similarity and differences in the views between individual managers. No direct references were made to Kelly's personal construct theory. Daniels, Johnson, et al. tested the homogeneity of managerial cognition and found diversity increases across company and functional boundaries, while Phythian and King (1992) identified key factors influencing tender decisions and the relationships among these factors by interviewing two managers closely involved in such tender activities.

The decision facing the IS researcher on this dimension is a simple one. The repertory grid is very attractive as a data gathering technique. The method permits the application of aspects of the cognitive literature other than Kelly's (Daniels, Johnson, et al., 1994), as well as theories beyond the field of cognitive science (Dutton et al., 1989; Moynihan, 1996; Phythian & King, 1992). Taking heed of Kelly's theory will permit richer insights into the subjective understandings of participants, based on their personal construct systems (Hunter, 1997; Latta & Swigger, 1992; Simpson & Wilson, 1999). Whether the IS researcher is interested in applying the theory behind the repertory grid technique or in the method alone does not directly impact on the design of the grid. The design of the repertory grid appears to vary with the research perspective taken—the second dimension in Figure 4.

Qualitative vs. Quantitative

On the second dimension, we distinguish research that is either qualitative or quantitative. The identification of emerging themes from elicited constructs is common in a qualitative approach using the repertory grid. Three of the examples in Table 1 used the technique in a qualitative manner. For example, Hunter (1997), when investigating how certain groups of individuals interpreted the qualities of "excellent" systems analysts, employed content analysis of the data gathered from individual interviews conducted using the repertory grid technique. The numeric component of the grid was only employed to conduct visual focusing at the end of each interview as a means of quickly assessing what had transpired during the interview and whether the research participant agreed with this initial assessment. While Hunter used computer software (COPE) to assist in the data analysis, it mainly represented a way to manipulate the data in support of identifying emerging themes. Similarly, Moynihan (1996) employed the repertory grid technique as a method to elicit interpretations from research participants of what aspects were considered important when deciding upon an approach to adopt for projects to be conducted for external clients. Unique grids were developed for each research participant. Then the data was analyzed from a qualitative perspective via content analysis at the construct level, where emerging themes were identified and categorized. Dutton et al. (1989) also adopted a qualitative approach by employing linguistic analyses of the research participants' responses to determine issue categories surrounding the identification of the range of strategies and frequency of use by decision makers. In these examples, the researchers took an open view toward gathering data and allowing themes or categories to emerge from the data as the project proceeded.

In contrast, the quantitative approach utilizes mathematical and/or statistical analyses of grid data (Daniels, Markoczy, & de Chernatony, 1994). These techniques are commonly used to explore the structure and content of an individual's construct systems (e.g., cognitive complexity and frame typification) or make comparisons between groups of individuals (Ginsberg, 1989). This approach was adopted by four of the examples in Table 1. For instance, Phythian and King (1992) assessed key factors relating to decisions about whether to proceed with a competitive tender by a large engineering organization. Statistical analyses (specifically, cluster analysis using FOCUS and correlation analysis) were conducted on individual and combined grids. This data was used to support the development of an expert support system, which was demonstrated to managers within the engineering organization. The conclusions were that the resulting ESS was a fair representation of the tender decision-making process which existed at the time. Daniels, Johnson, et al. (1994) tested the assumption of homogeneity of cognitions of competition in managers from the offshore pumps industry. The resulting cognitive maps, derived from cluster analysis, visual card sort, and principal components analysis, were compared using a self-rating technique and analyzed by applying Cochran's Q test, ANOVA, and Helmert contrasts to the data. The authors found that managerial cognitions of competition were diverse and that this diversity increased as company and functional boundaries were crossed. In another example, individual differences multidimensional scaling was applied to the data collected via the full context form of construct elicitation (Simpson & Wilson, 1999). This involved the sorting of the repertory of elements (factors taken into account when forming strategies) into discreet piles based on the participants' judgement of similarity or dissimilarity. The analysis produced normative maps that afforded some insights into the coherence of the strategic team within each participating organization. In the same study, grid data elicited through the minimum context form (i.e., triadic sort) was compared using correlation and cluster analysis. Similarly, Latta and Swigger (1992), exploring the commonality of construing among students and their instructor regarding user interface designs, applied cluster analysis and Spearman's rank order correlation to analyze the grids. The study revealed an overall correlation between the students' and the instructor's grids, promoting the utility of the repertory grid technique in modelling knowledge relating to the design of information systems.

Idiographic vs. Nomothetic

Within both the qualitative and quantitative perspectives, research using the repertory grid technique is either idiographic or nomothetic in nature. Early applications of the repertory grid were in clinical psychology, where the emphasis was on the idiographic characteristics of personal construct systems. The idiographic approach focuses on the subjective experiences of the individual and presents results in expressions and terms used by the individual. The resulting grid is considered "unique" in that there are no common elements or constructs employed in the elicitation process. For example, in the study of systems analysts, each participant was asked to name up to six systems analysts with whom s/he had interacted (Hunter, 1997). In this project, Hunter provided a role description (i.e., systems analysts interacted with) and asked each participant to specify examples that fit this category. The analysts named were not common among participants, and as such the resulting grids were not common in terms of the elements used. Similarly, Moynihan (1996) asked each participating project manager to make a list of systems development projects s/he had worked on as a project manager. If the project manager named more than nine projects, s/he was then asked to choose the three that were the most successful, the three that were the least successful, and three in between. Moynihan's research objective was to identify the situational factors project managers regard as important when planning new development projects and not to compare the subjective understandings of different project managers. As such, he did not supply a common set of systems development projects that would have permitted a comparative analysis of individual grids. In another example, each participant was asked to list the set of strategic issues that faced his/her organization at the time (Dutton et al., 1989). The 29 people interviewed named a total of 279 strategic issues. The first five issues mentioned by each participant were then used as the elements in the repertory grid process. The research objective in this instance was to identify the dimensions decision-makers in organizations use to sort strategic issues. Comparing grids was not the intent of this project.

In the three examples just discussed, data was analyzed using a qualitative perspective. Hunter (1997) and Moynihan (1996) both used content analysis to identify emerging themes in their respective projects. Instead of using content analysis, Dutton et al. (1989) applied linguistic analyses to the data they collected. In this example, linguistic analyses were used to classify groups of common constructs based on the participant's expressions and thus minimizing the interpretations of the researcher. These authors followed the rules guiding the use of linguistic analyses outlined in early works (Rosenberg & Sedlank, 1972; Sank, 1974). Another point to note is that two of the three examples did not apply any methods of linking elements and constructs in the repertory grid process (Dutton et al., 1989; Moynihan, 1996). These studies were primarily interested in the constructs and the labels attached to these constructs expressed by the participants. Using content and linguistic analyses, respectively, these authors were able to identify the themes or categories underlying the construct labels used by the participants. As such, rating, ranking, or dichotomizing elements along each elicited construct would have served no purpose. Hunter (1997), on the other hand, requested his participants to rate the named systems analysts against each of the qualities elicited using a 9-point scale. This rating exercise permitted the participants to differentiate between the individual systems analysts and identify the systems analyst most like their interpretation of "ideal" and "incompetent."

IS researchers interested in the idiographic characteristics of individual "unique" grids are not restricted to analyzing the elicited grid data purely from a qualitative perspective. Two examples in Table 1 illustrate projects that have applied quantitative analysis to idiographic repertory grids. For instance, in the study comparing the degree of coherence in strategic teams between companies, each participant was asked to produce a list of key factors in their business environment that was taken into account when forming strategies (Simpson & Wilson, 1999). This resulted in a list of factors for each participating company. Company F produced 20 factors while Company G 22. These factors were used as the elements in the repertory grid interviews in each company. The elicited data were then analyzed using multidimensional scaling, correlation, and cluster analyses. Similarly, Daniels, Johnson, et al. (1994) required each participant to state the companies s/he perceived to be competitors in the North Sea offshore pump industry. The data was then analyzed using various statistical tests.

In contrast, research comparing the grids of individuals or groups of individuals requires different decisions to be made concerning the elements and constructs in the repertory grid process. This nomothetic approach necessitates the use of a common set of elements and/or constructs to permit comparisons to be made between grids (Easterby-

Smith, 1980). Such research also tends to be quantitative in nature. For example, research to identify the similarities and differences in two managers' views on tender enquiry evaluations imposed a common set of tender enquiries as elements in the repertory grid process. This permitted the comparison of the construct systems of the two managers based on their personal experiences of similar events. In another example, a set of constructs was elicited from an instructor and then supplied as common constructs for a group of students to evaluate against a prescribed set of elements representing the features of online bibliographic retrieval systems (Latta & Swigger, 1992). This permitted the commonality of construing among students and between students and the instructor to be tested. In these examples, the reason for the use of common components in the repertory grid process was to compare grids. Other reasons supporting the use of supplied elements and/or constructs were mentioned earlier in this chapter.

An exception to this argument is demonstrated by Daniels, Johnson, et al. (1994), who successfully compared idiographically elicited grids with other idiographically elicited grids. In this study, the authors presented each manager with a booklet containing a variety of cognitive maps generated by visual card sort, cluster, and principal components analyses. These maps represented the manager's own maps and maps from a randomly selected member of the same company with the same management function, a randomly selected member of the same company with a different management function, a randomly selected member of a different company with the same management function, a randomly selected member of a different company with a different management function, and a map randomly generated from the manager's own named competitors. The manager was asked to rate the similarity of each of these maps to their own mental model on a 5-point fully anchored Likert-type scale. The resulting data were then analyzed using Cochran's Q test, ANOVA, and Helmert contrasts. A comprehensive introduction to the technique of rating the similarity between maps and issues of reliability and validity of the method are discussed elsewhere (Daniels, Markoczy, et al., 1994). This method of comparing grid data and resulting cognitive maps is particularly attractive to the IS researcher who does not necessarily wish to impose structure into the repertory grid process. It is an alternative to supplying a set of prescribed elements and/or constructs, which may limit the participants' responses.

Finally, none of the examples discussed in this section approached their studies using both qualitative and quantitative approaches. This does not imply that the repertory grid cannot lend itself to both qualitative and quantitative analysis of the collected data. For example, in one of the three studies classified in the qualitative quadrants in Figure 6 (Hunter, 1997), participants were asked to rate the elements along each of the elicited constructs. In this study, the data in the resulting grids could have been statistically analyzed to produce maps derived from cluster or factor analysis. Hunter did not design his study with the objective to compare the grids across his sample. By eliciting both elements and constructs, Hunter was setting the study to explore the idiographic characteristics of the participants' construct systems. Had Hunter set out to compare the similarity and differences in the grids across his sample, he would have had to use a common set of elements or constructs or both. The use of common elements and/or constructs permits comparison to be made and perhaps hypotheses tested. Alternatively, Hunter would have had to ask the participants to rate the similarity of a variety of maps, including his/her own.

CONCLUSION

We consider the repertory grid technique to be a valid and useful method that can be employed to investigate the subjective understanding at the level of the individual, group, or organization. We contend that in IS research a balance must be maintained between emphasis on organizational behaviour and subjective understanding. This balance can provide for more overall and integrative theories on the development, implementation, use, and management of IS in organizations. A better appreciation of the nature and extent of the subjective understanding can lead to improvements in the interpretive understanding and the subsequent positivist understanding (Lee, 1991) of the IS phenomenon. In terms of practical relevance, IS researchers and practitioners should give consideration to the qualities of the repertory grid as a tool for diagnosis and intervention. The method is a means of responding to calls for more relevance in IS research (Benbasat & Zmud, 1999; Robey & Markus, 1998). The properties of the cognitive map outcomes can help individuals to focus attention, trigger memory, highlight priorities, supply missing information, and reveal gaps in information, leading to more creative problem-solving (Fiol & Huff, 1992).

This chapter has demonstrated the flexibility of the repertory grid technique to support both qualitative and/or quantitative approaches to investigating the subjective understanding of human subjects in complex and socially dynamic organizations. With this technique, both qualitative and quantitative approaches need not be mutually exclusive. For instance, Hunter (1997) approached his study of systems analysts from a grounded theory perspective. The data collected using the repertory grid were analyzed to identify themes or qualities of an "excellent" systems analyst. In an extension of this investigation, the characteristics of "excellent" systems analysts were statistically tested to highlight the similarities and differences in the subjective understandings of Canadian and Singaporean research participants (Hunter & Beck, 1996).

Finally, we would like to conclude by reiterating two important points. The first is a word of caution. The repertory grid should not be considered a panacea to investigating the subjective understanding of individuals in an organizational setting. It can be used in conjunction with other methods—as a means of validating other techniques or as a "preliminary" phase to further interpretive or positivist investigations. The second is that the personal construct theory is one of several theories in cognitive science (Berkowitz, 1978). The repertory grid is one of several cognitive mapping methods available to the IS researcher (Huff, 1990). This chapter was written in an attempt to stimulate interest in the IS research community of the need for more cognitive emphasis in our field. Hopefully, IS researchers will be encouraged to further reflect on the virtues of applied theories and methods that can deliver utilizable and consumable outcomes to research and practice in IS.

REFERENCES

Bannister, D., & Fransella, F. (1980). *Inquiring Man: The Psychology of Personal Constructs* (2nd ed.). Harmondsworth, UK: Penguin Books.

Bannister, D., & Mair, J. M. M. (1968). *The Evaluation of Personal Constructs*. London: Academic Press.

Barley, S. R. (1986). Technology as an occasion for structuring: Evidence from observations of CT scanners and the social order of radiology departments. *Administrative Science Quarterly, 31*, 78-108.

Beail, N. (1985). An introduction to repertory grid technique. In N. Beail (Ed.), *Repertory Grid Technique and Personal Constructs* (pp. 1-26). Cambridge, MA: Brookline Books.

Bell, R. C. (1990). Analytic issues in the use of repertory grid technique. *Advances in Personal Construct Psychology, 1*, 25-48.

Benbasat, I., & Zmud, R. W. (1999). Empirical research in information systems: The practice of relevance. *MIS Quarterly, 23*(1), 3-16.

Berkowitz, L. (1978). *Cognitive Theories in Social Psychology*. New York: Academic Press.

Brown, S. M. (1992). Cognitive mapping and repertory grids for qualitative survey research: Some comparative observations. *Journal of Management Studies, 29*(3), 287-307.

Cohen, W. M., & Levinthal, D. A. (1990). Absorptive capacity: A new perspective on learning and innovation. *Administrative Science Quarterly, 35*, 128-152.

Daniels, K., de Chernatony, L., & Johnson, G. (1995). Validating a method for mapping manager's mental models of competitive industry structures. *Human Relations, 48*(9), 975-991.

Daniels, K., Johnson, G., & de Chernatony, L. (1994). Differences in managerial cognitions of competition [Special issue]. *British Journal of Management, 5*, S21-S29.

Daniels, K., Markoczy, L., & de Chernatony, L. (1994). Techniques to compare cognitive maps. *Advances in Managerial Cognition and Organizational Information Processing, 5*, 141-164.

DeSanctis, G., & Poole, M. S. (1994). Capturing the complexity in advanced technology use: Adaptive structuration theory. *Organization Science, 5*(2), 121-147.

Dunn, W. N., & Ginsberg, A. (1986). A sociocognitive network approach to organisational analysis. *Human Relations, 40*(11), 955-976.

Dunn, W. N., Cahill, A. G., Dukes, M. J., & Ginsberg, A. (1986). The policy grid: A cognitive methodology for assessing policy dynamics. In W. N. Dunn (Ed.), *Policy Analysis: Perspectives, Concepts, and Methods* (pp. 355-375). Greenwich, CT: JAI Press.

Dutton, J. E., Walton, E. J., & Abrahamson, E. (1989). Important dimensions of strategic issues: Separating the wheat from the chaff. *Journal of Management Studies, 26*(4), 379-396.

Easterby-Smith, M. (1980). The design, analysis and interpretation of repertory grids. *International Journal of Man-Machine Studies, 13*, 3-24.

Eden, C., Jones, S., Sims, D., & Smithin, T. (1981). The intersubjectivity of issues and issues of intersubjectivity. *Journal of Management Studies, 18*(1), 37-47.

Epting, F. R., Suchman, D. J., & Nickeson, K. J. (1971). An evaluation of elicitation procedures for personal constructs. *British Journal of Psychology, 62*, 512-517.

Fiol, C. M., & Huff, A. S. (1992). Maps for managers: Where are we? Where do we go from here? *Journal of Management Studies, 29*(3), 267-285.

Fournier, V. (1996). Cognitive maps in the analysis of personal change during work role transition. *British Journal of Management, 7*, 87-105.

Fransella, F., & Bannister, D. (1977). *A Manual for Repertory Grid Technique*. New York: Academic Press.

Gaines, B. R., & Shaw, M. L. G. (1980). New directions in the analysis and interactive elicitation of personal construct systems. *International Journal of Man-Machine Studies, 13*, 81-116.

Ginsberg, A. (1989). Construing the business portfolio: A cognitive model of diversification. *Journal of Management Studies, 26*(4), 417-438.

Griffith, T. L. (1999). Technology features as triggers for sensemaking. *Academy of Management Review, 24*(3), 472-488.

Griffith, T. L., & Northcraft, G. B. (1996). Cognitive elements in the implementation of new technology: Can less information provide more benefits? *MIS Quarterly, 20*, 99-110.

Huff, A. S. (1990). *Mapping Strategic Thought*. Chichester, UK: John Wiley & Sons.

Hunter, M. G. (1997). The use of RepGrids to gather interview data about information systems analysts. *Information Systems Journal, 7*, 67-81.

Hunter, M. G., & Beck, J. E. (1996). A cross cultural comparison of 'excellent' systems analysts. *Information Systems Journal, 6*, 261-281.

Jelinek, M., & Litterer, J. A. (1994). Toward a cognitive theory of organizations. In C. Stubbar, J. R. Meindl, & J. F. Porac (Eds.), *Advances in Managerial Cognition and Organizational Information Processing* (pp. 3-41). Greenwich, CT: JAI Press.

Jenkins, M., & Johnson, G. (1997). Linking managerial cognition and organizational performance: A preliminary investigation using causal maps [Special issue]. *British Journal of Management, 8*, S77-S90.

Keen, T. R., & Bell, R. C. (1980). One thing leads to another: A new approach to elicitation in the repertory grid technique. *International Journal of Man-Machine Studies, 13*, 25-38.

Kelly, G. A. (1955). *The Psychology of Personal Constructs*. New York: W. W. Norton.

Kelly, G. A. (1970). A brief introduction to personal construct theory. In D. Bannister (Ed.), *Perspective in Personal Construct Theory* (pp. 1-30). London: Academic Press.

Klein, H. K., & Myers, M. D. (1999). A set of principles for conducting and evaluating interpretive field studies in information systems. *MIS Quarterly, 23*(1), 67-93.

Krueger, R. A. (1988). *Focus Groups: A Practical Guide for Applied Research*. Newbury Park, CA: SAGE.

Langfield-Smith, K. (1992). Exploring the need for shared cognitive map. *Journal of Management Studies, 29*(3), 349-368.

Latta, G. F., & Swigger, K. (1992). Validation of the repertory grid for use in modeling knowledge. *Journal of the American Society for Information Science, 43*(2), 115-129.

Leach, C. (1980). Direct analysis of a repertory grid. *International Journal of Man-Machine Studies, 13*, 151-166.

Lee, A. S. (1991). Integrating positivist and interpretive approaches to organizational research. *Organization Science, 2*(4), 342-365.

Mancuso, J. C., & Adams-Webber, J. R. (1982). Anticipation as a constructive process: The fundamental postulate. In J. C. Mancuso & J. R. Adams-Webber (Eds.), *The Construing Person*. New York: Praeger.

Moynihan, T. (1996). An inventory of personal constructs for information systems project risk researchers. *Journal of Information Technology, 11*, 359-371.

Odell, L., Goswami, D., & Herrington, A. (1983). The discourse-based interview: A procedure for exploring tacit knowledge of writers in nonacademic settings. In *Research on Writing: Principles and Methods* (pp. 220-236). New York: Longman.

Orlikowski, W. J. (1992). The duality of technology: Rethinking the concept of technology in organizations. *Organization Science, 3*(3), 398-427.

Orlikowski, W. J., & Gash, D. C. (1994). Technological frames: Making sense of information technology in organizations. *ACM Transactions on Information Systems, 12*(2), 174-201.

Pervin, L. A. (1989). *Personality—Theory and Research* (5th ed.). New York: John Wiley & Sons.

Phythian, G. J., & King, M. (1992). Developing an expert system for tender enquiry evaluation: A case study. *European Journal of Operational Research, 56*(1), 15-29.

Porac, J. F., & Thomas, H. (1989). Competitive groups as cognitive communities: The case of Scottish knitwear manufacturers. *Journal of Management Studies, 26*(4), 397-416.

Reger, R. K. (1990). The repertory grid technique for eliciting the content and structure of cognitive constructive systems. In H. A. S. (Ed.), *Mapping Strategic Thought* (pp. 301-309). Chichester, UK: John Wiley & Sons.

Reger, R. K., & Huff, A. S. (1993). Strategic groups: A cognitive perspective. *Strategic Management Journal, 14*(2), 103-124.

Reich, B. H., & Benbasat, I. (2000). Factors that influence the social dimension of alignment between business and information technology objectives. *MIS Quarterly, 24*(1), 81-114.

Robey, D., & Markus, M. L. (1998). Beyond rigor and relevance: Producing consumable research about information systems. *Information Resources Management Journal, 11*(1), 7-15.

Rosenberg, S., & Sedlank, A. (1972). Structural representation of perceived personality trait relationships. In A. Romney, R. Shepherd, & S. Nerlove (Eds.), *Multidimensional Scaling: Theory and Application in the Behavioural Sciences* (Vol. 2, pp. 134-162). New York: Seminar Press.

Sank, L. I. (1974). Effective and ineffective managerial traits obtained as naturalistic descriptions from executive members of a super-corporation. *Personnel Psychology, 27*, 423-434.

Schein, E. (1987). *The Clinical Perspective in Fieldwork*. Newbury Park, CA: SAGE.

Shaw, M. L. G., & Thomas, L. F. (1978). FOCUS on education—An interactive computer system for the development and analysis of repertory grids. *International Journal of Man-Machine Studies, 10*, 139-173.

Simpson, B., & Wilson, M. (1999). Shared cognition: Mapping commonality and individuality. *Advances in Qualitative Organizational Research, 2*, 73-96.

Sims, H. P., Gioia, D. A., & Associates. (1986). *The Thinking Organisation*. San Francisco, CA: Jossey-Bass.

Slater, P. (1977). *Dimensions of Interpersonal Space*. London: John Wiley & Sons.

Stewart, V., & Stewart, A. (1981). *Business Applications of Repertory Grid*. UK: McGraw-Hill.

Stubbart, C. I. (1989). Managerial cognition: A missing link in strategic management research. *Journal of Management Studies, 26*(4), 325-347.

Swan, J. (1997). Using cognitive mapping in management research: Decisions about technical innovation. *British Journal of Management, 8*, 183-198.

Swan, J. A., & Newell, S. (1994). Managers' beliefs about factors affecting the adoption of technological innovation: A study using cognitive maps. *Journal of Managerial Psychology, 9*(2), 3-11.

Walton, E. J. (1986). Managers' prototypes of financial terms. *Journal of Management Studies, 23*, 679-698.

APPENDIX A

Personal Construct Theory
Corollaries

Fundamental Postulate: A person's processes are psychologically channelized by the ways in which he anticipates events (Kelly, 1955, p. 46).

People tend to behave like scientists attempting to understand and relate to their environment. They develop their own interpretation of reality, which they employ to interpret and predict current and future interactions with their environment.

1. Construction Corollary: A person anticipates events by construing their replications (Kelly, 1955, p. 49).
    People use their interpretations of previous events to predict how to react to future events.
2. Individuality Corollary: Persons differ from each other in their construction of events (Kelly, 1955, p. 55).
    Peoples' interpretations of events are never identical and may differ considerably.
3. Organization Corollary: Each person characteristically evolves, for his convenience in anticipating events, a construction system embracing ordinal relationships between constructs (Kelly, 1955, p. 56).
    People create their own personal system of constructs, which may be flexible depending upon the situation.
4. Dichotomy Corollary: A person's construction system is composed of a finite number of dichotomous constructs (Kelly, 1955, p. 59).
    Every construct is expressed in terms of a person's own use of labels to describe bipolar terms.
5. Choice Corollary: A person chooses for himself that alternative in a dichotomized construct through which he anticipates the greater possibility for extension and definition of his system (Kelly, 1955, p. 64).
    People try to improve the usefulness of the system of personal constructs.
6. Range Corollary: A construct is convenient for the anticipation of a finite range of events only (Kelly, 1955, p. 68).
    Individual constructs apply to a certain range of convenience.
7. Experience Corollary: A person's construction system varies as he successively construes the replications of events (Kelly, 1955, p. 72).
    People may revise their system of constructs based upon their new interpretations of events.
8. Modulation Corollary: The variation in a person's construction system is limited by permeability of the constructs within whose range of convenience the variants lie. (Kelly, 1955, p. 77).
    Some people are less willing to change their interpretations based upon new experiences.

9. Fragmentation Corollary: A person may successively employ a variety of construction subsystems, which are inferentially incompatible with each other (Kelly, 1955, p. 83).

    While people tend to employ a consistent pattern of personal constructs, there may be situations where contradictory action may be taken.

10. Commonality Corollary: To the extent that one person employs a construction of experience which is similar to that employed by another, his processes are psychologically similar to those of another person (Kelly, 1955, p. 90).

    There is the possibility that people do interpret the same events in a similar manner.

11. Sociality Corollary: To the extent that one person construes the construction processes of another, he may play a role in a social process involving the other person (Kelly, 1955, p. 96).

    People are able to interact well with others when they are able to understand others' interpretations.

Chapter XVI

Qualitative Research in Information Systems: An Exploration of Methods

M. Gordon Hunter
University of Lethbridge, Canada

ABSTRACT

The purpose of this chapter is to provide the researcher, who already is inclined to apply qualitative research, with an overview of methods. A representative sample of qualitative research methods is presented, which may be employed when conducting information systems research. These methods include Action Research, Case Study, Ethnography, Grounded Theory, and Narrative Inquiry. Examples of these research methods are also included, which provide a description of the method and references to more detailed presentations. Researchers should thoroughly explore these methods and become fully cognizant of when to appropriately apply each method. It is important to ensure that the chosen method addresses the research questions and supports the research objectives.

INTRODUCTION

This chapter discusses the use of qualitative research in the investigation of topics in information systems. A representative number of qualitative research methods are presented here for researchers to consider applying to their investigations. The purpose of this chapter is to provide the researcher who is already inclined to apply qualitative research with an overview of methods which may be considered for conducting research in the information systems subject area. The value of the chapter is that it represents an overview of the major qualitative research methods in information systems along with a discussion of an example of research that has been conducted within each topic area. This discussion provides the reader with an idea of how to go about conducting investigations using a particular qualitative research method.

This chapter does not compare qualitative and quantitative approaches. Indeed, there are many other venues where this debate continues. Further, this chapter does not discuss the pluralistic approach, where multiple methods are employed within a research project (Mingers, 2001). While this topic is fascinating and represents an exciting approach to conducting research, it is considered beyond the scope of this chapter. Thus, the focus of the presentation is to outline, for researcher consideration, aspects of qualitative research which may be adopted, where appropriate, in the investigation of information systems.

To begin, an overview of qualitative research, in general, is presented. After a review of the definition of qualitative research, a discussion is presented in support of why such approaches should be considered for information systems research. Then, the remainder of the chapter presents a discussion of the major qualitative research methods. The discussion of each method provides a description and references to more detailed presentations of each specific method.

WHAT IS QUALITATIVE RESEARCH?

Qualitative research is an interpretive approach to investigating subjects in their natural surroundings. Thus, qualitative researchers conduct their investigations "in the field." They spend time in organizations attempting to document situations and to garner organization members' interpretations of situations. The main emphasis of qualitative researchers is the personnel involved in organizations. So, qualitative researchers attempt to make sense of, or interpret, phenomena in terms of their meanings attributed by individuals. They must work closely with research participants. Thus, those individuals involved with the qualitative researcher are likely considered partners or fellow research participants, involved in the investigation of a research question.

A concern about conducting qualitative research relates to verification. In general, qualitative researchers tend to agree that replication is the best means to validate conclusions determined from qualitative research. Further concerns about verification relate to research bias and reliability.

Qualitative researchers become closely involved in research situations and with research participants. There arises then a concern about researcher bias. Thus, in an interview, questions may be posed in a certain way, or certain aspects of the discussion may be pursued more or less intensively. Some researchers would consider this flexibility to be beneficial, allowing the researcher to obtain relevant data. As Reason and Rowan (1981) suggest, "It is much better to be deeply interesting than accurately boring" (p. xiv). In the end, emphasis should be placed on the research method in order to counteract the potential introduction of bias.

When conducting qualitative research, measuring reliability is difficult. Pervin suggests reliability in the social sciences research context, "relates to the extent to which our observations are stable, dependable, and can be replicated" (Pervin, 1989, p. 271). That is, can a different person following the same method obtain the same results? Here again, the importance of the research method is emphasized.

A qualitative researcher will investigate a subject area and reach preliminary conclusions about a research question. Qualitative research is sometimes referred to as theory building. Subsequent investigations may replicate the research on a broader basis in an attempt to support or refute these initial findings. The most important consideration is that the research method adopted be chosen in light of the research objectives.

WHY EMPLOY QUALITATIVE RESEARCH IN INFORMATION SYSTEMS

Some time ago it was suggested that information systems, "will remain a doubtful science as long as it continues to strive to develop its stock of knowledge primarily through the practice of the so-called scientific method" (Klein & Lyytinen, 1985, p. 133). Galliers and Land (1987) responded with a taxonomy of information systems research approaches. Their revised taxonomy (Galliers, 1992), included here as Appendix A, divides approaches into "traditional" and "newer." Observations are associated with traditional approaches, while interpretations are associated with the newer approaches, which reflect the emphasis of qualitative researchers interacting with research participants. They recommend that information systems researchers should not blindly adopt a research method. The choice of research method should be made in relation to the research objectives. Hirschheim (1992) suggests "that information systems epistemology draws heavily from the social sciences because information systems are, fundamentally, social rather than technical systems" (p. 28).

Lee (2001) suggests that information systems research is more than the study of technology or behaviour. Rather, he suggests those information systems researchers must deal "with the phenomena that emerge when the technology and the behavioural interact, much like different chemical elements reacting to one another when they form a compound" (p. 247).

There is a growing interest among information systems researchers in various qualitative research techniques. Since 1991 the annual International Conference on Information Systems (ICIS) has held a series of panel discussions on aspects relating to qualitative research. These workshops represent an expanding forum for information systems researchers who are considering or actively applying qualitative research. The research results of Lending and Wetherbe (1992) suggest an increase in the application of qualitative research techniques, as indicated by journal publications. However, more recently, there has been a call amongst the information systems community for more of an emphasis on conducting qualitative research (Benbasat & Zmud, 1999).

SURVEY OF QUALITATIVE RESEARCH METHODS

There are a number of sources, as presented in the following paragraphs, of data regarding methods employed in conducting qualitative research in information systems. The following is a brief presentation of some of these sources.

Myers maintains a web site associated with ISWorld. The title of the site is Qualitative Research in IS. As Myers (1997) indicated early in the existence of this web site, "The goal was to create a single entry point on the Internet to support novice and experienced qualitative researchers in information systems" (p. 241). The site provides a vast amount of useful information about conducting qualitative research. The following is a list of the types of qualitative research discussed within the web site:

- Action Research
- Case Study
- Ethnography
- Grounded Theory

Each of the above topics includes links to more detailed discussions of each subject. Also, each of these topics is discussed further later in this chapter.

Recently, Trauth (2001) presented an edited compendium of issues and trends in qualitative information systems research. The manuscript discusses some methods (ethnography, Grounded Theory, critical research, and interpretive research) as well as some presentations about challenges and considerations when conducting qualitative research. Trauth comments, "A significant portion of established and emerging IS researchers are grappling with the issue of learning about new research methods even as they struggle to keep up with new information technologies. This is especially the case for qualitative methods" (p. i).

There are some journal articles which discuss the topic of qualitative research in information systems. For instance, a special issue of *MIS Quarterly* (March 1999) discussed the rigor and relevance of information systems research. Some of the discussion related to considerations for qualitative research. Further, Khazanchi and Munkvold (2000) presented a discussion about the nature of information systems as a discipline. They suggest that, while the study of information systems is relatively new, it can be developed into a recognized discipline with the judicious application of proven and acceptable research methods.

Before presenting a discussion of the specific qualitative research methods it should be noted that there are a number of approaches and perspectives which may be related to multiple methods. One example is critical social theory, which may be associated with both ethnography and action research. Cecez-Kecmanovic (2001) presents a definition of critical social theory. She suggests that "a critical social researcher studies the social life of people in order to help them change conditions and improve their lives" (p. 141). She continues by suggesting that information systems researchers must strive to investigate the relationship between the information system and its social context. Thus, she contends, it is incumbent upon the information systems researcher to identify the power relationship amongst the stakeholders and which groups or individuals may manipulate or dominate others.

Further, a general perspective on qualitative research is interpretive research. Klein and Myers (2001) present their definition of interpretive research. They suggest that the "foundational assumption for interpretivists is that most of our knowledge is gained, or at least filtered, through social constructions such as language, consciousness, shared meanings, documents, tools, and other artifacts" (p. 219). They further suggest that the context of information systems should be studied by attempting to understand associated phenomena and their meanings as ascribed by those individuals directly involved.

The following subsections discuss some of the many available qualitative research methods. Table 1 provides an overview of the discussion that follows.

Action Research

Action research is about investigating change. Cunningham (1993) suggests that action research is "a continuous process of research and learning in the researcher's long-term relationship with a problem" (p. 4). He further suggests that the action researcher must be prepared to experience the research problem as its context evolves within the problem. The intention of action research is to institute a process of change and then to draw conclusions from this process. More specifically, action research involves the collection of data about an organization in order to identify problems and their underlying causes. After devising and implementing solutions to the problems, further data are collected to determine the appropriateness of the original action and/or to devise subsequent action. This cyclical process may be continued to the satisfaction of the researcher and the organization. Finally, Cummings and Worley (2001) state, "A key component of most action research studies was the systematic collection of survey data that was fed back to the client organization" (p. 9).

The technology associated with information systems facilitates change. Thus, action research is an appropriate method to consider when conducting investigations in this area. The implementation of information systems is associated with the efforts of groups. Action research facilitates providing assistance to groups as they analyze problems and develop solutions (Mumford, 2001).

Table 1. Research Methods.

METHOD	DESCRIPTION	ARTICLE(S)
Action Research	Investigate the impact of change on an individual or group	Olesen and Myers (1999)
Case Study	Investigate a phenomenon in its environment	Butler and Fitzgerald (2001) Hasan et al. (2000)
Ethnography	Conduct primary observations over an extended period of time	Nandhakumar and Avison (1999)
Grounded Theory	Approach a research question without adopting a priori a research framework	Urquhart (2000)
Narrative Inquiry	Personal recital of facts relating to a specific person	Hunter and Tan (2001)

Olesen and Myers (1999) employed action research in their investigation of the relationship between the introduction of groupware into an organization and the consequent changes in individuals' work habits and the structure of the organization. Their reason for adopting action research was because "it enables a researcher to intervene in the organization while at the same time generate knowledge about the process." (p. 321). Their research perspective was interpretive, allowing them to concentrate their research on how individuals attempted to make sense of the specific situation. They employed a five-stage action research cycle (Susman & Evered, 1978). These stages include:

1. Diagnosing: identify the research question
2. Action Planning: determine the actions to be undertaken to address the research question
3. Action Taking: conduct and monitor the planned actions
4. Evaluation: determine if the actions have addressed the research question
5. Specifying Learning: document the knowledge obtained by conducting the project

Data were gathered from seven senior managers and four personal assistants through unstructured interviews and observation. Appropriate corporate documents were also obtained. The conclusions of this research related to process and content. From a process perspective the researchers felt that they were able to employ action research in a way that successfully contributed to addressing the specific research question. That is, the authors considered that their adopted research method allowed them to adequately investigate a work unit's response to the implementation of a specific software product. From a content perspective, while the product was installed successfully, the anticipated change in the organization did not come to fruition. In deed, "existing norms of communication and collaboration were reinforced" (Olesen & Myers, 1999, p. 327). So, the action research method allowed the researchers to delve into the situation beyond the surface responses to the introduction of new software and to determine the groups' internal reaction to an external change.

Case Study

Yin (1994) suggests that case studies are an empirical investigation of phenomena within their environmental context, where the relationship between the phenomena and the environment is not clear. A case, then, is examined in order to develop an understanding of an issue or to provide input into an existing theory or a new theoretical concept.

The unit of measurement in a case study is usually associated with the concept of an entity. Thus, a case study could be about an individual, a group, or an organization. It could also be about an event, such as the implementation of an information system. A research project employing the case study method may employ a single case or multiple cases. In this latter instance, conclusions could be determined based upon similarities and differences among the cases involved in the study.

Butler and Fitzgerald (2001) used a single case study method to investigate "the relationship that exists between user participation in systems development and the issue of organizational change surrounding the development and implementation of information systems" (p. 12). The important aspects of this research project were the relationship between user participation and the process of change and not change itself. Thus, an action research method was not adopted, and instead, a specific situation was investigated using the case study method.

The research philosophy consisted of a "constructivist research approach, incorporating the hermeneutic method ... [and a] ... qualitative, interpretive, case-based research strategy" (Butler & Fitzgerald, 2001, p. 16). The case consisted of two systems development projects within the same telecommunications company.

The two systems development projects were described with an emphasis on the documentation and analysis of the relationship between user involvement and the process of change. The results determined that:

- The organizational context influences user participation.
- Organizational specific policies and structures are necessary to facilitate change.
- User participation is influenced by project complexity, user/analyst relationships, and users' willingness to participate. User acceptance is affected by expected change, power relationships, and user commitment to change.
- It is difficult, if not dangerous, to attempt to separate the factors related to user participation and management of change.

The authors concluded that the organizational context provides the greatest impact on user participation and user acceptance and, consequently, on reducing resistance to change.

Another article included here employed a multiple case study approach. Hasan, Hyland, Dodds, and Veeraraghavan (2000) investigated how an organization may employ data to achieve its objectives through the development of multidimensional databases. Prototype information systems were developed which were intended to respond to a specific business situation. Data analysis followed an interpretive case study approach and was based upon a qualitative approach to group (researchers') discussions of the aspects of effective database development within four cases. Commonalities and differences among the four cases were employed in order to develop conclusions. The authors concluded that "the dimensional view of data [as opposed to the relational view] does provide users with an effective means of making sense of large quantities of data" (Hasan et al., p. 22).

Ethnography

Atkinson and Hammersley (1994) suggest that ethnography involves exploring the nature of phenomena, working with unstructured data, and analyzing data through the interpretation of the meanings attributed by research participants. The ethnographic research method involves primary observations conducted by the researcher over an extended period of time. This type of research is particularly appropriate for investigating the phenomena of social systems. Ethnography is increasingly employed as a research method for investigating information systems. The method is mainly employed to study the social aspects of work practices and the development and use of information systems (Schultze, 2001).

Nandhakumar and Avison (1999) employed an ethnographic method to the investigation of the information system development process in a large organization. The researchers employed this method in order to penetrate the guise of a standard system development approach, which they felt was simply in place to present an image of control. Ethnography involves detailed investigation of an entity within its specific context. In this situation, detailed qualitative data were gathered regarding the information system development practices within this specific context. Data were gathered using participant observation, including field notes and unstructured interviews. The authors concluded that "the development process is characterized by a continuous stream of intervention, bricolage, improvisation, opportunism, interruption and mutual negotiation as much as by regulatory, progress milestones, planning and management control" (Nandhakumar & Avison, p. 185). Further, with regards to the use of ethnography as a research method, the authors state:

> *We find that the use of an intensive field study approach using participant observation provides an effective means of understanding the complex social process of IS development. We wanted to investigate the IS development process from the perspective of the actors and to understand their interpretation of actions and perceptions, and the context within which these actions took place. For this, the researcher needs to have close access to the actors themselves to obtain their interpretations directly. (Nandhakumar & Avison, p. 185).*

Grounded Theory

The major proponents of Grounded Theory suggest it is "the discovery of theory from data systematically obtained from social research" (Glaser & Strauss, 1967, p. 2). They suggest a "category" emerges from the data and may stand by itself as a conceptual element. A "property," they suggest, is an aspect of a category. Both categories and properties are concepts indicated by the data and interpreted by the researchers.

Urquhart (2001) discusses how Grounded Theory may be employed either as a philosophical approach to research or as a technique for analyzing data. As a research philosophy, the researcher approaches a research question without adopting *a priori* a research framework or theoretical context. Grounded Theory is primarily a technique for analyzing data and includes the process of constant comparison of data with categories which have emerged from previous data. This constant comparison either generates new categories or supports previously identified categories. As Glaser and Strauss (1967) state, "By comparing where the facts are similar or different, we can generate properties of categories that increase the categories' generality and explanatory power" (p. 24). Eventually a situation of theoretical saturation is attained where no new categories emerge from the data.

Strauss and Corbin (1990) describe Grounded Theory's data analysis process via the terms "open," "axial," and "selective" coding. To begin, open coding is conducted by analyzing the data and identifying categories that represent conceptual groupings of data. Then, axial coding involves making connections between the categories to identify an overall theoretical framework. Also, within category data are analyzed to further elaborate on conditions, context, and consequences of associated data. Finally, selective coding represents completing the association of data for all emerging categories and the identification of core categories to support the conceptualization of the theoretical framework.

Urquhart (2000) has presented research which "takes a qualitative view of analyst-client dialogue and is designed to explore analyst-client interaction from a processual perspective" (p. 2). Urquhart contented that because the initial contact and exchange between analyst and client is verbal, communication skills are very important to ensure the appropriate interpretation is gleaned regarding the future system requirements. Participants in the research project were involved in the initial stages of system development or modification. They were asked to prepare a written one-page description of the situation and were then videotaped during an exploratory interview. Grounded Theory was employed to identify concepts used by participants in their initial contact regarding system requirements. Urquhart (2000) determined that analysts "recognized communication as playing a supremely important role in gaining thorough analyses of the system and were actively looking for enhanced ways to achieve this" (p. 11).

Narrative Inquiry

Narrative inquiry entails the documentation and analysis of individuals' stories about or personal accounts of a specific domain of discourse. As Swap, Leonard, Schields, and Abrams (2001) have suggested, employing research where participants relate stories about their personal experiences "would be more memorable, be given more weight, and be more likely to guide behavior" (p. 103). The narrative inquiry method allows the research participant to tell his or her own story. According to Tulving (1972), episodic memory relates to events which have been directly experienced, and it is these events which are most readily remembered.

Narrative inquiry has been defined as "the symbolic presentation of a sequence of events connected by subject matter and related by time" (Scholes, 1981, p. 205). Research employing the narrative approach (Vendelo, 1998) suggests the sequence of the story elements (Bruner, 1990) contribute to the appropriateness of the method. Czarniawska-Joerges (1995) further supports the importance of employing a sequential account when employing the narrative inquiry method.

Narrative inquiry has been employed extensively in other academic disciplines, such as behavioral science (Rappaport, 1993), fiction and film (Chatman, 1978), and strategic management (Barry & Elmes, 1997). However, it has been adopted into the information systems area to a lesser extent. Hirschheim and Newman (1991) employed narrative case studies and have suggested that the roles of myth, metaphor, and magic are alternative approaches which may assist in improving the understanding and interpreting of the social actions of developers and users involved in the development of information systems. Also, Boland and Day (1989) conducted a series of interviews to document information systems designers' interpretations of their experience. The authors concluded that a more thorough understanding had been gleaned of the information systems designers' structures of meaning employed during the design process.

Hunter and Tan (2001) employed narrative inquiry to identify the major career path impacts of information systems professionals. They interviewed a number of information systems professionals at various stages of their careers to determine why these individuals changed jobs. In order to ground the discussion in the research participants' personal experiences, individual resumes were employed as the main instrument to guide the interview and to elicit the narratives. The resume was employed to assist research participants to reflect upon their work experiences and report these experiences in a sequential account of events at they transpired throughout their careers. The resume approach has been used previously in information systems research (Young, 2000). The resume is readily available and an untapped source of data (Dex, 1991), as well as acting as a milestone reference to assist human memory recall (Baker, 1991). Based upon the transcripts of the interviews, common themes were identified. These themes represented two common trends for the profession. First, the information systems professionals interviewed tended to associate more closely with the profession than with a specific organization. Second, there was an increased desire to remain current with technology and to have experience with the leading-edge technologies. Hunter and Tan (2001) were able to provide recommendations and suggest implications for various stakeholders, including information systems professionals, and organizations.

CONCLUSION

This chapter has presented a series of methods which may be employed when conducting qualitative research. For each method presented a brief description has been provided along with a representative example of a publication which incorporated the specific method. There are many other research methods, too numerous to even attempt to list. In some cases, methods may be combined. Mingers (2001) proffers a pluralistic approach to information systems research, suggesting results may be richer and more reliable.

The methods discussed in this chapter have some common themes. First, they all adopt a social perspective to the area of investigation. That is, the methods would tend to be used when a researcher is interested in determining the perceptions about a subject, which may be held by an individual or group. Second, the methods support conducting an investigation within the context or environment of the entity being studied. So the individual or group is observed where they work. Or the individual or group is asked to describe their perceptions about a subject based upon their experiences. Third, each method supports the identification of underlying concepts associated with the entity under investigation. For instance, Olesen and Myers (1999), as discussed earlier, investigated how individuals interpret situations. They determined that even though change was expected through the implementation of an information system, in fact, existing norms were reinforced. Further, Butler and Fitzgerald (2001) found that user participation in information system development and implementation was contingent upon the organizational context.

While there were common themes amongst the research methods, it is also possible to identify some unique characteristics. In deed, it is these differences which may be the major contributing factor in a researcher's decision about which method to adopt. First, action research precipitates change in order to determine its impact. Olesen and Myers (1999) studied the changes in work habits resulting from the implementation of groupware. Second, a case study may be used to investigate a situation. Butler and Fitzgerald (2001) investigated user participation in the implementation of an information system at a specific organization. Third, ethnography may be employed when the researcher decides the best way to address a research question is to become deeply immersed in the subject or with the research participant. Nandhakumar and Avison (1999) became thoroughly involved in the development of an information system in order to proceed beyond the standard system development approach to determine what actually transpires. Fourth, Grounded Theory supports the statement of a research question and allows the answers, in the form of categories or themes, to emerge from the data. Urquhart (2000) investigated the initial communication between analyst and client regarding the identification of system requirements. Grounded Theory was used to attempt to uncover the underlying concepts of this communication. Finally, narrative inquiry permits the gathering of data by allowing the research participants to relate their own stories about their experiences. Hunter and Tan (2001) employed a novel technique by basing interviews on participants' resumes to gather their stories about major events throughout their careers.

There are many methods which may be employed when conducting qualitative information systems research. The methods presented in this chapter are only a sample of what is available to the qualitative researcher. Also, what has been discussed here represents an overview of the methods. It is incumbent upon the researcher to thoroughly explore these methods and to be fully cognizant of the reasons why one method may be more appropriate than another. Finally, the important consideration for any researcher when deciding which method to adopt is to ensure that the method chosen must address the research question in a way which supports the objectives of conducting the research.

REFERENCES

Atkinson, P., & Hammersley, M. (1994). Ethnography and participant observation. In N. K. Kenzin & Y. S. Lincoln (Eds.), *Handbook of Qualitative Research* (pp. 248-261). Thousand Oaks, CA: SAGE.

Baker, M. (1991). *Research in Marketing*. London: MacMillan.

Barry, D., & Elmes, M. (1997). Strategy retold: Towards a narrative view of strategic discourse. *Academy of Management Review, 22*(2), 429-452.

Benbasat, I., & Zmud, R. W. (1999). Empirical research in information systems: The practice of relevance. *MIS Quarterly, 23*(1), 3-16.

Boland, R. J., Jr., & Day W. F. (1989). The experience of systems design: A hermeneutic of organization action. *Scandinavian Journal of Management, 5*(2), 87-104.

Bruner, J. (1990). *Acts of Meaning*. Cambridge, MA: Harvard University Press.

Butler, T., & Fitzgerald, B. (2001). The relationship between user participation and the management of change surrounding the development of information systems: A European perspective. *Journal of End User Computing, 13*(1), 12-25.

Cecez-Kecmanovic, D. (2001). Doing critical IS research: The question of methodology. In E. M. Trauth (Ed.), *Qualitative Research in IS: Issues and Trends* (pp. 141-162). Hershey, PA: Idea Group.

Chatman, S. (1978). *Story and Discourse: Narrative Structure in Fiction and Film*. Ithaca, NY: Cornell University Press.

Cummings, T. G., & Worley, C. G. (2001). *Essentials of Organization Development and Change*. Cincinnati, OH: Thomson Learning.

Cunningham, J. B. (1993). *Action Research and Organizational Development*. Westport, CT: Praeger.

Czarniawska-Joerges, B. (1995). Narration or science? Collapsing the division in organization studies. *Organization*, *2*(1), 11-33.

Dex, S. (1991). *Life and Work History Analyses*. London: Routledge.

Galliers, R. D. (ed.) (1992). *Information Systems Research – Issues, Methods, and Practical Guidelines*. Henley-on-Thames, UK: Alfred Waller.

Galliers, R. D., & Land, F. F. (1987). Choosing appropriate information systems research methodologies. *Communications of the ACM*, *30*(11), 900-902.

Glaser, B. G., & Strauss, A. L. (1967). *The Discovery of Grounded Theory: Strategies for Qualitative Research*. New York: Aldine De Gruyter.

Hasan, H., Hyland, P., Dodds, D., & Veeraraghavan, R. (2000). Approaches to the development of multi-dimensional databases: Lessons from four case studies. *Database for Advances in Information Systems*, *31*(3), 10-23.

Hirschheim, R. (1992). Information systems epistemology: An historical perspective. In R. D. Galliers (Ed.), *Information Systems Research – Issues, Methods, and Practical Guidelines* (pp. 61-88). Henley-on-Thames, UK: Alfred Waller.

Hirschheim, R., & Newman, M. (1991). Symbolism and information systems development: Myth, metaphor and magic. *Information Systems Research*, *2*(1), 29-62.

Hunter, M. G., & Tan, F. (2001, May). Information systems professionals in New Zealand: Reflective career biographies. *International Conference of the Information Resources Management Association*, 132-133.

Khazanchi, D., & Munkvold, B. E. (2000). Is information systems a science? An inquiry into the nature of the information systems discipline. *Databases for Advances in Information Systems*, *31*(3), 24-42.

Klein, H. K., & Lyytinen, K. (1985). The poverty of scientism in information systems. In E. Mumford, R. Hirschheim, G. Fitzgerald, & A.T. Wood-Harper (Eds.), *Research Methods in Information Systems* (pp. 131-161). Amsterdam: North-Holland.

Klein, H. K., & Myers, M. D. (2001). A classification scheme for interpretive research in information systems. In E. M. Trauth (Ed.), *Qualitative Research in IS: Issues and Trends* (pp. 218-239). Hershey, PA: Idea Group.

Lee, A. S. (2001). Challenges to qualitative researchers in information systems. In E. M. Trauth (Ed.), *Qualitative Research in IS: Issues and Trends* (pp. 240-270). Hershey, PA: Idea Group.

Lending, D., & Wetherbe, J. C. (1992). Update on MIS research: A profile of leading journals and US universities. *Database*, *23*(3), 5-11.

Mingers, J. (2001). Combining IS research methods: Towards a pluralistic methodology. *Information Systems Research*, *12*(3), 240-259.

Mumford, E. (2001). Action research: Helping organizations to change. In E. M. Trauth (Ed.), *Qualitative Research in IS: Issues and Trends* (pp. 46-77). Hershey, PA: Idea Group.

Myers, M. D. (n.d.) Qualitative research in IS. Retrieved March 25, 2002 from: http://comu2.auckland.ac.nz/~isworld/quality.htm.

Myers, M. D. (1997). Qualitative research in information systems. *MIS Quarterly*, *21*(2), 241-242.

Myers, M. D. (2002). *Qualitative research in IS*. Retrieved March 25, 2002 from: www.qual.auckland.ac.nz.

Nandhakumar, J., & Avison, D. (1999). The fiction of methodological development: A field study of information systems development. *Information Technology and People, 12*(2), 176-189.

Olesen, K., & Myers, M. D. (1999). Trying to improve communication and collaboration with information technology: An action research project which failed. *Information Technology and People, 12*(4), 317-328.

Pervin, L. A. (1989). *Personality — Theory and Research* (5th ed.). New York: John Wiley & Sons.

Rappaport, J. (1993). Narrative studies, personal stories and identity transformation in the mutual help context. *Journal of Applied Behavioral Science, 29*(2), 239-256.

Reason, P., & Rowan, J. (eds.) (1981). *Human Inquiry – A Sourcebook of New Paradigm Research*. Chichester, UK: John Wiley & Sons.

Scholes, R. (1981). Language, narrative, and anti-narrative. In W. Mitchell (Ed.), *On Narrativity* (pp. 200-208). Chicago, IL: University of Chicago Press.

Schultze, U. (2000). A confessional account of an ethnography about knowledge work. *MIS Quarterly, 24*(1), 3-41.

Strauss, A., & Corbin, J. (1990). *Basics of Qualitative Research: Grounded Theory Procedures and Techniques*. Newbury Park, CA: SAGE.

Susman, G. I., & Evered, R. D. (1978). An assessment of the scientific merits of action research. *Administrative Science Quarterly, 23*(4), 582-603.

Swap, W., Leonard, D., Schields, M., & Abrams, L. (2001). Using mentoring and storytelling to transfer knowledge in the workplace. *Journal of Management Information Systems, 18*(1), 95-114.

Trauth, E. M. (2001). *Qualitative Research in IS: Issues and Trends*. Hershey, PA: Idea Group.

Tulving, E. (1972). Episodic and semantic memory. In E. Tulving & W. Donaldson (Eds.), *Organization of Memory* (pp. 381-404). New York: Academic Press.

Urquhart, C. (2000). Strategies for conversation and systems analysis in requirements gathering: A qualitative view of analyst-client communication. *The Qualitative Report, 4*(1/2). Retrieved in 2000 from: www.nova.edu/ssss/QR/QR4-1/urquhart.html.

Urquhart, C. (2001). An encounter with grounded theory: Tackling the practical and philosophical issues. In E. M. Trauth (Ed.), *Qualitative Research in IS: Issues and Trends* (pp. 104-140). Hershey, PA: Idea Group.

Vendola, M. T. (1998). Narrating corporate reputation: Becoming legitimate through storytelling. *International Journal of Management and Organization, 28*(3), 120-137.

Yin, R. K. (1994). *Case Study Research: Design and Methods* (2nd ed.). Thousand Oaks, CA: SAGE.

Young, J. (2000). *The career paths of computer science and information systems major graduates*. Unpublished doctoral thesis, University of Tasmania, Hobart, Australia.

APPENDIX A

Object	Modes of Traditional Empirical Approaches (Observations)					Modes of Newer Approaches (Interpretations)				
	Theorem Proof	Lab. Exper.	Field Exper.	Case Study	Survey	Forecasting & Futures Research	Simulation & Game/Role Playing	Subjective Argument.	Descriptive Interpretive (Including Reviews)	Action Research
Society	No	No	Possibly	Possibly	Yes	Yes	Possibly	Yes	Yes	Possibly
Organ./Group	No	Possibly (small grps.)	Yes	Yes	Yes	Yes	Yes	Yes	Yes	Yes
Individual	No	Yes	Yes	Possibly	Possibly	Possibly	Yes	Yes	Yes	Possibly
Technology	Yes	Yes	Yes	No	Possibly	Yes	Yes	Possibly	Possibly	No
Methodology	Yes	No	Yes	Yes	Yes	No	Yes	Yes	Yes	Yes
Theory Building	No	No	No	Yes	Yes	No	Yes	Yes	Yes	Yes
Theory Testing	Yes	Yes	Yes	Yes	Possibly	No	Possibly	No	Possibly	Yes
Theory Extension	Possibly	Possibly	Possibly	Possibly	Possibly	No	No	No	Possibly	Possibly

Information Systems Research Approaches: A Revised Taxonomy (Source: Galliers, 1992, p. 159)

Chapter XVII

Stories and Histories: Case Study Research (and Beyond) in Information Systems Failures

Darren Dalcher
Middlesex University, United Kingdom

ABSTRACT

Information systems development failures are prevalent in many domains and countries. The aim of this chapter is to explore some of the issues related to the study of such phenomena. Failure situations are not set-up in advance as the subject of studies. Analysing causes and relationships retrospectively depends on the ability to obtain rich and subjective contextual information that can be utilised for shedding a light on the circumstances that precipitate failures. This chapter makes the case for the use of case history and ante-narrative methods for understanding such rich and complex scenarios.

INTRODUCTION

Researchers with a keen interest in information systems' failures are faced with a double challenge. Not only is it difficult to obtain intimate information about the circumstances surrounding such failures, but there is also a dearth of information about the type of methods and approaches that can be utilised in this context to support such information collection and dissemination. The purpose of this chapter is to highlight some of the available approaches and to clarify and enhance the methodological underpinning that is available to researchers interested in investigating and document-ing failure phenomena in context-rich and dynamic environments. The focus of the discussion is on approaches to information systems failures that value the situational meanings and knowledge of participants and on a naturalistic research perspective, while at the same time advocating a mixture of quantitative and qualitative evidence and analysis.

The chapter begins by introducing forensic software engineering and the need to understand failures through the consolidation of a diverse range of subjective accounts offered by participants. Knowledge relating to failure is fragmented, distributed and hidden within the context, requiring a naturalistic enquiry process. Moreover, untan-gling causes is inherently pervasive due to emergent properties and the inability to delineate causes and effects. The solution in the form of case-based methods provides an approach that can capture subjective knowledge and situational meaning but requires a new perspective offered through detailed and chronological case histories of failures. The chapter concludes by proposing the supplementing of case histories with antenarrative inquiry, which extracts fragments of stories that emphasise the multiplicity of views and perceptions and their critical interactions during the lead-up to disaster. This supports the capturing of shared knowledge pertaining to failures, thereby enabling a better understanding of conflicts and issues as highlighted by stakeholders.

SETTING THE SCENE

The popular computing literature is awash with stories of IS development failures and their adverse impacts on individuals, organisations, and societal infrastructure. Indeed, contemporary software development practice is regularly characterised by runaway projects, late delivery, exceeded budgets, reduced functionality, and question-able quality, which often translate into cancellations, reduced scope, and significant rework cycles (Dalcher, 1994). Failures, in particular, tell a potentially grim tale. In 1995, 31.1% of U.S. software projects were cancelled, while 52.7% were completed late and over budget (cost 189% of their original budget) and lacked essential functionality. Only 16.2% of projects were completed on time and within budget; only 9% in larger companies, where completed projects had an average of 42% of desired functionality (Standish, 1995). The 1996 cancellation figure rose to 40% (Standish, 1997).

The cost of failed U.S. projects in 1995 was $81 billion; cost overruns added an additional $59 billion ($250 billion was spent on 175,000 U.S. software projects; however, $140 billion out of this was spent on cancelled or over-budget activities; Standish, 1995). In fact, Jones (1994) contended that the average U.S. cancelled project was a year late, having consumed 200% of its expected budget at the point of cancellation. In 1996, failed projects alone totalled an estimated $100 billion (Luqi & Goguen, 1997). In 1998, 28% of projects were still failing at a cost of $75 billion (Standish, 1998), while in 2000, 65,000 of U.S. projects were reported to be failing (Standish, 2000).

The Standish Group makes a distinction between failed projects and challenged projects. Failed projects are cancelled before completion, never implemented, or scrapped following installation. Challenged projects are completed and approved projects which are over budget and late and have fewer features and functions than initially specified. Lyytinen and Hirschheim (1987) identify correspondence failures (where the system fails to correspond to what was required), process failures (failure to produce a system or failure to produce it within reasonable budgetary and timescale constraints), interaction failures (where the system cannot be used or is not satisfactory in terms of the interaction) and expectation failures (where the system is unable to meet a specific stakeholder group's expectations). Many situations contain behavioural, social, organisational, or even societal factors that are ignored, and therefore the definition of failure needs to encompass a wider perspective. The general label *system failures* is often utilised in order to embrace a wider grouping of failures, including ones with undesirable side effects which may impact other domains and the organisational context (see, for example, Fortune & Peters, 1995). As information becomes more embedded in other domains, the scope and impact of failure becomes more wide-reaching. This was clearly evident from the extensive effort to minimise the impact of the "year 2000 bug" from any system containing computers and underscores our interest in using the term *IS failure* to a wider class of systems failures that merit investigating.

IS failure investigations start with extensive attempts to collate relevant evidence. Failure information tends to arrive from different sources, typically including anecdotal evidence and journalistic descriptions, reports of investigative committees, official public inquiries, audit reports, public account committee minutes and findings, case studies, and empirical surveys. In specific cases this may be augmented by internal documents, interviews, eyewitness accounts, direct observation, and archival records (and possibly physical artefacts). In most cases the researcher is exposed to specific information post hoc, i.e., once the failure is well established and well publicised and the participants have had a chance to rationalise their version of the story. Most of the available sources are therefore already in place and will have been set up by agencies other than the researcher.

The purpose of a forensic investigation is to explain a given failure by using available information and evidence. The term *forensic* is derived from the Latin *forensis*, which is to do with making public. Forensic science is the applied use of a body of knowledge or practice in determining the cause of death, nowadays extended to include any skilled investigation into how a crime was perpetrated. Forensic systems engineering is the postmortem analysis and study of project disasters (Dalcher, 1994). The work involves a detailed investigation of a project, its environment, decisions taken, politics, human errors, and the relationship between subsystems. The work draws upon a multidisciplinary body of knowledge and assesses the project from several directions and viewpoints. The concept of systems is a central tool for understanding the delicate relationships and their implications in the overall project environment.

The aim of forensic analysis is to improve the understanding of failures, their background, and how they come about (Dalcher, 1997). The long-term objectives are improving the state-of-the-practice and generating new insights into methods of managing complex projects. The knowledge generated is then fed back into the process via a double-loop learning system in order to improve the internal (organisational) or external (disciplinary) body of knowledge. Forensic systems engineering is thus primarily concerned with documentary analysis and (post-event) interviews in an effort to ascertain responsibility lines, causal links, and background information.

The primary mode of dissemination of findings, conclusions, and lessons is through the publication of case study reports focusing on specific failures. However, there are limited research methods to explore the dynamic and fragmented nature of complex failure situations. The armoury of research methods in this domain is often limited to main dissemination mode: case studies. Lyytinen and Hirschheim (1987) noted that more qualitative research methods were needed for IS failure research as well as more extensive case studies that explored problems in more detail and viewed solution arrangements in light of what transpired. The same methods also need to account for group issues and cultural implications. Sadly, 15 years on, the same constraints in terms of methods are still in evidence.

BACKGROUND: BEYOND THE OBJECTIVE

The choice of a research method is strongly coupled to the type of information that is available to the researcher. The choice of method determines what type of information will be sought for subsequent analysis. Furthermore, the type of information that is available will determine the types of analysis that may be conducted. However, the entire process must start with the research objective and how it is framed in terms of required information.

The positivist stance, prevalent in the natural sciences, is centred on the notion that all knowledge, in the form of facts, is derived from either observation or experience of real, objective, and measurable natural phenomena, thereby supporting the notion of quantitative analysis. Facts can thus be viewed as universal truths devoid of personal values and social interactions and independent of time and context. This enables researchers to focus on regularity, repeatability, and the verification and validation of causal relationships. The currency of such objective knowledge is the manipulation and metrification of objects and their relationships, expressed in the form of numbers to enable quantitative operations. This stance is difficult to sustain in failure research, where the actions, perceptions, and rationales of actors are not amenable to quantitative methods. (Note, however, that the actual findings and the factors leading to accidents can subsequently be modelled using quantitative notations.)

At the other extreme, (interpretivist, constructivist, or relativist) knowledge can be viewed as encompassing beliefs, principles, personal values, preferences, social context, and historical background, which are inevitably dynamic as they change with time (and context). Qualitative research methods originate in the social sciences, where researchers are concerned with social and cultural phenomena. Social interaction in human activity systems ensures intersubjectivity, as actors are forced to negotiate and agree on certain aspects. The humanistic perspective is outside the conventional positivist norm. The resulting emphasis is on the relevant interpretation of knowledge as held by participants in a social activity. Data sources utilised by researchers include observation, fieldwork, interviews, questionnaires, documents, texts, and the impressions and reactions of the researchers. Such qualitative perspective relies on **words** (Miles & Huberman, 1994), conveying feelings and perceptions, rather than numbers. Qualitative methods recognise the fact that subjects can express themselves and their feelings and, thereby, clarify the social and cultural contexts within which they operate. Meaning therefore needs to be "interpreted" in a process of "sense-making." Actions thus need to be understood in terms of intentions, which in turn are understood in their original context (Schutz, 1973). Indeed, Kaplan and Maxwell (1994) argue that the goal of understanding a phenomenon from the point of view of the main participants and their particular social, cultural, and institutional context is largely lost when the textual data are quantified.

Making sense of IS failures retrospectively is difficult. In general, there is very little objective quantitative failure information that can be relied upon. This makes the utilisation of quantitative methods less likely until all relevant information is understood. Indeed, a specific feature of failure is the unique interaction between the system, the participants, their perspectives, complexity, and technology (Perrow, 1984). Lyytinen and Hirschheim (1987) pointed out that failure is a multifaceted phenomenon of immense complexity with multiple causes and perspectives. Research into failures often ignores the complex and important role of social arrangement embedded in the actual context. This is often due to the quantitative nature of such research. More recently, Checkland and Holwell (1998) argued that the IS field requires sense-making to enable a richer concept of information systems. Understanding the interactions that lead to failures likewise requires a humanistic stance that is outside the conventional positivist norm to capture the real diversity, contention, and complexity embedded in real life. Forensic analysis thus relies on utilising qualitative approaches to obtain a richer understanding of failure phenomena in terms of action and interaction (as explored in subsequent sections).

(Note that triangulation, the mixing of quantitative and qualitative methods, offers the opportunity to combine research methods in a complementary manner in one study. A good example of such a mix in failure research would entail reliance on qualitative methods to capture the essence, context, and webs of interactions in the buildup to failure and complement the presentation by using more formal approaches to model the impact of such interactions.)

ISSUES, CONTROVERSIES, PROBLEMS: KNOWLEDGE IS HIDDEN WITHIN THE CONTEXT

Qualitative research methods are concerned with generating richer knowledge. However, knowledge is not something that exists and grows in the abstract (Boulding, 1956). It is a property of the interaction between agents and the environment and is tied to perspectives, intentions, and perceptions. Meaning is therefore not an intrinsic property of a message but depends on the code or set of alternatives from which the message comes (Ashby, 1960; Campbell, 1982; Lissack & Roos, 1999). In fact, Nadler (1985, p. 695) noted that "information is not a brick that can be thrown from one person to another with the exact same meaning."

Knowledge is deeply bound to its original context, which enables a "contextually correct" understanding. It is also strongly coupled to the time frame and, thereby, to the prevailing mindset. Only through the effective capturing of the precise context can information be evaluated against the rationale, motives, and assumptions that applied. Information about failure, much like evidence given by witnesses, can only be understood through the identification of position, perspective, and relationship. Any useful information must therefore be accompanied by additional contextual information that will shed light on its utility, validity, and relevance, and any methods adopted need to support the identification of such contextual knowledge.

The fact that a failure phenomenon is being investigated suggests that attention has already been drawn to the complexities, breakdowns, and messy interactions that such a situation entails (i.e., the investigation is problem-driven). Many such inquiries deal with subjective accounts, including impressions, perceptions, and memories. The aim of the researcher is to increase in a systemic way the understanding of a situation yet do so from a position that takes in the complexity of the entire situation and incorporates the different perspectives and perceptions of the stakeholders involved. Phenomenology can thus be described as the study of direct experience taken at face value and may utilise verbal, diagrammatic, or descriptive model forms (Remenyi, Williams, Money, & Swartz, 1998). The focus is on what the subject experiences and its expression in a language and mannerism that is loyal to that experience.

Methods used to research failures need to be systemic and able to get beneath how people describe experiences to the underlying structure and webs of interactions. Such methods need to:

- offer a holistic view unravelling a systems perspective on the entire topic of study, thus enabling researchers to ascend beyond the details—in failure research this enables the investigator the glimpse the "total system";
- be an inductive approach that enables the construction of meaning in terms of the situation and the development of general patterns that emerge from the cases under study;
- enable researchers to extend the boundaries of the system to capture interactions that may impact the failure; and
- support naturalistic enquiry, enabling phenomena to be understood in their naturally occurring settings.

Overall, the purpose of a failure research method is to enable the researcher to make sense of the complexity of detail and the complexity of interaction and chart the contributory role of different causes and issues in the buildup to failure. The next section continues to explore some of the unique characteristics of failure in terms of identifying causes and circular relationships that make the understanding of such phenomena even more complicated. These issues will need to be addressed in terms of any methods that can be used to highlight the nature and characteristics of failure phenomena.

Emergence and Simplistic Causality

Interestingly, many failure investigations try to reduce failure explanations to simple causal pairings (Lyytinen & Hirschheim, 1987), thereby ignoring the role of participants, their knowledge, their assumptions, and the overall environment. It is often noted that cause-event relationships do not tend to be "objective" (Checkland & Holwell, 1998; Lemon, 2001; Stake, 1995) and that neither time sequencing nor correlation are likely to provide a plausible proof of causality (Hage & Meeker, 1988). Interpretivism calls the possibility of uncovering causal links into question because all entities are in a state of "mutual shaping," so it is impossible to distinguish causes from effects (Thietart, 2001). Moreover, each failure is unique. In many cases, complex interactions between actors, systems, and failure causes play a part in creating a dynamic (and messy) mix. Therefore it is more important to try to understand the meaning that actors give to reality, as intentions, motivations, expectations, beliefs, perceptions, and fears are all grounded in the perception of reality. Failure research must proceed by taking into account the sum of all interactions and their dynamic colinear relationships.

The general phenomenon of emergence defies causal analysis, forcing greater emphasis on interactions. All systems are composed of inter-parts, and the system can only be explained as a whole. Accidents and failures display similar tendencies as unexpected and "interesting" interactions and properties emerge. When interactions occur in a certain way and order, they give rise to emergent (and often unexpected) patterns of behaviour. The complexity and interconnectedness of interacting components and agents thus gives rise to emergent phenomena. Emergence resulting from such synergies, intra-acting interactions, and nonlinear dynamics is represented by new properties, capabilities, and behaviours of the overall system. All too often emergent properties are neither designed nor planned. Slight changes in input or interaction patterns will thus lead to differences in emergence (i.e., unexpected new behaviours).

Proofs of causality are inevitably tenuous (Lowrance, 1976). Moreover, due to emergence and unexpected interactions, forming a direct link between cause and effect is rather complicated and somewhat misleading (Perrow, 1984). Cause-effect relationships involve uncertainties in both directions. In principle, separating cause from effect depends on the assumption of stability and minimum change within the environment. In practice, one is often faced with events (or potential events). A more realistic approach is to focus on an event and trace the range of causes and the effects that have resulted from them.

Cause ← Event → Effect

This approach enables the identification of multiple causes and multiple effects from the same event (as well as the detection of multiple events resulting from the same cause).

One of the major complications in failure investigations is in relating causes to effects (and possibly events) through extended time horizons (Dalcher, 2000). The implications of actions may not be witnessed for years or even generations. Delays between making a decision and observing the result distort the causal link between the two. As a result, people tend to associate a different level of severity to events occurring following a delay. The perceived severity is thus diminished, with the length of the delay further complicating the task of identifying patterns and interactions that contributed to a given failure. Failure researchers are thus required to provide adequate historical accounts of the interaction between actions, perceptions, and the passage of time.

SOLUTIONS: USING CASE STUDIES TO DESCRIBE REALITY

Having looked at some of the complications associated with capturing actions, reactions, and perspectives, it is now time to turn our attention to the main tool of forensic IT research, the case study. The term "case study" is an umbrella term used in different contexts to mean different things, which include a wide range of evidence capture and analysis procedures. Yin (1994, p. 13) defines the scope of a case study as follows:

A case study is an empirical inquiry that:

- investigates a contemporary phenomenon within its real-life context, especially when
- the boundaries between phenomenon and context are not clearly identified.

A case study can be viewed as a way of establishing valid and reliable evidence for the research process as well as presenting findings which result from research (Remenyi et al., 1998). According to Schramm (1971), the case study tries to illuminate a decision or a set of decisions and in particular emphasise why they were taken, how they were implemented, and with what results. A case study is likely to contain a detailed and in-depth analysis of a phenomenon of interest in context; in our case, the failure scenario.

The general aim of the case study approach is to understand phenomena in terms of issues in the original problem context. A case study allows the researcher to concentrate on specific instances in their natural setting and thereby attempt to identify the interacting perceptions, issues, and processes at work, ultimately resulting in in-depth understanding. Some of these interactions are likely to prove crucial to the success or failure of the organisation/system under scrutiny. Focusing on relationships and processes facilitates a holistic perspective, revealing underlying patterns and possibly some emergent properties. Many of these patterns remain hidden under normal conditions but can be prised open as a result of the special focus. (Note that case studies may contain rigour and application of careful logic about comparisons in the positivist tradition.)

In the context of failures, exploring a particular case or set of events entails attempting to provide the richest perspective of what transpired through the analysis of multiple subjective accounts of participants, the explanation of phenomena, and the retrospective identification of relationships. Case studies provide the mechanism for conducting an in-depth exploration. They often result from the decision to focus an enquiry around an instance or an incident (Adelman, Jenkins, & Kemmis, 1977), as they are principally concerned with the interaction of factors and events (Bell, 1999). Indeed, sometimes it is only the practical instances that enable one to obtain a true picture of the interaction (Bell). The combination of a variety of sources offers a richer perspective, which also benefits from the availability of a variety and multiplicity of methods that can be used to obtain new insights about this single instance. Crucially, the focus on a single incident thus enables the study of the particularity and complexity of a case, thereby coming to understand the activity within important circumstances (Stake, 1995).

Case studies are more likely to be used retrospectively rather than as an ongoing perspective (especially from a failure point-of-view), as researchers are unlikely to know the potential for useful results and interest from the outset. Case studies are useful in providing a multidimensional picture of a situation (Remenyi et al., 1998) in the context of historical description and analysis. The richness of detail can be controlled through the careful placement of systems boundaries and consideration of the wider system environment that is relevant to the phenomenon under study. Case studies can be utilised as a source of understanding which is tolerant of ambiguity, paradox, and contradiction. A case study is viewed as interpretative when events in the real world are observed, and then an effort takes place to make sense of what was observed, i.e., when one tries to make sense of a failure from the perspectives of participants. They also offer the potential for generating alternative explanations from the different stakeholder perspectives, thereby allowing the researcher to highlight contradictions and misunderstandings.

Case studies can be viewed as a comprehensive research strategy rather than as an information collection tool or a research design method. Information collection methods for case studies often use observation, document reading, and interviews, but other methods can be selected to suit the particular requirements of a case and the general strategy. Case study work needs to be self-contained, but researchers have the luxury of being able to expand the boundaries to incorporate emerging patterns and perceptions. The data, and indeed the analysis, are grounded in reality.

The main advantages of using case studies include:

- ability to identify and focus on issues
- richness of detail
- multiple perspectives
- multiple explanations (no absolute truth)
- cross-disciplinary remit
- ability to recognise and minimise inherent complexity
- ability to handle conflict, disparity, and disagreement
- ability to show interactions
- ability to observe emerging patterns
- conducted in real-life setting
- encompasses original problem context
- ability to deal with interpretations
- can extend the boundaries to include aspects of wider system environment
- can be accumulated to form an archive of cases

The main objections to their use include:

- sometimes viewed as soft data (but some argue it is hard research)
- biases inherent in accepting views and perceptions

- questions about generalisability of findings (especially from a single case), but it is possible to build a library of such cases
- issues regarding objectivity of approach and perceived lack of rigour
- negotiating access to settings
- boundaries are difficult to define, but this could also be a strength!
- mainly retrospective
- sometimes viewed as likely to take too long and result in massive documentation
- the observer effect
- reliability of conclusions
- there is little control over events, but this may also be a strength

In summary, case studies are ideal for exploring interactions between people and their understanding of a situation. The richness of the data obtained by multiple means from multiple perspectives provides a real insight into the main issues at play. The time dimension (sequencing) is critical to understanding interactions and identifying their impacts. Actions (and reactions) can only be understood in context, and case studies create the context for understanding them. Emergence often defies causal analysis, forcing a greater emphasis on interactions; however, case studies enable the identification of networks of issues that people are likely to act on. The generally liberal use of the term *case study* requires a tighter definition of its meaning in failure research. The next section sets the role of case studies within the context of IS failure research.

RECOMMENDATIONS: CASE HISTORIES TO REPLACE CASE STUDIES

While there may be a tradition of using case studies within the IS community, this is perhaps more often borrowed from the MBA culture than as a result of self-conscious effort to adopt them as a research approach (Cornford & Smithson, 1996; Walsham, 1995). Indeed, the case study is typically used more in its capacity as a teaching tool than as a **research tool**. The shift to studying the impact of issues within the organisational context renders case studies particularly useful for investigating failure scenarios. However, the use of the term often leads to some confusion. Case studies have been used to adopt an idiographic (Cornford & Smithson, 1996), an interpretivist (Stake, 1995; Walsham, 1993), a constructive (Jankowicz, 2000), or even a positivist (Benbasat, Goldstein, & Mead, 1987; Yin, 1984, 1993, 1994) stance.

After Walsham (1993) and Myers (1994), we take the view that interpretivist case studies develop deeper understanding of IS phenomena. The shift from technical to organisational issues (Benbasat et al., 1987) necessitates a deeper look at how people act on interpretations and perceptions. Generating explanatory models enables expressions of patterns, judgements, and values that provide a systemic clue to the unfolding of events.

Case studies are typically used to explore issues in the present and the past and are comprised of ethnographic studies, single case studies, and comparative case studies

(Jankowicz, 2000), as well as action research, evaluative, exploratory, explanatory, and descriptive case studies (Bassey, 1999). In our experience there is a need to add the failure case study as a special example of a case study focusing primarily on the background, context, perception, interactions, and patterns, especially as the failure investigation is likely to take place *after* the (failure) event. We thus propose the use of the label *case histories* to refer to the specialised historical research studies focusing on failure incidents.

Case histories are concerned with providing the background and context that are required to endow words and events with additional meaning. Background refers to previous history of the system itself, while context refers to interactions with the environment. As failures are time- and place-dependent, the case history framework enables readers to obtain an understanding of the intimate context surrounding the main event. The primary tool available to the community is the case histories of failures (derived from the use of the case study method). These represent a detailed historical description and analysis of actual processes. Their value is in tracing decisions (and recorded rationale) to their eventual outcomes by utilising techniques borrowed from decision analysis and systems engineering. Indeed, the historical description and presentation of a chronology of events are based on the recognition that real life is ambiguous, conflicting, and complex.

Case histories highlight complexities and trade-offs that are embedded in the acquisition and development processes or in the operation and interaction mode. They also help in the identification, definition, and assessment of pervasive problems in a given application domain. Maintaining repositories of forensic case histories is a form of risk management and, hopefully, mitigation that can be applied to future undertakings (Dalcher, 2002). Failures are crucial to the development of a mature and responsible discipline that responds to crucial issues that emerge from past failures. Case histories thus aid in understanding the role and significance of failures.

Recommendations

Case histories contain observations, feelings, and descriptions. They can be used to construct, share, dispute, and confirm meanings, interpretations, and scenarios in the context of real events. Such observations must be systematically processed and structured. Their validity depends on the procedures used to obtain the information. Where possible, multiple sources of evidence should be used to support the emerging story. A mix of methods for obtaining the information will also enhance the value of the result. The use of alternative perspectives enables the analyst to consider conflicts and varying perceptions and their role in the unfolding story. Finally, case histories should be composed in an engaging manner to provide convincing reading (Remenyi et al., 1998) with a clear and concise story.

It is now clear that case histories provide more than a straightforward chronology of events. Rather than simply highlight a chronicled sequence of happenings, they convey a story encompassing a specific perspective, focus, and possibly some inevitable biases. The interpretation plays a key part in transmutating the chronicle into a meaningful story with plot, coherence, and purpose. However, constructing a convincing narrative of a complex story with competing meanings, alternative perspectives, and inherent prejudices is a challenge in itself.

FUTURE TRENDS: STORIES
ARE NARRATIVE INQUIRY

As we have seen, failures, in common with other organisational activities, are based on stories. The verbal medium is crucial to understanding behaviour within organisations and systems, and researchers are thus required to collect stories, grounded in practice, about what takes place (Easterby-Smith, Thorpe, & Lowe, 2002; Gabriel, 2000). The result is the transformative plotting of scattered events to uncover hidden patterns and unexplored meanings (Denning, 2001; Kearney, 2002). Similarly, understanding failures often entails the retrospective untangling of complicated webs of actions and events and emergent interaction patterns. Failure storytelling can thus be understood as a combination of narrative recounting of empirical events with the purposeful unlocking of meaningful patterns or a plot.

Historically, storytelling has been an acceptable form of conveying ideas, experience, and knowledge of context. It plays a key role in communicating the cultural, moral, or historical context to the listener. Indeed, Arendt (1958) argued that the chief characteristic of human life is that it is always full of events, which ultimately can be told as a story. There are even strong claims that the narrative is the main mode of human knowledge (Bruner, 1986, 1990; Schank, 1990), as well as the main mode of communication (Boje, 1991; Denning, 2001; Fisher, 1984, 1987; Schank). Moreover, children are often initiated into culture (and its boundaries) through the medium of storytelling, offering models for emulation or avoidance.

In practice, the essence of any good case study revolves around the ability to generate an effective story line, normally with a unique style, plot, or perspective. In a large case, a general theme can be obtained from selected excerpts weaved together to illustrate a particular story. Personal stories that form part of a case study can thus be viewed as a valid source of data, organised to make sense of a theme or problem. This is particularly useful when the researcher is trying to portray a personal account of a participant, a stakeholder, or an observer in an incident, accident, or failure. The implication is that the need to address personal aspects of interaction and story (that remains a problem in IS research) is fulfilled by the development of a research-valid narrative. Indeed, Remenyi et al. (1998) contend that a story, or a narrative description, is valid if the resulting narrative adds some knowledge. Furthermore, White (1973, p. 27) describes a story as "the process of selection and arrangement of data from the unprocessed historical record in the interest of rendering the record more comprehensible to an audience of a particular kind" by inserting a sense of perspective and purpose.

A narrative can be structured to give a voice to the researcher, to the narrator, to the participants, to the stakeholders, or to cultural groups, traditions, or ideas. In the context of research it is not concerned with the development of a reflective autobiography or life story but rather with the analysis and devolvement of themes that emerge from a medley of events (Bell, 1999; Carr, 2001; Polkinghorne, 1987; White, 1973). Researchers are thus concerned with how information interpreted from a story can be structured in such a way as to produce valid research findings. This form of narration can be particularly useful in uncovering motives and rationales and linking them to the actual consequences and their impact on stakeholder groups. It also suggests an understanding of implied causes and emergent interactions.

Understanding IS failures is therefore more complicated than the discovery of a simplistic chronology of events. Failure researchers collect subjective accounts extracted from participants and observers. Developing narratives relies on trust between the researcher and the storyteller. Storytellers reveal personal feelings and motivations which may compromise their position or interests. Sharing the information and making it public suggest that the storyteller is prepared to release certain details about themselves and their position publicly. This may have ethical research implications (as well as the potential for organisational, or even legal, complications). Shared stories imply shared concepts, shared vocabularies, and shared perceptions (or as a minimum, the ability to see where the sharing stops).

Narratives are neither discovered nor found: they are constructed. Narrative inquiry is evolving into an acceptable research approach in its own right in the social sciences and in management research circles (Bell, 1999; Boje, 2001; Czarniawska, 1998; Easterby-Smith et al., 2002; Gabriel, 2000). The story format provides a powerful way of knowing and linking disparate accounts and perspectives. The main pitfall with this approach revolves around the narrative structure which is developed by the storyteller. If the initial storyteller is not the researcher, care should be taken to eliminate personal biases in terms of outcomes and actions (but these should remain as descriptions of feelings, reactions, and motivation). Follow-up questions can thus provide the mechanism for clarifying context, background, rationale, or sequence or, more generally, for "objectifying" and "time sequencing" the events. When different accounts are combined, the story line benefits from the richness of multifaceted insights.

Developing a narrative requires plot as well as coherence, as a story is made out of events and the plot mediates between the events and the story (Boje, 2001; Carr, 2001; Kearney, 2002). In failure stories, the plot often emanates from the actions and perceptions of participants emerging out of the flux of events, in (direct) contradiction with expectations. The storyteller is concerned with the perspective and purpose of participants as well as with the plausibility of the emerging plot. The combination of plot, purpose, and perspective dictates the selection of elements, the filling in of links, and the removal of "irrelevant" noise.

Postmodern interpretation contends that most real-life stories are fragmented, nonlinear, multivariate, and incoherent. This has already been highlighted as a feature of failure stories. Such stories also tend to be dynamic, polyphonic (multi-voiced), and collectively produced, as they occur in asymmetrical, random, and turbulent environments. The stories are not plotted as such and they appear to flow, emerge, and network, offering complex clustering of events, emergent phenomena, causes, and effects. Moreover, the accounts are often subjective, counterintuitive, and contradictory. This leads to interacting, and conflicting webs of narratives, characterised by coincidences, predicaments, and crises.

Generally, stories appear to be improperly told, as a story is an "ante" state of affairs, existing previously to a carefully constructed narrative (Boje, 2001). The **antenarrative**, or the "real" story, is the fragmented, messy and dynamic, multi-vocal, multi-plotted, multi-version, and complex tale. Indeed, modern storytellers look for new ways and mediums for weaving and depicting a multi-vocal reality, as exemplified by Mike Finggis's digitally shot film *Time's Arrow,* where the screen is split in four to allow for four separate perspectives and sub-stories that occasionally intersect or overlap. In the tradition of postmodern inquiry, a real-life researcher is often faced with fragments rather than a whole story to tell, and many of the fragments may reflect contrary versions of reality. This is potentially more acute when the accounts attempt to justify roles of participants in the lead-up to disaster. It would also appear from past analysis that there are hierarchies of stories and stories that exist within or interact with other stories. Using the terminology provided by Boje, the purpose of narrative methods is to take a complex situation characterised by collective (yet often conflicting) memory and an antenarrative and construct the plot and coherence that can be used to narrate the story of interest.

The reality in failure stories is of multistranded stories of experiences and reactions that lack collective consensus. Indeed the discipline of decision making has also recognised that making choices is about forming and selecting interpretations from a mosaic of possibilities (March, 1994, 1997; Weick, 1995). Not surprisingly, disasters or traumatic stories are hard to narrate, understand, and justify. Stories have three basic properties: time, place, and mind (Boje, 2001), which interact and build up as the story evolves. In forensic case histories, these are further clarified through the identification of the background and context, which clarify and justify the interpretation in the context of the emerging phenomena.

Boje (1991, 2001) and Kearney (2002) contend that the current view is of sequential single voice stories and implies excessive reliance on the hypothetical-deductive approach (akin to simplistic causal pairings). The answer is not to develop Harvard case studies but to rewrite stories as polyvocal tapestries enabling different perceptions and interpretations to exist, thereby explaining webs of actions and interactions. What is new in this approach is the antenarrative reading, which enables narrative analysis methods to be supplemented by antenarrative methods, allowing previously fragmented and personal storytelling to be interpreted as a unified whole. This focus offers alternative discourse analysis strategies that can be applied where qualitative story analyses can help to assess subjective, yet "insightful" knowledge in order to obtain "true" understanding of complex interactions.

CONCLUSION

With the benefit of hindsight it is possible to reconstruct a systematic retelling of events that have led to a failure. The narrated structure provides an explanation as to how and why failures occur. The purpose of the structure is to make sense of a rich tapestry of interactions and connections by following an identified story line that chronicles and links the relevant issues within the environment. This can lead to a rich explanation or justification grounded in the original perception of the problem environment. Indeed, recounted life may prise open perspectives that would have been inaccessible using ordinary methods and thinking arrangements. Moreover, failure tends to highlight missing and incorrect assumptions and faulty defensive mechanisms and can therefore serve as a pretext to updating the frame of reference or the context for understanding.

This chapter focused on the qualitative research methods available in the domain of IS failure. Failures are often dynamic and confusing, requiring a holistic approach to resolution. Investigating and making sense of IS failures is still a relatively immature discipline with little awareness of alternative approaches for identifying and capturing that knowledge.

Case studies have been used as the traditional means of transmitting knowledge about past failures. However, this is often done with little consideration for the terminology, implications, and multiple meanings associated with case studies and therefore calls for additional refinement and for the discovery of richer and more diversified alternative approaches. Case histories are a special instance of a case study looking at the factors involved in failures in context and at the dynamic interrelationships between them. They can be described as a problem-driven research tool focusing on the "holistic totality" in a naturalistic setting. Narrative methods (and antenarrative reading) provide an additional facet for addressing the fragmented nature of failure stories. Their great strength is in offering an alternative to sequential, single-voiced stories, thereby giving a voice to a multiplicity of perspectives. Narrative methods thus offer a new meta-tool for the armoury of the IS failure community.

Combining case histories with narrative descriptions is likely to lead to clearer failure stories that can account for contradictions and misunderstandings. It is hoped that by developing our understanding of methods that help in capturing and structuring histories and in telling stories we will also improve our ability to learn from such experiences. Indeed, the methods discussed in this chapter form the front end required for understanding and capturing knowledge in action (which could be supplemented by more formal methods to model their impact through a process of triangulation).

As for the future, good stories can also benefit from pictures. Once we have mastered the techniques of telling complex modern stories, we need to focus on composing that information. Even the most gripping story needs to be made attractive and believable. Textual information needs additional support not only in "emplotting" and in maintaining coherence and perspective but also in ascertaining the plausibility of constructed stories and in differentiating between noise and narrative. Developing improved techniques for organising or visualising knowledge (such as Net maps) can therefore help in untangling some of the fragmented strands as well as in making the stories more readable and understandable, as well as ultimately more appealing.

REFERENCES

Adelman, C., Jenkins, D., & Kemmis, S. (1977). Rethinking case study: Notes from the Second Cambridge Conference. *Cambridge Journal of Education*, 6, 139-150.

Arendt, H. (1958). *The Human Condition*. Chicago, IL: University of Chicago Press.

Ashby, W. R. (1960). *Design for a Brain* (2nd ed.). London: Chapman & Hall.

Bassey, M. (1999). *Case Study Research in Educational Settings*. Buckingham, UK: Open University Press.

Bell, J. (1999). *Doing Your Research Project: A Guide for First-Time Researchers in Education and Social Science* (3rd ed.). Buckingham, UK: Open University Press.

Benbasat, I., Goldstein, D. K., & Mead, M. (1987). The case research strategy in studies of information systems. *MIS Quarterly*, *11*(3), 369-386.

Boje, D. M. (1991). The storytelling organization: A study of story performance in an office-supply firm. *Administrative Science Quarterly*, *36*, 106-126.

Boje, D. M. (2001). *Narrative Methods for Organisational & Communication Research*. London: SAGE.

Boulding, K. E. (1956). General systems theory—The skeleton of science. *Management Science, 2*, 197.

Bruner, J. (1986). *Actual Minds, Possible Worlds*. Cambridge, MA: Harvard University Press.

Bruner, J. (1990). *Acts of Meaning*. Cambridge, MA: Harvard University Press.

Campbell, J. (1982). *Grammatical Man: Information, Entropy, Language, and Life*. New York: Simon & Schuster.

Carr, D. (2001). Narrative and the real world: An argument for continuity. In G. Roberts (Ed.), *The History and Narrative Reader* (pp. 143-156). London: Routledge.

Checkland, P., & Holwell, S. (1998). *Information, Systems and Information Systems—Making Sense of the Field*. Chichester, UK: John Wiley & Sons.

Cornford, T., & Smithson, S. (1996). *Project Research in Information Systems: A Student's Guide*. Basingstoke, UK: Macmillan.

Czarniawska, B. (1998). *A Narrative Approach to Organization Studies*. London: SAGE.

Dalcher, D. (1994). Falling down is part of growing up; the study of failure and the software engineering community. In *Proceedings of the 7th SEI Education in Software Engineering Conference* (pp. 489-496). New York: Springer-Verlag.

Dalcher, D. (1997). The study of failure and software engineering research. In *Proceeding of the UK Software Engineering Association Easter Workshop* (pp. 14-19). London: Imperial College.

Dalcher, D. (2000). Feedback, planning and control—A dynamic relationship. In *FEAST 2000* (pp. 34-38). London: Imperial College.

Dalcher, D. (2002). Safety, risk and danger: A new dynamic perspective. *Cutter IT Journal, 15*(2), 23-27.

Denning, S. (2001). *The Springboard: How Storytelling Ignites Action in Knowledge-Era Organizations*. Boston, MA: Butterworth-Heinemann.

Easterby-Smith, M., Thorpe, M., & Lowe, A. (2002). *Management Research* (2nd ed.). London: SAGE.

Fisher, W. R. (1984). Narration as a human communication paradigm: The case of public moral argument. *Communication Monographs, 51*, 1-22.

Fisher, W. R. (1987). *Human Communication as Narration: Towards a Philosophy of Reason, Value and Action*. Columbia, SC: University of South Carolina Press.

Fortune, J., & Peters, G. (1995). *Learning from Failure: The Systems Approach*. Chichester, UK: John Wiley & Sons.

Gabriel, Y. (2000). *Storytelling in Organizations: Facts, Fictions and Fantasies*. Oxford, UK: Oxford University Press.

Hage, J., & Meeker, B. F. (1988). *Social Causality*. London: Unwin Hyman.

Jankowicz, A. D. (2000). *Business Research Projects* (3rd ed.). London: Business Press.

Jones, C. (1994). *Assessment and Control of Software Risks*. Englewood Cliffs, NJ: Prentice Hall.

Kaplan, B., & Maxwell, J. A. (1994). Qualitative research methods for evaluating computer information systems. In J. G. Anderson, C. E. Aydin, & S. J. Jay (Eds.), *Evaluating Health Care Information Systems: Methods and Applications* (pp. 45-68). Thousand Oaks, CA: SAGE.

Kearney, R. (2002). *On Stories*. London: Routledge.

Lemon, M. C. (2001). The structure of narrative. In G. Roberts (Ed.), *The History and Narrative Reader* (pp. 107-129). London: Routledge.

Lissack, M., & Roos, J. (1999). *The Next Common Sense: Mastering Corporate Complexity Through Coherence*. London: Nicholas Brealey.

Lowrance, W. W. (1976). *Of Acceptable Risk: Science and the Determination of Safety*. Los Altos, CA: William Kaufmann.

Luqi, & Goguen, J. A. (1997). Formal methods: Promises and problems. *IEEE Software*, *14*(1), 73-85.

Lyytinen, K., & Hirschheim, R. (1987). Information systems failures: A survey and classification of the empirical literature. *Oxford Surveys in Information Technology*, *4*, 257-309.

March, J. G. (1994). *A Primer on Decision Making*. New York: Free Press.

March, J. G. (1997). Understanding how decisions happen in organisations. In Z. Shapira (Ed.), *Organisational Decision Making* (pp. 9-34). Cambridge, UK: Cambridge University Press.

Miles, M. B., & Huberman, A. M. (1994). *Qualitative Data Analysis: An Expanded Sourcebook*. Thousand Oaks, CA: SAGE.

Myers, M. D. (1994). A disaster for everyone to see: An interpretive analysis of a failed project. *Accounting, Management and Information Technology*, *4*(4), 185-201.

Nadler, G. (1985). Systems methodology and design. *IEEE Transactions on Systems, Man, and Cybernetics*, *15*(6), 685-697.

Perrow, C. (1984). *Normal Accidents, Living with High-Risk Technologies*. New York: Basic Books.

Polkinghorne, D. (1987). *Narrative Knowing and Human Sciences*. Albany, NY: State University of New York Press.

Remenyi et al. (1998). *Doing Research in Business and Management: An Introduction to Process and Method*. London: SAGE.

Schank, R. C. (1990). *Tell Me a Story: Narrative and Intelligence*. Evanston, IL: Northwestern University Press.

Schramm, W. (1971). *Notes on case studies of instructional media projects*. Working paper for the Academy for Educational Development. Washington, DC.

Schutz, A. (1973). On multiple realities. In *Collected Papers I: The Problem of Social Reality* (pp. 207-259). The Hague, The Netherlands: Martinus Nijhoff.

Stake, R. E. (1995). *The Art of Case Study Research*. Thousand Oaks, CA: SAGE.

Standish Group. (1995). *Chaos 1995*. Dennis, MA: Standish.

Standish Group. (1997). *Chaos 1997*. Dennis, MA: Standish.

Standish Group. (1998). *Chaos 1998*. Dennis, MA: Standish.

Standish Group. (2000). *Chaos 2000*. Dennis, MA: Standish.

Thietart, R.-A. (2001). *Doing Management Research: A Comprehensive Guide*. London: SAGE.

Walsham, G. (1993). *Interpreting Information Systems in Organizations*. Chichester, UK: John Wiley & Sons.

Walsham, G. (1995). Interpretive case studies in IS research: Nature and method. *European Journal of Information Systems*, *4*(2), 74-81.

Weick, K. E. (1995). *Sensemaking in Organisations*. Thousand Oaks, CA: SAGE.

White, H. (1973). *Metahistory*. Baltimore, MD: John Hopkins University Press.

Yin, R. K. (1984). *Case Study Research: Design and Methods*. Newbury Park, CA: SAGE.

Yin, R. K. (1993). *Application of Case Study Research—Design and Methods*. Newbury Park, CA: SAGE.

Yin, R. K. (1994). *Case Study Research: Design and Methods* (2nd ed.). Newbury Park, CA: SAGE.

Chapter XVIII

Using Critical Realism in IS Research

Sven A. Carlsson
Jönköping International Business School, Sweden

ABSTRACT

Different strands of postmodern, poststructuralist, postrealist, and nonpositivistic approaches and theories have gained popularity in information systems (IS) research. Since most of these approaches have a flat treatment of the agency/structure dimension, focus almost exclusively on micro phenomena, and reject objectivist elements, it can be argued that they are problematic to use in IS research. An alternative approach and philosophy is critical realism, which suggests, for example, that social reality is not simply composed of agents' meanings but that there exist structural factors influencing agents' lived experiences. Critical realism starts from an ontology which identifies structures and mechanisms through which events and discourses are generated as being fundamental to the constitution of our natural and social reality. This is in direct contrast to a constructivist ontology. This chapter presents critical realism and Derek Layder's critical-realism-based adaptive theory and exemplifies how they can be used in IS research.

INTRODUCTION

Commentators on IS research have pointed out weaknesses in positivist, realist, and quantitative approaches for research on the design, development, and use of ICT-based information systems (IS). The commentators have called for the use of alternative approaches and theories. In response, IS researchers have used different types of postmodern, poststructuralist, and postrealist approaches and theories, for example, grounded theory, structuration theory, ethnography, and actor-network theory. Most of the alternative approaches and theories are heavily oriented towards interpretations and agents' meanings. Although the alternatives overcome some problems associated with traditional positivist and realist approaches and theories, they at the same time are problematic to use in IS research. For example, they treat the agency/structure dimension in a collapsed and flat manner, they have in some cases an exclusive focus on micro phenomena, and they reject objectivist elements. As will be discussed, the alternatives' focuses and rejections can be problematic in developing theories on the design, development, and use of ICT-based IS. Given that we in the last years have seen an increase in published IS research utilizing postmodern, poststructuralist, postrealist, and nonpositivistic approaches and theories, these alternative approaches and theories, as well as IS research based on them, need to be scrutinized. (For simplicity, we will refer to these different approaches and theories as "post-approaches" and "post-theories" when distinction is not required.)

The purpose of this chapter is threefold. First, to point out some of the limitations and weaknesses in different post-approaches and post-theories to the study of design, development, and use of ICT-based IS. Second, to present critical realism and discuss how it overcomes some of the problems associated with the different forms of post-approaches and post-theories. Third, to present and exemplify how Derek Layder's (1998) adaptive theory approach can be used in IS research—Layder's adaptive theory builds on critical realism.

Research in the IS field can, from a research approaches perspective, be characterized as quite broad. Our concern here is primarily theory development and theory testing in IS research, but we will briefly discuss how theories can feed into design science and constructive research, for example, how they can feed into the design or construction of a new systems development method. We will not explicitly address pure conceptual analytical research but discuss it as an element of an empirical research process. (For classifications and discussions of different IS research approaches see Galliers, 1991; Järvinen, 1999, 2000; March & Smith, 1995; and Walls, Widmeyer, & El Sawy, 1992.)

The remainder of the chapter is organized as follows: the next section sets the scene by briefly presenting and discussing different responses to the cry for alternatives to positivist and realist approaches. The section also points out some limitations and weaknesses in the postmodern, postrealist, and poststructuralist approaches and theories. Next we present critical realism as an alternative approach and discuss how it overcomes the noted problems. This is followed by a presentation of Derek Layder's adaptive theory approach. We also exemplify how critical realism and adaptive theory approach can be used in IS research. The final section presents conclusions and suggests further research.

POST-APPROACHES AND POST-THEORIES IN IS RESEARCH: PROBLEMS IN PARADISE

In recent years, several researchers have argued for the need of post-approaches and post-theories in IS research (Hirschheim & Klein, 1989; Iivari, 1991; Orlikowski & Baroudi, 1991; Walsham, 1993, 1995). In response to this call, researchers have used, for example, qualitative approaches, interpretive approaches, grounded theory, and theories like Anthony Gidden's structuration theory.

Several IS scholars have suggested grounded theory as an alternative to positivistic approaches, and a number of IS studies using grounded theory have been published—for examples, see Michael Myers's "Qualitative Research in Information Systems" at http://www.qual.auckland.ac.nz/ or Trauth (2001). Generally, grounded theory is an approach to the analysis of qualitative data aiming at generating theory out of research data by achieving a close fit between the two (Glaser & Strauss, 1967). Said Strauss and Corbin (1998), "Theory that was derived from data, systematically gathered and analyzed through the research process. In this method, data collection, analysis, and eventual theory stand in close relationship to one another." Although positive to some of the ideas in grounded theory, Derek Layder points out major weaknesses in grounded theory. Layder (1993) says that the grounded theory approach "must break away from its primary focus on micro phenomena. The very fixity of this concentration is a factor which prevents grounded theory from attending to historical matters of macro structure as a means of enriching contemporary or, as I [Layder] shall call them, present-centred forms of research on micro phenomena. It should be possible to augment the processual and dynamic analyses of interactional phenomena by a parallel focus on the historically antecedent forms that provide their institutional backdrop." Transferred to IS research this means that researchers using grounded theory must "identify" the influences of macro structural features on behavior and interactions through what they are able to "directly observe." This means that macro phenomena have no validity to IS researchers using grounded theory unless these macro phenomena emerge directly from field data. Research suggests that macro phenomena, like national culture, influence IS designers (Hunter & Beck, 1996) and how IS are used and are evaluated (Leidner, Carlsson, Elam, & Corrales, 1999; Tan, Watson, & Wei, 1995). These macro phenomena (structural/systemic factors) can hardly emerge in IS research focusing on agents' perceptions, meanings, and actions. Other weaknesses pointed out by Layder include how power can be handled in grounded theory. Grounded theory focuses on situated and interpersonal aspects. This means that a researcher using grounded theory will most likely miss the importance of power "behind the scenes" of activity. To exemplify, group support systems (GSS) researchers stress the importance of anonymous communication as a way to support equal participation and to even out power differences. In most cases this is discussed without noting the setting—the immediate arena for social activities—as well as the wider context. That is, there is no discussion of the power structure in the setting that ultimately has an impact on a decision group's activities and the possibility to implement a decision. To put it differently, by neglecting the setting one misses the

Figure 1. Structurational Model of Technology (Orlikowski, 1992, p. 410).

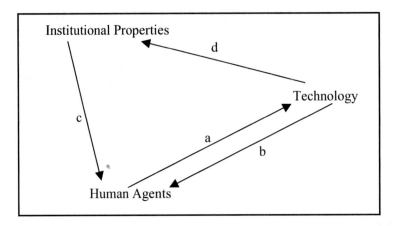

interplay between structural and interactional dimensions of power. The importance of structural dimensions in understanding the relationships between IS design, IS use, and power has been pointed out by, for example, Markus and Bjørn-Andersen (1987) and Davenport and Prusak (1997).

A theory favored by some IS researchers is Anthony Gidden's (1984) structuration theory. Most notably is Orlikowski's work on applying structuration theory to the development and use of IS in organizations (Orlikowski, 1992, 2000). Figure 1 depicts Orlikowski's structurational model of technology and shows the relationship between technology, human agents, and institutional properties.

According to Orlikowski (1992), technology is identified as the "product of human action" (Arrow a), coming into existence and being sustained through human action and being constituted through use. Only through the appropriation of technology by humans, therefore, does it exert influence. However, technology is also "the medium of human action" (Arrow b). Technology constrains and enables social practices. Institutional properties influence human agents (Arrow c)—"institutional conditions of interaction with technology." Arrow d reflects the influence of technology in reinforcing or transforming organizations' institutional properties—"institutional consequences of interaction with technology."

Structuration theory overcomes some of the problems associated with positivist and realist theories, but Giddens's view on the relationship between agency and structure is problematic when studying ICT-based information systems. Jones (1999) after reviewing IS research based on Giddens's structuration theory concludes that "it is evident that the specific attempts to adapt structuration to incorporate material aspects of IS have encountered a number of serious problems which remain as yet unresolved." The problem is Giddens's conception of structure which means that structure cannot be separated from agency. It means "a single-level social ontology that conflates 'agency' and 'structure' in such a way that they are analytically rendered down to localized social practices bereft of any institutional underpinnings or contextualization. The ontological status and explanatory power of 'structure'—i.e., as a concept referring to relatively enduring institutionalised relationships between social positions and practices located at different levels of analysis that constrain actors' capacities to 'make a difference'— is completely lost in a myopic analytical focus on situated social interaction and the local conversational routines through which it is reproduced" (Reed, 1997). Furthermore, Giddens "vehemently opposes objectivism in all guises. Such a dismissal of objectivism is premature and unwarranted in so far as it fails to recognize that some form of objectivism is necessary since it is the only possible way of registering the distinctive and partly independent characteristics of systemic phenomenon" (Layder, 1998). Layder, Ashton, and Sung (1991), in reflecting on their use of structuration theory to study the transition from school to work among British 18- to 24-year-olds, conclude that "empirically structure and action are interdependent ... but partly autonomous and separate domains. In this respect our findings lead us to conclude that the empirically applicability of structuration theory concerning the interconnection between structural and individual variables is somewhat more limited than has hitherto been acknowledged."

Actor-network theory is another of the postmodern alternatives used in IS research which shares with the other alternatives its focus on agency and the local, contingent, and indeterminate.

Some researchers have advocated that IS researchers should integrate positivist and interpretive approaches (Lee, 1991; Trauth & Jessup, 2000), integrate case study and survey research methods (Gable, 1994), or combine qualitative and quantitative methods (Kaplan & Duchon, 1988). Although these suggestions have some similarities with what critical realism and Layder propose, the suggestions are not based on a specific philosophy of/for social sciences, and the issue of ontology is not addressed—some researchers mix approaches and methods based on quite different ontological views. The philosophy for science we advocate, critical realism, starts from an ontology which identifies structures and mechanisms through which events and discourses are generated as being fundamental to the constitution of our natural and social reality. This is in direct contrast to a constructivist ontology. The approach we advocate is based on Layder's philosophy and framework for social science (Layder, 1990, 1993), which belongs to what is called critical realism. Layder (1993) says: "Put very simple, a central feature of realism is its attempt to preserve a "scientific' attitude towards social analysis at the same time as recognizing the importance of actors' meanings and in some way incorporating them in research. As such, a key aspect of the realist project is a concern with causality and the identification of causal mechanisms in social phenomena in a manner quite unlike the traditional positivist search for causal generalizations." From an epistemological stance, concerning the nature of knowledge claim, the realist approach is nonpositivistic, which means that values and facts are intertwined and hard to disentangle.

Summarizing, from an IS research perspective there are at least three major problems with the use of different strands of post-approaches and post-theories. First, their fascinations with the voices of those studied have led to an increase in IS research as mere reportages and local narratives ("any narrative will do"). In some cases this has led to what can best be characterized as an interpretive morass. Second, their exclusive focus on agency leads to their ignoring of the structural (systemic) dimension—the agency/structure dimension is collapsed, leading to a flat treatment of the dimension. Third, their rejection of objectivist elements leads to problems when researching artifacts like ICT-based information systems. We are not claiming that the criticized approaches and theories cannot be useful in IS research, but that they have a number of unnoted problems and limitations and that they certainly not are panaceas.

Jones (1999), Walsham (1995), and Mingers (2001a) have pointed out some problems with post-approaches and post-theories in IS research. They have suggested that the development of a "position" based on critical realism could be a valuable contribution to IS research. The next section presents critical realism.

AFTER THE "POST-ERA": CRITICAL REALISM

The approach we advocate is based on Layder's philosophy and framework for social science (Layder, 1990, 1993, 1997, 1998), which belongs to what is called critical realism. Critical realism was developed as an alternative to traditional positivistic models of social science as well as an alternative to post-approaches and post-theories (Archer, 1995; Archer, Bhaskar, Collier, Lawson, & Norrie, 1998; Bhaskar, 1978, 1989, 1998; Harré & Secord 1972; Lòpez & Potter, 2001).

Critical realism can be seen as a specific form of realism. Its manifesto is to recognize the reality of the natural order and the events and discourses of the social world. It holds that "we will only be able to understand—and so change—the social world if we identify the structures at work that generate those events and discourses. ... These structures are not spontaneously apparent in the observable pattern of events; they can only be identified through the practical and theoretical work of the social sciences" (Bhaskar, 1989). Bhaskar (1978) outlines what he calls three domains: the real, the actual, and the empirical (see Table 1). The real domain consists of underlying structures and mechanisms, and relations; events and behavior; and experiences. The generative mechanisms, residing in the real domain, exist independently of but capable of producing patterns of events. Relations generate behaviors in the social world. The domain of the actual consists of these events and behaviors. Hence, the actual domain is the domain in which observed events or observed patterns of events occur. The domain of the empirical consists of what we experience; hence, it is the domain of experienced events.

Bhaskar argues that "real structures exist independently of and are often out of phase with the actual patterns of events. Indeed it is only because of the latter we need to perform experiments and only because of the former that we can make sense of our performances of them. Similarly it can be shown to be a condition of the intelligibility of perception that events occur independently of experiences. And experiences are often (epistemically speaking) 'out of phase' with events—e.g., when they are misidentified. It is partly because of this possibility that the scientist needs a scientific education or training. Thus I will argue that what I call the domains of the real, the actual and the empirical are distinct" (Bhaskar, 1978). Critical realism also argues that the real world is ontologically stratified and differentiated. The real world consists of a plurality of structures that generate the events that occur and do not occur (called generative mechanisms).

As noted above, Layder is positive to some of the ideas in grounded theory and in general to empiricism (although not to extreme empiricism as "pure" grounded theory).

Table 1. Ontological Assumptions of the Critical Realist View of Science (Bhaskar, 1978, p. 13). (The Xs indicate the domain of reality in which mechanisms, events, and experiences, respectively, reside, as well as the domains involved for such a residence to be possible.)

	Domain of Real	Domain of Actual	Domain of Empirical
Mechanisms	X		
Events	X	X	
Experiences	X	X	X

Layder also "borrows" ideas from middle-range theory (Merton, 1967). According to Merton, middle-range theories are "intermediate to general theories to general theories of social systems [often called grand theories—an example is structuration theory] which are too remote from particular classes of social behavior, organization and change to account for what is observed and to those detailed orderly descriptions of particulars that are not generalized at all." Layder points out the strengths as well as the weaknesses of middle-range theory. A strength is its focus on macro phenomena. A weakness is its rigid notion of social science (positivistic), which is quite different from a critical realism view and what Layder presents.

Layder developed his philosophy and framework primarily for being used in theory generation and development and less so for theory testing. The framework can be used for generating both substantive and formal theories. The former is theory "developed for a substantive area such as patient care, race relations, professional education, geriatric lifestyles, delinquency or financial organizations," and formal theory is theory "developed for a formal or conceptual area of sociological inquiry such as status passage, stigma, deviant behaviour, socialization, status congruency, authority and power, reward systems, organizations or organizational careers" (Glaser & Strauss, 1971). Layder says that his framework can also be used in studies that have information gathering or descriptive aims.

Layder suggests a stratified or layered framework of social organization. The framework includes macro phenomena, like structural and institutional phenomena, as well as micro phenomena, like behavior and interaction. Figure 2 depicts Layder's framework and describes levels (elements/sectors) of potential areas of interest in research on social organization—including research on the design, development, and use of ICT-based IS. As the figure suggests, Layder's framework reflects a greater appreciation of the multifaceted nature of the empirical world than do middle-range theory and grounded theory. These tend to exclusively focus on one or two of the elements.

We will briefly present the different elements and, for convenience, start with the self and work towards the macro elements. The first level is *self*, which refers "primarily to the individual's relation to her or his social environment and is characterized by the intersection of biographical experience and social involvements" (Layder, 1993). Self focuses on how an individual is affected by and responds to social situations. In encountering social situations, individuals use strategies, based on their "theories" (mental models), to handle the situations. These strategies and how they are used can be addressed in research. How individuals emotionally and intellectually perceive, describe, and understand specific situations are also important areas to address. In general, the self and situated activity have as their main concern "the way individuals respond to particular features of their social environment and the typical situations associated with this environment" (Layder, 1993).

In *situated activity* the focus is on the dynamics of social interaction. The area of self focuses on how individuals are affected and respond to certain social processes, whereas situated activity focuses on the nature of the social involvements and interactions. This means that the interaction and the process have features that are the result of how the participating individuals' behaviors intermesh and coalesce. Situated activities vary considerably along a number of dimensions, for example, along the dimensions "time" and "place."

Self and situated activity can be treated as separable elements in research, but they are in practice hard to separate. It is hard to separate selves from the social situation in which they are embedded, but by separating them a researcher can focus on: (1) how individuals respond to and are affected by their social interactions and situations and (2) the nature of the social interactions themselves—for example, how users react to a specific type of computer-mediated communication system and the nature of the computer-mediated communication. The topics addressed at the self and situated activity levels can be subjective as well as objective "components and characteristics."

Figure 2. Research Map (Adapted from Layder, 1993, p. 72).

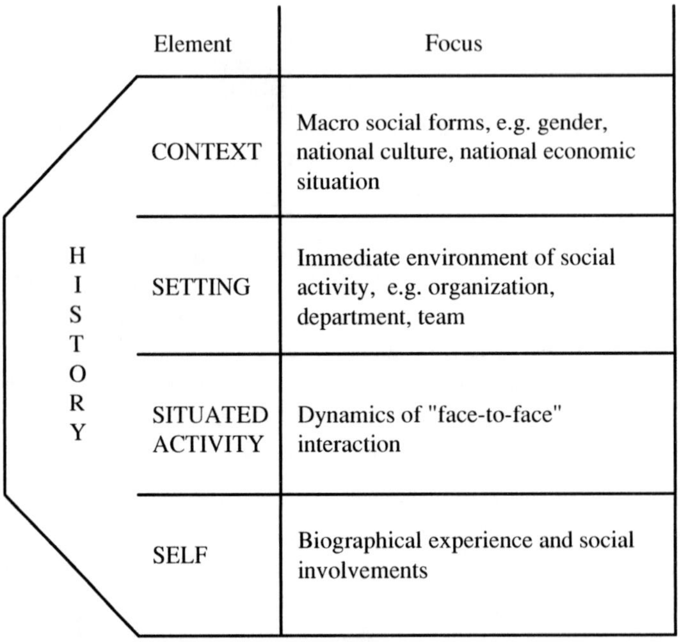
Element
Focus
CONTEXT
Macro social forms, e.g. gender, national culture, national economic situation
SETTING
Immediate environment of social activity, e.g. organization, department, team
SITUATED ACTIVITY
Dynamics of "face-to-face" interaction
SELF
Biographical experience and social involvements
HISTORY

The focus in *setting* is on the intermediate forms of social organization. A setting provides the immediate arena for social activities. A setting can be things like the culture of the organization, artifacts like ICT-based IS that are used in situated activities, power, and authority structures. It should be stressed that setting is not just a particular pattern of activity. Seeing setting and context as particular patterns of activity is a characteristic feature of grounded theory and other approaches that draw on interactionist or constructivist perspectives. Layder (1993) sees setting and context as "rather different but *complementary* aspects of social life, and that, in principle, full and equal weighting should be given to each in field research."

The wider macro social forms that provide the more remote environment of social activity are referred to as the *context*. Although there is not a clear border between settings and context and some social forms straddle the two elements, it can be fruitful to distinguish them. In general, context refers to large-scale and society-wide features. Macro elements that have been used in research include gender, national culture, and national economic situation.

Viewing the design, development, and use of ICT-based IS as layers of social organization that are interdependent has two major advantages. It enables a researcher to be sensitive to the different elements with their distinctive features. In general, IS research based on post- approaches and post-theories does not distinguish between the different layers. They handle features of the different layers in more or less the same way, and they do not express their underlying assumptions about the interdependence between the layers other in fairly simple "causal" relationships. Layder's framework also stresses that the layers operate on different "time scales." For example, computer-based communication is a social activity (a situated activity) that, within a certain time span, is a continuous process. In describing and explaining the design, development, and use of such a system, a researcher has to "understand" the way such a process unfolds over time and how this process is related to the other elements and their changes over time. This means that a researcher has to view the operation of the elements not only vertically but also horizontally.

Although critical realism has influenced a number of social science fields—e.g., organization studies (Reed, 1997, 2001; Tsang & Kwan, 1999; Tsoukas, 1989)—its presence in the IS field is almost invisible. Noteworthy are Mutch (1997) and Dobson (2001), who argue for the use of critical realism in IS research and discuss how critical realism can overcome problems associated with post-approaches and post-theories. Mingers (2001a) used ideas from critical realism to argue for the use of pluralist methodologies in IS research. He also used an approach influenced by critical realism in reviewing the use of multimethod research in the IS literature (Mingers, 2001b). Carlsson and Leidner (1998) used critical realism to develop a model for contextual design of management support systems (MSS). They argued that the proposed model can be used to structure, describe, and analyze the "social organization" where a MSS is used or is to be used and that the model can be used to increase designers' and other stakeholders' understanding of the "social organization" where MSS design takes place.

USING CRITICAL REALISM AND ADAPTIVE THEORY IN IS RESEARCH

Critical realism has primarily been occupied with philosophical issues and fairly abstract discussions, and there has been less focus on how to actually carry out empirical research. Regarding empirical research rooted in critical realism, the works of Derek Layder and Margaret Archer (1995) are noteworthy. Derek Layder's (1998) *adaptive theory* is an approach for primarily generating theory in conjunction with ongoing empirical research. It has its roots in critical realism and attempts to combine the use of preexisting theory and theory generated from data analysis in the formulation of research as well as in actual empirical research. Adaptive theory builds on some of the strengths of existing approaches, but it also overcomes some of the weaknesses, noted above, in these different types of post-approaches and post-theories.

Figure 3 depicts the different elements of the research process according to Layder. There is not some necessary or fixed temporal sequence. Instead the different elements are loosely and flexibly positioned in relation to each other. Layder stresses that theorizing should be a continuous process, accompanying the research at all stages.

To exemplify how Layder's adaptive theory can be used in IS research, we will use a study on the use of executive information systems (Carlsson & Leidner, 1998a; Carlsson, Leidner, & Elam, 1996; Leidner & Carlsson, 1998; Leidner & Elam, 1995; Leidner, Carlsson, & Elam, 1995; Leidner, Carlsson, Elam & Corrales, 1999). The overall purpose of the study was to increase our understanding on the development and use of executive information systems (EIS) and contribute to the cumulative knowledge related to EIS.

Layder's adaptive theory approach has eight overall parameters. One parameter says that adaptive theory "uses both inductive and deductive procedures for developing and elaborating theory" (Layder, 1998). The adaptive theory suggests the use of both forms of theory generation within the same frame of reference and particularly within the same research project and time frame. In our project we used both forms of theory generation. Based on previous EIS studies and theories as well as Huber's (1990) propositions on the effects of advanced ICT on organizational design, intelligence, and decision making, we generated a number of hypotheses (a deductive procedure). These were empirically tested. In the same project we also used an inductive procedure. Although previous theories as well as the results from other parts of the project were fed into the inductive procedure, we primarily used an inductive approach to from the data generate patterns of EIS use.

Another parameter says that adaptive theory "rests upon an epistemological position which is neither positivist nor interpretivist" (Layder, 1998). Adaptive theory, in order to look for the most powerful forms of explanation, draws upon both positivist and interpretivist theories. In an effort to transcend the limitations of the theories, adaptive theory occupies the intermediate ground between both theories. In our study this was, in part, accomplished by using and combining traditional positivistic re-search—hypotheses testing—with interpretive research.

One parameter says that adaptive theory "embraces both objectivism and subjec-tivism in terms of its ontological presuppositions" (Layder, 1998). The adaptive theory conceives the social world as including both subjective and objective aspects and mixtures of the two. In our project, one objective aspect was the ICT used in the different

Figure 3. Elements of the Research Process (Layder, 1998).

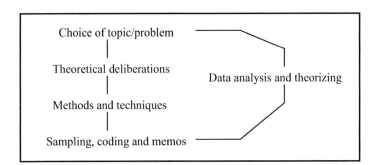

EIS—viewed as a generative mechanism—and one subjective aspect was perceived effects of EIS use. (This can be contrasted with views based in structuration theory, which views technology as "instantiations.")

Two other parameters say that adaptive theory "assumes that the social world is complex, multifaceted (layered) and densely compacted" and "focuses on the multifarious interconnections between human agency, social activities and social organization (structures and systems)" (Layder, 1998). The idea that the world comprises both subjective and objective features means that adaptive theory assumes that "the social world is complex and dense. Furthermore, it also assumes that the texture of this complexity and density is formed from the multifarious interconnections between agency and structure" (Layder, 1998). In our study we focused on the interconnections between agency and structure. We addressed self, e.g., perceptions of EIS; situated activity, e.g., use of EIS in day-to-day work; setting, e.g., organizational structure and culture; and context, e.g., national culture and economic situation. We found, for example, that national culture influenced how EIS were used and how they were perceived. We also found "interconnections" between EIS use and organizational strategy and organizational structure. The "effects" of these generative mechanisms "showed up" in the domain of experienced events.

Our study and the results (theory) were influenced, e.g., by Huber's propositions and the theory saying that EIS are systems for providing top managers with critical information, as well as by Robert Quinns' competing values approach (Quinn, 1988; Quinn, Faerman, Thompson, & McGrath, 1996; Quinn & Rohrbaugh, 1983). The latter theory was brought in to theorize around the data from the interpretive part of the study. Adaptive theorizing was ever-present in the research process. Theorizing was done before hypotheses testing was done. We used theories about national culture (extant theory) to generate hypotheses (theorizing) on how national culture (context) could influence how EIS were used and perceived (situated activity and self). Also, in the interpretive part, theorizing was present. It was present in generating questions—using extant theory and the results from hypotheses testing—as well as in analyzing the collected data. Our study led to our argument that it is a misconception to think of EIS as systems that just provide top managers with information. We think part of the problem lies in the use of the word *information*. EIS are systems that do more than provide information. EIS are systems that support managerial cognition and behavior—providing information is only one of several means—as well as it can be one important means in organizational change. The above is related to the parameter saying that adaptive theory "both shapes and is shaped by the empirical data that emerges from research. It allows the dual influence of extant theory (theoretical models) as well as those that unfold from (and are enfolded in) research. Adaptive theorizing is an ever-present feature of the research process" (Layder, 1998).

We can also envision that critical realism can make major contributions in: (1) IS evaluation research, (2) artifact construction and design science, and (3) studies on IS discourses.

Information systems evaluations are of critical concern to practitioners and academics (Bjørn-Andersen & Davis, 1988; Farbey, Land, & Targett, 1995, 1999; Symons, 1991). IS evaluation research, as its name implies, is concerned with the evaluation of different aspects of IS. It can be considered a special case of evaluation research. In IS evaluation the essential question asked is: Has the IS (that is, the intervention) achieved its anticipated goals? The IS field was early influenced by the experimental evaluation school, in which, for example, a group is exposed to the IS evaluated and another group—the control group—is not exposed to the IS. Later, qualitative IS evaluation approaches emerged, for example, approaches based in the pragmatic evaluation school and the constructivist evaluation school. The latter two belong to what can be labeled postmodern evaluation approaches. The critique voiced earlier applies to these evaluation approaches. In contrast to these approaches, Pawson and Tilley (1997) and Kazi (2003) advocate evaluation approaches which draw on the principle of critical realism and which see "the outcome of an intervention as the result of generative mechanisms and the contexts of those mechanisms. A focus of the former element entails examining the causal factors that inhibit or promote change when an intervention occurs [like the implementation of an ERP system]. Pawson and Tilley's approach is supportive of the use of both quantitative and qualitative research methods" (Bryman, 2001). In line with the development in evaluation research, it can be argued that IS evaluation approaches based on the principle of critical realism can be worth developing and exploring.

Another area where critical realism might be useful is in design research and constructive research. Layder, being a sociology scholar, does not address this area. Carlsson and Leidner (1998) used Layder's framework—described earlier in this chapter and summarized in Figure 2—to develop a contextual IS design model. They argue that the design model can be used in a number of ways, for example:

- To support stakeholders in their development of "theories" of the situated activity, setting, and context an IS is to be implemented in
- For understanding an IS design process by supporting stakeholders in identifying and describing the different elements and dimensions that enable (opportunities) and constrain the process

A further area where critical realism can bring in some fresh thoughts are in "IS discourse" research. IS discourses are critical to the advancement of the academic IS field as well as to IS practice, but the discourses are too seldom discussed. Reed (2000) argues that "Discourses—such as the quantitatively based discourses of financial audit, quality control and risk management—are now seen as the generative mechanisms through which new regulatory regimes 'carried out' by rising expert groups—such as accountants, engineers and scientists—become established and legitimated in modern societies. What they represent is less important than what they do in facilitating a radical reordering of preexisting institutional structures in favour of social groups who benefit from the upward mobility which such innovative regularity regimes facility" (Reed, 2000). Two areas where discourse analysis based on the principle of critical realism can be worth developing and exploring are:

- Discourse analysis of the academic IS field
- Analysis of information systems and especially ICT-based IS from a discourse perspective according to Reed's view on discourse analysis

CONCLUSIONS AND FURTHER RESEARCH

In this chapter we have pointed out some limitations and weaknesses in different strands of post-approaches and post-theories for studying the design, development, and use of ICT-based information systems. Critical realism was proposed as an alternative to these approaches, and we presented Layder's adaptive theory and exemplified how it can be used in IS research. Critical realism and adaptive theory have a number of interesting features and consequences. Further IS studies based on them can form a valuable contribution to IS research and the IS field. Our suggestions make no claims as to being the final word in the debate about how to research the design, implementation, and use of ICT-based information systems, but critical realism and adaptive theory can lead to a stream of research that can bring new knowledge to the IS field.

REFERENCES

Archer, M. (1995). *Realist Social Theory: The Morphogenetic Approach*. Cambridge, UK: Cambridge University Press.

Archer, M., Bhaskar, R., Collier, A., Lawson, T., & Norrie, A. (eds.) (1998). *Critical Realism: Essential Readings*. London: Routledge.

Bhaskar, R. (1978). *A Realist Theory of Science*. Sussex, UK: Harvester Press.

Bhaskar, R. (1989). *Reclaiming Reality*. London: Verso.

Bhaskar, R. (1998). *The Possibility of Naturalism* (3rd ed.). London: Routledge.

Bjørn-Andersen, N., & Davis, G. B. (eds.) (1988). *Information Systems Assessment: Issues and Challenges*. Amsterdam: North-Holland.

Bryman, A. (2001). *Social Research Methods*. Oxford, UK: Oxford University Press.

Carlsson, S. A., & Leidner, D. E. (1998a). Contextual design of management support systems. In D. Berkeley, G. Widmeyer, P. Brezillon, & V. Rajkovic (Eds.), *Context Sensitive Decision Support Systems* (pp. 88-105). London: Chapman & Hall.

Carlsson, S. A., Leidner, D. E., & Elam, J. J. (1996). Individual and organizational effectiveness: Perspectives on the impact of ESS in multinational organizations. In

P. Humphreys, L. Bannon, A. McCosh, P. Migliarese, & J. C. Pomerol (Eds.), *Implementing Systems for Supporting Management Decisions: Concepts, Methods and Experiences* (pp. 91-107). London: Chapman & Hall.

Davenport, T. H., & Prusak, L. (1997). *Information Ecology.* Oxford, UK: Oxford University Press.

Dobson, P. J. (2001). The philosophy of critical realism—An opportunity for information systems research. *Information Systems Frontier, 3*(2), 199-201.

Farbey, B., Land, F. F., & Targett, D. (1995). A taxonomy of information systems applications: The benefits of evaluation ladder. *European Journal of Information Systems, 4*(1), 41-50.

Farbey, B., Land, F. F., & Targett, D. (1999). IS evaluation: A process for bringing together benefits, costs, and risks. In W. L. Currie & B. Galliers (Eds.), *Rethinking Management Information Systems* (pp. 204-228). Oxford, UK: Oxford University Press.

Gable, G. (1994). Integrating case study and survey research methods: An example in information systems. *European Journal of Information Systems, 3*(2), 112-126.

Galliers, R. D. (1991). Choosing appropriate information systems research approaches: A revised taxonomy. In H.-E. Nissen, H. Klein, & R. Hirschheim (Eds.), *Information Systems Research: Contemporary Approaches and Emergent Traditions* (pp. 327-345). Amsterdam: North-Holland.

Giddens, A. (1984). *The Constitution of Society.* Cambridge, UK: Polity Press.

Glaser, B. G., & Strauss, A. L. (1967). *The Discovery of Grounded Theory.* Chicago, IL: Aldine.

Glaser, B. G., & Strauss, A. L. (1971). *Status Passage.* London: Routledge.

Harré, R., & Secord, P. (1972). *The Explanation of Social Behavior.* Oxford, UK: Blackwell.

Hirschheim, R., & Klein, H. K. (1989). Four paradigms of information systems development. *Communications of the ACM, 32*(10), 1199-1216.

Huber, G. P. (1990). A theory of the effects of advanced information technologies on organizational design, intelligence, and decision making. *Academy of Management Review, 15*(1), 47-71.

Hunter, M. G., & Beck, J. E. (1996). A cross-cultural comparison of 'excellent' systems analysts. *Information Systems Journal, 6*(4), 261-281.

Iivari, J. (1991). A paradigmatic analysis of contemporary schools of IS development. *European Journal of Information Systems, 1*(4), 249-272.

Järvinen, P. (1999). *On Research Methods.* Tampere, Finland: Opinpaja OY.

Järvinen, P. (2000). Research questions guiding selection of an appropriate research method. In *Proceedings of the Eighth European Conference on Information Systems* (pp. 124-131).

Jones, M. (1999). Structuration theory. In W. L. Currie & B. Galliers (Eds.), *Rethinking Management Information Systems* (pp. 103-135). Oxford, UK: Oxford University Press.

Kaplan, B., & Duchon, D. (1988). Combining qualitative and quantitative methods in information systems research: A case study. *MIS Quarterly, 12*(4), 571-586.

Kazi, M. A. F. (2003). *Realist Evaluation in Practice.* London: SAGE.

Layder, D. (1990). *The Realist Images in Social Science.* London: Macmillan.

Layder, D. (1993). *New Strategies in Social Research.* Cambridge, UK: Polity Press.

Layder, D. (1997). *Modern Social Theory.* London: UCL Press.

Layder, D. (1998). *Sociological Practice: Linking Theory and Social Research*. London: SAGE.

Layder, D., Ashton, D., & Sung, J. (1991). The empirical correlates of action and structure: The transition from school to work. *Sociology, 25*, 447-464.

Lee, A. S. (1991). Integrating positivist and interpretive approaches to organizational research. *Organization Science, 2*(4), 342-365.

Leidner, D. E., & Carlsson, S. A. (1998). Les bénéfices des systèmes d'information pour dirigeants dans trois pays. *Systèmes d'Information et Management, 3*(3), 5-27.

Leidner, D. E., & Elam, J. J. (1995). The impact of executive information systems on organizational design, intelligence, and decision making. *Organization Science, 6*(6), 645-665.

Leidner, D. E., Carlsson, S., & Elam, J. J. (1995). A cross-cultural study of executive information systems. In *Proceedings of the 28th Annual Conference on System Sciences, III*, 91-100.

Leidner, D. E., Carlsson, S. A., Elam, J. J., & Corrales, M. (1999). Mexican and Swedish managers' perceptions of the impact of EIS on organizational intelligence, decision making, and structure. *Decision Sciences, 30*(3), 633-658.

Lòpez, J., & Potter, G. (eds.) (2001). *After Postmodernism: An Introduction to Critical Realism*. London: Athlone.

March, S. T., & Smith, G. F. (1995). Design and natural science research on information technology. *Decision Support Systems, 15*, 251-266.

Markus, M. L., & Bjørn-Andersen, N. (1987). Power over users: Its exercise by system professionals. *Communications of the ACM, 30*(6), 498-504.

Merton, R. (1967). *On Theoretical Sociology*. New York: Free Press.

Mingers, J. (2001a). Combining IS research methods: Towards a pluralist methodology. *Information Systems Research, 12*(3), 240-259.

Mingers, J. (2001b). *The paucity of multimethod research: Review of the IS literature* (Working paper). Coventry, UK: University of Warwick, Warwick Business School.

Mutch, A. (1997). Critical realism and information systems: An exploration. In the *Seventh Annual BIT Conference*.

Orlikowski, W. J. (1992). The duality of technology: Rethinking the concept of technology in organizations. *Organization Science, 3*(3), 398-427.

Orlikowski, W. J. (2000). Using technology and constituting structures: A practice lens for studying technology in organizations. *Organization Science, 11*(4), 404-428.

Orlikowski, W. J. & Baroudi, J. J. (1991). Studying information technology in organizations: Research approaches and assumptions. *Information Systems Research, 2*(1), 1-28.

Pawson, R., & Tilley, N. (1997). *Realistic Evaluation*. London: SAGE.

Quinn, R. E. (1988). *Beyond Rational Management: Mastering the Paradoxes and Competing Demands of High Performance*. San Francisco, CA: Jossey-Bass.

Quinn, R. E., & Rohrbaugh, J. (1983). A spatial model of effectiveness criteria: Towards a competing values approach to organizational analysis. *Management Science, 29*, 363-377.

Quinn, R. E., Faerman, S. R., Thompson, M. P., & McGrath, M. R. (1996). *Becoming a Master Manager* (2nd ed.). New York: John Wiley & Sons.

Reed, M. I. (1997). In praise of duality and dualism: Rethinking agency and structure in organizational analysis. *Organization Studies, 18*(1), 21-42.

Reed, M. I. (2000). The limits of discourse analysis in organizational analysis. *Organization, 7*, 524-530.

Reed, M. I. (2001). Organization, trust and control: A realist analysis. *Organization Studies, 22*(2), 210-228.

Strauss, A., & Corbin, J. M. (1998). *Basics of Qualitative Research: Techniques and Procedures for Developing Grounded Theory*. Thousand Oaks, CA: SAGE.

Symons, V. J. (1991). A review of information systems evaluation: Content, context and process. *European Journal of Information Systems, 1*(3), 205-212.

Tan, B. C. Y., Watson, R. T., & Wei, K.-K. (1995). National culture and group support systems: Filtering communication to dampen power differentials. *European Journal of Information Systems, 4*(1), 82-92.

Trauth, E. (2001). The choice of qualitative methods in IS research. In E. Trauth (Ed.), *Qualitative Research in IS: Issues and Trends* (pp. 1-19). Hershey, PA: Idea Group.

Trauth, E., & Jessup, L. (2000). Understanding computer-mediated discussions: Positivist and interpretive analyses of group support system use. *MIS Quarterly, 24*(1), 43-79.

Tsang, E. W., & Kwan, K.-M. (1999). Replication and theory development in organizational science: A critical realist perspective. *Academy of Management Review, 24*(4), 759-780.

Tsoukas, H. (1989). The validity of idiographic research explanations. *Academy of Management Review, 14*(4), 551-561.

Walls, J. G., Widmeyer, G. R., & El Sawy, O. A. (1992). Building an information system design theory for vigilant EIS. *Information Systems Research, 3*(1), 36-59.

Walsham, G. (1993). *Interpreting Information Systems in Organizations*. Chichester, UK: John Wiley & Sons.

Walsham, G. (1995). Interpretive case studies in IS research: Nature and method. *European Journal of Information Systems, 4*(1), 74-81.

About the Authors

Michael E. Whitman, PhD (mwhitman@kennesaw.edu), is an associate professor of information systems in the Department of Computer Science and Information Systems at Kennesaw State University, Georgia, USA. He is also the director of the master of science in information systems and director of the Center for Information Security Education and Awareness at KSU. Dr. Whitman received his PhD in management information systems, an MBA and a bachelor's degree in management from Auburn University. Dr. Whitman's current research interests include information security, security policy, computer use ethics, and IS research methods. He has published articles on these topics in journals such as *Information Systems Research, Communications of the ACM, Information & Management*, the *Journal of International Business Systems*, and the *Journal of Computer Information Systems*. He has delivered frequent presentations at national and regional conferences, including the Americas Conference on Information Systems, the Decision Sciences Institute, and the Southern Association for Information Systems. Dr. Whitman recently published two texts in *Information Security: Principles of Information Security* (Course Technology, 2003) and *Hands-On Information Security Lab Manual* (Thomson Custom Publishing, 2003).

Amy B. Woszczynski, PhD (awoszczy@kennesaw.edu), is an assistant professor of information systems in the Department of Computer Science and Information Systems at Kennesaw State University, USA. She received her PhD in industrial management from Clemson University, her MBA from Kennesaw State University, and a bachelor's degree in industrial engineering at Georgia Tech. Dr. Woszczynski's current research interests include pedagogy and curriculum to improve the success rate of students in the first programming course, individual differences in the information systems classroom, diversity in the IT workforce, and research methods in information systems. She has published articles on these topics in journals such as *Computers in Human Behavior* and *Industrial Management and Data Systems*. She has delivered frequent presentations at national and regional conferences, including the Americas Conference on Information Systems, the Southern Association for Information Systems, and the Southeast Informs.

* * *

Thilini Ariyachandra (thilinia@arches.uga.edu) is a PhD candidate in the MIS Department at the University of Georgia, USA. She received a BSc in finance and banking with a minor in computer information systems at the University of South Alabama. Her current research interests include data warehousing technology and effectiveness of information systems in organizations. She has published in *Information Systems Management* and in the proceedings of the *International Conference on Cultural Attitudes towards Technology and Communication* and the *Americas Conference on Information Systems*.

John C. Beachboard joined the Computer Information Systems faculty at Idaho State University (USA) in 2001. He completed a PhD in information transfer and an MS in information resources management at the School of Information Studies, Syracuse University. He holds an MS in business administration from Boston University and a BS in public administration from the University of Arizona. Dr. Beachboard has taught graduate courses in research methods for information management and IT project management and undergraduate courses in strategic IS management and systems architectures. He has held staff and management positions developing, implementing and operating information/telecommunications systems for the Department of Defense. He is keenly interested in the development, application, and effectiveness of information technology management policies in the private and public sectors.

Marie-Claude Boudreau (mcboudre@terry.uga.edu) is an assistant professor of MIS at the University of Georgia, USA. She received a PhD degree in CIS from Georgia State University, a Diplôme d'Enseignement Supérieur Spécialisé from l'École Supérieure des Affaires de Grenoble, and an MBA from l'Université Laval in Québec. Her current research investigates the consequences of information systems in organizations. She has published in *MIS Quarterly, Information Systems Research, JMIS, Communications of the AIS, The Academy of Management Executive, AMIT, Information Technology & People,* and conference proceedings.

Sven A. Carlsson (sven.carlsson@jibs.hj.se) is a professor of informatics at Jönköping International Business School, Sweden. His research interests include the use of ICT to support management processes, knowledge management, and the use of ICT in electronic value chains and networks. Mr. Carlsson was previously a professor of informatics at the School of Economics and Management, Lund University. He has been a visiting scholar at the University of Arizona, Tucson, National University of Singapore, and Marshall School of Business, University of Southern California. He is a regional editor for *Knowledge Management Research & Practice* and is on the editorial board for *Electronic Journal of Business Research Methods* and *Journal of Decision Systems*. His articles have appeared, among others, in *Journal of Management Information Systems, Decision Sciences, Information & Management,* and *Journal of Decision Systems*.

Chris Coulston received BS, MS, and PhD degrees in computer science and engineering from the Pennsylvania State University (USA) in 1991, 1994, and 1999, respectively. In 1999 he joined the Electrical and Computer Engineering Department at Penn State Erie (USA), the Behrend College, where he is currently an assistant professor. His research interests are in teaching methodologies, hypertext metrics, and computational complexity.

Darren Dalcher leads the Software Forensics Centre (SFC), a specialized institute at Middlesex University (UK) that focuses on systems failures, software pathology, and project failures. Before becoming leader of the SFC, Dr. Dalcher directed the Forensic Systems Research Group at South Bank University, where he organized and disseminated the notion of systems forensics. Dr. Dalcher obtained his PhD in software engineering from King's College, University of London. In 1992, he founded the Forensics Working Group of the IEEE Technical Committee on the Engineering of Computer-Based Systems (ECBS), an international group of academic and industrial participants formed to share information and develop expertise in failure and recovery. Dr. Dalcher is active in a number of international committees and steering groups. He is heavily involved in organizing international conferences and has delivered numerous keynote addresses and tutorials.

Gerardine DeSanctis (PhD, Texas Tech University) is the Thomas F. Keller Professor of Business Administration in the Fuqua School of Business at Duke University, USA. Her interests are in the general areas of computer-mediated work and management of information technology. Most of her research has examined the impacts of electronic communication systems on teams and organizations. She also has studied the evolution of online learning communities and e-communication overload. She currently serves as an associate editor for *MIS Quarterly*. She is on the advisory board for *Information Systems Research* and is a member of the editorial board for the *Journal of Organizational Behavior*. In the past, she has served as a senior editor for both *Organization Science* and *MIS Quarterly*. Recent coedited books include *Shaping Organization Form: Communication, Connection, and Community* and *Information Technology and the Future Enterprise*.

Roberto Evaristo is an assistant professor in the Information and Decision Sciences Department at the University of Illinois, Chicago, USA. He is currently involved in several projects related to the management of distributed projects, with work done in Japan, the U.S. and Europe. He has published in outlets such as *Communications of the ACM, International Journal of Project Management, Database, Journal of Global Information Management, Competitive Intelligence Review, European Management Journal, Human Systems Management, Journal of Organizational Computing and Electronic Commerce, International Information Systems*, and elsewhere. He also serves on the editorial board of the *Journal of Global Information Management* and the *Journal of Global Information Technology Management*.

R. Brent Gallupe is a professor of information systems and director of the Queen's Executive Decision Center at the School of Business, Queen's University at Kingston, Canada. He also holds an ongoing visiting professor appointment at the University of Auckland, New Zealand. His current research interests are in computer support for groups and teams, global information systems, and knowledge management systems. His work has been published in such journals as *Management Science, MIS Quarterly, Information Systems Research, Academy of Management Journal, Sloan Management Review,* and *Journal of Applied Psychology*.

Susan Gasson is an assistant professor in the College of Information Science and Technology at Drexel University, Philadelphia, Pennsylvania, USA. Following a career in data communications systems design and consultancy, she earned an MBA and a PhD from Warwick Business School in the UK. Dr. Gasson's research interests include social cognition and knowledge management in complex collaborative processes and the codesign of business and IT systems. Her empirical research has emphasized the use of qualitative methods, including a longitudinal grounded theory study of collaborative framing processes in cross-domain information system design and case studies of the problems underlying human-centered and traditional IS design approaches.

David Gefen (gefend@drexel.edu) is an assistant professor of MIS at Drexel University, Philadelphia, Pennsylvania, USA, where he teaches Strategic Management of IT, Database Analysis and Design, and VB.NET. He received his PhD in CIS from Georgia State University and a master of sciences in MIS from Tel-Aviv University. His research focuses on psychological and rational processes involved in ERP and e-commerce implementation management. Dr. Gefen's wide interests in IT adoption stem from his 12 years of experience in developing and managing large information systems. His research findings have been published in *MISQ, JMIS, The DATA BASE for Advances in Information Systems, Omega: the International Journal of Management Science, JAIS, eService Journal,* and a paper in *CAIS* that is on the AIS ISWorld Exemplary Works on Information Systems Research.

Varun Grover is the William S. Lee Distinguished Professor of IS at the College of Business & Behavioral Sciences, Clemson University (USA). Previously he was a Business Partnership Foundation fellow and professor of Information Systems at the University of South Carolina. Dr. Grover has published extensively in the information systems field, with more than 150 publications in refereed journals. Four recent articles have ranked him among the top five researchers based on publications in major IS journals over the past decade. His work has appeared in journals such as *Information Systems Research, MIS Quarterly, Journal of MIS, Communications of the ACM, Decision Sciences, IEEE Transactions,* and *California Management Review.* He is currently an associate editor for a number of journals, including *MISQ, JMIS, JOM, Database,* and *IJEC* and on the board of editors of five others.

M. Gordon Hunter is an associate professor in information systems in the Faculty of Management at the University of Lethbridge, Canada. Dr. Hunter has previously held academic positions in Canada, Hong Kong, and Singapore and visiting positions in Germany, USA, and New Zealand. He has a bachelor of commerce degree from the University of Saskatchewan in Canada. He received his doctorate from Strathclyde Business School in Glasgow, Scotland. Dr. Hunter is an associate editor of the *Journal of Global Information Management.* He serves on the editorial board of the *Journal of Global Information Technology Management,* and the *Journal of Information Technology Cases and Application.* He has conducted seminar presentations in Canada, USA, Asia, New Zealand, Australia, and Europe. His current research interests relate to the productivity of systems analysts with emphasis upon the personnel component, including cross-cultural aspects, and the effective use of information systems by small business.

Kun Shin Im is a professor of information systems at Yonsei University, Seoul, Korea. He holds a PhD in MIS at the University of South Carolina and a PhD in accounting at Yonsei University. His research interests include organizational effectiveness of information technologies, valuation of Internet firms, applications of accounting information systems, and development of constructs for IS performance measures. His work has been published in *Information Systems Research*, *Journal of Information Technology Management*, and other journals.

Leigh Jin is an assistant professor in the Department of Information Systems and Business Analysis at San Francisco State University, California, USA. She earned her doctorate in computer information systems in 2002 from Georgia State University. She received her MBA and BBA in management information systems from Beijing University of Aeronautics and Astronautics. Her recent research interests include virtual organizations and open source community development.

Elena Karahanna is an associate professor of MIS at the Terry College of Business, University of Georgia, USA. She holds a PhD in MIS from the University of Minnesota. Her current research interests include the adoption, use, and infusion of information technologies, the effect of media choice and use on individuals and organizations, IS leadership, and cross-cultural issues. Her work has been published in *MIS Quarterly*, *Management Science, Organization Science, Data Base, the Journal of Organizational Computing and Electronic Commerce*, and elsewhere. She currently serves on the editorial boards of *MIS Quarterly*, *Journal of AIS*, the *European Journal of Information Systems*, and *Computer Personnel*.

Michael J. Masterson received his PhD in management information systems from Auburn University in Auburn, Alabama. His research interests include theory development in information systems, strategic management of information technology, and research design and applied statistical methodology. Dr. Masterson has published case studies in *The Handbook of Enterprise Operations Management* and numerous conference proceedings. Dr. Masterson is currently on active duty with the United States Air Force. His current assignment is as the military advisor to the chief academic officer, Headquarters Air University, Maxwell AFB, Alabama, USA.

Joe McDonagh is director of executive education at Trinity College, Dublin, Ireland. He works in the fields of organization development and information technology, specializing in the management of large-scale IT-enabled business change. He teaches on executive degree programmes at Trinity College Dublin and at a number of business schools in Europe and America. He works on consultancy and executive development with many European and American multinationals as well as providing advice to governments. He has extensive commercial experience with large corporations and publishes widely on the management of large-scale IT-enabled business change. He lives in Dublin with his wife Majella and two sons, Colin and Sean.

Marshall Scott Poole (PhD, University of Wisconsin) is a professor of speech communication and professor of business administration at Texas A&M University, USA. He has conducted research and published extensively on the topics of group and organizational communication, computer-mediated communication systems, conflict management, and organizational innovation. He has coauthored or edited seven books, including *Communication and Group Decision-Making*, *Research on the Management of Innovation*, and *Organizational Change and Innovation Processes: Theory and Methods for Research*. He has published in a number of journals, including *Management Science*, *MIS Quarterly*, *Human Communication Research*, *Academy of Management Journal*, and *Communication Monographs*. He currently is a senior editor of *Information Systems Research* and *Organization Science*.

R. Kelly Rainer, Jr., is the George Phillips Privett Professor of Management Information Systems at Auburn University in Auburn, Alabama, USA. He received his PhD from the University of Georgia. He has published articles in leading academic and practitioner-oriented journals. His research interests include information technology in education (particularly higher education) and various aspects of information technology infrastructure. He is coauthor (with Efraim Turban and Richard Potter) of *Introduction to Information Technology* (2nd ed., John Wiley & Sons).

Julie Rennecker is an assistant professor in the Information Systems Department at Case Western's Weatherhead School of Management (USA). Her work explores the interplay between workers' embeddedness in their material and socially proximal work environments and their participation in virtual work groups. She is particularly interested in the often invisible influences of the relationships, power dynamics, and practicalities of situated work on individuals' understanding of and contribution to virtual project teams and how these individual actions translate into team and organizational-level consequences. Her research-to-date has been in the automotive and energy industries.

Daniel Robey is a professor and John B. Zellars Chair of Information Systems at Georgia State University (USA), holding a joint appointment in the Departments of Computer Information Systems and Management. He earned his doctorate in administrative science in 1973 from Kent State University. Professor Robey is editor-in-chief of *Information and Organization* and serves on the editorial boards of *Organization Science*, *Academy of Management Review*, *Information Technology & People,* and the John Wiley series on Information Systems. His current research includes empirical examinations of the effects of a wide range of technologies on organizational structure and patterns of work. It also includes the development of theoretical approaches to explaining the development and consequences of information technology in organizations.

Mark Srite is an assistant professor of MIS at the University of Wisconsin-Milwaukee, USA. His current research interests include the acceptance, adoption, and use of information technologies, cross-cultural IT issues, and group decision-making. His work has been published in *Decision Support Systems*, the *Journal of Global Information Management*, and elsewhere.

The J. Mack Robinson Distinguished Professor of IS at Georgia State University (GSU) (USA), **Detmar W. Straub** has conducted research in Net-enhanced organizations and e-commerce, computer security, technological innovation, and international IT. He holds a DBA (MIS; Indiana) and a PhD (English; Penn State). He has published more than 100 papers in such journals as *MIS Quarterly, Management Science, Information Systems Research, CAIS, JAIS, Organization Science, CACM, JMIS, Journal of Global Information Management, Information & Management, Academy of Management Executive,* and *Sloan Management Review.* He is currently an assistant editor (*Management Science; Information Systems Research*) and a senior editor (*DATA BASE*). Former coeditor of *DATA BASE for Advances in Information Systems* and an associate editor and associate publisher for *MIS Quarterly,* he has consulted widely in industry in the computer security area as well as technological innovation. He teaches courses at GSU in electronic commerce strategy, IT strategies for management, IT outsourcing, international IT, and computer security management.

Felix B. Tan is professor of Information Systems at the School of Computer and Information Sciences, Auckland University of Technology in New Zealand. He serves as the editor-in-chief of the *Journal of Global Information Management.* He is also the vice president of research for the Information Resources Management Association and the editor of the ISWorld Net's EndNote Resources page. Dr. Tan's current research interests are in electronic commerce, business-IT alignment, global IT, management of IT, cognitive mapping and narrative methodologies. His research has been published in *MIS Quarterly, Journal of Global Information Management, Journal of Information Technology* as well as other journals and refereed conference proceedings. Dr. Tan has more than 20 years experience in IT management and consulting with large multinationals, as well as University teaching and research in Singapore, Canada and New Zealand.

Theresa. M. Vitolo received a BSE degree in industrial engineering and a PhD degree in information science from the University of Pittsburgh in 1978 and 1985, respectively. Teaching in systems-related fields since 1986, she joined the Computer and Information Science Department at Gannon University (USA) in 1999. In addition to teaching, she has worked as a systems analyst/programmer on a variety of systems development projects. Her interests include intelligent interface design, motivated system energetics, and other issues in the field of human-computer interactions.

Index

International Journal of IT Standards & Standardization Research(JITSR)

The International Source for Advances in IT Standards and Standardization Research

ISSN:	1539-3062
eISSN:	1539-3054
Subscription:	Annual fee per volume (2 issues): Individual US $85 Institutional US $145
Editor:	Kai Jakobs Technical University of Aachen, Germany

Mission

The primary mission of the *International Journal of IT Standards & Standardization Research* is to publish research findings to advance knowledge and research in all aspects of IT standards and standardization in modern organizations. Furthermore, the *International Journal of IT Standards & Standardization Research* will be considered as an authoritative source and information outlet for the diverse community of IT standards researchers. JITSR is targeted towards researchers, scholars, policymakers, IT managers, and IT standards associations and organizations.

Coverage

JITSR will include contributions from disciplines in computer science, information systems, management, business, social sciences, economics, engineering, political science, and communications. Potential topics include: technological innovation and standardization; standards for information infrastructures; standardization and economic development; open source and standardization; intellectual property rights; economics of standardization; emerging roles of standards organizations and consortia; conformity assessment; standards strategies; standardization and regulation; standardization in the public sphere; standardization in public policy; tools and services related to standardiztion; and other relevant issues related to standards and standardization.

For subscription information, contact:

Idea Group Publishing
701 E Chocolate Ave., Ste 200
Hershey PA 17033-1240, USA
cust@idea-group.com
www.idea-group.com

For paper submission information:

Dr. Kai Jakobs
Technical University of Aachen, Germany
Kai.Jakobs@i4mail.informatik.rwth-aachen.de